APPLETON-CENTURY HANDBOOKS OF LITERATURE

Albert C. Baugh, Editor

ENGLISH LITERATURE
FROM DRYDEN TO BURNS

ENGLISH LITERATURE

from DRYDEN TO BURNS

ALAN DUGALD McKILLOP

Professor of English
The Rice Institute

New York

APPLETON-CENTURY-CROFTS, INC.

8105

PREFACE

In the study of the rich expanse of English culture from the Restoration of Charles II to the outbreak of the French Revolution a great deal has been accomplished in recent years, and the literature of the subject multiplies. It is the purpose of this manual to give the student some timely aid in the earlier stages of his acquaintance with the period by putting at his disposal something less elaborate than full-scale literary history and biography, something more highly developed than an elementary syllabus. Sketches of authors and brief sections on general topics have been provided in the hope that brevity and directness will compensate for the inevitable dogmatic tone and over-simplification. A principal danger in this plan is that under compression the minor authors may appear to be treated in a routine and colorless way; but if at first they seem to be—to use Rossetti's unsympathetic comment on Gilfillan's *British Poets*—"the usual array of nobodies from Addison and Akenside down to Zany and Zero," it can be said with confidence that they improve on further acquaintance. The bibliographies are merely suggestive and highly selective; much valuable material has gone unrecorded here, but the brief suggestions offered are enough to guide the student to the finer and more elaborate bibliographical tools which are now at hand. And after all, an alert consciousness of current scholarship must go along with a direct and independent reading of the literature itself. To promote and guide such a reading program is the primary purpose of this book.

I am particularly indebted to Professor Albert C. Baugh for suggesting that there might be a place for a manual on this plan, and his criticism and advice while the project

was under way proved to be most helpful. My general indebtedness to the large and able group of scholars in this
field is at once too obvious and too great for full record,
though it is of course implied, however inadequately, in the
bibliographical references. The coöperation of the pub-
lishers, particularly in making available the large collection
of illustrations gathered by the late Professor J. W. Cun-
liffe, is gratefully acknowledged. Other illustrations have
been drawn for the most part from the Rice Institute Library, with a few additional sources specifically recorded.
The maps of London are simplified tracings made by
Charles B. Wilson from the "'Correct Plan" in the *London
Magazine,* 1761.

ALAN DUGALD McKILLOP

CONTENTS

>>>

ILLUSTRATIONS

>>>

ENGLISH LITERATURE
FROM DRYDEN TO BURNS

POLITICAL HISTORY (1660-1702)

>>>

The restoration of the Stuart king Charles II to the throne in 1660 was a national act; it was hailed with enthusiasm by Englishmen of different classes and opinions. They wanted relief from the rigor of Puritan rule or protection from the anarchy that threatened them after the death of Cromwell. Now the King was to have his own again, and the landed gentry and aristocracy were once more in power. But in practice the Restoration was interpreted as the victory of a party. Parliament was controlled by Anglican squires who passed a series of acts called the Clarendon Code (Corporation Act, 1661; Act of Uniformity, 1662; Conventicle Act, 1664; Five Mile Act, 1665) by which Dissenters were excluded from municipal corporations, clergymen who refused to accept ordination and the Book of Common Prayer were deprived of their livings, religious assemblies ("conventicles") not according to the form of the Church of England were prohibited. Thus the line was drawn sharply between Anglican and Dissenter. The distinction was social, economic, and political, as well as religious; the Anglican interest included the land-owning gentry and aristocracy and their dependents, that is, most of the rural population; the Dissenters included especially the trading and industrial population in town and city. Such divisions are perhaps inevitable; Americans and English alike find it natural that the nation should divide into two fairly evenly balanced great parties which unite only in time of imminent national danger. The implications of this situation and the rules of this game were worked out by trial and error in the England of the late seventeenth century.

Charles II, witty and intelligent though he was, did not provide leadership which could permanently satisfy national needs. Rochester's burlesque epitaph runs:

> Here lies a great and mighty King
> Whose promise none relies on;
> He never said a foolish thing,
> Nor ever did a wise one.

The profligacy of his court was notorious; his mistresses and his boon companions were a public scandal, and still do too much to color our idea of the whole period. Brilliant and

CHARLES II

dissolute courtiers like George Villiers, Duke of Buckingham, and John Wilmot, Earl of Rochester, were much in the public eye. English Puritans then and later have found it hard to judge Charles aright. He showed a marked interest in toleration because of his private attachment to the Catholic Church; he had a lively but superficial interest in science and literature, though he was never a good patron. In his public life he may be described as a clever and unscrupulous politician who wanted to keep himself in power.

The honeymoon period of the Restoration was soon over. A naval war against the Dutch, caused by the struggle for sea power and commercial advantage, culminated in a successful Dutch attack on the British fleet in the Medway. At almost the same time England was distressed not only by this unpopular and disastrous war but by the Great Plague, in which perhaps a fifth of the population of London died (1665), and the Great Fire which laid the old City in ruins from the Temple to the Tower (September, 1666). The war and the Fire are the themes of Dryden's *Annus Mirabilis* (1667). Charles's principal minister had been the elder states-man Edward Hyde, Earl of Clarendon, whose gravity was out of key with the Court and who was now dismissed as a politi-cal scapegoat. In his place the King put a group of unscrupu-lous ministers known as the "Cabal" (Clifford, Ashley, Buck-ingham, Arlington, Lauderdale). Abroad English interests were threatened by the rising power of Louis XIV. Since Holland was the principal continental opponent of France, a Triple Alliance—England, Holland, Sweden—was formed against Louis in 1668, but in 1670 Charles concluded the Treaty of Dover with Louis, binding himself openly to aid France against Holland and secretly to receive subsidies from Louis and to declare himself a Catholic at an oppor-tune time. This deal made Charles partly independent of Parliament, which could control the King only by con-trolling his revenues; the diplomatic and political situa-tion thus created was terribly dangerous for England. Another unpopular Dutch war followed. Pro-French and pro-Catholic policies ran contrary to national feelings and prejudices, which were further influenced by the fact that Charles's brother James, Duke of York and heir to the throne, was an avowed Catholic. When Charles tried to favor Catholics and Dissenters at the same time by issuing a Declaration of Indulgence (1672), public opinion forced its withdrawal, and Parliament passed a Test Act (1673) requiring all office-holders to take communion in the Angli-can form and thus applying further the principles of the Clarendon Code. Now an opposition developed under the leadership of Anthony Ashley Cooper, Earl of Shaftesbury, and the public, particularly the Whig stronghold of Lon-

don, was driven to frenzy by the excitement of the Popish
Plot (1678; see below, *Absalom and Achitophel,* pp. 40-42).
The state was in serious danger, for it was not certain that
acute political differences could be settled by parliamentary
process, without sedition or revolution. There was a violent Tory reaction after Charles took the Whig leaders off
guard by dissolving Parliament at Oxford in the spring of
1681. He extended the power of the Crown by getting control of local government in the principal cities and towns,
and at the time of his death in 1685 he dominated the
situation completely.

His brother, who succeeded as James II, was unable to
prolong and extend the Tory triumph, and soon lost his
throne. He was an open and uncompromising Catholic,
and kept up the connection with Louis XIV. A Whig and
Protestant rebellion in Somerset under Monmouth was put
down, attended by the barbarous trials conducted by Chief
Justice Jeffreys; but James tried to force Catholicism on the
prelates of England and the universities, and thus antagonized the very leaders on whom he had to rely for support.
When the Church of England refused to go along with
him he tried to effect a strange political alliance between
Dissenters and Catholics by including them in two attempted Declarations of Indulgence which would give them
more freedom of worship (see below, *The Hind and the
Panther,* p. 38). At the same time his interest in building
up a large standing army indicated an obvious plan to im-
pose his measures by force on an unwilling nation. The
situation reduced to absurdity the favorite Tory doctrines
of the divine right of kings and the duty of passive obedience; these doctrines were now turned against the very
Church which had preached them so zealously. The result
was the "Glorious" or "Bloodless" Revolution of 1688;
James fled to France, and Tories and Whigs, Anglicans and
Dissenters united to call to the throne the Dutch prince

William of Orange, grandson of Charles I, husband of James's Protestant daughter Mary, and leader of the Protestant powers of the Continent against Louis XIV. The Revolution, like the Restoration, was carried out by a temporary coalition which expressed the settled will of the nation, but it differed from the Restoration in establishing a firm constitutional basis for settlement. The Bill of Rights (1689) set up the limited monarchy of Britain as it has continued to the present day. Parliament was confirmed in complete control of the Army and of finance. The Toleration Act granted freedom of worship to Dissenters (not to Catholics, Unitarians, or Jews), though the Test Acts, making nominal acceptance of Anglican doctrine and ritual a requirement for holding public office, remained in force. Despite the stability of this settlement, the Jacobites, those who maintained the indefeasible right of the House of Stuart to the throne and who longed to bring back James's son (the Old Pretender) and later his grandson (the Young Pretender), remained a powerful political influence for generations.

William himself was an unsociable foreigner, not personally popular, more interested in pushing anti-French policies on the Continent than in settling political issues in England. His foreign policy was in line with British interests, but a large part of the nation, including the Tory landowning class, was hostile or indifferent to his European commitments. He decisively defeated the forces of James at the battle of the Boyne in Ireland (1690). To carry on his continental war he had to rely on Whig ministers to deal with Parliament, and thus cabinet government began to emerge in the 1690's. The House of Commons ruled, normally expressing the will of the powerful landed aristocracy, but ultimately responsible to public opinion, subject to violent fluctuations of mood, and not yet fully amenable to party control and management. The Whig oligarchy which eventually got the upper hand was sluggish and selfish, but made alliance with the new forces of business and finance; under its auspices the Bank of England was established and modern government credit financing began. Queen Mary died in 1694. Though the war against France ended in 1697 with the Peace of Ryswick, William was engaged in the diplomatic moves which preceded the War of the Spanish Succession when he died in 1702, and was succeeded by James's other Protestant daughter Anne.

The general trend of English public life in this period was toward moderation and compromise. Yet sharp political and religious controversies continued, and when the censorship was suspended (1679-1685) and finally allowed to lapse (1695), political satire and invective found extravagant utterance. The London populace was still swept by sudden and violent waves of feeling as in the Popish Plot and on later occasions. An extreme Tory, or High Flyer, was very likely a Jacobite as well, and might be considered a menace to the state. Similarly a Dissenter might be regarded as a potential rebel, one who wanted to revive the "Good Old Cause" of the Puritan Commonwealth. At the same time a certain moderation was observed in acts, if not in language. Opponents were not "liquidated," or completely deprived of civil rights. In fact the rights of the subject were confirmed: the Habeas Corpus Act was passed in 1679, and heresy was no longer a capital offense.

Political theories which based the state on the existence of absolute power or undivided sovereignty were not generally accepted. Thomas Hobbes taught that by the social contract individuals had surrendered all power to the state and could never get it back again. Yet his defense of absolute power in his *Leviathan* (1651) as the only alternative to anarchy was not fully congenial even to royalists, though it had an intellectual power and a cynical brilliancy which might commend it to freethinkers at court. Much more popular in the King's party was the doctrine of non-resistance or passive obedience preached by the Church of England, the doctrine of the divine right of kings affording religious sanction for the maintenance of political order. But the policies of James II forced on the ruling classes the Whig doctrine that all powers in the state should be limited. John Locke, in his *Two Treatises of Government* (1690), drew up what was practically the official Whig justification of the Revolution. Absolute power, whether of the king or of the mob, is to be checked. Man enjoys natural rights, not least among them the right to own and control property. The social contract sets up a government with police powers, but this government can claim authority only so long as it can guarantee the citizen actual enjoyment of his fundamental rights. The theory was acceptable because it identified the independence of the natural man with the rights of the property owner to freedom from interference either from king or people, from above or below. As to the natural goodness of man, the theory was noncommittal: man's goodness and rationality were hoped for in social and political relations, but the doctrine of limited powers, the principle of checks and balances, guarded against the possibility that man might actually be tyrannical and unjust. Locke thus offered an acceptable compromise, of decisive influence for British and American political thought. His defense of religious toleration is thoroughly in the spirit of the age; speculative theology, differences of religious dogma, should not come within the range of the limited powers of the state, save that Catholics and atheists are excluded as politically dangerous. Public peace and order are more important than the passionate pursuit of absolute truth. Similarly, in the field of political action, campaigning and debating take the place of the threat of force. The trend toward moderation is best expounded by the eminent Lord Halifax in his *Character of a Trimmer* (probably written about 1685), a defense of the English constitution and the Church as embodying the very spirit of reasonable compromise. This was the lesson taught by the troubled reigns of Charles II and James II and handed on to later generations.

G. M. Trevelyan, *England under the Stuarts* (15th ed., London, 1930); Godfrey Davies, *The Early Stuarts* (Oxford, 1937); *Bibliography of British History, Stuart Period, 1603-1714* (Oxford, 1928); G. N. Clark, *The Seventeenth Century* (Oxford, 1929); *The Later Stuarts, 1660-1714* (Oxford, 1934); K. Feiling, *History of the Tory Party, 1640-1714* (Oxford, 1924); A. S. Turberville, *Commonwealth and Restoration* (London, 1936); David Ogg, *England in the Reign of Charles II* (2v, Oxford, 1934); Arthur Bryant, *King Charles II* (London, 1931); Louise F. Brown, *The First Earl of Shaftesbury* (New York, 1933); F. S. Ronalds, *The Attempted Whig Revolution of 1678-1681* (Urbana, 1937); C. L. Grose, "Charles the Second of England," *American Historical Review*, XLIII (1938). 533-41; G. M. Trevelyan, *The English Revolution, 1688-1689* (New York, 1939); T. B. Macaulay, *History of England from the Accession of James II,* ed. Sir Charles Firth (6v, London, 1913-15); Sir Charles Firth, *A Commentary on Macaulay's History of England* (London, 1938); C. L. Grose, *Select Bibliography of British History, 1660-1760* (Chicago, 1939); G. P. Gooch, *Political Thought in England from Bacon to Halifax* (London, 1914-15); H. J. Laski, *Political Thought in England from Locke to Bentham* (London, 1920); W. A. Dunning, *History of Political Theories from Luther to Montesquieu* (New York, 1938); Z. S. Fink, *The Classical Republicans* (Evanston, 1945).

SOCIAL HISTORY (1660-1702)
>>>

When we think of Restoration society, Charles II and his courtiers and mistresses come to mind, dissolute gallants and frivolous ladies. No doubt the nation was deeply affected by this situation; it made a great difference that

many members of the ruling classes were given over to a
selfish and vicious pursuit of pleasure. This side of the
age is given more than due prominence in Restoration
comedy and in society gossip such as we find in the
Mémoires de la vie du Comte de Grammont by Anthony
Hamilton. But other aspects of the age are fully documented in the great diaries of Pepys and Evelyn, and in
abundant letters and memoirs. There is a marked contrast
between the surface play of fashionable life on the one
hand, and on the other the underlying interests and the
normal daily life of the nation. There were many devout
Englishmen—humble men for whom John Bunyan and
George Fox spoke, men of higher culture who could appreciate the style and the substance of great divines like Isaac
Barrow, Robert South, and Richard Baxter. Sermons and
devotional literature were in great demand, and it was the
golden age of the English pulpit. There has never been a
period in English history when eminent clergymen made
more important contributions to philosophy, science, and
literature. Virtuosi among the laymen and scholars among
the divines helped to make this an age of great intellectual
achievement. And if the solid Englishmen with moderate
sized or small estates did not share fully in this drama of
ideas, neither did they participate in the corruption of the
Court. English society was solidly founded on the family.
Among the property-owning classes marriages were arranged in terms of property and money; girls married
young, immediately undertook elaborate household duties,
and raised large families under strict religious and social
discipline. In these respects our own age is much more unstable than seventeenth-century England. At the same
time, it is true that Restoration England was much more
worldly than Cromwellian England; the reign of saints,
idealists, and fanatics was over.

The kingdom was governed by the owners of landed

estates, the peers in the House of Lords, the gentry in the House of Commons. Some new men got estates during the Commonwealth period, and in general those with new wealth bought land, built up an estate and a family, and reënforced a class that held tenaciously to economic and social power. The country gentry or squires continued to be the backbone of society in a nation predominantly rural, and gave the whole national life a Tory and Anglican coloring. Small freehold farmers or "yeomen" were still numerous. The smaller landowners were destined to play a less important part in the England of the future, but their decline had barely begun. The squire, who was usu-ally a justice of the peace (see p. 96) ruled the parish and the village along with the parson. The famous third chap-ter of Macaulay's *History* describes the typical squire of 1685 as a fox-hunting and ale-drinking boor, but later his-torians such as Sir Charles Firth and G. M. Trevelyan point out that there were various degrees of wealth and culture among the landed families. From this class came many military officers, government officials, and holders of good livings in the Church. Literary culture in the country was pretty well limited to the gentleman's library and the clergyman's study, but a squire or yeoman who was inter-ested in books and current pamphlets could get them. News was circulated largely by handwritten newsletters until the 1690's. There was little printed matter in circulation among the people except religious books and some chapbooks and broadside ballads. The games, festivals, and recreations tra ditional among the folk continued through the century; even the Puritans had not been able to keep people from playing games on Sunday, dancing, and haunting alehouses. Cockfighting was a popular sport. On the whole, class dis-tinctions were fixed, but not oppressive. The nobility and gentry lived in their country houses for a large part of the year; Sprat could say in 1667 that whereas the French "prefer the pleasures of the town," the English prefer "those of the field." Travel was not easy; the best roads were unfit for heavy traffic and were improved only slowly. The gentry traveled in great discomfort in clumsy six-horse coaches without springs. The ordinary way of traveling, and the quickest, was on horseback, and post horses were regularly supplied for travel on the main roads. Travel was becoming more common, and regular stage-coach services were established from many points to London. The squires came to town more than ever before, and all phases of the national life centered in London.

It was in this generation, indeed, that London was becoming a world center of trade and commerce. Perhaps we pay too much attention to the political troubles of the time, and not enough to the tremendous growth of business. The government fostered foreign trade according to the mercantile system; that is, it tried to stimulate exports of manufactured goods but not of raw materials, and to restrict imports to essential raw materials and commodities not produced at home. This principle governed the relation of Britain to her colonies. A Parliament composed of landowners did all it could to protect English shipping, commerce, and industry. Political leaders were more likely to listen to City magnates, representative of big business, than to small squires. The growth of trade developed the Empire and ultimately did much to change the structure of English society and to alter social standards. The effect of the rise of the middle or trading class will be considered later (see pp. 94-95). Meanwhile it should be noted that many members of the landowning classes were connected with mercantile and commercial interests, and that in spite of the contempt for shopkeeping citizens which appears in much Restoration literature, trade had an honored place in the English economy.

The traditional opposition between the tradesman or

merchant of the City and the fashionable courtier was intensified by the growing importance of trade and commerce. The extravagant styles and ostentatious vices of the fashionable were no doubt overemphasized then as they are now. Styles in dress changed for men from the Elizabethan cloak, doublet, and hose to loose surcoat, waistcoat,

and knee breeches. Gentlemen and soldiers wore hats with large plumes. Gallants and would-be gallants carried swords. "A strange effeminate age," wrote the surly Oxford antiquarian Anthony à Wood in 1663, "when men strive to imitate women in their apparel, viz., long periwigs, patches in their faces, painting, short wide breeches like petticoats, muffs and their clothes highly scented, bedecked with ribbons of all colours." [1] Wigs were a new fashion, and came to be worn by almost all men with any pretence to respectability; gentlemen would have several, including an expensive one for dress occasions. The

THE MONUMENT
Built 1671-77, from a design by Wren, to commemorate the Great Fire. From an anonymous engraving in the Guildhall Library, London.

beaux carried wig combs, and combed their great white periwigs in public.

Another traditional opposition, that between town and country, was also intensified by the rapid growth of Lon-

[1] *Life and Times of Anthony à Wood,* ed. L. Powys (London, 1932), p. 113.

don. The City itself was rebuilt with astonishing speed after
the Great Fire of 1666; the crowded medieval town from
the Tower to the Temple was wiped out and replaced by
modern brick buildings along the lines of the old streets
and lanes. Many of the principal landmarks date from this
period—the Monument commemorating the Fire, a new
Bethlem Hospital in Moorfields, a new Royal Exchange,
and above all Wren's new St. Paul's dominating London
from Ludgate Hill, and his fifty-two city churches replac-
ing eighty-nine that had been burned. Thus London largely
assumed the appearance which it kept until the incendiary
bombs of the Second World War wrought a change comparable to that of 1666. Merchants and shopkeepers lived
at their places of business; the poor were huddled in large
slum areas, particularly in the sections just outside the city
walls. There was a traffic problem, and the streets of the
rebuilt city were crowded with wagons, coaches, sedan
chairs, hawkers, and hard-pressed pedestrians. Fashion
moved westward; some of the first of the new squares so
characteristic of modern London were laid out just after
the Restoration, such as Soho Square and Bloomsbury
Square. Whitehall was the principal residence of the king
and the executive headquarters of the government. The
pattern of London pleasure resorts was now set for a century to come. Innumerable allusions in the dramatists and
diarists enable us to reconstruct the pastimes of the town.
The most fashionable resorts in Charles II's reign were the
Mulberry Garden (on the site now occupied by Buckingham Palace), Hyde Park, and the Mall in St. James's Park,
a favorite place for evening promenades. To these should
be added Whitehall itself, and, of course, the playhouses.
New Spring Gardens, later Vauxhall, had just been opened
at Lambeth. In the fields and country towns to the north,
such as Islington and Tottenham, the citizens took their
Sunday outings. Especially fashionable eating houses were

Locket's at Charing Cross and the French House (Chatelin's) in Covent Garden. The New Exchange, an arcade on the south side of the Strand, where millinery, ribbons, cosmetics, etc. were sold, brought fashionable frivolities into the City. More characteristic of the City, however, were innumerable taverns, ordinaries (eating houses, but also the scene of much gambling), and coffee houses. Coffee, in-

INTERIOR OF A LONDON
COFFEE HOUSE
From *Vulgus Britannicus,* 1710.

troduced like tea and chocolate in the middle of the seventeenth century, soon became a popular beverage; the first coffee house was opened in Oxford in 1650, in London in 1652, and the coffee houses in part superseded the ale houses and became places of daily resort for many of the citizens. Here a man for a penny or so could smoke a pipe, drink a dish of coffee, receive and write letters, read pamphlets and newspapers, and talk with the other habitués. The patrons would usually be a mixed company drawn from the neighborhood and the busy streets, though naturally men of similar occupations and opinions tended to gather together. The coffee house thus promoted the club. Political clubs were common, especially in the years of the Popish Plot, and the gathering of wits at Will's in Covent Garden, sometimes referred to as "the Wits' Coffee House," became the most prominent literary club of the age. The coffee house met the needs of London life for over a hun-

dred years, and its endless conversation and sociability
continued to be of great importance for the diffusion of
news and general information and the expression of political and literary judgments.

H. D. Traill, *Social England,* iv (New York, 1909); G. M.
Trevelyan, *English Social History* (New York, 1942); Dorothy
Hartley and M. M. Elliot, *Life and Work of the People of Eng-
land: Seventeenth Century* (London, 1928); Louis B. Wright,
Middle-Class Culture in Elizabethan England (Chapel Hill,
1935); L. L. Schücking, *Die Familie im Puritanismus* (Leipzig,
1929); Arthur Bryant, *The England of Charles II* (London,
1934); *Postman's Horn* (London, 1936); Joan Parkes, *Travel in
England in the Seventeenth Century* (London, 1925); Sir Walter Besant, *London in the Time of the Stuarts* (London, 1903);
T. F. Reddaway, *The Rebuilding of London after the Great
Fire* (London, 1940).
See also references to Clark, Davies, Macaulay, Ogg, Trevelyan, Turberville, under Political History (1660-1702) above,
p. 8, Pepys and Evelyn below, pp. 57-60, and many of the references under Social History below, pp. 119-120.

SEVENTEENTH-CENTURY THOUGHT
▶▶▶

The importance of the formal doctrines of an age for
the student of literature cannot be made clear by a mere
statement of the views of scientists, philosophers, and theologians; the problem is to understand how the general
intelligence accepts and interprets technical ideas, and
assimilates them with what it already has. Popular thought
is never identical with science, philosophy, or theology,
though it is closely related to all three. Locke and Newton
are mere names to innumerable people whose outlook has
been deeply affected by their work. We must ask then how
science, philosophy, theology, and literary criticism meet and
interact. This may seem to be a hopeless task, even though

history treats the age as a unit. The historian's problem is not solved by giving a general situation a name, yet a simple notion of what the name denotes may be helpful.

Recent writers [1] have described the Renaissance world-view, the view of Shakespeare and Spenser, as the vision of an ordered universe imaginatively accepted, a world in which man could feel at home. This vision was accepted with the reverence due to tradition, with the assent of the intellect, and at the same time with imaginative enthusiasm. For example, in John Case's *Sphaera Civitatis* (1588) the sphere of state is identified with the concentric spheres of Ptolemaic astronomy: Elizabeth is the outer sphere, the *primum mobile*; her counselors are the fixed stars; the royal virtues are the seven planets, and all turns about immovable justice. Here cosmological, political, and ethical ideas are combined in a system which may seem to us to be mere analogy, but which was accepted both as an imaginative construction and as a statement of general truth. The seventeenth century viewed such a picture with different eyes. Political struggles and civil wars in England, France, and Holland, the Thirty Years' War in Germany, growing divergences of religious doctrine, social and economic change, the irruption of ideas from the new science —all combined to make men ask more urgently: On what grounds can order be discovered, maintained, or restored in such a world? Though many answers were given, the foremost philosophers of the age—Descartes, Spinoza, and Leibniz—found a rule of reason guaranteed by or identified with God and the nature of things. This rule operated alike in the individual, in society, and in the physical universe. A characteristic document is Grotius' treatise *De Jure Belli et Pacis* (1625), which bases jurisprudence on a universal rational law consonant with human nature. This order differed from the old order accepted by tradition in

[1] Basil Willey, Hardin Craig, Theodore Spencer, E. M. W. Tillyard.

that it was thought out anew, on the basis of a priori principles and mathematical method. Men of course continued to live their lives largely by custom, prescription, and inherited belief, but they felt a new need to square life and reality with reason. There was a weakening of belief in supernatural sanctions and in the power of imagination, and it is probable that this was a cause rather than an effect of the new rationalism. But it is impossible to assign a simple cause for a profound change in ways of thinking. When we say that western man became more worldly and more rational, we are merely describing a change, not explaining it.

The familiar description of neo-classicism in histories of literature emphasizes both authority and reason: neo-classicism tries to square the two standards, to make sure that the rule imposed by authority is rationally valid. In science the conflict of authority and reason was acute; ancient tradition was in direct opposition to new methods of experiment and research, and here the superiority of the moderns over the ancients seemed to be clear. Philosophy, like science, might seem to make a clean break with authority, but the prestige of older philosophies was still great, and the need to come to terms with religion was very strong. In religion and literary criticism the conflict was important, but far less extreme than in science; the authority of revelation or the great ancients might be held to conform to an eternal standard ratified by reason.

The world conceived by imagination is a unity; the world conceived by reason is broken up by sharp distinctions, and such pairs as mind and matter, imagination and reason, man and nature, the intellect and the senses, society and the individual, are so decisively separated that it is hard to get them together again. Yet as the seventeenth century grew more complicated, the need for unity was greater than ever. This is the origin of the most pressing philo-

sophical problems of the age. The system of the great
French thinker René Descartes set up self-evidence as the
test of truth, and mathematical clarity and consistency as
the standard of knowledge; the world-picture was a rational
order in knowledge and a mechanical order in nature. This
was thoroughly in the spirit of the anti-authoritarian side
of the century, but went too far to suit the English mind.
It set up a sharp dualism, and thus raised the problem of
how to connect mind and matter, God and Nature. English
thought found more congenial guidance in Bacon, who
emphasized the observation of external nature for man's
use, and challenged the waning authority of the scholastic
philosophy inherited from the Middle Ages without in
theory putting man absolutely on his own in the universe
with nothing but a scientific method. Thomas Hobbes also
went too far for the English in accepting the mechanical
universe presented by the new science, and in supposed
conformity to the conception of a merely material universe
in motion, reducing human life to the egoistic movements
of will and passion in the individual and the downright
assertion of absolute power by the state (*Leviathan,* 1651).
Thus a universal mechanical law of nature was made the
basis for positive or institutional law. But this doctrine
overemphasized absolute power at the expense of reason;
the general tendency was to argue, whether in Church or
State, in art or science, that valid reason gave actual power.
Thus an important group of conservative and academic
thinkers known as the Cambridge Platonists (Benjamin
Whichcote, Henry More, Ralph Cudworth, and others) emphasized the divinity of reason and put religious truth in
a setting of calm meditation; they used the weight of philosophical and religious tradition to support an appeal to
reason. Except for More, they are connected with academic
scholarship rather than the new science, and they do not
include a philosopher of the first rank, but their influence

on the liberal and rational religion of later generations was considerable. Shaftesbury was the true heir of the Cambridge group (see below, p. 129). Their influence overlaps with the tendency toward inclusiveness and toleration in the Church called "latitudinarianism." In the immediate future ritual and dogma were to lose ground to calm reason and liberalism. But something is lost when the enthusiasm and scholarship of the Cambridge men cool down to the plain sense of the famous Archbishop Tillotson:[1]

> Reason is the faculty whereby revelations are to be discerned. ... All revelation from God supposeth us to be men and to be endued with reason. ... Whatever doctrines God reveals to men are propounded to their understandings.

The characteristic reconciliation of authority and experience in English thought is worked out by John Locke in his *Essay concerning Human Understanding* (1690). Locke wants to free the mind from the dictation of absolute authority, and to find rational certainty in morals and religion comparable to that yielded by the new science; but he approaches this problem not as a radical or revolutionary but as a practical Englishman. So he starts by saying that we get all ideas from experience, either of the external world or of the workings of the mind. He opposes innate ideas because they seem to be impositions of arbitrary authority. (The Cambridge Platonists, on the other hand, accepted innate ideas as a manifestation of the clear light of reason, and thus as a link between man and God.) The senses give us knowledge both of the primary qualities which really exist in the external world, solidity, extension, figure, and motion, and of the secondary qualities which exist only in our sense experience, such as color and sound. The assertion of primary qualities means that Newton's material universe, subject to mathematical law, is real.

[1] "Of the Trial of the Spirits," in *Sermons* (London, 1757), II. 31.

Despite a vein of cautious skepticism, Locke keeps the established scheme of God, man, and nature; within man he finds a self which maintains its integrity and has the power to discover and obey God's law, and, with less certainty, to know the external world. "We have the knowledge of our own existence by intuition, of the existence of God by demonstration, and of other things by sensation."[1] His political philosophy has already been briefly noted above (p. 7). Locke does not let speculation lead him to extreme conclusions. His most original contribution is his emphasis on the workings and content of man's mind, so that human nature as revealed in experience becomes the principal theme of philosophy; in other words, philosophy tends to become psychology and ethics. This might lead to skepticism or naturalism; man's knowledge could be regarded as mere sense experience, without validity beyond itself, or man could be regarded as purely a creature of nature, a part of the material world. Locke himself does not draw such conclusions. He tries to give both the senses and reason, external nature and human nature, a place in his scheme, just as he seeks in politics to reconcile the rights of the individual with the power of the state, and in religion the claims of reason with the authority of the Bible and the Church. In other words, he accepts and assumes the great metaphysical principle of "harmony." Indeed it is "harmony" rather than "reason" which dominates much of the popular thought of the time. Locke is the least daring of seventeenth-century philosophers, and he handed on his inconsistencies and compromises for later generations to work over in the fields which we should now call ethics, political science, and psychology. His sober utilitarian attitude set the tone in English and American thought for a hundred years, and helped to create the climate in which eighteenth-century didactic literature flourished.

[1] *Essay* (Oxford, 1894), II. 304.

> Philosophy consists not
> In airy schemes, or idle speculations;
> The rule and conduct of all social life
> Is her great province. Not in lonely cells
> Obscure she lurks, but holds her heavenly light
> To senates and to kings, to guide their councils,
> And teach them to reform and bless mankind.
> (Thomson, *Coriolanus*, iv, i)

SCIENCE

The methods and achievements of the new science were of crucial importance for the seventeenth-century mind. A great western European fund of new discoveries and new methods was formed. The Elizabethan Gilbert did pioneer work in magnetism and electricity, Harvey discovered the circulation of the blood (1628), and other great advances were made in anatomy and physiology. The compound microscope and the telescope offered not only new facts but the vision of an infinite universe, and thus gave a tremendous stimulus to the imagination. The air pump, barometer, thermometer, and many other instruments were invented and in the second half of the century fostered a passionate interest in experiment. It was the golden age of the amateur scientist and the virtuoso. Most important of all, developments in mathematics—analytic geometry by Descartes, calculus by Pascal and later by Newton and Leibniz—gave the scientist new and indispensable tools, and set up a standard of precision and certainty which the philosopher tried to attain in other fields. The Copernican system of astronomy, published in 1543, had not been fully accepted for several generations, but Kepler's more exact formulation of the laws of the motion of the planets (1621) and Galileo's pioneer use of the telescope and his findings in mechanics led directly to Newton's formulation of the law of gravitation as a universal principle (*Philosophiae Naturalis Principia Mathematica*, 1687). This became the su-

TITLE-PAGE OF BACON'S *INSTAURATIO MAGNA*,
LONDON, 1620.

This volume contains the *Novum Organum,* the formulation of Bacon's
scientific method. The engraving represents a ship sailing beyond the
Pillars of Hercules, traditionally the western limits of the world. The
Latin motto is from Daniel xii.4: "Many shall run to and fro, and
knowledge shall be increased."

preme example of a universally valid natural law established both by observation and by precise reasoning and calculation; it confirmed the belief, at once traditional and rational, that the universe was governed by Divine Reason and Power, and directly or indirectly it influenced the preacher, the poet, and the man on the street.

Bacon had anticipated this scientific movement in the large, and though the plans and methods he recommended were never followed in detail his influence was of great importance for English science. He emphasized the collection rather than the selection of facts, and did not attach enough importance to the use of mathematics, or to the work of the pioneering scientist who frames and tests hypotheses. But his teachings were congenial to the English mind: he taught distrust of mere words and baseless speculation; he encouraged the organization of research by groups, as in Salomon's House in his utopian *New Atlantis,* and he emphasized the practical ends of science. The little group of scientists who began to meet in London in 1645 and at Oxford in 1648, carried the Baconian program into the Restoration period and became the nucleus of the Royal Society, organized at Gresham College, London, in 1660, and chartered by the King in 1662. Bacon's influence can be distinguished from the more speculative and a priori thinking of Descartes, and it is wholly apart from the sterile traditionalism of the universities. The Royal Society was the project of gentlemen who gathered evidence about "all the works of nature or art," independently of the schools. Its program represented organized research—continuous, cumulative, and coöperative, in order, said the secretary Oldenburg.[1]

that such productions being clearly and truly communicated, desires after solid and useful knowledge may be further enter-

[1] Introduction to *Philosophical Transactions* (1665), quoted by C. R. Weld, *History of the Royal Society* (London, 1848), I. 180.

tained, ingenious endeavours and undertakings cherished, and those addicted to or conversant in such matters may be invited and encouraged to search, try, and find out new things, impart their knowledge to one another, and contribute what they can to the grand design of improving natural knowledge and perfecting all philosophical arts and sciences—all for the glory of God, the honour and advantage of these kingdoms, and the universal good of mankind.

While Lord Robert Boyle, one of the chief ornaments of the Society, was laying the foundations of modern chemistry he was dwelling on the utility of science and above all the support which science gave to religion. The program was closely connected in its origin with the practical and utilitarian side of Puritanism, and continued with the approval and support of many in the ruling classes and the Church. Sprat's *History of the Royal Society* (1667) emphasizes practicality, piety, and patriotism, and in its famous words about the style required by the new science, "a close, naked, natural way of speaking," points to the concurrent change in English prose style. Scientific achievement gave new meaning to the idea of progress, and strengthened the moderns against the ancients, man's future and its possibilities against the past and the weight of tradition. This optimistic progressivism was combined with a belief in an experimentally verified rational pattern of the universe. New findings were thought to strengthen the old argument that the universe is the work of an infinitely wise Artificer; microscopy gave new vividness to the old conception of a chain of being extending without break from the animalcule to God; the telescope revealed an infinite and unthinkably majestic universe; Newtonian physics showed in actual operation precise mathematical law which was taken to be ultimately an act of the divine will. The forces which actuated the universe were not merely mechanical and material; magnetism and gravity were conceived in terms of an ethereal medium which was incorporeal, indeed divine, and such ideas seemed to make possible the reconciliation of the new science with many traditional religious and philosophical ideas. Divine law governed spirit and matter with absolute regularity. The new views did not have entirely free course; they were sometimes limited by doubts about the power of human reason, and old beliefs in witchcraft, astrology, alchemy, special providences, still lingered on, but the age witnessed the pervasion of scientific ideas far beyond the range of their technical application.

E. Bréhier, *Histoire de la philosophie*, II, i (Paris, 1929); Preserved Smith, *History of Modern Culture*, I (New York, 1930); Basil Willey, *The Seventeenth Century Background* (London, 1934); Hardin Craig, *The Enchanted Glass* (New York, 1936); Theodore Spencer, *Shakespeare and the Nature of Man* (New York, 1942); E. M. W. Tillyard, *The Elizabethan World Picture* (New York, 1944); R. F. Jones, *Ancients and Moderns* (St. Louis, 1936); *Seventeenth-Century Studies Presented to Sir Herbert Grierson* (Oxford, 1938); E. A. Burtt, *The Metaphysical Foundations of Modern Physical Science* (London, 1925); Martha Ornstein, *The Rôle of Scientific Societies in the Seventeenth Century* (Chicago, 1928); Sir Henry Lyons, *The Royal Society, 1660-1940* (Cambridge, 1944); A. Wolf, *History of Science, Technology, and Philosophy in the 16th and 17th Centuries* (London, 1935); C. S. Duncan, *The New Science and English Literature in the Classical Period* (Menasha, 1913); Katharine B. Collier, *Cosmogonies of Our Fathers* (New York, 1934); Grant McColley, ed., *Literature and Science* (Chicago, 1940); Marjorie Nicolson, "The Early Stage of Cartesianism in England," *Studies in Philology*, XXVI (1929), 356-74; "The 'New Astronomy' and English Literary Imagination," *ibid.*, XXXII (1935), 428-62; *The Microscope and English Imagination* (Northampton, 1935); "The Telescope and Imagination," *Modern Philology*, XXXII (1935), 233-60; W. E. Houghton, Jr., "The English Virtuoso in the Seventeenth Century," *Journal of the History of Ideas*, III (1942), 51-73, 190-219; R. W. Frantz, *The English Traveller and the Movement of Ideas*, University of Nebraska Studies, XXXII-XXXIII (1932-33); G. N. Clark, *Science and Social Welfare in the Age of Newton* (Oxford, 1937).

LITERARY TYPES AND STANDARDS
>>>

What kind of literature was required and produced by this age? Without elaborate critical campaign or controversy, change occurred in response to a felt need in the field of prose. Sprat, we have seen, speaks of the plain style required by the new science; Burnet and many others speak of the new plain style favored by Restoration preachers. The widening of the reading public had much to do with this important change: popularization encouraged simplification, and this tendency had already appeared in the style of the Puritan preachers and in much utilitarian and popular writing. The change of prose style extended to literary criticism, journalism, and political and philosophical discussion. The pamphlet and the essay were in favor, small units of prose calculated to enlighten and persuade. If the appeal was to tradition and prejudice, it must still be clothed in the garb of reason; the reader must be taken to be a sensible man, not a fanatic, enthusiast, radical, or pedant.

Poetry was more easily classified by type than prose, and established types remained. The great symbols of the Renaissance imagination still persisted. *Paradise Lost* (1667) promptly won admiration even among Restoration courtiers, but of course it was the product of the preceding age. When the Restoration tried to attain sublimity, as in the heroic plays and in attempts at epic, its voice became hollow and its style bombastic. The same insincerity appeared in the most pretentious lyric form cultivated during the period, the Pindaric ode developed by Abraham Cowley, which aspired to enthusiasm and inspiration. In the prefatory note to *Gondibert* (1651) Hobbes and Davenant had already said that an epic poem should be clear and rational and should avoid the supernatural. Cowley said the same thing in his lines in praise of this poem:

> Methinks heroic poesy till now
> Like some fantastic fairy-land did show,
> Gods, devils, nymphs, witches' and giants' race,
> And all but man in man's chief work had place.
> Thou like some worthy knight with sacred arms
> Dost drive the monsters thence, and end the charms.
> Instead of those dost men and manners plant,
> The things which that rich soil did chiefly want.

Enthusiasm and heroism gave way before the study of men and manners, of human nature operating within the limits of a fixed literary and social code. This was already the direction of French classicism, and the early residence of Charles II in France and the vogue of French fashions and standards in his reign have been taken to indicate a decisive influence. It may be noted that the height of classicism in France was reached from 1660 to 1685; that is, the first quarter-century of the reign of Louis XIV corresponds exactly to the reign of Charles II. Cases of direct influence appear: Corneille is of importance for dramatic criticism, Boileau for criticism and satire. Yet at most the French influence only gave articulation and color to a change already under way in England. There was already a neo-classical tradition in western Europe derived ultimately from the Italian critics of the Renaissance. France was doing far more than England to develop this tradition, and had assumed leadership, but after all one literature takes from another only what it is predisposed to take. We must not therefore consider Restoration literary types and theories as mere derivatives of the French, though there was a considerable debt to French criticism. And of course French remained the international language of diplomacy, society, and culture for over a century to come.

Classicism bases literature on the permanent and universal elements in human nature, that is, on man's long-run experience of his own powers and limitations; in such experience moderation, self-control, the need to come to terms with other men, clear communication, count for most. But this human universal is to be realized in a given society. Thus there is ambiguity in the classical watchword *decorum*; it means properly the way in which particular characters, events, and actions, as presented in literature, illustrate universal truths or principles, but it often comes to mean conformity to conventional and apparently arbitrary rules. Given traditions and given fashions always have something arbitrary about them; universal standards and the current situation are never completely reconciled. The poetic forms most in favor in the classical period took a somewhat detached attitude toward the situation at the moment; though they met what were supposed to be the needs of a rational society, they did this by keeping in theory to an ideal of generality and clarity. The irregular, the particular, the casual, and the confused were censured. The ground for this censure was an exacting aesthetic ideal, but it was likely to be stated in moral terms. The things excluded and disapproved were nevertheless interesting, and hence the popularity of satire, which could treat of these things in order to disapprove them. From the general classical position follows also the development of the verse-essay, later the descriptive-didactic poem, and the decline of the lyric.

The course of imaginative poetry may be measured by its relation to the two great Elizabethans, John Donne and Ben Jonson. Donne, esteemed by modern criticism one of the greatest English poets, combined intense religious and amatory feeling with restless and ingenious thought, expressing both at once in the daring and sometimes extravagant figures of speech which are called "conceits" and

which earned for him and his school the nickname "metaphysical poets." This complexity was called "wit" in the
seventeenth century. Ben Jonson's example in lyric, on the
other hand, encouraged clear expression and formal structure. Both poets encouraged the use of reason, but Donne's
reason led to complication, Jonson's to simplicity. Social,
intellectual, and philosophical changes led to the triumph
of the neo-classical ideal of simplicity and formality, and
to the campaign, furthered by Dryden and carried on later
by Addison, Pope, and many others, against "false wit."
The conceit, which at its best may be a true expression of
imaginative power, became a mark of false or affected verse.
This change appears in the career of Abraham Cowley
(1618-1667). Educated at Westminster and Cambridge,
Cowley was a moderate royalist, and spent several years as
an exile in Paris. He worked intelligently but imitatively
in various forms, undertaking a religious epic in the unfinished *Davideis,* writing love poems in the cycle called *The
Mistress,* largely imitative of Donne, and about 1650 essay-
ing Pindaric odes. The set of his mind was toward moderation and common sense; his conceits and rhetorical flights
appear to be merely decorative. At the Restoration he was
disappointed in his hopes of patronage, and spent the last
few years of his life in retirement at Chertsey. It is not surprising to find him setting forth *A Proposition for the
Advancement of Experimental Philosophy* (1661), praising
in verse the Royal Society, of which he was a member, and
expounding a meditative Epicurean philosophy in his prose
essays. In his career we can see the turn away from exu-
berance.

The case of Edmund Waller (1606-1687) is somewhat
different. He had a long career as a member of Parliament,
was involved in a royalist plot in 1643, later made his
peace with Cromwell, and changed again at the Restoration. His occasional verse, couched in the heroic couplet,

nicely balanced and regularly closed at the end of every
second line, clear and commonplace in content, made him
the chief exponent of the new style in verse. Ben Jonson's
example, Fairfax in his translation of Tasso, Sandys in his
Ovid, Denham in his famous poem *Cooper's Hill* (1642),
all contributed to the development of the closed couplet.
Waller kept clear of the ardors and complexities of the
school of Donne. Though he wrote some pleasant lyrics,
his turn was for occasional and epistolary verse with a
mildly didactic tone. He represented the side of the age
which we may call at once sober and superficial.

> Though poets may of inspiration boast,
> Their rage, ill-governed, in the clouds is lost.
> He that proportioned wonders can disclose,
> At once his fancy and his judgment shows.
> Chaste moral writing we may learn from hence,
> Neglect of which no wit can recompense.
>> ("Upon the Earl of Roscommon's
>> Translation of Horace")

The age of Dryden and Pope greatly overrated Waller, and
called him "the parent of English verse."

Many critics, notably the supposedly prosaic Hobbes,
paid tribute to the power of imagination; judgment or common sense never suppressed creative power—call it imagination or what we will—in the work of major artists like
Dryden and Pope. The opposition between imagination
and reason is parallel to the oversharp dualistic distinctions of seventeenth-century philosophy. In practice the relation between the two is much like the relation between
liberty and social order: everyone is in favor of both, but
may then go on to exalt one at the expense of the other.
There was a tendency to stress the intellectual content of
verse, that is, to try for the qualities verse might have in
common with ideally clear, harmonious, and logical prose.
But rhetorical tradition, if nothing else, set up an absolute

distinction between prose and poetry. The distinguishing marks of poetry then became meter and diction. Hence the emphasis on smooth "numbers," the rigorous polishing and balancing of the heroic couplet, and hence also the increasing prominence of poetic diction. During the seventeenth century, starting at least as early as Sylvester's widely influential translation of Du Bartas and Sandys's Ovid, and developing through Milton and others down through Dryden and far beyond, there grew up a store of terms and phrases, drawn largely from Latin poetry, which were systematically used to elevate and decorate verse, to give it dignity, elegance, generality, and at the same time a kind of logical precision. The diction cannot be described in detail here, but it includes the free use of certain words taken from the Latin, often in their literal sense ("devolve," "error," "obvious"), participial adjectives ("swelling tide"), adjective plus noun denoting genus ("bleating kind," "finny tribe," "plumy people"), excessive fondness for certain monosyllables with long vowels, especially in the riming position ("store," "main," "train"). This style probably appears at its worst in descriptions of external nature; in the best poets it does not altogether supplant a plain and direct style.

Without undertaking an elaborate survey of literary types, we may note that after 1660 satire takes such various forms as to defy classification. Its basic purpose was to show in what endless ways man falls short of the standards set by right reason. The satirist always professed just indignation, though he was often delivering a personal attack, whether playful, malicious, or savage. An age of political and religious controversy, with a highly concentrated social life, found endless occasion for such writing. Andrew Marvell's career shows the trend: his beautiful meditative lyrics are of the mid-century, his political satires are of the Restoration. John Sheffield, Earl of Mulgrave, in his *Essay upon Satire* makes the traditional connection with the Roman models, distinguishing between the savage manner of Juvenal and Persius and the urbane manner of Horace, and on the whole expressing a preference for the latter. Oldham used the Juvenalian style (see p. 48), and Marvell's anti-court satires, though less savage, are unbridled; Horatian suavity was hardly reached until the eighteenth century. But Butler and Dryden were virtually independent of Roman models in their satiric triumphs. Satire in the broad sense includes adaptations of prose forms, such as the character, the essay, the controversial pamphlet, and prose fiction. Marvell's *Rehearsal Transpros'd* (1672–73), the most successful satire between Butler and Oldham, attacks the intolerant Archdeacon Samuel Parker in witty and flexible prose.

Somewhat similar though not identical reasons underlie the development of burlesque literary forms, the deliberate cultivation of incongruity between subject and style, a pretentious style being used for low matter or high matter being treated in undignified style. This might be done for the purpose of expressing a cynical or satirical view of mankind, as in Butler's *Hudibras,* or it might be a playful campaign against extravagant literary projects and pretensions, or merely a light exercise in technique and style. Every literary form had its burlesque antitype—epic, tragedy, opera, pastoral, lyric, romance—and the process was extended during the eighteenth century.

The interest in analysis and exposition, fortified by the traditional idea that poetry ought to teach as well as delight, led to the development of the group of types included under the terms *verse-essay* or *verse-treatise,* the georgic (conceived broadly as a poem telling how to do something), and later the descriptive-didactic poem. If the age had rigid ideas about poetic form and diction, it sometimes seemed to have curiously indiscriminate ideas about poetic subject matter. The maintenance of the right attitude and style on the part of the poet, it was felt, could make any subject eligible for the appropriate type of poetry. Of course a somewhat similar attitude marked the masters of the new prose also, but prose was less hampered than verse by traditional requirements of genre and style. The new attitude was sober yet flexible, moderately strict without sacrificing geniality and good manners, relatively plain in style and light in touch, and disposed to assume easily accessible common ground between writer and reader.

F. Baldensperger, "Romantique: ses analogues et ses équivalents," *Harvard Studies and Notes,* XIX (1937). 13-105; A. Beljame, *Le Public et les hommes de lettres en Angleterre, au dix-huitième siècle, 1660-1744* (Paris, 1881); René Bray, *La Formation de la doctrine classique en France* (Paris, 1927); L. Charlanne, *L'Influence française en Angleterre au dix-septième siècle* (Paris, 1906); A. F. B. Clark, *Boileau and the French Classical Critics in England, 1660-1830* (Paris, 1925); R. S. Crane, "Neo-Classical Criticism," in *Dictionary of World Literature,* ed. J. T. Shipley (New York, 1943); E. Gosse, *From Shakespeare to Pope* (Cambridge, 1885); R. F. Jones, "The Attack on Pulpit Eloquence in the Restoration," *Journal of English and Germanic Philology,* XXX (1931). 188-217; "Science and English Prose Style in the Third Quarter of the Seventeenth Century," *Publications of the Modern Language Association,* XLV (1930). 977-1009; "Science and Language in England of the Mid-Seventeenth Century," *Journal of English and Germanic Philology,* XXXI (1932). 315-31; A. H. Nethercot, *Abraham Cowley, the Muse's Hannibal* (London, 1931); H. Peyre, *Le Classicisme français* (New York, 1942); R. L. Sharp, *From Donne to Dryden* (Chapel Hill, 1940); J. E. Spingarn, ed., *Critical Essays of the Seventeenth Century* (3v, Oxford, 1908-09); C. D. Thorpe, *The Aesthetic Theory of Thomas Hobbes* (Ann Arbor, 1940); S. Vines, *The Course of English Classicism* (London, 1930); Ruth C. Wallerstein, "The Development of the Rhetoric and Metre of the Heroic Couplet," *Publications of the Modern Language Association,* L (1935). 166-209; George Williamson, *The Donne Tradition* (Cambridge, Mass., 1930); "The Restoration Revolt against Enthusiasm," *Studies in Philology,* XXX (1933).

571-603; "The Rhetorical Pattern of Neo-Classical Wit," *Modern Philology*, XXXIII (1935). 55-81; "Senecan Style in the Seventeenth Century," *Philological Quarterly*, XV (1936). 321-51; Paul S. Wood, "Native Elements in English Neo-Classicism," *Modern Philology*, XXIV (1926). 201-08; "The Opposition to Neo-Classicism in England between 1660 and 1700," *Publications of the Modern Language Association*, XLIII (1928). 182-97.

JOHN DRYDEN (1631-1700)

>>>

The career of John Dryden shows us the taste and thought of the Restoration, its political, intellectual, artistic, and religious struggles and tensions, variously expressed in the work of a supremely competent writer. His individual genius won him high place, but it was always genius in account with the age. He began as a docile young student under the Commonwealth, taking his political and literary ideas from his surroundings; he ended in opposition, a Catholic and a Tory, but meanwhile he had always been moved to write not only to meet the general taste of the times but to meet special demands and occasions—plays for the fashionable public, poems on current events, complimentary verses, timely satiric and didactic poems, critical essays pointed for self-defence and clarification of current issues. Thus he wrought out literary models and standards which his age accepted, and which were in large part to

DRYDEN

meet the tastes of the English public for a century to come. The man remains something of a mystery, for biographical facts are meager, but his achievement in letters is of the first importance. The age of Dryden gives the key to the age of Pope and the age of Johnson.

Dryden was born in the parish of Aldwincle All Saints, Northamptonshire, in 1631. His father was a small landed proprietor who took the Puritan side. He was educated at Westminster School and Trinity College, Cambridge, and seems to have had some minor employment with a kinsman in Cromwell's government (1656-58). Aside from some juvenile verses on the death of a schoolfellow Lord Hastings, full of the conceits of the metaphysical school, his first piece was *A Poem upon the Death of his Late Highness Oliver* (1659). Within two years he was hailing the return of Charles II in *Astraea Redux* (1660) and lines *To His Sacred Majesty. A Panegyrick on his Coronation* (1661). He was content, not necessarily in a bad sense, to follow popular opinion. We have little detail about the beginnings of his literary career in London; he may have done hackwork for the bookseller Henry Herringman, and he was already acquainted with Sir Robert Howard (whose sister Elizabeth he married in 1663), an active dramatist and one of the proprietors of the King's Company. Dryden was soon writing regularly for this company; an author seeking the favor of the newly restored court and aristocracy would naturally turn to drama. After an undistinguished beginning in comedy, he collaborated with Howard in *The Indian Queen* (produced 1664, published 1665), and himself wrote the sequel *The Indian Emperor* (produced 1665, published 1667), beginning his notable, though not entirely fortunate, work in the heroic play (see p. 67). The plague closed the theaters in 1665-66, and Dryden retired during this time to Charlton, Wiltshire. Here he wrote of the strange and disastrous events of these months in *Annus Mirabilis* (1667). A more significant work of these years was the essay *Of Dramatic Poesy* (1668), the first notable achievement of the new prose and of Dryden's intellectual power.

For ten years Dryden's energy was divided between comedy and the heroic play. In the *Defence of an Essay of Dramatic Poesy* (1668) he confesses that he writes what the public wants, and that he does not feel comedy to be his strong point, but there is reason to believe that he took the heroic play more seriously. After *Tyrannic Love* (produced 1669, published 1670) his work in this form reached its height in *The Conquest of Granada* (produced 1670-71, published 1672). These bombastic and artificial rimed plays drew Dryden away for a time from his natural bent. Meanwhile he was defending his work in important prefaces; his vigorous prologues and epilogues, written for his own plays and others too, are also a link between his dramatic practice and his criticism. But the critical current was turning against literary extravagance. The success of the famous burlesque written by Buckingham and others, *The Rehearsal* (produced 1671, published 1672), is a symptom rather than a cause of this change, which appears in the growing sobriety of Dryden's *Aureng-Zebe* (produced 1675, published 1676), and in his return to his Shakespearean allegiance in *All for Love* (produced 1677, published 1678). The bombast or "fustian" of the heroic plays went the way of the conceits of metaphysical poetry, but meanwhile these rhetorical exercises had given Dryden final mastery of the heroic couplet.

Dryden was now making a modest living from his plays; he had become a shareholder of the King's Company in 1668. He was appointed poet laureate and historiographer in 1670, the former retroactive to 1668. The literary and social life of the capital involved the writers of the day in quarrels and feuds largely inflamed by the rivalries of the great patrons, such men as Rochester, Mulgrave, Buckingham, and Dorset. Thus Dryden had a tedious controversy with Elkanah Settle, a mediocre writer of heroic plays, whose *Empress of Morocco* was a center of dispute in 1673 and who was backed by Rochester (see p. 414). In December, 1679, Dryden was badly beaten up by hired bullies because of his supposed authorship of some lampoon or satire. It used to be thought that Rochester was responsible; though this is very doubtful, the "Rose Alley Ambuscade" provides us with an ugly glimpse of the Restoration gangster at work.

In the political excitement of the Popish Plot and the Exclusion Bill (see pp. 40-42), bitter personal and partisan controversy was fused with an intense interest in the highest issues of Church and State. Dryden had always had an intelligent layman's interest in ideas; he belonged to the Royal Society and paid some attention to the new science (see the lines *To My Honour'd Friend Dr. Charleton*, 1663), but probably he had always been more interested in that zone of controversy where religion and politics met. Now the result was twofold: the application of his keen intelligence to the problems of the time led to new achievements in satire and verse-essay, and he was forced as never before to take stock of his own religious and political opinions. *Mac Flecknoe* (probably written about 1678; published 1682) is a purely personal attack on Shadwell, but *Absalom and Achitophel* (1681) and *The Medal* (1682) are supreme examples of satire that combines animus against individuals with what may be called a drama of contending ideas. In siding with the Court against the Whigs led by Shaftesbury Dryden followed his personal inclination and took his color from his associates, but he also came to consider political and religious issues more seriously. A Tory in politics, he was still defending the position of the Church of England in *Religio Laici* (No-

vember, 1682), but on the death of Charles II and the
accession of the Catholic James II, the poet too became a
Catholic, and affirmed this position in *The Hind and the
Panther* (April, 1687). In the former poem he defended
the Church of England against deists and freethinkers,
without extended reference to Dissenters; in the latter, the
noble Hind is the Catholic Church, the Panther is the still
noble but faulty Church of England, and the hated enemies
of both (the Baptist Boar, the Independent Bear, the
Presbyterian Wolf) are the dissenting sects. Thus Dryden
laid himself open to the charge that he was trying to get
on the winning side and keep court favor—a charge constantly repeated by contemporary satirists and later biographers. Recently, however, Bredvold's important study of
the history of Dryden's mind and opinions has shown that
we must think of him, in his own words, as "naturally inclined to skepticism in philosophy," and that in distrust of
man's own power to know and judge aright, he was anxious to find an absolute authority in Church and State.
Theology calls this position "fideism." His change in 1660,
his position in the crisis of 1678-82, his quest for authority
in *Religio Laici*—all point toward the Catholic position
which he assumed in 1686. His official appointments under
Charles were renewed under James, but it cannot be shown
that he got much money or prestige from his conversion.
Moreover, he appears not to have sympathized with the
drastic steps which James took to reëstablish Catholicism;
like other moderate English Catholics he would have preferred a conciliatory policy toward the Church of England.
It was, of course, impossible for him to change again when
Protestantism and limited monarchy triumphed with the
Revolution of 1688. He never took the oath of allegiance
to William and Mary, lost his official appointments, and
resolutely turned again to the business of making his living by his pen.

Though Dryden is not a vivid personality for us, he gains in dignity and mellowness in his later years. His candor appears in his admission of the justice of Jeremy Collier's attack on the viciousness of the Restoration stage. He did not withdraw from the arena, but he no longer thought of himself as a controversialist and fighter. He was by no means a social outcast, and was befriended and admired by men of all parties, particularly by Dorset. From his favorite seat in Will's Coffee House he laid down the law among the wits of the town.

In the last decade of his life he continued to write plays, competently if not with the highest distinction. The turn for rhetorical and eloquent lyric which had appeared in the lines *To the Pious Memory of the Accomplisht Lady Mrs. Anne Killigrew* (1686) and *A Song for St. Cecilia's Day* (1687) reached its height in *Alexander's Feast* (1697). But in the long run his command of verbal harmonies appears to better advantage in his vigorous and resonant heroic couplets. He gave much time and attention to translation, and one of his important achievements was the establishment of standards and methods by which the work of classical and other authors was recast and adapted to the taste of the eighteenth century. What was wanted, according to Dryden, was something not so free as mere paraphrase or imitation, or so close to the original as word for word translation ("metaphrase"). He had begun work of this sort in the 1680's, in the first volumes of the miscellany called "Tonson's"; he now went on to translate Juvenal and Persius (1693), and, most important of all, Virgil (1697), in a version which itself became a classic and remained for the eighteenth century a model of meter and diction. In the *Fables* (1700) he applied his skill as translator and adapter with brilliance and versatility to Chaucer, Boccaccio, Homer, and Ovid. The famous Preface to the *Fables* shows his final development as a critic, his combi-

nation of literary insight and experience with personal
power. Thus he could write:

What judgment I had increases rather than diminishes; and
thoughts, such as they are, come crowding in so fast upon me
that my only difficulty is to choose or to reject, to run them into
verse, or to give them the other harmony of prose: I have so
long studied and practised both that they are grown into a habit,
and become familiar to me.

In the last months of his life he was planning to translate
Homer, "a poet more according to my genius than Virgil."
He died in 1700, and was buried near Chaucer in West-
minster Abbey.

DRYDEN'S SATIRES

Two of the strongest motives in Restoration politics were
fear of France and fear of Catholicism. Since Charles II
was secretly committed to France and attached to the
Catholic faith, while his brother and presumptive heir to
the throne, the Duke of York, was openly Catholic, public
excitement about the succession to the throne was very
great, and led to the formation of an opposition party led
by Anthony Ashley Cooper, Earl of Shaftesbury, who
played on the nation's fear of popery from the time he
went into opposition in 1674. His party backed as Protestant claimant to the throne one of Charles's illegitimate
sons, James, Duke of Monmouth. Then in 1678 came the
fantastic stories of Titus Oates about a Catholic plot to
kill the King and seize the government. The magistrate
Sir Edmund Berry Godfrey, before whom he gave his testimony, was mysteriously murdered. The secretary of the
Duke of York was executed among others for supposed
complicity in the plot. Oates's testimony became more and
more sensational. "Scoops," "exposures," and wild rumors
were spread by broadsides, pamphlets, and word of mouth

as effectively as in the later days of yellow journalism, and the public was swept by a wave of hysteria. Meanwhile something like a two-party system was forming: the Court party got the nickname "Tory"; the opposition "Country" or "Patriot" party was labeled "Whig." The immediate purpose of the Whigs was to pass the Exclusion Bill blocking the succession of the Duke of York, but Charles caught the Whig leaders off guard by suddenly dissolving Parliament at Oxford in March, 1681, and by the end of the year there was a reaction in favor of the Court. In July Shaftesbury was arrested and sent to the Tower. At this point *Absalom and Achitophel I* was published (November, 1681), a partisan utterance perhaps suggested by the King himself and at the same time an immortal satire. Dryden keenly analyzes the characters of the leaders of the opposition, Achitophel (Shaftesbury) and Zimri (Buckingham), and gives us a classic study of human nature in politics. We may contrast with these analytical portraits Dryden's broad and contemptuous caricatures, such as Shimei (Slingsby Bethel). His treatment of David (Charles) is of course flattering; his attitude toward Absalom (Monmouth) is cautious and conciliatory. His general position is that there must be a loyally accepted authority to keep the state from anarchy; this is Toryism, but not the extreme doctrine of divine right and non-resistance. The versatile satire ranges from savage assault to eloquent discussion of first principles, from invective to verse-essay. To appreciate the quality of Dryden's work we have to compare it with the next best satires of 1681, Oldham's *Satires upon the Jesuits*. The narrative element is slight: Dryden takes from Samuel 2:14-18 the story of Absalom's rebellion against David, abetted by the shrewd old counselor Achitophel, a parallel which had already been used by contemporary writers. There is no dramatic action, and the conspiracy comes to a somewhat abrupt end with the final speech of

David, but the whole poem is intended to be a partisan pamphlet rather than a narrative.

Shaftesbury was acquitted by a jury of London Whigs the week after *Absalom and Achitophel I* was published. A medal was struck in honor of this occasion, and Dryden satirized the Whig triumph in *The Medal, A Satire against Sedition* (March, 1682), a short piece notable for its attack on democracy, the tyranny of the crowd. This piece was answered by *The Medal of John Bayes* (May, 1682), probably to be attributed to Shadwell. *Mac Flecknoe* was published at some time during this year, and was long considered to be a reply to *The Medal of John Bayes*. But a reference in the newspaper *The Loyal Protestant,* February 9, 1681-82, shows that *Mac Flecknoe* had been written by that time. It is a purely personal attack on Shadwell, seems to refer exclusively to plays produced in or before the 1670's, and may have been written shortly after the death of Richard Flecknoe, whose successor on the throne of Dulness Shadwell is. Thus Dryden inverts the familiar scheme of the "session of the poets" or "assizes of Parnassus," in which various poets contend for Apollo's prize, the laureateship. But here a booby prize is awarded and the poem is centered about the caricature of Shadwell as a dunce, drawn with magnificent unscrupulousness. Dryden's last great fling at personal satire was in the portraits of Og (Shadwell) and Doeg (Settle) in *Absalom and Achitophel II* (November, 1682) ; the rest of this piece was written by Nahum Tate.

OF DRAMATIC POESY, AN ESSAY (published 1667, dated 1668)

If Dryden's preoccupation with the stage led him to do much second-rate work, we must also remember that it gave the stimulus which made him a great critic. The drama was the chief theme of Restoration criticism, a theme which Dryden made his own. *Of Dramatic Poesy* shows the poise of his temperament, his interest in reconciling the free imaginative drama and robust humor of the Elizabethans with the stricter neo-classical standards largely transmitted from France. The work is truly an essay; that is, it weighs ideas and tries them out. The new classical criticism tended to be dry and mechanical, to apply formulas and catchwords. Dryden pays due attention to formulas and catchwords, but his position is that such things have meaning only as they operate in the judgment and experience of cultivated authors and critics. It is significant that this first important piece of modern English literary criticism is a dialogue with four speakers, Crites (Dryden's brother-in-law Sir Robert Howard), Eugenius (Charles Sackville, Lord Buckhurst, later Earl of Dorset), Lisideius (Sir Charles Sedley), Neander ("New man," Dryden himself). Crites is for the ancients in general against the moderns, Eugenius for the moderns in general against the ancients, with some preference for the English, Lisideius for the French, on the ground that they are stricter in the observance of the classical code than the ancients themselves, Neander for the English drama, whether it be the freedom of Shakespeare or the disciplined regularity of Ben Jonson, as against the more regular French. A subordinate issue, but one which occasioned lively debate between Dryden and Howard before and after the *Essay,* is the question of rime in plays; Crites favors blank verse, Neander rime, which was the mark of the heroic play and was further defended by Dryden against Howard in the *Defence of an Essay of Dramatic Poesy* (1668). Another opposition which runs through the *Essay* is between the Elizabethan and the Restoration drama, with the balance inclining in favor of the Elizabethan. A little later Dryden came to value contemporary style and wit more highly, but eventually he returned to his underlying belief in the primacy of

Shakespeare. The general tone of his criticism is well described by Courthope:[1]

Dryden's Prefaces have all of them, beneath the surface, a parliamentary air; they are the product of active debate in real life. . . . They are also essentially the work of occasion. Some owe their being to innovations on the stage, others to political crises, others again to the enterprise of booksellers; but all imply the existence of a society divided between rival parties, resolved to question, to enquire, to dispute; to give and take blows from opposite sides; an atmosphere, in fact, such as that which prevailed in Will's Coffee-house in the stormy era of the Restoration and the Revolution.

The result is not an authoritarian or dictatorial neoclassicism, but a compromise calculated to appeal to men of moderation and good sense who share the same cultural background.

Hugh Macdonald, *John Dryden: A Bibliography* (Oxford, 1939); J. M. Osborn, "Macdonald's Bibliography of Dryden," *Modern Philology*, xxxix (1941-42). 69-98, 197-212, 313-19; *Works,* ed. Scott-Saintsbury (18v, Edinburgh, 1882-93); *Poetical Works,* ed. W. D. Christie (London, 1870; Globe edition); ed. G. R. Noyes (Boston, 1908; Cambridge edition); *Poems,* ed. J. Sargeaunt (London, 1910); ed. B. Dobrée (London, 1934; Everyman's Library); *Essays,* ed. W. P. Ker (2v, Oxford, 1900); *Poetry and Prose,* ed. D. Nichol Smith (Oxford, 1925); *The Best of Dryden,* ed. L. I. Bredvold (New York, 1933); *The Songs of John Dryden,* ed. C. L. Day (Cambridge, Mass., 1932); *Dramatic Works,* ed. M. Summers (6v, London, 1931-32); *Selected Dramas,* ed. G. R. Noyes (Chicago, 1910); *Letters,* ed. C. E. Ward (Durham, 1942); G. Saintsbury, *Dryden* (London, 1881; English Men of Letters); J. M. Osborn, *John Dryden: Some Biographical Facts and Problems* (New York, 1940); A. W. Verrall, *Lectures on Dryden* (Cambridge, 1914); Allardyce Nicoll, *Dryden and his Poetry* (London, 1923); Alan Lubbock, *The Character of John Dryden* (London, 1925); Mark Van Doren, *The Poetry of John Dryden* (New York, 1932); T. S. Eliot, *John*

[1] W. J. Courthope, *History of English Poetry*, v, 83.

Dryden, the Poet, the Dramatist, the Critic (New York, 1932); L. I. Bredvold, *The Intellectual Milieu of John Dryden* (Ann Arbor, 1934); Mildred Hartsock, "Dryden's Plays: A Study in Ideas," in *Seventeenth Century Studies, Second Series,* ed. R. Shafer (Princeton, 1937); P. H. Frye, "Dryden and the Critical Canons of the Eighteenth Century," *University of Nebraska Studies,* VII (1907). 1-39; G. Thorn-Drury, "Dryden's *Mac Flecknoe,*" *Modern Language Review,* XIII (1918). 276-81; "Some Notes on Dryden," *Review of English Studies,* I (1925). 79-83, 187-97, 324-30; Ruth Wallerstein, "To Madness Near Allied; Shaftesbury and His Place in the Design and Thought of *Absalom and Achitophel,*" *Huntington Library Quarterly,* VI (1943). 445-71; "Dryden and the Analysis of Shakespeare's Techniques," *Review of English Studies,* XIX (1943). 165-85; J. M. Bottkol, "Dryden's Latin Scholarship," *Modern Philology,* XL (1943). 241-54; E. N. Hooker, "The Purpose of Dryden's *Annus Mirabilis,*" *Huntington Library Quarterly,* X (1946). 49-67; G. Davies, "The Conclusion of Dryden's *Absalom and Achitophel,*" *ibid.,* 69-82; S. H. Monk, "Dryden Studies: A Survey, 1920-1945," *ELH,* XIV (1947). 46-63.

SAMUEL BUTLER (1613-1680)
>>

    Samuel Butler grew up near Worcester, was educated there, and is said to have been secretary to several Puritan justices—whence his strong dislike of the fanatics of the Commonwealth. The first two parts of his famous satire *Hudibras* were probably written some years before the Restoration and published respectively in 1662 (dated 1663) and 1663 (dated 1664); a third part followed tardily in 1677 (dated 1678). *Hudibras* delighted the taste of the town because of its attack on the Puritans, but it brought more fame than fortune to its author, and he remained an obscure office-holder until his death in 1680. He became a signal instance of neglected genius, and the tradition, as John Dennis later put it with considerable exaggeration, was "that Butler was starved at the same time that the King had his book in his pocket."

The poem presents the adventures and arguments of a knight Hudibras, representing the Presbyterians, and his squire Ralpho, who holds the opinions of the Independents. A letter of Butler's says that the original of Hudibras was "a west country knight, then a colonel in the Parliamentary Army and a Committee Man, with whom I became acquainted lodging in the same house with him in Holborn." [1] He adds that Ralpho was this colonel's clerk. This supports the tradition that Sir Henry Rosewel of Devonshire was Butler's original, rather than Sir Samuel Luke of Bedfordshire (see *Hudibras*, 1, i, 896). There is little action in the poem: Hudibras undertakes to stop a bear-baiting, and later woos a wealthy widow and consults the astrologer Sidrophel. Instead of the epic breadth of his model *Don Quixote,* Butler gives us merely an elaborate running commentary on human folly, couched in harsh and grotesquely rimed octosyllabic couplets. His burlesque method is to present all human interests and activities in a sequence of grotesque images. War, politics, theology all reduce to a series of wrong-headed arguments and ignoble brawls. Like Swift after him, he portrays man as a perverse quarrelsome animal inevitably led astray by greed and selfishness, com-

BUTLER

---

[1] R. B. Quintana, "The Butler-Oxenden Correspondence," *Modern Language Notes*, XLVIII (1933). 1–11.

plicating what is really simple and obscuring the truth by endless talk and controversy. His other pieces of satire and his pungently written prose *Characters* show that his animus was directed not merely against the Puritans but against the infinite variety of folly to be observed in mankind at large. A Cavalier could be as big a fool as a Puritan.

Historically Butler connects with the Renaissance tradition of burlesque erudition directed against scholastic learning and pedantry in general, seen in richer and more genial form in Rabelais and Cervantes; he also connects with the old comedy of humors, with the burlesque of classical epic models by such French writers as Scarron, and broadly with the traditional idea that satire should be written in a harsh and rugged style. His merits are his great skill in ingenious versification and comic riming, his coinage of striking phrases and lines, and his use of his out of the way learning for surprising figures and analogies. For these qualities the eighteenth century greatly admired him, and he was one of the most quoted and imitated of English poets for a hundred years. Jonathan Swift was in some ways his greatest follower. Students of American literature will find a remarkable example of Butler's influence in John Trumbull's *McFingal* (1775).

Hudibras, ed. A. R. Waller (Cambridge, 1905); *Characters and Passages from Notebooks,* ed. A. R. Waller (Cambridge, 1908); *Satires and Miscellaneous Poetry and Prose,* ed. René Lamar (Cambridge, 1928); René Lamar, "Du nouveau sur l'auteur d'*Hudibras*," *Revue anglo-américaine,* I (1924). 213-27; E. S. de Beer, "The Later Life of Samuel Butler," *Review of English Studies,* IV (1928). 159-66; Richmond Bond, *English Burlesque Poetry, 1700-1750* (Cambridge, Mass., 1932); Dan Gibson, "Samuel Butler," in *Seventeenth Century Studies,* ed. R. Shafer (Princeton, 1933); E. A. Richards, *Hudibras in the Burlesque Tradition* (New York, 1937).

JOHN OLDHAM (1653-1683)

>>

Oldham was the son of a nonconformist clergyman in Gloucestershire, matriculated at St. Edmund's Hall, Oxford, and taught school at Croydon, Kent, where he is said to have been visited by Rochester, Sedley, and Dorset because of their interest in his early verse. He then became a tutor in several families, entered into the literary life of the town, and won great contemporary fame by his *Satires upon the Jesuits: Written in the Year 1679. Upon Occasion of the Plot* (1681). These pieces followed Persius, Juvenal, and the rugged satire of the Elizabethans, and expressed violent Protestant partisanship in the excitement over the Popish Plot. Oldham died of smallpox at the age of thirty. He seems to have avoided personal feuds and enmities, and the great Tory poet Dryden overlooked political and religious differences to pay him a magnificent tribute in verses *To the Memory of Mr. Oldham* (1684). But despite high literary competence, Oldham's harsh and exaggerated indignation lessens the permanent value of his work. He fell into neglect during the eighteenth century, and was omitted from Johnson's collection of the poets.

H. F. Brooks, "Bibliography," *Proceedings of the Oxford Bibliographical Society*, v (1936). 1-38; *Poetical Works*, ed. R. Bell (London, 1854); W. M. Williams, "The Genesis of John Oldham's *Satyrs upon the Jesuits*," *Publications of the Modern Language Association*, LVIII (1943). 958-70.

SIR CHARLES SEDLEY (1639-1701)
CHARLES SACKVILLE, LORD BUCKHURST,
EARL OF DORSET (1643-1706)
JOHN WILMOT, EARL OF ROCHESTER (1647-1680)
>>>

Sedley, Sackville, and Rochester were among the most notorious of Charles II's associates, leaders of the fashionable younger set at court. All three could write a careless and elegant kind of cavalier lyric; good examples are Sackville's "Song Written at Sea," Sedley's "Love still has something of the sea" and "Phyllis is my only joy," and Rochester's "Upon Drinking in a Bowl." Along with Etherege and the versatile Duke of Buckingham they were the most distinguished of those whom Pope calls "the mob of gentlemen that wrote with ease." They were men of genuine literary culture, not mere dabblers and poseurs.

Anthony à Wood sums up Sedley's life immediately after the Restoration by saying that he "lived mostly in the great city; became a debauchee, set up for a satirical wit, a comedian, poet, and courtier of ladies." [1] Prior put it mildly when he wrote of Sackville that "in an age when pleasure was more in fashion than business, he turned his parts rather to books and conversation than to politics." [2] The group was too cynical to be ardently royalist,—they knew the Court too well. Sedley and Dorset lived to sober up, turn Whig, and take part in the Revolution. Dorset's chief claim to a place in literary history is as the great patron of Restoration authors, Dryden, Shadwell, Otway, Lee, Etherege, Congreve, Dennis, Prior, and many minor writers

[1] *Athenae Oxonienses,* quoted by V. de S. Pinto, *Sir Charles Sedley,* p. 51.
[2] Dedication to *Poems on Several Occasions* (1709).

such as Tom D'Urfey. Dryden in particular had good reason to praise his generosity. He set the example for the great Whig patrons of the reign of Queen Anne, Halifax and Somers.

DORSET

Rochester's career was brief and meteoric; at the end of his extravagant life he died repentant and made a good end, as Bishop Burnet reported in a famous tract, *The Life and Death of the Earl of Rochester* (1680). On the surface Rochester is a careless and cultured young aristocrat. His *Allusion to Horace, The Tenth Satire of the First Book* is an early example of the fitting of contemporary English matter into the Horatian framework. It expresses the somewhat supercilious attitude of Rochester's coterie:

> I loathe the rabble. 'Tis enough for me
> If Sedley, Shadwell, Sheppard, Wycherley,
> Godolphin, Butler, Buckhurst, Buckingham,
> And some few more whom I omit to name,
> Approve my sense, I count their censure fame.

Thus the satirist praises his friends at the expense of other writers who are dismissed contemptuously—Dryden, Crowne, Otway, Settle, and Lee. Modern students find in Rochester an interesting representative of a lost generation, ironically conscious that he was wandering in a waste land; he may be overrated just now for this reason. Along with cavalier grace, he shows at times a brutal cynicism and a disposition to reflect on the ugly realities which underlie

a life of sensual pleasure. Thus his most important poem
is the *Satire against Mankind* (1675), which is indebted to
a satire of Boileau's but has a deeper personal coloring
and a broader philosophical background. Here Rochester
treats what satirists and moralists considered the central
issue, man's animality and his dubious claim to rationality.
Rochester belittles reason as a guide, and the aspirations
of fanatical theologians to attain a knowledge of divine
truth; he praises the sure operation of instinct in animals
as contrasted with the extravagance of human reason and
human passion. Thus he shows himself aware of a vein of
thought, to be found in Plutarch and Montaigne and destined to reappear in Swift, which exalts the life of the lower
animals as moderate, constant, and self-sufficient, above the
irrational career of man. Rochester's philosophy is Epicurean; true reason, as opposed to the false reason of the
theologians and philosophers, aims at maintaining and re-
newing the pleasures of the senses. Yet he does not settle
down contentedly with such a program, but suggests, somewhat in the manner of Butler and Swift, that man cannot
live up to a sensible idea of moderation.

Collected Works of John Wilmot, Earl of Rochester, ed. J. Hay-
ward (London, 1926); *A Satire against Mankind and Other
Poems*, ed. H. Levin (Norfolk, Conn., 1942); J. Prinz, *John Wil-
mot Earl of Rochester* (Leipzig, 1927); V. de S. Pinto, *Rochester.
Portrait of a Restoration Poet* (London, 1935); K. B. Murdock,
The Sun at Noon (New York, 1939) [contains biographical sketch
of Rochester]; *The Rochester-Savile Letters, 1671-1680*, ed. J. H.
Wilson (Columbus, 1941); J. F. Moore, "The Originality of
Rochester's *Satyr Against Mankind*," *Publications of the Mod-
ern Language Association*, LVIII (1943). 393-401; J. H. Wilson,
"Rochester's 'Session of the Poets,'" *Review of English Studies*,
XXII (1946). 109-16; *Poetical and Dramatic Works of Sir Charles
Sedley*, ed. V. de S. Pinto (2v, London, 1928); V. de S. Pinto,
Sir Charles Sedley, 1639-1701 (London, 1927); Brice Harris,
Charles Sackville, Sixth Earl of Dorset (Urbana, 1940).

SIR WILLIAM TEMPLE (1628-1699)
>>>

Temple earned a place in history as a diplomat; he had much to do with negotiating the Triple Alliance of England, Holland, and Sweden against France in 1668, and the Treaty of Nimiguen (1678), ending the war between France and a continental alliance; furthermore he helped to arrange the marriage of William and Mary in 1677. But he withdrew in disgust from public life during the political crisis of 1679, and thereafter lived in retirement at Sheen and later at Moor Park, Surrey. An eminent virtuoso, moved by intellectual curiosity and by a desire of exercising his mind and his style, he wrote well if not profoundly on a variety of subjects and was long admired as a stylist. Johnson went so far as to say that "Temple was the first writer who gave cadence to English prose."

More important for the modern student are the fresh suggestions for cultural history which Temple passed on to the eighteenth century. The essay *Of Heroic Virtue* draws illustrative matter from Arabian, Chinese, Peruvian, and "Scythian" culture; in particular it dwells on the hardy valor and love of liberty of the northern peoples, and thus sets an important theme for later writers. His reference to the irregularity of Chinese gardening is important in aesthetic history (see pp. 248-49). *Of Poetry* contains the famous passage on *humor* as a unique English quality, produced by special conditions of society and climate. *On the Original and Nature of Government* shows marked speculative power in deriving society not from the "social contract" which was then assumed by most social scientists, but from a natural extension of patriarchal authority in the family. In the *Essay upon Ancient and Modern Learning* he mixes ill-advisedly in the controversy which had been stirred up by the praise of the moderns in France by Perrault and Fontenelle. Temple defends the ancients, not because he is a devotee of classical culture, but because his view of history as a series of cycles leads him to deny the dogma of progress. He seriously underrates modern scientific achievement. The controversy in England led to Wotton's *Reflections upon Ancient and Modern Learning* in reply to Temple, Boyle's edition of the Epistles of Phalaris, which Temple had praised as an example of the merit of the ancients, and Bentley's crushing demonstration that Phalaris was spurious. Bentley's work, unlike the amateur efforts of the other participants, is a monument of learning. Meanwhile Temple's young secretary Jonathan Swift had written *The Battle of the Books* (see p. 143), nominally on his master's side. The relation between Temple and Swift has been misinterpreted as that of a somewhat pompous and selfish elderly man to a powerful and proud young genius. While Swift could never be completely satisfied with the easy going virtuosity of Temple, he acquired many important ideas and attitudes during his years at Moor Park, and Temple was on the whole a good patron to him.

Many eighteenth-century editions of *Works; Essays on Ancient and Modern Learning and on Poetry,* ed. J. E. Spingarn (Oxford, 1909); *Early Essays and Romances,* ed. G. C. Moore Smith (Oxford, 1930); Clara Marburg, *Sir William Temple: A Seventeenth Century 'Libertin'* (New Haven, 1932); Homer E. Woodbridge, *Sir William Temple: The Man and His Work* (New York, 1940); *The Letters of Dorothy Osborne to William Temple,* ed. G. C. Moore Smith (Oxford, 1928).

JOHN BUNYAN (1628-1688)

>>

Bunyan, like the other great Puritan Milton, represents attitudes formed before 1660. At the same time Bunyan's work shows the power of Dissent to develop, under the influence of the Bible, a plain style universally acceptable and destined to meet the needs of a great reading public to come. Bunyan also shows post-Restoration Dissent grimly struggling against political disabilities and making its great contribution to the national culture. And beyond all this, he represents the plain sturdy English Puritan in such a way as to transcend the limitations of time and circumstance.

Bunyan was born at Elstow, Bedfordshire, of humble though not poverty-stricken parents, and followed his father's trade of brazier or whitesmith (called "tinker"). He served in the Parliamentary forces from 1644 to 1647 at Newport Pagnell, Buckinghamshire. On his return to Elstow and his marriage, his thoughts turned seriously to religion and he became a devout Churchman, reading the Bible and a few pious works and engaging in serious self-examination. This period is described in *Grace Abounding,* one of the most important of religious autobiographies, which may well exaggerate the magnitude of his sins, but not the intensity of his religious struggles. In 1653 he joined the nonconformist congregation of John Gifford at Bedford, and soon began to preach and to carry on religious controversy. The first of his numerous publications was *Some Gospel Truths Opened* (1656). His own congregation was Baptist, and he had bitter disputes with the Quakers, but his spirit was not narrowly sectarian, and his imagination and his humane grasp of religious truth eventually enabled him to write of the Christian life in terms acceptable to all mankind. His homely style was in the tradition of popular preaching. Innate practicality and shrewdness kept him from the wild extravagances of the sects. He shows from the first his great power of using visualized homely detail for the purpose of religious teaching: "I saw, through grace, that it was the blood shed on Mount Calvary that did save and redeem sinners, as clearly and as really with the eyes of my soul as ever, methought, I had seen a penny loaf bought with a penny" (*The Doctrine of the Law and Grace Unfolded,* 1659).[1]

The Restoration persecution of nonconformists led to the imprisonment of Bunyan in Bedford Jail from 1660 to 1672, when he was released by Charles's Declaration of Indulgence (see p. 3), and became pastor of Bedford Meeting. During his imprisonment he had published many religious works; the most important is *Grace Abounding* (1666). In 1675 he was imprisoned again for six months. Now began the time of his greatest literary achievement. *Pilgrim's Progress,* planned earlier, was written during this second imprisonment and published in 1678. Other important works of this period were *The Life and Death of Mr. Badman* (1680) and *The Holy War* (1682). The second part of *Pilgrim's Progress* appeared in 1684.

Saving only the parables of the New Testament, *Pilgrim's Progress* is the most popular allegory in literary history. It has gone through innumerable editions and been translated into more than a hundred languages. Bunyan's earnestness and practicality kept him to a statement of the essentials of the religious life in terms of the adventures of a journey. The basic scheme is simple, and need not have a literary origin, though Bunyan no doubt thought of the adventures in popular romances he had read in early life. Much of his content, however, is drawn from the actualities of life

1 *Works* (3v, London, 1862), I. 549.

about him. The style is straight from the Bible, mingled with seventeenth-century colloquial English. The realism is so systematic as to make Bunyan a forerunner of the great novelists. He was scarcely influenced by literary ambitions or critical fashions; he had little consciousness of style and technique as distinct from subject-matter, yet he tells us that he wrote *Pilgrim's Progress* to please himself—"I did it mine own self to gratify"—thus confessing perhaps to the self-conscious pleasure of the artist. In the stark realism of *Mr. Badman* we have an unrelenting plainness which points toward Defoe; in *The Holy War* a much more elaborate and artificial allegory of the siege of Mansoul by Diabolus. *Pilgrim's Progress* long competed with *Robinson Crusoe* for universal popularity and complete adoption by the folk. The authors of both books were long despised or underestimated by literary people. But if we compare the two men we see that, though both have an equal grasp of plain facts and plain words, something is lost when we turn from Bunyan's spiritual integrity to the shopkeeping ethics of Defoe.

Pilgrim's Progress, ed. J. B. Wharey (Oxford, 1928); *Pilgrim's Progress and Mr. Badman*, ed. G. B. Harrison (London, 1928); *Pilgrim's Progress and Grace Abounding*, ed. E. Venables (Oxford, 1900); *Grace Abounding and Pilgrim's Progress*, ed. J. Brown (Cambridge, 1907); *Mr. Badman and Holy War*, ed. J. Brown (Cambridge, 1905); J. Brown, *John Bunyan, 1628–1688: His Life, Times, and Work* (rev. ed., London, 1928); G. O. Griffith, *John Bunyan* (London, 1927); G. B. Harrison, *John Bunyan* (London, 1928); J. B. Wharey, *A Study of the Sources of Bunyan's Allegories* (Baltimore, 1904); "Bunyan's Mr. Badman and the Picaresque Novel," *University of Texas Studies in English*, IV (1924); Harold Golder, "John Bunyan's Hypocrisy," *North American Review*, CCXXIII (1926). 323-32; W. Y. Tindall, *John Bunyan, Mechanick Preacher* (New York, 1934).

SAMUEL PEPYS (1633-1703)

>>

Samuel Pepys has become the best-known character of his time; in his famous diary we can relive the life of a citizen of Restoration London. He was an ordinary man in some ways—a busy, inquisitive government clerk recording for nine years everything that he thought and did, but a genius too, in his quick response to the many aspects of life, his aptitude for catching the salient detail of every moment. "I staid up till the bellman came by with his bell under my window, as I was writing of this very line, and cried 'Past one of the clock, and a cold, frosty, windy morning.'" His hopes and fears and discomforts, his love of music and the theater, his domestic pleasures and troubles, his casual amours—all are set down without reserve, and with such enthusiasm and vividness as to give distinction to the commonplace.

These details stand out against the great historical events which Pepys saw and in which he had a share. The son of a London tailor, he was well educated at St. Paul's and Cambridge, and appears as a protégé of Edward Montagu, afterwards first Earl of Sandwich. At the Restoration he was made Clerk of the King's ships and of the Acts of the Navy, and became an efficient and indispensable administrator of naval affairs at a crucial period. Though he took perquisites and presents, he was far superior to the typical office-holder of his time; the history of the Navy during these years was inglorious, but Pepys did what he could. He was President of the Royal Society in 1684 and 1685, and Secretary of the Admiralty from 1684 to 1688. Throughout his career he was closely associated with the Duke of York, afterwards James II, and went out of office after the

Revolution of 1688. He left his collections of books, broadside ballads, and manuscripts, including the famous diary, to his own college, Magdalene, Cambridge, where the visitor to the Pepysian Library may still see them in bindings and cases of Pepys' own design. He accumulated large

The condition of the State was thus ·viz·. The Rump after being disturbed by my Lord Lambert. was lately returned to sit again. The Officers of the Army all forced to yield — Lawson lies still in the River. & Monk is with his Army in Scotland.

PEPYS FACSIMILE WITH TRANSCRIPTION

masses of letters and official documents which have been used by recent biographers to reconstruct his important career as a public official.

His later years are well described in Evelyn's *Diary,* May 26, 1703:

This day died Mr. Samuel Pepys, a very worthy, industrious and curious person, none in England exceeding him in knowledge of the navy, in which he had passed through all the most considerable offices, Clerk of the Acts and Secretary of the Admiralty, all which he performed with great integrity. When King James II went out of England, he laid down his office, and would serve no more; but withdrawing himself from all public affairs, he lived at Clapham with his partner, Mr. Hewer, formerly his clerk, in a very noble house and sweet place, where he enjoyed the fruit of his labors in great prosperity. He was universally beloved, hospitable, generous, learned in many things, skilled in music, a very great cherisher of learned men of whom he had the conversation. His library and collection of other curiosities were of the most considerable, the models of ships especially. Besides what he published of an account of the navy, as he found and left it, he had for divers years under his hand the History of the Navy, or *Navalia,* as he called it.

Pepys kept his diary from New Year's, 1660, to May 31, 1669, when he gave it up because of failing eyesight. It consists of about three thousand pages written in Shelton's shorthand, a well-known system of the time. This can hardly be called a secret code, but the diary was thus made inaccessible to the ordinary reader, and evidently Pepys wrote only for himself. The diary was first transcribed early in the nineteenth century by a Cambridge student named John Smith; Lord Braybrooke published about a quarter of the text in 1825, Mynors Bright published much more in 1875, and Henry B. Wheatley published the whole, except for some expurgations, in 1893–99. Pepys' method obviously contrasts with John Evelyn's, who wrote more formal entries and carefully revised his text. Indeed, most diarists, like all letter-writers, have a reader in mind; the complete spontaneity and frankness of Pepys are so rare as to give him a unique place in literature.

Diary, ed. H. B. Wheatley (10v, London, 1893–99); *Correspondence and Papers,* ed. J. R. Tanner (3v, London, 1926-29); H. B. Wheatley, *Samuel Pepys and the World He Lived In* (New York, 1880); J. R. Tanner, *Mr. Pepys: An Introduction to the Diary together with a Sketch of his Later Life* (London, 1925); Arthur Ponsonby, *Samuel Pepys* (New York, 1928; English Men of Letters); Arthur Bryant, *Samuel Pepys* (3v, Cambridge, 1933–38); Clara Marburg, *Mr. Pepys and Mr. Evelyn* (Philadelphia, 1935).

JOHN EVELYN (1620-1706)

>>

Evelyn's famous *Diary* is not an intimate day by day record like Pepys', but a series of memoirs drawn up in the form of a journal, mingling earlier and later impressions and judgments. From 1643 to 1652 Evelyn resided on the Continent, thus keeping out of trouble at home, and the first third of the *Diary* is devoted to a record of this protracted grand tour. Thereafter he lived at Sayes Court, Deptford, indulging his taste for planting and his miscellaneous interests as a virtuoso. After 1660 the *Diary* gives a remarkable record of the Restoration as seen by a respectable and intelligent man who was loyal to the King but who could not approve the licentiousness of the Court. Evelyn was a prominent member of the Royal Society, and did some work as a public official, especially in caring for the casualties of the Dutch War. But he preferred to mind his books and his garden. His miscellaneous writings, though sometimes defective in style and in technical grasp, testify to the breadth of his interests—*Sculptura* (1662), on engraving; *Kalendarium Hortense* (1664) or garden calendar; *Sylva* (1664), on the planting of trees; *Fumifugium* (1661), on the smoke-nuisance in London, and others. The *Diary*, the most important item in a large mass of manuscript collectanea, is one of the best-known sources for the Restoration period.

Geoffrey Keynes, *John Evelyn. A Study in Bibliophily and a Bibliography of his Writings* (Cambridge, 1937) ; *Diary*, ed. W. Bray (2v, London, 1818) ; ed. H. B. Wheatley (4v, London, 1879); ed. A. Dobson (3v, London, 1906) [variant texts, none reliable]; Arthur Ponsonby, *John Evelyn* (London, 1933); G. B. Parks, "John Evelyn and the Art of Travel," *Huntington Library Quarterly*, x (1947). 251-76. [Forthcoming complete edition of the *Diary* by E. S. de Beer.]

ater, the house was roofed and lighted by chandeliers. Physically the stage was a compromise between the Elizabethan and the modern; an outer stage projecting into the pit still remained, but the essential feature of the modern stage, the proscenium arch, divided this outer stage from an inner stage, and was provided with a curtain. The curtain was not used as in the modern theater; in general it was kept up during the performance, not lowered and raised between acts. Exits and entrances were ordinarily made through doors, one or two on each side, situated under the proscenium arch. Above the outer pair of doors were windows. Scenes were usually changed by closing or opening flat sets. Scenery was used on the inner stage; there was a great increase in the use of spectacular settings, and this is connected by historians of the theater with a deterioration of serious drama itself. Certainly the interest in decoration and spectacle conflicted with the classicist's demand for observance of the unities of time, place, and action. The use of scenery ultimately came from court performances in the time of James I and Charles I, and was now transferred to the public stage. Even before the reopening of the theaters Davenant's pioneer productions showed what an important part scenic and musical effects were soon to have (*The First Days Entertainment at Rutland House,* May 23, 1656; *The Siege of Rhodes Made a Representation by the Art of Prospective in Scenes and the Story sung in Recitative Music,* September, 1656; *The Cruelty of the Spaniards in Peru* and *The History of Sir Francis Drake,* at the Cockpit in Drury Lane, 1658 and 1659). Beside the introduction of scenery the great innovation of the Restoration stage was of course the employment of actresses in place of the Elizabethan boy actors.

The audience occupied the pit, the middle and upper galleries, and the boxes. The Elizabethan custom of sitting on the stage was discouraged and more or less completely

forbidden after the Restoration, but reappeared at the end
of the century and continued into the next. Gallants took
full advantage of their privileges and made public nui-
sances of themselves. Gentlemen claimed the right to see

ADMISSION CHECKS FOR THE DORSET GARDENS THEATER
Above, an upper gallery check of 1671 with the coronet and monogram
of the Duke of York; below, a pit check of 1684 when the house was
known as the Queen's.

one act free, and the general public at first had free entrance after the third act, but at the end of the century a
small fee called "after-money" was collected. Allured particularly by the actresses, gallants often went behind the
scenes to the "music room" or "green room." One corner
of the pit, regularly occupied by noisy and ostentatious
gallants, was called "fop corner." Prostitutes haunted pit
and galleries in masks, and orange women hawked their

wares. As in Elizabethan times, performances began in mid-afternoon, but toward the end of the century the hour became later.

Acting styles were naturally more realistic in the comedy of manners than in tragedy, where Betterton, the great leader of the profession, cultivated a formal and stately manner. The actresses contributed charm and talent, but one does not have to be a Puritan to add that their influence was not always good. Their rôles were of great importance and encouraged the development of what was called the "she-tragedy"; even the delivery of the prologue or epilogue by the cleverest actress in the company might be an important part of the program. Costumes were elaborate, but not adapted to the supposed time and place of action, though such characters as orientals and Indians would wear exotic garb, and there seems to have been a stock military costume, helmet and armor, for Greek and Roman characters. Conventions were established and persisted: thus heroic characters wore a large plumed hat or headdress; kings and generals carried truncheons; villains and murderers wore black wigs and indeed entire suits of black. It is always important to keep in mind the externals of Restoration drama. As Edward Howard complained in 1671, "Scenes, habits, dancing, or perhaps an actress, take more with spectators than the best dramatic wit." [1]

Restoration dramatists manipulated established forms to meet the tastes of their audiences. An Elizabethan repertory was maintained after a fashion; Shakespeare's plays were acted in altered and mutilated form; the comedies of Beaumont and Fletcher were "the most frequent entertainments of the stage," said Dryden in 1668, and Ben Jonson's comedy of humors was greatly admired. When new dramatic types appear in this period, it seems reasonable to suppose

[1] Preface to *Six Days Adventure*, quoted by C. V. Deane, *Dramatic Theory and the Rhymed Heroic Play*, p. 63.

that they connect with the English dramatic situation in the middle of the seventeenth century, which up to recent times has not been well understood. Earlier accounts exaggerated the break in dramatic tradition caused by the closing of the theaters, and the importance of foreign, especially French, influences. We now know that there was no complete break and no sudden transformation by foreign influence, even though there were important changes in tone and style.

HEROIC PLAY AND TRAGEDY

In serious drama an important development was the emergence of the heroic play. This type may be described in the words of Professor Clark as "a wholly serious play, composed in rimed verse, with a tone befitting heroic poetry, and concerned with the lofty sentiments of persons in high station." The heroic tone means in practice a declamatory style, sometimes wildly extravagant but always controlled by logic and rhetoric rather than spontaneous feeling. The lofty sentiments are called forth by violent conflicts between love and honor, with lovers changing their minds and kings and rebel leaders changing sides and policies in the affairs of some remote and exotic kingdom, such as Peru, Granada, or Agra. The plays usually avoid tragic endings, but aspire to tragic elevation of character; much of their popularity must have been due to the opportunity they gave for spectacular settings and stage effects. The rimed couplets were a fashion of the 1660's and 1670's rather than an essential feature. This artificial and pretentious form has been variously connected with the bombastic strain in Elizabethan drama, especially in Marlowe, with a somewhat similar vein in the dramatic romances of Beaumont and Fletcher, with the French heroic romances which were highly popular in England, with traditional epic heroism, and with Italian opera. "An heroic play ought

to be an imitation, in little, of an heroic poem," wrote
Dryden in his *Essay of Heroic Plays* prefixed to *The Conquest of Granada* (1672). As Professor Harbage points out,
we have here to do with a diffused heroic ideal, variously
realized in the sources just enumerated, and already brought
on the English stage in the "cavalier drama" cultivated by
the aristocracy in the reigns of James I and Charles I. The
little-known cavalier plays of that period have essentially
the same features as the notorious heroic plays of the age
of Dryden. The type can be made out in Davenant's *Siege
of Rhodes* (1656), is cultivated in the rimed tragedies of
Roger Boyle, Earl of Orrery, in the early 1660's,[1] under
strong collateral influence from French romance appears
fully developed in Dryden and Howard's *Indian Queen*
(produced 1664), rises to heights of rant in Dryden's *Tyrannic Love* (produced 1669), achieves magnificence of style
in Dryden's *Conquest of Granada* (produced 1670 and
1671), and becomes more rational and formal in Dryden's
Aureng-Zebe (produced 1675). The movement dies down
in the late 1670's, but leaves a legacy of turgidity and rant
to later English tragedy. The heroic play may be described
as a deliberate attempt to be romantic and heroic in an
unromantic and unheroic age, an age that was drawing a
sharp line between imagination and reason. The adjective
romantic appears just when this distinction is made, and
seems to have been coined in the middle of the century to
denote an artificial cultivation of the imaginary or fictitious.
The Rehearsal (1671), by the Duke of Buckingham and
others (probably Thomas Sprat, Samuel Butler, and Martin Clifford) , attacked among various dramatic fashions the
extravagances of the heroic plays; it had been originally
planned in the 1660's as an attack on Davenant and Sir

---

[1] *The Black Prince* and *Henry the Fifth*. Not produced and published until 1664 and later, but possibly written earlier and circulated
in manuscript.

Robert Howard, but finally centered on Dryden ("Bayes"). The success of *The Rehearsal* did not eradicate the deep love of bombast or the popularity of spectacular effects on the stage. There was, however, a strong counter-movement, and the extravagance of the love-and-honor poet became proverbial, like the extravagance of the French heroic romance. *The Rehearsal* later became the model for a series of brilliant dramatic burlesques, down to Sheridan's *Critic* (1779). The vogue of the heroic play must have been closely connected with the popularity of exaggerated styles in acting. The mode encouraged not only bombast but the extravagant expression of the tender emotions; this dual aspect is ridiculed in the rough verses of Thomas Shadwell:

> A dull romantic whining play,
> Where poor frail woman's made a deity,
> With senseless amorous idolatry,
> And sniveling heroes sigh, and pine, and cry.
> Though singly they beat armies, and huff kings,
> Rant at the gods, and do impossible things,
> Though they can laugh at danger, blood, and wounds,
> Yet if the dame once chides, the milk-sop hero swoons.
>   (Epilogue to *The Virtuoso*, 1676)

The return to blank verse in tragedy about 1677, notably Dryden's *All for Love* (produced 1677, published 1678), though it does not mean the complete submergence of the heroic, marks the heightening of various influences which may be loosely described as Elizabethan. Good writing, even in the most artificial kinds of literature, is not completely controlled by formula, and in *All for Love* we have the Shakespearean theme of Antony and Cleopatra subjected to Restoration rhetoric and reason without losing its vitality. Antony becomes the great example of the conflict of love and honor. Dryden achieves a mingling of Elizabethan nobility with artificial heroism and fairly strict neo-classical form, a synthesis which was beyond the reach of his ablest contemporaries.

In the excitement attending the Popish Plot the dramatists became intensely partisan, and plays with marked political intention were written by Dryden, Lee, Otway, and
Crowne for the Tories, by Settle and Shadwell for the
Whigs, but politics did not lead to any intellectual or
artistic triumphs in the drama.

Aristotle's definition of tragedy set forth as essential the
appeal to pity and terror. With this Renaissance criticism
had combined the idea of admiration, which may be taken
as the keynote of the heroic play. Thus Dryden had defended the heroic play by arguing that, like the epic, it
was not bound by the limits of the true and the probable.
The extreme of artificial elevation could not be maintained
for long, and the analogy with the epic failed, but the two
emotions of Aristotle's definition could be connected with
the harsh and the tender passions of the love and honor
play. The two aspects are differentiated in the work of the
pathetic Otway and the ranting Lee.

Thomas Otway (1652-1685). Otway, a clergyman's son
educated at Winchester and Christ Church, Oxford, was
drawn into the life of the town as an unsuccessful actor
and as a writer of rather undistinguished comedies and
one significant historical play—*Don Carlos*, 1676. His
Caius Marius (produced 1679, published 1680) curiously
puts the plot of *Romeo and Juliet* into a Roman setting,
but marks his change to blank verse and the Elizabethan
poetic vein. His high reputation rests on two plays, *The
Orphan* (1680) and *Venice Preserved* (1682). A hopeless
love for the actress Mrs. Barry, who created the rôle of
Monimia in *The Orphan* and of Belvidera in *Venice Preserved*, deeply colored his private life. He died in poverty
in 1685. His career suggests a cross between a "university
wit" of the Elizabethan period and an unfortunate young
poet of the romantic age.

The Orphan tells of the love of the twin brothers Castalio and Polydore for the hapless Monimia; Polydore, not knowing that Castalio is actually married to her, takes his brother's place by stealth on the wedding night. The half-accidental disaster and the painfully intense feeling anticipate the sentimental turn the English drama was soon to take; the substitution of a pathetic and domestic for a heroic theme similarly anticipates the tendency of later tragedy to seek a middle class level. *Venice Preserved* deals with friendship, outraged love, and political action. Pierre, who enters into a conspiracy to free Venice from senatorial tyranny, involves his friend Jaffeir, who offers his wife Belvidera as a hostage for his good faith. When Belvidera is grossly insulted by one of his confederates, Jaffeir betrays the plot, but atones for his disloyalty by taking his place on the scaffold beside his friend. The theme of the conspiracy connects the play with the excitement of the Popish Plot; the work is Tory in spirit, and contains a gross caricature of Shaftesbury. In general it transposes the love and honor theme of the heroic play to a finer level of poetry and psychology, and thus offers a technical parallel to Dryden's *All for Love;* its wide appeal came from its combination of high Roman conceptions of political and personal loyalty (as in *Julius Caesar* and *All for Love*) with Otway's characteristic softness and pathos.

Nathaniel Lee (1649?-1692), an almost exact contemporary of Otway, made the transition from the rimed heroic play to blank verse in 1677 with *The Rival Queens,* presenting the rivalry of Roxana and Statira for the love of Alexander the Great, a plot drawn not so much from classical antiquity as from French heroic romance (La Calprenède, *Cassandre*). He collaborated with Dryden in *Oedipus* (1678) and *The Duke of Guise* (1682). Undisciplined in his life and his writing, he went mad for a time and was confined in Bedlam. Along with a strong heroic vein, he represents

a return to Elizabethan models, perhaps with special influence from the Jacobean tragedies of Ford and Webster.
He indulges to the full his taste for extravagant diction,
rant, and spectacular scenic effects. "In what raptures,"
wrote Colley Cibber later, "have I seen an audience at the
furious fustian and turgid rants in Nat Lee's *Alexander
the Great!* ... When these flowing numbers came from the
mouth of a Betterton, the multitude no more desired sense
to them than our musical connoisseurs think it essential in
the celebrate [*sic*] airs of an Italian opera." [1]

The rather rough division of heroic and pathetic which
appears in the contrast between Lee and Otway was pro-
longed into the next century. The pathetic came to dominate the heroic in John Banks (*The Unhappy Favourite,
or The Earl of Essex,* 1681; *Vertue Betray'd, or Anna
Bullen,* 1682), and in Thomas Southerne (*The Fatal Marriage,* 1694; *Oroonoko,* 1696). There was a general falling
off in original drama after the union of the companies in
1682 and the partisan paroxysms of the stage during the
excitement of the Popish Plot. In the following years opera
gained ground with a public interested in music and spectacle; comedy, as we shall see, held and consolidated its
gains, while tragedy lost its vitality. Persistent criticism of
rhetorical and bombastic tragedy was of little real aid in
preserving and developing serious drama in the eighteenth
century.

Heroic Play and Tragedy: Bonamy Dobrée, *Restoration Trag-
edy, 1660–1720* (Oxford, 1929) ; L. N. Chase, *The English Heroic
Play* (New York, 1903) ; B. J. Pendlebury, *Dryden's Heroic Plays*
(London, 1923); C. V. Deane, *Dramatic Theory and the Rhymed
Heroic Play* (London, 1931); W. S. Clark, "The Sources of the
Restoration Heroic Play," *Review of English Studies,* IV (1928).
49-63; "The Definition of the Heroic Play in the Restoration
Period," *ibid.,* VIII (1932). 437-44; Alfred Harbage, *Cavalier Drama*
(New York, 1936); A. E. Parsons, "The English Heroic Play,"

[1] *Apology*, Ch. IV (2d ed., London, 1740), I. 88-89.

Modern Language Review, XXXIII (1938). 1-14; Roger Boyle, Earl of Orrery, *Dramatic Works,* ed. W. S. Clark (2v, Cambridge, Mass., 1937) ; Thomas Otway, *Works,* ed. M. Summers (3v, London, 1926) ; ed. J. C. Ghosh (2v, Oxford, 1932) ; R. G. Ham, *Otway and Lee, Biography for a Baroque Age* (New Haven, 1931); W. B. Van Lennep, "Nathaniel Lee," *Harvard University Summaries of Theses, 1934* (Cambridge, Mass., 1935), pp. 337-41; John Banks, *The Unhappy Favourite,* ed. T. M. H. Blair (New York, 1939); J. W. Dodds, *Thomas Southerne, Dramatist* (New Haven, 1933).

COMEDY

Restoration drama, intended for a limited and special audience, develops specialized types—the heroic play and, even more characteristic, a new comedy of manners. The age which Dryden described in *The Secular Masque* as "a very merry, dancing, drinking, laughing, quaffing, and unthinking time" was hospitable to comedy. At the reopening of the theaters various kinds of comedy were cultivated. Dryden's early plays show us the situation. *The Wild Gallant* (produced 1663) seems to be a remaking of a farce by the Jonsonian Richard Brome. *The Rival Ladies* (1664) takes a complicated Spanish plot and mixes heroic verse with intrigue; this mixture was called tragicomedy, of which *Secret Love, or The Maiden Queen* (produced 1667), based on Scudéry's *Grand Cyrus,* is the best example in Dryden's work. With Davenant he did Shakespeare's *Tempest* over in 1667, a literary atrocity. In *Sir Martin Mar-All* (written by Newcastle and revised by Dryden; produced 1667) and *An Evening's Love, or The Mock-Astrologer* produced 1668) appears the practice of making inferior adaptations from Molière and the comedies of the younger Corneille. *Marriage à la Mode* (produced 1671), with a slight slant toward the heroic, is dominated by a bright comic intrigue. The use of scabrous sexual themes appears in *The Assignation* (produced 1672) and *The Kind Keeper.*

or Mr. Limberham (produced 1678). In *The Spanish Friar*
(produced 1680) Dryden attains a brilliant success in low
comedy. When he returns to comedy ten years later in
Amphitryon (from Plautus and Molière) and *Don Sebas-
tian,* he shows competence but no further advance. The
mere desire to try what would please the public led to
eclecticism.

Jonson's comedy of humors was a distinct and powerful
influence; the technique of making each character represent a dominant humor, a single obsession or absurdity, was
a practical device which enabled the dramatist to get quick
and direct effects. John Wilson's Jonsonian comedies (*The
Cheats,* produced 1662, published 1664; *The Projectors,*
1665) have merit. The invention of humors was likely to
be combined with mere bustle and farce, as in the
plays of Thomas Shadwell (see p. 82). Jonsonian humors
formed a solid substratum for realistic comedy and later
for comic fiction. In the long run the humors were plastic
enough to be variously combined with realism, high or low
comedy, satire, or even sentiment. But humorous sketches
of character had somehow to be tied up with plots, and, in
the more philosophical kind of comedy, related to a social
system. A vein of intrigue on the early Restoration stage,
as in Sir Samuel Tuke's *Adventures of Five Hours* (1663,
much admired by Pepys) and in several of Dryden's comedies is associated with the Spanish "cloak and sword"
comedy. In addition to French and Spanish sources, the
plots of Fletcher's comedies also contribute here; Restoration plays are too often mere tangles of trick and stratagem. Aphra Behn, best known for her famous romance
Oroonoko (see p. 397), was one of the most competent
writers of the comedy of intrigue (e.g., *The Rover,* I, 1677;
II, 1680). Bustling farces, variously combined with intrigues
and humors, were always acceptable. Here we get into the
extra-literary tradition of the art of getting laughs. It is

significant that Shakespeare's romantic comedies found little favor, and that the more favored pieces of Beaumont
and Fletcher seem to have been those in which comic dialogue outweighed romance. Molière's comedies were well
known and frequently adapted, but not in such a way as
to approach Molière's penetrating analysis of human nature. No English writer of comedy, George Meredith complained later, has succeeded like Molière in arousing
"thoughtful laughter."

Yet from amid the complex of social and literary influences there appears a unique result, the Restoration comedy
of manners, denounced as the reflection of a vicious society by the intolerant clergyman Jeremy Collier and by
moralistic critics like Steele and Macaulay in later times,
admired as a sheer creation of fancy detached from the
actual social situation by Charles Lamb, admired as a consistent reflection of a society based on a philosophy of pleasure by John Palmer and Bonamy Dobrée. Attention here
centers almost exclusively on what we may call the "big
five"—Etherege, Wycherley, Congreve, Vanbrugh, Farquhar.
Of these only the first two worked in the reign of Charles
II; all Congreve's plays were produced in William's reign,
and Vanbrugh and Farquhar carry over into the reign of
Queen Anne. As Thorndike puts it: "By the end of the
century the mode is no longer that of the Rochesters and
Sedleys, and the comedy of Congreve, Farquhar, and Vanbrugh is in some degree the perfection of a literary and
dramatic tradition rather than the mirror of its age." [1]

This kind of comedy certainly represents the society of
the time in the sense that that society produced it and
enjoyed it. The fashionable characters frankly confess and
act upon their own frivolity, malice, and sensuality, and in
a socially realistic setting these avowals strike later audiences and readers as particularly immoral. But according

[1] A. H. Thorndike, *English Comedy*, p. 277.

to their own standards the characters get away with it if they express and illustrate their principles in the proper style. The type is most easily identified in terms of speech and bearing, what Dryden called in 1668 "the courtship [courtliness], raillery, and conversation of plays." Unlike the comedy of Molière, this style puts excessive emphasis on verbal fencing and repartee. The code assumes the existence of illicit love, which is accepted when carried on in the right manner. "Wit be my faculty and pleasure my occupation," cries Bellmour in Congreve's *Old Bachelor*. Wit enables people of true fashion to play the game according to the rules; foolish characters break into the charmed circle and comedy lashes their follies, which are judged as violations of good form, not as violations of moral law. Most people, in fact, are outside the charmed circle—dull citizens, country folk, professional men, and stock comic types like the miser, the hypocrite, and the amorous middle aged woman. Special derision was reserved for the mere beau or fop who tried to ape the style of the true gallant. The code was exceedingly precarious, could be practised only by a small minority, and could hardly be maintained for long even in the dramas that are supposed to illustrate it. It is an extreme reaction from chivalry, from love and honor; it is anti-cavalierism with the ideals of exclusiveness and stylistic elegance retained. Hints of this attitude can be detected in the "easy dialogue" of some of Fletcher's young libertines, and in the careless grace of cavalier lyric, but it remained for Charles II's court to develop it into a system.

George Etherege (1635?-1691) . Such a development could not take place except when a courtier with literary talent but without excessive literary or intellectual preoccupations was given a free hand. Sir George Etherege was in this ideal position. He owed more to his early residence in France and to his court connections than to his desultory studies. "Sir George was a fair man, but spoiled his face with drinking," wrote the antiquarian Oldys.[1] A typical Restoration courtier, an associate of Rochester, Dorset, and Sedley but rather less of a man of letters, he did not cudgel his brains, but with a touch of genius attained "courtship" and "easy dialogue." His first play, *The Comical Revenge* (1664), resorts at times to broadly farcical effects, but his second, *She Would If She Could* (1668), displays well-matched wit combats between gallant and lady, developed in natural dialogue and set against the fashionable background of the town, "the plays, the Park, and Mulberry Garden." *The Man of Mode, or Sir Fopling Flutter* (1676) introduces the classic case of the fop against whose extreme affectations the ease, elegance, and wit of Dorimant (perhaps Rochester) and Medley (perhaps Sedley) are measured. The rôle of Sir Fopling was often imitated, as by John Crowne in *Sir Courtly Nice* (1685) and by Vanbrugh in the Lord Foppington of his *Relapse*. Etherege's famous play long remained the most notable example of the virtues and faults of its kind. But he wrote nothing more of importance. Under James II he was made English envoy at Ratisbon (Regensburg); he lived in Paris after the Revolution of 1688, and died there.

William Wycherley (1641?-1715). Of all these dramatists William Wycherley subjected the mode in which he worked to the severest criticism. A young cavalier, educated in France and then at Oxford and the Temple, he enjoyed some court favor and became a lover of the Duchess of Cleveland, one of the mistresses of Charles II. His earlier comedies, *Love in a Wood, or St. James's Park* (produced 1671, published 1672), and *The Gentleman Dancing-Master* (produced 1672, published 1673) sustain unevenly Etherege's man-about-town attitude, though with less gayety and more coarseness. *The Country Wife* (1675) is a bril-

[1] Quoted by V. de Sola Pinto, *Sir Charles Sedley,* p. 67 n.

liant, ingenious, and indecent farce, yet Wycherley is inclined to present vice, infidelity, and jealousy not lightly but with the scornful intensity which was traditional for satire. He does not, like Hippolita in *The Gentleman Dancing-Master,* praise his own time as "a pleasant, well-bred, complaisant, free, frolic, good natured, pretty age." He describes the man about town as a false wit who resents the presentation of his kind on the stage and thinks of the dramatist as his enemy.[1] Thus he comes close to breaking the spell of elegant un-moral comedy. His contemporaries thereafter regarded him as a great satirist, and there is good ground for this estimate, but it is going too far to consider him as an austere moralist. This vein is continued in his last comedy, *The Plain Dealer* (produced 1676, published 1677). Here the surly Manly, who is distantly related to Alceste, the hero of Molière's *Misanthrope* (1666), reviles the follies of the world, not in the even tones of common sense, but in brutal and outrageous fashion. Perhaps the meaning of the *Misanthrope,* a difficult play, is that we must not use an absolute standard of rational perfection to judge the imperfect but necessary conventions of society; Wycherley's Manly, however, is a misanthrope who despairs of reason and human nature. There is a tendency in Restoration satire, marked in Rochester, Butler, and Wycherley, to give up hope in the presence of human irrationality. Rochester and Wycherley, and Mandeville after them, were influenced by the anti-rationalism of the French *libertins.* In spite of his marriage with the wealthy Countess of Drogheda, Wycherley spent several years in a debtors' prison. Though he lived on to a somewhat degenerate old age to become the correspondent and adviser of the youthful Pope, his important work was done by 1676.

William Congreve (1670-1729). The strength of the

[1] Cf. Sparkish in *The Country Wife,* especially III, ii.

Restoration code is shown by its consummate treatment, almost a generation later, in the brief and brilliant series of Congreve's comedies. Though born in Yorkshire, he spent his early life in Ireland and was educated at Kilkenny Grammar School and at Trinity College, Dublin. In Lon-

CONGREVE

don he scored a spectacular success with his first comedy, *The Old Bachelor* (produced January, 1693). Dryden said that he had never seen such a first play, and renewed his praise on the production of *The Double-Dealer* (October, 1693, published 1694). Betterton's new company opened the theater in Lincoln's Inn Fields with Congreve's third comedy, *Love for Love* (1695). Next came a highly successful tragedy, *The Mourning Bride* (1697), now forgotten except for Dr. Johnson's praise and the familiar quotations beginning "Music has charms to soothe a savage breast," and "Heaven has no rage like love to hatred turned." His last comedy, *The Way of the World* (1700), had only moderate success at first. Though Congreve lived on for thirty years, he wrote no more. The close of his career as a dramatist marks the end of an epoch. He held profitable government posts, enjoyed the patronage of the Duchess of Marlborough and the favor of Mrs. Bracegirdle the actress, associated on equal terms with Pope and Swift, and according to Voltaire's possibly exaggerated report took a characteristic Augustan attitude: "He spoke of his works as of trifles that were beneath him, and hinted to me in our first conversation that I should visit him upon no other foot than that of a gentleman who led a life of plainness and simplicity" [1]

Congreve is for easy elegance, like Etherege, but his mind is keener and his style more finished. From Wycherley he takes over elaborate plot machinery, but not the fierce indignation of the satirist. At all times he shows himself the supreme master of witty dialogue, though follies verging on wickedness predominate in *The Double-Dealer,* grotesque humors in *Love for Love.* The familiar cast of characters reappears in his plays—foolish old men, quarrelsome and amorous widows, coxcombs and beaux, pert servants, silly young girls, with a fringe of grotesque characters, and, finally, dominating the scene, the hero and heroine who live up to the sparkling dialogue. As we pass from *Love for Love* to *The Way of the World,* the merely eccentric and foolish characters lose their importance. Mirabell the hero and Millamant the heroine in Congreve's last play, one of the important parts which he wrote for the charming Anne Bracegirdle, represent the consummation of his interest in true wit, and here the Restoration code reaches its supreme expression at the moment when it is passing away forever.

Sir John Vanbrugh (1664-1726). Vanbrugh (pronounced "Vanbrook" or "Vanbroog" in his own time) was of Flemish descent, resided in France from 1683 to 1685, then entered the Army and was for a time a prisoner of war in France. He indicated his general position by writing the genially cynical *Relapse* (produced 1696, published 1697), a sequel to Cibber's *Love's Last Shift* (see p. 83). His *Provoked Wife* (produced in 1697 with an all-star cast—Betterton, Mrs. Barry, and Mrs. Bracegirdle) is a return to a boisterous and free style of comedy and only secondarily to the moral license of the Restoration. Such a rough vein

---

[1] *Letters concerning the English Nation,* ed. C. Whibley (London, 1926), Letter XIX, p. 140.

of humor has always been possible on the English stage, and the Sir John Brute of this play long remained a favorite part. As a dramatist Vanbrugh worked at some dis-

VANBRUGH
From the *Universal Magazine*.

advantage after Collier's attack, which selected *The Relapse* for special mention (see pp. 83-84). He turned to the profession of architecture, and combined his two professions in 1705 by building the Haymarket Theater for Betterton's company and there presenting his later plays, *The Confederacy* and *The Mistake.* Castle Howard, Yorkshire, and Blenheim Palace, built by the nation for Marlborough at Woodstock, near Oxford, are the chief examples of his heavy baroque style:

> Lie heavy on him, earth, for he
> Laid many a heavy load on thee—

ran the satirical epitaph. Yet his contemporaries in the reign of Anne were right in recognizing his worth as an artist and a wit. His unfinished comedy, *A Journey to London,* finished by Cibber and produced in 1728 as *The Provoked Husband,* shows how imperfectly his lusty vein blended with the new moralizing comedy.

George Farquhar (1677 or 1678-1707). Farquhar was a scapegrace at Londonderry School and Trinity College, Dublin, acted at the Smock Alley Theater, Dublin, and on making his way to London successfully launched two comedies, *Love and a Bottle* (produced 1698, published 1699), and the popular *Constant Couple* (produced 1699, published 1700); then in 1701 its inferior sequel *Sir Harry Wildair,* and in 1702 two relatively unimportant plays, *The Inconstant* and *The Twin Rivals.* From 1700 he was in the Army, seeing service in Holland and serving as a recruiting officer in various parts of England. This experience colored his last two comedies, *The Recruiting Officer* (1706) and *The Beaux' Stratagem* (1707). He died just as the latter play was being produced through the good offices of his best friend, the actor Wilks.

Farquhar is gay rather than robust; he carries into the early eighteenth century something of the quality of Etherege and Congreve, but he moves away from cynicism, and shows a healthy interest in various aspects of life outside the narrow circle of the town. It may even be said that the germ of sentiment infects his good natured rakes. His Irish wit gives him an easy mastery of dialogue and makes his last two plays particularly delightful performances. He has a gayety and good nature which invite comparison with those other Anglo-Irishmen, Steele and Goldsmith and Sheridan, and undoubtedly influenced their dramatic work. With Farquhar the cycle of Restoration drama had run its course, and with the death of the actor Betterton in 1710 an even half-century of dramatic history, dating from the reopening of the theaters, came to an end. Of the great writers of comedy it may be noted that each expresses his individual talent in a few plays produced within a few years. The concentrated comedy of manners contrasts with the diffused and versatile talents of Dryden, who stands outside this tradition. A dozen important plays adequately represent the whole cycle from Etherege to Farquhar. Many of the conventions of this comedy came down into the eighteenth century, but it is fair to say that England had no second Congreve not only because of the new requirements imposed by changing social and moral standards, but because the art of Congreve at his best was too exacting.

Thomas Shadwell (1642?-1692). Shadwell had a prominent place in the Restoration theater and in personal and
political controversy, though there has always been considerable difference of opinion about his literary merit.
After his education at Gonville and Caius (pronounced
"Keys") College, Cambridge, and the Middle Temple, he
became from 1668, when he produced *The Sullen Lovers,*
one of the most active London playwrights *(The Humorists,* produced 1670; *Epsom Wells,* produced 1672). He set
up as a specialist in humors, a follower of Ben Jonson,
though he also borrowed freely from Molière. His somewhat naïve idea that the principal business of a writer of
comedy is to collect and describe new humorous types suggests the limits of his critical and dramatic power; but he
achieves some success in a rough, vigorous, caricatured realism, and thus documents the life of his time. *The Virtuoso*
(1676) satirized the supposed follies of the new science.
In and after 1678 he was at personal and political odds
with Dryden, and is principally but unjustly remembered
as the gross lumbering Og of *Mac Flecknoe* and *Absalom
and Achitophel II.* He was remarkably successful in getting
patronage, and after the Revolution he followed Dryden as
poet laureate and historiographer royal. His best plays are
of this time—*The Squire of Alsatia* (1688), and *Bury Fair*
(1689). Sir Walter Scott was a great admirer of Shadwell,
and used the low-life scenes of the former play in *The Fortunes of Nigel.*

REFORMATION OF MANNERS

Meanwhile Puritan middle class standards had been re-
asserting themselves and gaining more political and social
weight after the Revolution of 1688. From the extreme
Puritan point of view, of course, plays could never be reformed. One of the bad results of the licentiousness of
Restoration comedy was that it permanently alienated the

middle class and confirmed a moralistic opposition to the
theater that has lasted until our own day. The public sentiment that lay behind the Societies for the Reformation
of Manners, formed in and after 1692 with the approval of
the Queen and given to an extremely censorious view of
such offenses as swearing and Sabbath-breaking, would thoroughly disapprove of the theater. Soon comedy was forced
to compromise, though the traces of moral improvement
which appear in the 1690's are not so marked as to make
a "thorough godly reformation." Colley Cibber's *Love's
Last Shift* (1696) is usually taken as a turning point; the
last act, in which the libertine repents and reforms, is in a
moralizing vein which emphasizes the natural goodness of
the human heart, the vein later called "sentimental." But
in Cibber it is combined with much intrigue and flippancy
in the old style. We shall see that the new note was sounded
more clearly by Steele (see p. 161). This reaction from
Restoration cynicism was so natural that Cibber cannot be
given exclusive credit for it; rakes might easily reform to
make a happy ending, and virtuous heroines had always
been pathetic and charming. Allardyce Nicoll and Miss
Lynch point out that the sentimental note appears before
Cibber in some of D'Urfey's comedies (*The Virtuous Wife,*
1679; *Love for Money,* 1691; *The Richmond Heiress,* 1693).
But from the time of Cibber these themes are taken into a
fairly continuous if not consistent program.

The claim that the drama was subject to moral law was
more insistently made by the Reverend Jeremy Collier in
his famous tract, *A Short View of the Immorality and Pro-
faneness of the English Stage* (1698). Collier had a basis
in formal Aristotelian criticism for his attack: the drama
should teach virtue by exhibiting poetic justice and decorum (a consistent presentation of characters according to
their fundamental qualities and their social status). His
judgments have the rigidity and severity of the formalist

critic Thomas Rymer. At the same time he repeats the
Puritan polemic against the stage in general; he finds im-
propriety or even blasphemy in trifling things; and he
seems to be unwilling to allow the dramatist to describe
vice and folly. In detail his criticisms are absurd. Yet he
made his point; Restoration comedy was at times gratu-
itously lewd and cynical. Dryden admitted that Collier had
a strong case, and the new men, Congreve, Vanbrugh, and
Farquhar, had to meet Collier on his own premises and
were soon busily explaining that their comedies were written with moral intent. Bigoted as Collier was, the trend of
opinion he represented made it henceforth impossible for
any dramatist to work on exactly the same assumptions as
Congreve.

Restoration comedy: C. S. Paine, *The Comedy of Manners,
1660–1700, A Reference Guide* (Boston, 1941); N. B. Allen,
The Sources of John Dryden's Comedies (Ann Arbor, 1935);
D. H. Miles, *The Influence of Molière on Restoration Comedy*
(New York, 1910); J. Wilcox, *The Relation of Molière to
Restoration Comedy* (New York, 1938); *Dramatic Works of
Wycherley, Congreve, Vanbrugh, and Farquhar,* ed. Leigh Hunt
(London, 1840); *Representative English Comedies,* eds. C. M.
Gayley and A. Thaler, IV (New York, 1936); George Meredith,
An Essay on Comedy, ed. L. Cooper (New York, 1918); John
Palmer, *The Comedy of Manners* (London, 1913); Bonamy
Dobrée, *Restoration Comedy, 1660–1720* (Oxford, 1924); H. T. E.
Perry, *The Comic Spirit in Restoration Drama* (New Haven,
1925); Kathleen Lynch, *The Social Mode of Restoration Com-
edy* (New York, 1926); E. E. Stoll, "Literature and Life," in
Shakespeare Studies (New York, 1927); Sir George Etherege,
Works, ed. H. F. B. Brett-Smith (2v, Oxford, 1927); William
Wycherley, *Works,* ed. M. Summers (4v, London, 1924); W. Con-
nely, *Brawny Wycherley* (New York, 1930); William Congreve,
Works, ed. M. Summers (4v, London, 1923); J. C. Hodges, *Wil-
liam Congreve the Man* (New York, 1941); Sir John Vanbrugh,
Works, eds. B. Dobrée and G. Webb (4v, London, 1927–28);
L. Whistler, *Sir John Vanbrugh, Architect and Dramatist, 1664–
1726* (London, 1938); P. Mueschke and J. Fleisher, "A Re-

evaluation of Vanbrugh," *Publications of the Modern Language
Association*, XLIX (1934). 848–89; George Farquhar, *Works*, ed.
C. Stonehill (2v, London, 1930); Thomas Shadwell, *Works*, ed.
M. Summers (5v, London, 1927); A. S. Borgman, *Thomas Shadwell* (New York, 1928); J. W. Krutch, *Comedy and Conscience
after the Restoration* (New York, 1924); Sister Rose Anthony,
The Jeremy Collier Stage Controversy, 1698–1726 (Milwaukee,
1937); G. S. Alleman, *Matrimonial Law and the Materials of
Restoration Comedy* (Wallingford, Pa., 1942).

General references for Restoration theater and drama: A. W.
Ward, *History of English Dramatic Literature*, III (2d ed., London, 1899); G. H. Nettleton, *English Drama of the Restoration
and Eighteenth Century, 1642–1780* (New York, 1914); Allardyce Nicoll, *Restoration Drama, 1660–1700* (2d ed., Cambridge,
1928); Malcolm Elwin, *The Playgoer's Handbook to Restoration Drama* (London, 1928); John Downes, *Roscius Anglicanus*,
ed. M. Summers (London, n. d.); Leslie Hotson, *The Commonwealth and Restoration Stage* (Cambridge, Mass., 1928); Eleanore
Boswell, *The Restoration Court Stage, 1660–1702* (Cambridge,
Mass., 1932); M. Summers, *The Restoration Theatre* (London,
1934); *The Playhouse of Pepys* (London, 1935); *Bibliography
of the Restoration Drama* (London, 1935); A. Harbage, *Annals
of English Drama, 975–1700* (Philadelphia, 1940); C. L. Woodward and J. G. McManaway, *A Check List of English Plays,
1641–1700* (Chicago, 1946); E. L. Avery, "Tentative Calendar of
Daily Theatrical Performances, 1660–1700," *Research Studies of
the State College of Washington*, XIII (1945). 225–83; A. Harbage, *Thomas Killigrew, Cavalier Dramatist, 1612–83* (Philadelphia, 1930); *Sir William Davenant, Poet Venturer, 1606–1668*
(Philadelphia, 1935); A. H. Nethercot, *Sir William D'Avenant,
Poet Laureate and Playwright-Manager* (Chicago, 1938); E. J.
Dent, *Foundations of English Opera* (Cambridge, 1928); Autrey
Nell Wiley, *Rare Prologues and Epilogues, 1642–1700* (London,
1940); *Songs from the Restoration Theater*, ed. Willard Thorp
(Princeton, 1934).

POLITICAL HISTORY (1702-1760)
>>>

From the Revolution of 1688 through the eighteenth
century England was ruled by a series of personally dull
monarchs who could not maintain the social and intellectual importance of the Court. William III was succeeded
by Anne, the second Protestant daughter of James II. She
was firm in a moderate Tory position and in devotion to
the Church. Religious and political differences still cut
deep, but self-interest and national interest kept Englishmen from extreme intolerance and violence. In foreign
affairs, England was confronted with the issue of the Spanish succession: Louis XIV was trying to put his grandson
on the Spanish throne, and this meant a disturbance of the
balance of power on the Continent and a threat to British sea
power and trade. William had tried to compromise with
Louis in two successive Partition Treaties, dividing Spanish
territories among three claimants, France, the Empire, and
Bavaria, but Louis would not keep to these agreements.
The Tories had opposed intervention on the Continent,
but when Louis occupied the Spanish fortresses in Holland
and on the death of James II recognized his son, the Old
Pretender, national sentiment accepted as inevitable the
war for which William had been preparing. Thus Protestant and anti-Jacobite sentiment and economic and political interests put England at the head of a Continental
coalition, including Dutch, Austrians, and Bavarians,
against the aggressive Louis. This in turn placed at the
forefront of English and European affairs the great gen-

eral John Churchill, Duke of Marlborough, who broke
French military power by an unparalleled series of victories
on the Continent (Blenheim, 1704; Ramillies, 1706; Oude-
narde, 1708; Malplaquet, 1709). This War of the Spanish
Succession determined the course of politics at home; the
majority headed by Godolphin, who regularly acted with
Marlborough, gradually ceased to be a moderate Tory coalition and came to follow the Whig line; on the dismissal
of Robert Harley, a moderate Tory, in 1708, it became a
party government. In domestic affairs Godolphin's government put through a political union with Scotland (1707),
in order to help business in both countries. At this time
Marlborough and his wife Sarah Jennings, the Queen's
closest friend, virtually governed England. Marlborough,
the supreme figure in the history of the British Army, was
also a brilliant, calculating, and cold politician who has
been bitterly attacked by the Whig historian Macaulay (see
also Thackeray's *Henry Esmond*) but stoutly defended by
his great descendant Winston Churchill. It should be remembered that both military and diplomatic affairs were
under his control.

Thus the war came to be considered a Whig affair, as it
dragged on after a reasonable peace offer by Louis had
been rejected in 1709 and as taxes fell heavily on Tory
landowners. Meanwhile the domineering Duchess of Marlborough was superseded in the Queen's favor by Abigail
Hill, later Mrs. Masham, a kinswoman and an agent of the
Tory Harley. In 1710 a change in national feeling expressed
itself in violent Tory and High Church demonstrations,
when the government tried to prosecute the extremist Tory
preacher Henry Sacheverell. The Queen's dismissal of the
Whig ministers was followed by a Tory victory at the polls.
Since most of the major writers were in politics, this over-
turn must be considered a landmark in literary as well as
political history, and its effect on the careers of Addison,

Steele, Swift, Defoe, Prior, Pope, Arbuthnot, Gay, Rowe, Congreve, and others should be kept in mind. The new government under Robert Harley, Earl of Oxford, and the brilliant and unscrupulous Henry St. John, Viscount Bolingbroke, took office with a clear mandate to negotiate peace. The result was the Peace of Utrecht (1713), which gave Britain Gibraltar and Minorca in the Mediterranean, and Nova Scotia, Newfoundland, and the Hudson Bay territory in America, besides a share with Spain in the slave trade (the Asiento). But the Tories were badly out of touch with business men and Dissenters, and their leaders, particularly Bolingbroke, were closely tied up with the Jacobites. When Anne died in 1714, Bolingbroke was impeached and fled to France, Harley and others were indicted, and the Tory party virtually disappeared for two generations as a force in practical politics.

An act of 1701 had secured the succession after Anne to the Elector of Hanover, a descendant of James I on his mother's side. The Elector accordingly came to the English throne in 1714 as George I. There was no serious opposition, though a Jacobite rebellion was put down in Scotland in 1715. A mediocre German prince, with little interest in his new kingdom, George I necessarily put the power into the hands of the Whig leaders who stood ready to take over. After a period of uncertainty and disagreement the general direction of Whig policy became clear: to govern through the House of Commons, which was controlled by the Whig oligarchy; to adopt a conciliatory policy toward the traditional enemies France and Spain; to encourage commerce and shipping; to avoid drastic changes of every kind; and to make sound finance the principal business of government. Thus it was the practical ability of the Whig leader Sir Robert Walpole that got England out of the financial difficulties caused by the collapse of the South Sea Company, the end of the orgy of speculation known as the "South Sea Bubble." Walpole was a John Bull type, a coarse Norfolk squire with little culture or idealism, but of unsurpassed political and administrative talents. The situation called for a leader who could get different factions to work together, manipulate the members of the House, and avoid antagonizing public opinion any more than was necessary. In these respects Walpole was peerless; he based his policies on a working agreement between the business class and the landowning class; he used both Dissenters and Church as political tools, and of course he gave bribes. He kept power for twenty years by a skilful appeal to individual and national self-interest. Though powerful, he was no dictator; he backed down, for example, on Wood's halfpence (see p. 139), and on his sound but unpopular Excise Bill (1733), which would have checked smuggling and increased revenue by substituting an easily collectible tax for the import duties on wine, tobacco, and other articles. There was a great outcry about what would now be called "bureaucracy."

Walpole had against him not only the Tories, who were too strongly Jacobite to count for much, but a powerful group of dissident Whigs. William Pulteney was from 1725 the leader of this faction, sometimes called the "Country Party"; seconded by Carteret and Chesterfield and aided by the Tory Bolingbroke after his return from exile. Later a younger group called "the Patriots" carried on—William Pitt, Lyttelton, Richard Grenville, Lord Cobham. The Whig magnates wanted to keep control, and just as they had opposed the royal prerogative so they now opposed the concentration of power in the hands of a first minister. Walpole on the whole understood the needs and the temper of the nation better than they. But since he reflected the indifference of merchants and squires to literary culture, it happened that the principal friends and patrons of literature were in opposition, and practically all the able writers of the time, both the survivors of the age of Queen Anne and the new men who came to the fore—Thomson, Johnson, Fielding, Akenside, and many others. Pope's daring *Epistle to Augustus* was leveled against George II himself. Swift's *Gulliver's Travels,* Fielding's *Jonathan Wild,* and Gay's *Beggar's Opera* are only the most famous of innumerable literary attacks on Walpole. Bolingbroke's journal called the *Craftsman* was from 1726 the principal organ of the opposition. Walpole, on the other hand, hired obscure journalists and paid government subsidies to various papers. Government censorship was not severe; although expressed Jacobite opinions were prosecuted, and although there was an attempt to censor the stage (Licensing Act of 1737), there was large freedom of speech. As in our own day, we must distinguish the violence of partisan controversy from the actualities of economics and politics. Brilliant satirists and eloquent legislators prophesied doom, yet the nation survived and prospered.

Court intrigue could not make head against Walpole. When George I was succeeded by George II in 1727, it was thought that he might fall out of favor, but with the support of the clever Queen Caroline he continued to govern. It was almost a rule in the Hanoverian era for the heir apparent to be in opposition, and for a time Walpole's enemies gathered about Frederick, Prince of Wales. In the late 1730's the tide began to turn against the first minister. Public opinion obliged him, against his own inclinations, to declare war against Spain in 1739, though he mistakenly continued to hold office until 1742. The great Whig peace was over. "It was Walpole's long rule," says Trevelyan, "that gave the eighteenth century in England that peculiar sense of domestic peace and stability which is often regarded as its chief characteristic. Rest after three generations of strife was Sir Robert's gift to Britain."

The governments which immediately succeeded Walpole,

headed first by Carteret and then by the Duke of Newcastle and his brother Henry Pelham, had no constructive imagination, continued to govern by a corrupt use of patronage, and involved England in a half-hearted intervention on the Continent against France in the War of the Austrian Succession, which ended in 1748. Meanwhile English reverses, particularly the defeat at Fontenoy, encouraged the Young Pretender Charles Edward to try his fortune. In 1745 he landed in the Highlands, held court at Edinburgh, and marched as far south as Derby, but was forced to retreat across the Border and finally defeated at Culloden (1746). The panic caused by this last Jacobite uprising brought home even to ardent Tories the fact that England's national interests were now completely bound up with the House of Hanover, though the lost cause continued to be a theme of Scottish song and romance down to our own day.

This was the romance of the past; the romance of the future was to be the continued expansion of the British Empire. The foundation in commerce and finance had been strengthened by Walpole, but the fuller realization of the imperial idea was to be the work of William Pitt. Imperialist expansion brought France and Britain into direct conflict. After Braddock's defeat at Fort Duquesne (1755) and the loss of the indispensable Mediterranean naval base Minorca the next year, it was clear that the Newcastle government could not carry on, and George II was forced to call on the brilliant young Pitt, who proved to be the greatest war minister, with now the possible exception of Winston Churchill, in the history of Britain. From the beginning of the Seven Years War (1756) his purpose was to fight defensively against France on the Continent and at the same time to maintain and extend the Empire against the French in India and America. Though he had long opposed English meddling on the Continent, he found that his policy required an alliance with Frederick the Great of

WILLIAM PITT THE ELDER
Reproduced by permission of *The Century Magazine*.

Prussia, who was threatened with destruction by an Aus-
trian-Russian-French coalition. But Pitt's greatest achievement was to fire the imagination and the spirits of his
countrymen. The tide turned in India in 1757 with Clive's
victory at Plassey—a decisive event in the long struggle of

the East India Company with French competitors and native Indian rulers—and later with Wolfe's capture of Quebec, the breaking of French naval power at Quiberon Bay, and many other victories on land and sea. England fought successful wars on three continents, and Pitt was a national hero. Yet at the accession of George III Pitt's program of offensive warfare was checked, the young minister gave up office, and the Peace of Paris brought the Seven Years War to an end in 1763.

G. M. Trevelyan, *England under Queen Anne* (3v, London, 1930–34); Winston Churchill, *Marlborough: His Life and Times* (6v, New York, 1933-38); W. T. Morgan, *English Political Parties and Leaders in the Reign of Queen Anne, 1702–1710* (New Haven, 1920); *Bibliography of British History, 1700–1715* (5v, Bloomington, 1934–42); C. G. Robertson, *England under the Hanoverians* (London, 1911); Sir Charles Petrie, *The Four Georges* (Boston, 1935); Basil Williams, *The Whig Supremacy, 1714–1760* (Oxford, 1939); Keith Feiling, *The Second Tory Party, 1714–1832* (London, 1938); Wolfgang Michael, *England under George I* (2v, London, 1936–39); F. S. Oliver, *The Endless Adventure* (3v, Boston, 1931–34) [Walpole's career]; W. L. Dorn, *Competition for Empire, 1740–1763* (New York, 1940).

See also above, p. 8, references to G. N. Clark, Davies' *Bibliography*, Feiling, Grose; and below, pp. 318-19.

SOCIAL HISTORY (1702-1789)
>>

A brief sketch of social history cannot easily be subdivided. Much of what has been said about the Restoration holds good for the eighteenth century; though significant changes take place, there is an underlying coherence and stability, and at the same time enough freedom to give play to individual character and enterprise. In control were the great landowners, representing the largest concentration of wealth and of political and social power. They made up for the most part the governing Whig oligarchy, and employed a large number of agents in their affairs. Throughout the period the relation of great man to dependent, of patron to patronized, is of high importance for the administration of the business of great estates, politics, the professions, education, and the arts. We hear more of these relationships than of the relation of capital to labor, of employer to employed. The merchants, financiers, and contractors of the City were also powerful, and, of course, wanted government in their own interest. The typical country gentleman or squire was against the government or court, and so usually was the small business man of the City. The lower classes in town and country, employed as servants or laborers, had no political voice, but were an important part of the social scene.

Much of the history of the time is to be understood in terms of "the rise of the middle class," but that phrase needs to be made more precise. The middle class would certainly include business men and tradesmen and the large professional groups, and thus occupies a broad area between the great magnates above and the laborers below. The "merchant," that is, a dealer engaged in wholesale foreign trade, stood as the representative of the new power of the middle class, and was praised by writers like Steele, Defoe, Richardson, and Lillo.

Among the employments of human life, that of the merchant (whose good is the good of all men) should by all be held in the first esteem; it is he who enlarges the interests of his country; it is he who by his credit makes his fellow-citizen everywhere at home, and extends the offices, advantages, and civilities of acquaintance and neighborhood to all parts of the habitable world.[1]

The composite character of the middle class, its varied

[1] Steele, *An Account of the Fish-Pool*, 1718.

interests and connections with high and low, made it most representative of the national life. The gentry and the upper middle and professional classes were linked in vari ous ways; thus it had been common for the younger sons of squires to be apprenticed to merchants and to the larger tradesmen, though the practice did not increase. A snobbish dislike of business persisted, and self-made men sought gentility by purchasing land and building fine country houses. Conversely the older families were willing to marry their sons to City heiresses, and thus new money was taken into the aristocracy. The new fortunes were largely made in foreign and colonial trade. The West Indian landlord and the "nabob" from India stood for upstart wealth, luxury, and corruption. The peerage remained exclusive until the end of the century, when additional peers were freely created. But the gentry was not exclusive, and the whole system might be described as snobbish, plutocratic, and elastic. Class lines were fluid between upper middle class and gentry, though not between labor and the middle class. Faulty and unjust though the whole system was, it carried with it a strong sense of political moderation and respect for law and order. All classes were conservative and patriotic and rejoiced in "freedom," in what Blackstone called "our matchless constitution." The class struggle was still to come. Thus England withstood the shock of the American and the French Revolutions.

THE COUNTRY AND THE PROVINCES

This stable social order combined the old ways of life of rural England with new cultural, social, and economic forces developed in the great metropolis of London and in the new industries of the provinces. The ruling classes had vital contacts with both town and country: the magnate had his country house or houses and his town house; the newly rich citizen got a country estate; the squires came to town for the season, and as the century advanced the tradesman tried to get a suburban "box." The elegances of the town extended to the country; the new palatial country seats, in the latest architectural style, had libraries and often important art collections. The art of landscape gardening was extensively practised in their grounds and parks. The great estates were a principal feature of the counties, and were often more important than the towns. Less pretentious mansions, manors, halls, lodges, villas, and cottages also dotted the countryside. The richest landowners and many of the squires could leave details to agents and spend their time as they pleased, in politics, sport, dissipation, or individual hobbies, though naturally some of the nobility and many of the gentry took a real interest in farming.

Local government was in the hands of the landowners; theoretically the vestry administered affairs in the annual parish meeting, but actually the parish officers took orders from the justice of the peace, an unpaid magistrate holding his commission directly from the Crown. Usually the justice of the peace was the squire himself, and the office passed from father to son. The justice of the peace might be benevolent, like Sir Roger de Coverley and Fielding's Squire Allworthy, or he might be a petty tyrant, as in many English novels from Fielding to Dickens. He was likely to be severe on vagrants and poachers. The game laws restricted hunting to squires, their heirs, and substantial freeholders and leaseholders, and prohibited the sale of game; these statutes were savagely enforced because of the sporting interests of the squires. The life of the parish centered about the great house: the squire probably controlled the clergyman's living, his tenants tilled the soil, his servants were a large and important group, and the village tradesmen depended on his favor.

In the south and east the typical parish centered in a village, usually near the great house, with a group of houses around the church; in the north and west the population was more widely dispersed over the countryside. Towns of various sizes, all small according to our standards, were scattered through the counties. Cathedral towns and county towns had great dignity and charm. Many of them were residential and social centers, drawing genteel tenants and purchasers both from city and country. The famous resorts may best be considered in connection with the social life of London, and the great new business and manufacturing centers of the West Midlands in connection with the Industrial Revolution.

The villages housed much industry. The great woolen industry in particular was scattered throughout the land in small towns and villages and even isolated cottages and farms, but principally in Norfolk, Lancashire, and the West Riding of Yorkshire, and in innumerable villages of the Southwest. Trading centers like Norwich, Leeds, Halifax, and Bristol depended on this industrial hinterland. London stood for commerce, finance, and fashion; the provinces stood for agriculture and industry. The woolen interests, the most powerful of the older industries, were glorified in Dyer's *Fleece* (1757). Long before they had pushed through laws checking the importation of the printed cotton fabrics of the East (calico, dimity, and so forth), and even requiring that corpses be buried in woolen; but the final result was to stimulate the cotton manufacture in England, and fustian (linen and cotton mixed) was widely used.

The expansion of the textile industry was supported by foreign markets made possible by British sea power; a prime motive of national policy was to extend markets for British fabrics. For the first time commodities were carried in large bulk for the use of whole populations, and imports of tea, sugar, tobacco, cotton, and silk were paid for in the long run by manufactures. To meet increased demand, industry was gradually mechanized in the second half of the century. Hargreaves' spinning jenny, in use in the 1760's, Arkwright's water frame, and Watt's first patent for a steam engine (1769) mark the beginning of the new era. The factory system was first fully developed in the cotton industry, which became the classic example of the Industrial Revolution; woolen manufacture passed more gradually from the cottage to the factory or "mill." The new industrial plants centered in the West Midlands because of the abundant supply of water power and of the coal necessary for steam

THE DUKE OF BRIDGEWATER'S AQUEDUCT OVER THE
MERSEY, NEAR MANCHESTER
From the *Gentleman's Magazine*, 1766.

power and for the smelting of iron. Water power was still of primary importance; the age of iron was just beginning. The great ugly cities which were the heart of British business grew rapidly—Manchester for cotton, Birmingham and Sheffield for iron and the metal working industries, Leeds and Halifax for wool. Liverpool was the principal port for the whole region. In Staffordshire were the famous Wedgwood potteries. The growth of industry required better transportation. A system of canals built in the second half of the century carried a huge volume of imported and domestic commodities and in particular brought coal to the manufacturing centers. The Duke of Bridgewater was a pioneer in this development. Canals were to this period what railroads were to the nineteenth century. At the same time travel became easier and more comfortable with the building of new turnpikes and the use of faster and lighter vehicles. The mail coaches continued to be an important part of English life until the second quarter of the nineteenth century.

An agricultural revolution also took place in the eighteenth century because it became necessary to produce more food for a rapidly increasing population. Through a great part of the country the open-field system of cultivation had been followed; that is, the common fields were divided into narrow strips for individual cultivation, the same farmer cultivating scattered strips, and uncultivated land was used in common. But owners by means of enclosure acts continued to incorporate these open fields into closed fields which could be more efficiently cultivated, and also withdrew from public use much uncultivated land. At the same time, more and more of the land was taken into large well-managed estates. Agricultural methods improved greatly, especially in the region extending from London to Norfolk. Crop rotation, better fertilizers and implements, and improvements in breeding and feeding livestock made it possible for British agriculture to provide a larger food supply. But with these changes the small squires and yeomen tended to disappear toward the end of the century, and the new improvements worked hardships on the poor. The wages of agricultural labor did not rise in this period of increasing prosperity for the middle and upper classes. The population displaced by the agricultural revolution moved to town, the poor to work in the new mills and factories, the abler and more fortunate to make their way in business, industry, and the professions.

LONDON LIFE AND THE WORLD OF FASHION

The size of the capital was overwhelming, ten per cent of the population of England and Wales as against five per cent now. Rough estimates of population are for England five and a half to six million in 1700, six and a half million in 1750; for London about 675,000 at both dates. In 1801 the first census gave 9,200,000 for England, 900,000 for London. France in the eighteenth century had twenty-three to twenty-four million, Paris five to six hundred thousand. Commentators usually considered the monstrous growth of London a bad thing, a principal cause of the supposed increase in crime, vice, and luxury. London grew rapidly from 1660 to 1700, despite plague and fire, and again in the second half of the eighteenth century. During the first half of the century the population remained stationary, in part, perhaps, because of the ravages of gin-drinking. Yet there was great physical expansion throughout the period. East of the City was the great port, with its warehouses and docks, and north of the City a growing industrial area. Fashion moved westward into the region bounded by St. James's Park on the south and Hyde Park on the west. During the Restoration period Soho and Leicester Fields were fashionable squares; the next half century added Cavendish, Berkeley, Hanover, and Grosvenor Squares. Here, near the parks, were the new mansions of the rich and the aristocratic. The city-planning of the period went on into the early nineteenth century with the extension of the fine system of squares in Bloomsbury and the laying out of Regent's Park and Regent Street. The old City within the walls linked industrial east and fashionable west. Many new city churches were built after the Great Fire and in the early eighteenth century, and other great public buildings were completed. The London of literature centered west of St. Paul's, around Temple Bar, Covent Garden, and the

TEMPLE BAR

The gateway built by Wren 1670-72, removed in the nineteenth century. This point, where the Strand ends and Fleet Street begins, marks the ancient boundary between Westminster to the west and the City proper to the east. Here the heads of traitors were exposed on spikes.

Strand, a region of coffee houses, taverns, and theaters, and extended still farther west, of course, to the haunts of fashion. In the absence of convenient streets and bridges, the river until after 1750 continued to be a main thoroughfare. Streets were still narrow and dirty, with "kennels" (gutters) in the middle, and not regularly provided with sidewalks. People used hackney coaches and sedan chairs, and at night respectable citizens were often accompanied by a servant with lantern or torch.

The coffee house was still the important social center for various classes and groups. Wits, authors, and actors frequented the coffee houses in the Covent Garden neighborhood—Will's, Button's, and the Rose. Child's and the Grecian were associated with the learned professions, Jonathan's in Exchange Alley with stockbrokers, Lloyd's in Lombard Street with those interested in marine news. Groups of *habitués* naturally formed clubs such as are de-

CHARING CROSS ABOUT 1707
The statue is of Charles I. Note the sedan chair stand and the posts placed for the protection of pedestrians.

scribed in the *Tatler* and the *Spectator*. The coffee house was to eighteenth-century London what the café has been to Paris. The tavern, primarily a place to eat and drink, was somewhat different in tone, though it is hard to draw the line.

Townspeople spent much time in public rather than at home, and places of public resort were of great importance. The parks, the Mall in St. James's Park for promenades, the Ring in Hyde Park for those in coaches and on horse-back, were frequented, particularly on Sunday, by the populace as well as the fashionable classes. The New Exchange in the Strand, where pretty shopgirls offered millinery and other articles of fashion for sale, was a favorite haunt of gallants and ladies. Vauxhall, or Spring Gardens, was opened at the Restoration, though its glory dates from the years after 1730, and Ranelagh, the other notable place

THE JUBILEE BALL AT RANELAGH GARDENS, APRIL 26, 1749.
From a print in the Bristol Museum.

of the kind, was opened in 1742. Each of these gardens had a main building or "rotunda," and here the public could enjoy excellent music, refreshments, fireworks, and in general an opportunity to see and be seen. Supper parties were a special feature at Vauxhall; the more genteel Ranelagh offered light refreshments, promenade concerts, and masquerades. Masquerades were introduced by an enterprising Swiss named Heidegger in the reign of George I, and were often denounced as dangerous hotbeds of intrigue.[1] Similar in tone were the balls and concerts ("ridottos") given by Mrs. Cornelys in Soho Square in the 1760's, and entertainments of this kind were also given in the Pantheon, opened in 1772. Fanny Burney's *Evelina* affords a delightful view

INTERIOR OF THE PANTHEON

of London resorts in this decade. There were innumerable resorts in the suburbs, some of them spas where people went to take the waters. The humble citizen could thus enjoy a Sunday outing, if only at a suburban tavern with

[1] Masquerade scenes are common in novels, e.g., *Pamela, Grandison, Tom Jones, Cecilia.*

a small garden and a bowling green. The great fairs were popular and boisterous; Mayfair was abolished about 1710, but Bartholemew Fair lasted until the middle of the century.

Prominent in social life were the resort towns whither the upper and middle classes crowded in the season, that is, in autumn and winter. These were almost all spas, Bath the greatest of them all, along with Tunbridge Wells, Epsom, Harrogate, Scarborough, Cheltenham, Bristol Hot Springs. At first health resorts, these towns became more and more fashionable. With Beau Nash as master of ceremonies, Bath became a second social capital, and except for London has been more thoroughly described than any other city of the time, by Richardson, Smollett, Sheridan, Burney, Anstey, Austen, and many others. Favorite gathering places in these towns were the pump rooms and the circulating libraries, which came to have some of the manifold attractions of an American drugstore. Seaside resorts, except Scarborough, did not become popular until late in the century, when such places as Margate, Brighton, and Weymouth came into favor because of new ideas about the medicinal value of sea-bathing and sea air.

Fashionable manners and costumes are fully recorded in comedies, novels, essays on the model of the *Tatler* and the *Spectator*, satires on the model of *The Rape of the Lock*, and prints and caricatures. The luxury trades played an important part in London life—jewelers, dyers, coach-makers, hairdressers and wigmakers, milliners, mantua-makers, trunk makers, cabinet makers, saddlers, makers of watches and clocks. Much of the frivolity and elegance of the Restoration persisted, though costumes were somewhat less elaborate. Men's garments were of brilliant colors, and gold and silver embroidery was freely used. Men of fashion wore coats of knee length, elaborate waistcoats, knee breeches and silk stockings, lace at wrist and neck, the

whole topped with an expensive wig and a cocked hat.
There was much variation in detail; thus in George II's
time the beau wore a smaller hat and a shorter coat with
capes. Trousers did not take the place of breeches and stockings until the 1790's. There were numerous accessories—
watch, ring, snuff box, cane, in the earlier period a muff,
often a toothpick case and pocket mirror, regularly a sword
worn at the side and ornamented with a ribbon or tassel
(sword-knot), reduced to a small dress sword late in the
century. But swords were not worn in the country. A fashionable wardrobe was very expensive. The wig alone
entailed great expense, care, and one would think incon-
venience. The trades of barber and wigmaker were usually
combined. The style of the wig varied greatly with the fashion. The enormous periwig with flowing curls gave way to
the full-bottomed wig early in the eighteenth century. The
bag-wig, with hair gathered in a bag or knot, came in in
the second quarter, and the bob-wig, made to imitate the
natural hair, was common at times. After the middle of
the century men came more and more to wear their own
hair, powdered and in a queue. At home men relaxed in
night-caps and dressing gowns, called "nightgowns," though
worn by day and even out of doors and in coffee houses.
Fashions for women were too complex for brief description; the hoop-skirt (crinoline) was in and out of fashion
through the whole period. Riding habits were at times
fashionable for general wear. Headdresses were very elaborate, sometimes very high, involving much powder and
pomatum (scented ointment). Women often adorned their
faces with beauty patches. Important accessories, besides
innumerable varieties of jewelry and ornament and abundant laces and ribbons, were fan, snuff box, and etui-case
(tweezer-case). Powder, paint, perfumes, and washes were
lavishly used, sometimes by men as well as women.

We get the impression that the leisure classes really were

at leisure, with an endless round of parties, formal and informal, and endless dining, card playing, conversation, and
letter writing. Almost everybody gambled, whether in fashionable assemblies or humbler social gatherings and raffle
shops. The Groom Porter's, an allowed resort kept by an
official of the royal household, seems to have been a principal gambling place early in the century. Later we hear
of fortunes won and lost at the fashionable clubs in the
neighborhood of St. James's St., Almack's (later Brook's),
White's, and Boodle's. The brilliant statesman Charles James
Fox was one of the heaviest gamblers of his time. Gentlemen were still expected to defend their honor in duels,
despite the long continued moral campaign against dueling
(cf. Steele's *Conscious Lovers,* Richardson's *Sir Charles
Grandison*). Heavy drinking among men was the rule rather
than the exception; the upper classes drank imported wines,
Spanish, Portuguese, and French. At the beginning of the
century interest in sport had not reached the heights it
later attained, but horses and dogs became increasingly a
cult of the ruling class. The principal racing centers were
Newmarket, Epsom, Ascot, and Doncaster, and classic races
like the Derby were established in the course of the century. Fox hunting became the principal diversion of the
country gentleman, though hare hunting continued to be
very popular. Cricket, not yet professionalized, was a popular sport in which boys and men of all classes took part.
The cruel sports of bull-baiting and cockfighting were ple-
beian but popular. Professional boxers, who fought with
bare fists, became of absorbing interest to a sporting cli-
entèle.

Much of what has been said about costume and manners
applies only to the fashionable. Contemporary descriptions
dwelt, as they always do, on extreme styles and fads. The
sober citizen, then as now, dressed plainly and went about
his business quietly. The general result was to mark class

distinctions by differences of style and manner, and this
continued down to later times.

THE LOWER CLASSES—PHILANTHROPY AND REFORM

Of the life of the lower and middle classes we have comparatively little on literary record, and when an interest in
the poor and humble develops late in the period, sentimental sympathy gives a colored and untrustworthy picture.
In the City shopkeepers on a large or small scale usually
lived at their places of business. The industrial and working districts might house the respectable and obscure, or
verge on the misery to be found in London's worst slums.
The security we think of as characteristic of the eighteenth
century extended only to property owners, and the growth
of wealth and luxury widened the gap between the rich
and the poor. The poor could hardly better themselves,
and were victims of every economic depression and every
alternation of war and peace. They were repeatedly told by
good citizens like Defoe and Franklin that only their vices
were keeping them down. "Alms are the wages of idleness"
(*Spectator* No. 232).

Wherever the responsibility might lie, the concentration
of population bred poverty and crime. The great slums
and particularly the "Liberties," out of reach of the police,
afforded hideouts for criminals. Highway robbery was common; there was a certain romance attached to the dashing
bandit who rode on Bagshot Heath or the Great North
Road. Drunken bullies roved the streets at night, assaulted
helpless citizens, and beat up the watch. In the country
smuggling and poaching were characteristic crimes—the former really a major industry.

The great curse of London life in the first half of the
century was cheap gin. To increase the consumption of
grain, the distilling of gin had been encouraged; gin drinking increased so rapidly in the 1720's that laws to check the

traffic by taxing and licensing were passed even by an inert
government, and after several attempts the evil was lessened
by an act of 1751. Hogarth contrasts the pleasure and prosperity of *Beer Street* with the horrors of *Gin Lane*. The law
would scarcely move to carry out reforms, but it treated
crime with the greatest severity. More and more offenses
were made capital, almost two hundred by the end of the
century. But the threat of severe punishment did not check
crime. The criminal was not caught, or juries would not
convict, or for certain felonies he could claim benefit of
clergy and get off with a branding. Executions were public, and hanging days were holidays in London. The prisoner rode in a cart from Newgate to Tyburn, at the
northeast corner of Hyde Park, while the bell of St. Sepul-
chre's tolled and the people crowded streets, windows, and
temporary stands. Pirates were hanged at Execution Dock,
Wapping. Though Johnson approved of such spectacles,
the procession to Tyburn was abolished in 1783. "Cheats,
perjurers, libellers, and blasphemers" were sentenced to
stand in the pillory (thus Defoe in 1703); "vagrant idle
fellows" were put in the stocks. The prisons were horrible
places, Newgate perhaps the worst. Women were sent to
Bridewell. Large numbers of unfortunate debtors were
thrown into prison along with the criminals. "Gaol fever"
(typhus) often ravaged prisons and hospitals. Even the sluggish social conscience of the time was moved, and Oglethorpe's Committee of 1729, praised in Thomson's *Winter,*
revealed "the horrors of the gloomy gaol." Jail scenes became common in fiction.[1] John Howard's investigation of
the state of the prisons came late in the century. Up to
1775 many criminals were transported to the American
colonies. Thereafter they were crowded into the prison
ships or hulks on the Thames. But throughout the period

[1] Defoe's *Moll Flanders,* Fielding's *Amelia,* Mackenzie's *Man of
Feeling.*

there were relatively few convictions, and a relatively small part of the population was in jail; the number would have been even smaller had it not been for the poor debtors.

Under Walpole and Lord Hardwicke there were moderate legal reforms: archaic law French and Latin were superseded by English, the rights of defendants were better protected and the rules of equity improved; prosecution for witchcraft was forbidden, and acts of indemnity protected Dissenters against the provisions of the Test and Corporation Acts. There was a sincere effort to protect individual rights. But what was needed was a more efficient administration of institutions and laws, and also far-reaching humanitarian reform. Eighteenth-century inertia tolerated established injustice and incompetence. The parish authorities were responsible for poor relief, and passed along vagrants and poor likely to become public charges, unless such people could claim permanent residence or "settlement." Under a law of 1722 workhouses were established where the poor might work and partly pay their way. Overseers of the poor also farmed out this kind of labor. There was a theoretical distinction between workhouses, and poorhouses for the sick and incapable, but the two were often combined, as in the house described in Crabbe's *Village* (1783). Destitute children were bound out as apprentices and sometimes cruelly treated (see Crabbe's "Peter Grimes"). Infant mortality was terrible, sometimes as high as 75 per cent in general and as high as 90 per cent for parish children. The crowded London parishes had a heavy burden of poor relief, and legislation to have the work done by competent paid officials, and to board out and bind out poor London children in the country improved matters in the second half of the century. The magistracy of Henry Fielding at Bow Street (1748-1754) was a landmark in London social history; though Fielding advocated severe punishments, he tried to protect the poor by legal aid, to get at the causes of crime, and to improve public order by developing an efficient police force instead of the incompetent watch which had feebly patrolled the streets. His work was continued by his blind brother Sir John Fielding, who presided at Bow Street from 1754 to 1780.

Throughout the age the indifference to social injustice and cruelty contrasts sharply with the Englishman's sensitiveness about political rights. The parish and the national government could carry out social reforms only within narrow limits; there was a wide field for private philanthropies and charities. The philanthropic spirit was increasingly in evidence from the late seventeenth century, and though it never worked on such a large scale as to provide full relief, its persistence and spread are important signs of the times, and show us the good side of sentimentalism. Better a humanitarianism which might become maudlin than the callous cruelty which was so common. Notable projects were Oglethorpe's plan for the Georgia colony as a relief for poor debtors, the opening of the Foundling Hospital to receive abandoned children, the provision of medical care for the poor through the opening of hospitals and dispensaries. The cruel treatment of the insane was not much improved, and up to the middle of the century people paid admission to Bedlam to laugh at the antics of the inmates. Humanitarian zeal occasionally appeared in the middle and upper classes, as with Oglethorpe, William Hay's labors for poor relief, Jonas Hanway's good work for poor London children, and Howard's heroic travels and labors in prison reform. Representative of widening sympathies were the opening of charity schools, the Magdalen Charity for penitent prostitutes, the Thatched House Society for the relief of those imprisoned for small debts, the Marine Society for putting homeless boys into the navy, the growth of the antislavery movement. There was a rapid growth of humane feeling for animals. The philanthropist and humanitarian won more and more approval in literature and in life. *Guardian* No. 79 remarked in 1713 that such charities were characteristic of "the middle kind of people" rather than of those of "fashion and power," and this continued to be true. The ruling classes and the Church gave little official sanction to organized philanthropy.

STANDARDS OF LIVING

There was a general improvement in physical comfort and in economic and social standards, obvious and elaborate for the rich, gradual for the poor. Public health by our standards was still bad, but the decline of the death-rate gave evidence that it was improving. The sick were often attended by apothecaries, not physicians; the latter could be consulted by the apothecaries, and their fees were high. The plague ceased, but smallpox continued until vaccination became general in the mid-century. The fearful rate of infant mortality and the unsanitary conditions in jails and hospitals improved only very slowly.

The old-fashioned heavy meals of meat, fish, bread, cheese, ale, and beer were gradually modified. Upper class menus became more elaborate and varied. The introduction of potatoes and the greatly increased consumption of sugar and tea changed the diet of the common people. Coffee and chocolate lost ground relatively, and tea, much of it smuggled, came to be, as it still is, the national beverage. Oranges, lemons, and limes became popular, and the pineapple was considered the greatest of delicacies. Pipe tobacco and snuff were used more and more. The use of imported luxuries was a matter for national pride:[1]

Our ships are laden with the harvest of every climate: our tables are stored with spices, and oils, and wines; our rooms are filled with pyramids of China, and adorned with the workman-

[1] *Spectator* No. 69.

ship of Japan: our morning's draught comes to us from the
remotest corners of the earth: we repair our bodies by the drugs
of America, and repose ourselves under Indian canopies.

Aristocracy and middle class kept a large number of servants, who played a more prominent part on the social scene
than they do now. The staff of a great house would include
butler, steward, housekeeper, footmen, valet, cooks, page,
kitchenmaids, chambermaids, housemaids, gardeners, coach-
man, grooms, ostlers, and so forth. In an age of increasing
prosperity servants' wages were being raised, and we hear
much of their insolence, ingratitude, and imitation of their
betters.[1] When a guest dined in high life the servants stood
in line at his departure to receive their tips ("vails").

All this led to incessant moralizing about luxury among
high and low. Servants no longer knew their place, country
people dressed like city people and drank tea every day,
and laborers ate meat more than once a week—such were
the complaints of those concerned with public morals. At
this point economics and morals sometimes conflicted, for
what was good for business might be bad for morals; the
ensuing debate on luxury may be followed in Mandeville,
Goldsmith, Johnson, and many other writers. Denunciation
of luxury has much the same place in economic moralizing
that denunciation of "faction" (party spirit) and corruption has in political moralizing. The official attitude of
satirist and moralist sometimes obscures the age's underlying satisfaction with things as they are, but this comes out
in the progressivism and complacency of the apologists for
luxury.

In the middle classes there was an accompanying refinement of manners which came to lay excessive emphasis on
propriety. Those who think that the Victorians invented
prudery should consider the outcry against the exhibition
of casts of famous statues, such as the Venus de Medicis,

[1] See James Townley's amusing farce, *High Life below Stairs* (1759).

in the rooms of the Royal Academy in 1780. The fashionable aristocracy continued their free manner of living down to the days of the Regency, and the most that can be said for the populace is that their manners became somewhat less brutal and boisterous. But the standards of the coming age were more and more largely determined by the middle classes.

ARMY AND NAVY

For the most part the Englishman took security and prosperity as a matter of course, and accepted calmly the growth of British sea-power, the continuing tradition of British navigation and discovery, and somewhat reluctantly the necessity of defending the Empire by military force. Overseas trade called for a great merchant marine defended by a strong navy. The forests were cut down to build ships, "the wooden walls of England." But conditions in the Navy were bad throughout the century; Smollett's unsavory descriptions in *Roderick Random* of life aboard a man-of-war are accurate and first-hand. Naval administration was honeycombed with graft, and the men suffered from bad sanitation, bad food, and brutal floggings. Impressment was necessary to get men; sailors in port or even at sea, released criminals, ordinary citizens were seized by press gangs, sent to guardships, and then put into active service. But in general the officers were well trained and competent. In time of war they might make modest fortunes by sharing prize money, the profits from captured merchant vessels. English seamanship scored a triumph in Anson's voyage around the world from 1740 to 1744, an amazing feat combining warfare and navigation, and later in Cook's explorations in the Pacific, whither English and French explorers were drawn in the 1760's in quest of a great southern continent. Cook rediscovered New Zealand, landed in Australia, and discovered New Caledonia and the Hawaiian Islands, where he was killed. The colonization of Australia by convicts began in 1788. The full consequences of this period of exploration for military and naval history have just appeared in the great Pacific campaigns of 1942-1945.

Unlike the powers of the Continent, the island kingdom could afford the luxury of being anti-militarist. The seventeenth century had given the English a deep distrust of standing armies; politics was colored by fear of arbitrary military rule. The Army was dependent on Parliament, which not only voted supplies but every year reenacted the Mutiny Bill, on which army discipline depended. William and Marlborough built up an effective army, but it was kept down after the Peace of Utrecht, quartered in ale-houses at home and miserably supported and lodged in the colonies. Even the expansion of the militia was opposed. From 1740 on England was almost continually at war; the soldier was a familiar figure, but he was not admired or idealized. The seamy side of army life in 1745 is vividly presented by Hogarth in *The March of the Guards to Finchley*. Sterne's subtle and sympathetic treatment of the old soldier in the characters of Uncle Toby and Corporal Trim is highly exceptional. The Army was recruited largely from the poorer classes, even from criminals under sentence of transportation. After discharge the soldier or sailor was not given a bonus or rehabilitation by a grateful country; if he was disabled he might be lodged in Greenwich Hospital, for sailors, or Chelsea Hospital, for soldiers, but he might become an outcast or vagrant. The old soldier as a tramp or beggar is a common subject in late eighteenth-century art and literature.

EDUCATION

The schools, like other established institutions, settled down into a dull routine in the eighteenth century. The demand for a practical modern education, deriving from

Baconian doctrine and reiterated during the seventeenth century, was not met by the universities. Oxford and Cambridge showed no interest in intellectual freedom and educational progress and very little interest in scholarship and research. Cambridge was intellectually more alive, with Bentley in Greek, for example, at the beginning of the century, and Richard Porson at the end. Sir William Blackstone was the great ornament of Oxford in law. Many of the ablest scholars were outside the universities—headmasters of the public schools, learned clergymen or lawyers, or simply independent students like Gibbon. Professorships were few, with nominal duties. The instruction offered by the Fellows of the colleges, acting as tutors, was dull and desultory. Undergraduates were mostly idle upper class youths; there were also some studious lads of humbler origin, destined mostly for the Church, and a certain number of poor boys earned their way by menial tasks—servitors at Oxford and sizars at Cambridge. Walpole, Gray, Gibbon, Adam Smith, Coleridge, and many others complain of how little the universities had to offer.

Some gentlemen had a respectable knowledge of Latin, less frequently of Greek, and classical tradition colored literary patronage and the taste of the élite reading public. Most of this classical learning, but little else, was got at grammar schools, that is, secondary schools. Prominent in the education of the ruling classes were the most important grammar schools, called "public schools," such as Winchester, Eton, Westminster, and St. Paul's, with Harrow and Rugby rising into prominence, but these public schools did not yet dominate the English social system as they came to do in the nineteenth century. The schools in the City on charitable foundations were still prominent, though not at their most flourishing point—Charterhouse, Merchant Taylors', Christ's Hospital. Much of the education of boys of high rank was by private tutors who lived in the family.

Boys of the upper and middle classes were often sent to small private academies, that is, tutored and boarded in small groups by a private teacher, often a clergyman. Many of these establishments were very poor. After school and university, the boy of good family might be sent on a grand tour of the Continent lasting two or three years; accompanied by a tutor, he would spend considerable time in France and Italy, perhaps returning through Germany and the Low Countries. This was not a tour in the modern sense; the plan was to give the pupil familiarity with continental languages and manners, with some smattering of history and politics and possibly of fine arts and commerce. Locke, Addison, Pope, Richardson and many others complain that the system did not work. "Our young English travellers," wrote Chesterfield, "generally distinguish themselves by a voluntary privation of all that useful knowledge for which they are sent abroad." [1]

Since Dissenters were excluded from the public schools and universities by the Test Act, they opened their own academies, primarily to train for the ministry, but also, since many Dissenters were in business, to meet the needs of practical life. They gave the best school education to be had during this period; their curriculum emphasized English, inductive logic, and science, and the teaching was often good. Morton's academy at Stoke Newington, attended by Defoe, was well known; there were also, among many others, Doddridge's at Northampton, John Taylor's at Warrington, where Priestley and John Aikin taught, and Samuel Jones's at Tewkesbury, attended by Joseph Butler. Isaac Watts and William Godwin were educated in such academies. Many of their students, particularly those who were to become clergymen, lawyers, or physicians, afterwards attended the universities of Edinburgh, Glasgow, Utrecht, and Leyden. The academies were viewed with hos-

[1] Letter of January 2, 1752. *Letters,* ed. Dobree, v, 1809.

tility by the Tories, and were inclined to encourage political liberalism and religious heresy, especially unitarianism. Partly for this reason they did not attract endowments and eventually died out.

Primary education usually began with a "dame's school," such as is described in Shenstone's *Schoolmistress*. In the late seventeenth century, under the auspices of the Society for Promoting Christian Knowledge, began the famous charity schools, planned to give only a rudimentary education, with a strong religious accent, to children so poor as to be considered public charges. Great care should be taken, it was agreed, not to educate the poor above the state in which Providence had placed them. These schools were opened in large numbers in the first quarter of the century; in 1729 there were reported to be 132 in London and over 1400 in England and Wales. The schools in London and Bristol were the best. All respectable and pious people praised and supported them, and the clergy preached many a sermon on their behalf. Somewhat similar to the charity schools in spirit were the Sunday schools begun by Robert Raikes at Gloucester in 1780, which spread rapidly in the last years of the century and gave some elementary education to children who worked in the factories. Mrs. Trimmer and Hannah More promoted schools of industry for unemployed children. The self-supporting lower classes sent their children to inferior private schools at a charge of a few pence a week. There was little or no education for the lower classes at the secondary level; thus no provision was made for the general education of apprentices in their spare time.

Throughout the period the education of women lagged; in girls' schools the emphasis was at first on the useful—needlework, reading, writing, and a little arithmetic, but as the prosperity and social ambitions of the middle class increased more ornamental accomplishments were added, such as dancing, drawing, music, and a smattering of French.

R. J. Allen, *The Clubs of Augustan London* (Cambridge, Mass., 1933); *Life in Eighteenth Century England* [portfolio of prints] (Boston, 1941); J. Ashton, *Social Life in the Reign of Queen Anne* (London, 1883); A. Barbeau, *Life and Letters at Bath in the XVIIIth Century* (New York, 1904); Sir Walter Besant, *London in the Eighteenth Century* (London, 1902); J. B. Botsford, *English Society in the Eighteenth Century as Influenced from Oversea* (New York, 1924); D. Defoe, *A Tour thro England and Wales* (2v, London, n. d.; Everyman's Library); M. Dorothy George, *England in Johnson's Day* (London, 1928); *England in Transition: Life and Work in the Eighteenth Century* (London, 1931); *English Social Life in the Eighteenth Century* (London, 1923); *London Life in the XVIIIth Century* (London, 1925); A. D. Godley, *Oxford in the Eighteenth Century* (New York, 1908); Dorothy Hartley and M. M. Elliot, *Life and Work of the People of England: Eighteenth Century* (London, 1931); L. C. Jones, *The Clubs of the Georgian Rakes* (New York, 1942); M. G. Jones, *The Charity School Movement* (Cambridge, 1938); Chester Kirby, "The English Game Law System," *American Historical Review*, XXXVIII (1933). 240-62; W. S. Lewis and others, *Private Charity in England, 1747-1757* (New Haven, 1938); *Three Tours through London in the Years 1748, 1776, 1797* (New Haven, 1941); E. Lipson, *The Economic History of England*, III: *The Age of Mercantilism* (London, 1931); H. McLachlan, *English Education under the Test Acts* (Manchester, 1931); P. Mantoux, *The Industrial Revolution in the Eighteenth Century* (London, 1928); D. Marshall, "The Domestic Servants of the Eighteenth Century," *Economica*, IX (1929). 15-40; *The English Poor in the Eighteenth Century* (London, 1926); J. E. Mason, *Gentlefolk in the Making* (Philadelphia, 1935); Irene Parker, *The Dissenting Academies* (Cambridge, 1914); Constantia Maxwell, *Dublin under the Georges, 1714-1830* (London, 1936); *Country and Town in Ireland under the Georges* (London, 1940); Julia Patton, *The English Village, 1750–1850* (New York, 1919); M. H. Perkins, *The Servant Problem and the Servant in English Literature* (Boston, 1928); M. Phillips and W. S. Tomkinson, *English Women in Life and Letters* (London, 1927); M. J. Quinlan, *Victorian Prelude* (New York, 1941); A. E. Richardson, *Georgian England* (London, 1931); E. S. Roscoe, *The English Scene in the Eighteenth Century* (New York, 1912); W. C. Sydney, *England and the English in the Eighteenth Century* (2v, New York, 1891) ; J. G. Southworth, *Vauxhall Gardens* (New York, 1941) ; *Tricks of the Town*, ed. R. Straus (New York, 1928) ; J. Sutherland, *Background for Queen Anne* (London, 1939); H. D. Traill and J. S. Mann, *Social England,* IV-V (London, 1909); G. M. Trevelyan, *English Social History* (New York, 1942) ; A. S. Turberville, *English Men and Manners in the Eighteenth Century* (Oxford, 1926) ; ed. *Johnson's England* (2v, Oxford, 1933) ; J. B. Williams, *Guide to Printed Materials for English Social and Economic History, 1750-1850* (2v, New York, 1926) ; James Woodforde, *Diary of a Country Parson,* ed. J. Beresford (5v, London, 1924-31); W. Wroth, *The London Pleasure Gardens of the Eighteenth Century* (London, 1896); Iris Brooke and James Laver, *English Costume of the Eighteenth Century* (London, 1931).

EIGHTEENTH-CENTURY THOUGHT
>>>

The seventeenth century had been a period of epoch-making scientific discovery, the building of great philosophical systems on the basis of reason, and the settlement of violent conflicts in Church and State. The eighteenth century did not make comparable scientific discoveries or undertake to build new systems; it tried to cash in on the speculative profits of the seventeenth century and to put ideas to work. The great German thinker Leibniz carried into the eighteenth century the ideals of the seventeenth: he constructed a bold and speculative system on the idea that reality must be reason in action, leading to the conclusion that God has necessarily made this "the best of all possible worlds" (*Théodicée,* 1710); and as a rational reformer he sought to bring about the actual unification of science, religion, and society. But it has already been said that the dominant strain in eighteenth-century English thought derives from Newton plus Locke. Under the influence of Locke, English philosophy tends to break up into the practical discussion of questions of education, morals, psychology, sociology, and economics. Newton's system was interpreted as vindicating the great principle of harmony or rational order in morals, society, politics, and religion. The brilliant achievements of Newtonian physics led men to expect that simple laws could be found which would be valid for these fields also, and Locke's sober program of descriptions and analyses was continued. The conclusions which would emerge would not be radical or revolutionary; they would give a rational description of things as they are, and would thus appeal to "reasonable" men.

The line of thought in which philosophers are most interested often differs from the line of popular thought. To consider the first briefly, both Newton and Locke assumed a principle of causality which established the existence of matter as the cause of sensation and likewise the existence of God as the cause of the order of nature. The greatest English philosophers of the eighteenth century, Berkeley and Hume, centered attention on the problem of knowledge formulated by Locke, particularly the question of our knowledge of causes. Locke had said that all our knowledge of the external world is by way of sensation, content of consciousness; Berkeley went on to say that since this is so, since all our knowledge is of ideas, the conception of material substance is meaningless, and God remains the sole guarantor of an external world. Hume took the last step and reduced human knowledge to a mere series of impressions, with no certain reference to what is outside the content of consciousness at a given moment, and thus landed in complete theoretical skepticism. Whereas Berkeley had argued against the existence of matter, on the ground that we have no knowledge of such a cause, Hume extended the argument to mind and to God. This con-

STATUE OF NEWTON BY
ROUBILIAC
At Trinity College Chapel,
Cambridge.

clusion if consistently maintained meant the destruction of the vision of world-order and world-harmony. But things did not go so far; even in Hume, skepticism in action meant a shrewd limitation of knowledge to what is actually found in experience. The wider influence of the empirical philosophy popularized a psychology based on the association of ideas and a hedonistic ethics (see pp. 132-33). The Scottish common sense school (notably Thomas Reid) which set about refuting Hume did not contribute much to the advance of technical philosophy, but long dominated the widely influential Scottish universities and to a large extent the minds of educated men in Great Britain and America.

Thus both technical and popular English thought shrank from the extreme conclusions that might be drawn from Locke, and, it may be added, from Newton. Just as Locke's theory of knowledge eventually led to the skepticism of Hume, so Newtonian mechanics eventually led to the exclusion of mind and the vision of a purely mechanical and material universe. England would not go all the way here either. The men who brought out the dramatic and explosive possibilities of eighteenth-century thought were French. The English temperament shrank from radical thought, and a relatively liberal government and society gave a certain amount of toleration to such radical thought as did appear. The French mind is always disposed to push ideas to their extreme logical consequences, and the heavy-handed censorship exercised by Church and State in eighteenth-century France aggravated this tendency. Thus we get the paradox that a French scholar like Hazard (*La crise de la conscience européenne*) can describe the early eighteenth century as deeply skeptical, while English historians dwell on its complacency and self-assurance. The primacy in European popular thought passed to the brilliant *philosophes* of the mid-century, to Voltaire and the Encyclopedists centered about Diderot, who had learned much in England and bettered the instruction. Technically Voltaire is a moderate deist; actually he is a bitter, subtle, shrewd opponent of those established institutions, first of all the Church, which perpetuate dogma, prejudice, and ignorance. Diderot and the French materialists (La Mettrie, d'Holbach, Helvétius) dwell on the materialistic and antireligious implications of science. Rousseau, operating with the same terms as Locke and the English moralists, puts intense personal experience and biting social and political criticism into the familiar idea of "natural goodness." If a good way of life is to be worked out on the basis of man's actual needs and the lessons of experience, then the educational system (*Emile*) and the personal and political relations of civilized western man (*Nouvelle Héloïse, Contrat Social*) need to be drastically overhauled, though this does not mean that Rousseau actually proposes to escape from civilization and be a noble savage (see below, p. 363).

The thinkers who rely on critical reason in the midcentury are often grouped under the term *Enlightenment* (from the German "Aufklärung"). With its emphasis on propaganda to spread the light of reason, the term applies to Voltaire and Diderot and many others, not so closely to Rousseau, and with varying degrees of appropriateness to Hume, Adam Smith, Franklin, and Jefferson.

DEISM

Deism may be described as an attempt to base religion on truth discovered in nature and by reason. In the spirit of the age, the deists appeal from arbitrary authority to reason, but since they are largely concerned with weakening or discrediting the Christian revelation, they differ from the rationalizing divines and the Newtonian physico-theologists who likewise seek and find God's plan in nature. The deists were often treated as moral and social outcasts, and the bitter hostility of the orthodox obscured the fact that the basic distinction was one of emphasis, and that almost all were agreed in exalting reason and reducing the irrational, mysterious, and supernatural elements in religion. This should be kept in mind when we read the attacks on deists or "freethinkers" by Swift, Addison, Steele, Fielding, and others. The deists were trying to identify a universal element in religion, one on which all reasonable beings can and do agree. This element, they assumed, would prove to be the core of Christianity. Revelation might be parallel to or might confirm this basic natural and rational religion. The compromiser Locke (*Reasonableness of Christianity,* 1695) would keep both natural and revealed religion, and teaches that one can abide by reason and yet accept miracles, the Fall and the Atonement, and the inspiration of the Scriptures. More clearly deistic is Toland's position in *Christianity not Mysterious* (1696); revelation is only of the intelligible or reasonable, but Toland does not say that this means modification or abandonment of Christianity. In general deists agreed that nature taught that there was a personal God, and a future life with rewards for good and punishments for evil. Charles Blount in the 1690's and later Thomas Woolston (*Six Discourses on Miracles,* 1727-29) represented a more markedly anti-Christian approach. On the negative side they attacked the miracles and thus the credibility of the Bible story. Matthew Tindal's work, with its self-explanatory title, *Christianity as Old as the Creation, or the Gospel a Republication of the Religion of Nature* (1730), was the most important utterance of the later deism and aroused violent controversy. Besides Sherlock's *Trial of Witnesses* (1729), Law's *Case of Reason* (1731), Conybeare's *Defense of Revealed Religion* (1732), and innumerable other pieces, such major works as Berkeley's *Alciphron* (1732) and Butler's *Analogy of Religion* (1736) were called forth by Woolston and Tindal. Starting from the deist's position that a natural religion could be clearly discovered, Butler connected natural and revealed religion by "analogy"; both run parallel, and depend on probability rather than certainty; Christianity can therefore claim as much rational sanction as is possible in the field of religion.

Outside this field of controversy, deistic tendencies blended with cool rational orthodox views, with the current emphasis on Christianity as a system of moral behavior, as in the influential sermons of the latitudinarian Archbishop Tillotson. Deism also stimulated biblical scholarship by insisting on a critical examination of texts. As a philosophy it lacked imaginative color and emotional depth, and may be said to represent the impoverished side of neo-classicism. Its shallow optimism lacked the "tragic sense of life" which we find in more somber minds like Butler and Johnson. Its conception of a rigid reason which does not admit of progress lost out in an age which was becoming interested in the changing perspectives of history. It appealed to the head rather than the heart, and never reached the masses who were moved by the evangelical revival. But its position in liberal thought, its coherence and utility as a program of life, may be seen in the careers of two great American deists, Franklin and Jefferson, and in the history of unitarianism in Old and New England.

ETHICS

The turn away from metaphysical speculation, the weakening of purely supernatural sanctions in religion, the interest in man as a social animal and in the useful ends of literature—all these and related causes fill the period with discussion of morals. Many literary types are developed or modified to suit this interest—the essay in verse or prose, the satire in verse or prose, the novel, the drama, the descriptive-reflective poem. The work of the moralists carries over with unusual directness into literature, and into fields which we now think of as distinct from ethics—psychology, sociology, political science, economics, and aesthetics. It was, of course, traditional to apply moral standards to the presentation of human character, but it was a new thing to pay so much attention to the problem of identifying and defining the good as actually found in the individual and in society. This interest was now shared as never before by the professional philosopher and the popular writer.

Does the good have its ultimate basis outside individual interest or desire? Is it absolute or relative? The answers were given partly in terms of inherited philosophies and religions, Christianity, Platonism, Stoicism, adjusted to newer conceptions of reason or natural law, and partly in terms of the new interest in psychology, in what man finds actually happening in his mind. Both the love of simple order and the respect for tradition sought to identify the good with some universal ideal like reason; at the other extreme, a factual report on human nature might show man to be selfish and sensual. Thus in the philosophy of Hobbes, a materialistic world-view was associated with a picture of man as a predatory animal restrained from an unbridled exercise of his selfish will only by the police power of the state. Moreover, Hobbes taught, the state exercises this power not in the realization of an ideal or by virtue of divine or natural right, but because of a selfish calculation of advantage. Hobbes raised two issues sharply: (a) Is the good absolute, or relative to human desire? (b) If relative to human desire, is it approved on selfish or unselfish grounds? His clean-cut position came into direct conflict with established tradition and with the English tendency to compromise. The chief task of the typical Eng-

lish moralist of the next century was to answer Hobbes.
The age was reluctant to think of the good as arbitrarily
willed by the individual, the state, or even God himself.

The Cambridge Platonists upheld an absolute standard
based on divine reason and congruous with human nature
(see above, pp. 18-19). Emphasis on man's natural participation in and approval of this world-plan made for an optimistic view of human nature, and at the same time the
good was described as having useful and pleasant consequences for man. Thus the good is absolutely valid, and
from the point of view of man's interests it is also vindi-
cated by an end-product of happiness. Richard Cumberland
in his *De Legibus Naturae* (1672) took this position in
reply to Hobbes. Locke the compromiser is on both sides
of the main issues; with his emphasis on the test of experience he can say, "Things are good or evil only in respect
to pleasure or pain." Yet sensations and feelings point to
a world ordered by God according to law, and Locke is
rationalist enough to argue that moral laws may be de-
duced with mathematical certainty. In his practical exposition of morals, however, God rather than mathematical
certainty gives the guarantee. In spite of his rationalistic
vein, Locke fathers the hedonistic and the utilitarian in
English morals—the doctrine that the good is what is "good
for" something in the sense of ultimately producing pleasure. Yet the late seventeenth and early eighteenth centuries
also harbored the other tendency, to equate morals with
mathematics, to think of social relations as logical relations,
and to deduce morals a priori from the fitness or congruity
of things. This appears in the theologian Samuel Clarke
and was expounded in popular form in William Wollaston's *Religion of Nature Delineated.* (There were busts of
Clarke, Wollaston, Newton, and Locke in Queen Caroline's famous Hermitage at Richmond.) Both deists and
orthodox divines showed considerable interest in thus try-

ing to explain morality in terms of identity, equivalence, proportion, and consistency.

Anthony Ashley Cooper, Third Earl of Shaftesbury (1671-1713). Shaftesbury, the grandson of Dryden's "Achitophel," was not a great original thinker, but he expounded key ideas which he passed on from the seventeenth to the eighteenth centuries and his influence on English literature was extensive. His philosophic writings were collected under the title *Characteristicks of Men, Manners, Opinions, Times* (1711). Shaftesbury was tutored by Locke, and in Holland he came under the influence of the critical and skeptical Bayle, but his views go back to the doctrine of Plato and the Stoics, the ancient idea of a rational and divine world order, as formulated just before him by the Cambridge Platonists. Man does not merely experience sensations—as the extreme empirical position attributed to Locke would teach, though Locke himself does not keep to this position—his knowledge of the world is an imitation of the

SHAFTESBURY

divine forms, at once true, beautiful, and good, which lead us through nature to God. These forms give the standards by which we judge all things; they are, in the language of the time, "innate ideas," but they are not merely abstract ideas; they call into play man's feelings and senses, not merely his understanding. Thus man has an inner sense of the true, the good, and the beautiful, yet these principles do not depend on man's experience, but are absolutely valid. He finds in the universe the actual realization of his ideals. Indeed, by his inner knowledge (intuition) and expression of these ideals he contributes to their realization, and thus the creative artist takes a central position in Shaftesbury's system. (English empiricism, making man the passive recipient of sense impressions, had little interest in and was unable to account for the creative artist.) In the field of ethics, Shaftesbury's teaching postulates a harmony between the individual and society, and the expression or realization of this harmony is the benevolence to which man is naturally prompted. This is of course in direct opposition to Hobbes' teaching that man is essentially non-social and egoistic. Man has natural taste and natural goodness, though he must cultivate and develop these inborn powers.

Shaftesbury recommends and tries to illustrate a genteel and genial way of thought. He associates Christian dogma with fanaticism and controversy, and turns from the Hebraic to the Hellenic strain, recommending classic moderation and enlightened enthusiasm. He would substitute urbane irony and ridicule for controversy, and even teaches that "ridicule is the test of truth," that is, that no truth is exempt from challenge. Freedom of thought and speech is the first requisite for man's enlightenment. This is his version of the Whig doctrine of liberty, which takes the form of the doctrine that arts and sciences flourish best in free states. In general he encouraged the age to think well of man and the universe, and to indulge an enthusiasm at once religious, philosophical, poetic, and political. The underlying conception of man's natural goodness was, of course, not peculiar to Shaftesbury. From Renaissance humanism and beyond, the assertion of man's power to conceive and perform the good, as against the Augustinian doctrine of man's utter sinfulness, had appeared in the rational theologians of the seventeenth century, the Cambridge Platonists and others. Shaftesbury's influence was somewhat restricted by his marked hostility to Christianity, but he offered an optimistic over-simplification of the facts of life which was much to the taste of the age, and his prestige was great. Montesquieu's remark is well known, that the four great poets of the world were Plato, Montaigne, Malebranche, and Shaftesbury. By way of Hutcheson and others he widely influenced eighteenth-century ethics, he gave the impulse to the eighteenth-century development of aesthetics, and his conception of a free enthusiastic spirit contemplating the wonders of creation was directly applied in poetry by Pope, Thomson, Akenside, and John Gilbert Cooper. Later Shaftesbury was the philosophic sponsor of a critical school in Germany which opposed mere empirical and rational formulas with an exaltation of enthusiasm and creative genius.

Bernard Mandeville (1670-1733). The seventeenth-century opposition between Hobbes and the benevolist divines was repeated in the eighteenth-century opposition between Mandeville and Shaftesbury. Mandeville was born in Holland and practised medicine in London. His *Grumbling Hive* (1705), an expression of his social and economic views in doggerel verse, was reissued with his larger book *The Fable of the Bees; or Private Vices Public Benefits* (I, 1714, II, 1729). Here he describes man as naturally selfish and sensual; society and business simply serve man's appetites, and actual happiness, success, and prosperity consist in selfish satisfaction, no matter how we camouflage our motives. Luxury and vice are what we really want and are moreover "good for business." To be sure, Mandeville professes to believe that real virtue would be free from any taint of selfishness, and then goes on to conclude that there is no real virtue in the world. This seems to be a curious recognition of absolute standards, but what Mandeville really intends is to reduce absolute standards to absurdity. He is an extreme hedonist and utilitarian. On these grounds he

defends luxury, extravagance, the liquor traffic, even pros-
titution. He thus points out the contradiction between
the conventional exhortations to frugality and abstinence
and the dominant interest in prosperity and luxury. Mandeville was influenced by French cynics and skeptics (La
Rochefoucauld, Bayle), and his views were far too drastic
for English moralists, but they fell in with the satirists'
picture of man and with orthodox views of the corruption
of human nature. They could be used to construct a utilitarian theory in ethics and also to support the economic
doctrine of laissez faire, that society prospers most when
the individual is given a free hand. They encouraged later
emphasis on the "economic man," the individual who in-
variably seeks his own profit. Mandevillian elements can
be found in some of the greatest writers of the time, in
Swift and Fielding and Johnson.

LATER ETHICS

A more subtle psychology would show both self-regarding
and altruistic elements in human nature, though the facile
contrast between selfishness and benevolence appears constantly in the popular thought of the time. The ethics of
the theologian Butler balanced the observed facts of selfishness and benevolence, and set over the passions a moni-
tor conscience representing not only reason but moral
compulsion of divine authenticity. But the general trend
was away from absolute doctrines and toward empiricism
and utilitarianism, a description of the good in terms of
actual human experiences and desires. Religion continued
to color thinking about morals, and God was invoked by
the pleasure-pain moralists, first, because as the Creator he
gave his sanction to such a scheme, and second, because in
case the virtuous man suffers more pain than pleasure in
this life, the balance will be redressed in a future life.
This was orthodox doctrine; we often find it in the authors

of the time (Young, Richardson), and it was restated by the late eighteenth-century theologian William Paley, whose books were generally used in British and American colleges. Leaving heaven and hell out of account, other ways were devised of explaining how the moral life was based on pleasurable and painful sensations. The principle of the association of ideas was used by Hartley and others to show how moral judgments, like Locke's compound ideas, were built up out of simple elements of sense experience. Studying results rather than origins, Jeremy Bentham (*Principles of Morals and Legislation,* 1780, 1789) tried to determine the exact value of acts and policies by ascertaining the quantity of pleasure or pain produced. This calculation of results was associated in the later British utilitarian school with a practical reform movement in legislation. In the mid-century Hume, the consistent empiricist, could find no rational standard of the good, merely a "sentiment" which approved the good, and so carefully did he keep to the findings of experience that he could not fully explain the sentiment in terms of utility (pleasure and pain); in Hume, as for his age, the instinctive social and altruistic quality of human nature is a central fact, on which the great structures of society must be based. The same is true for his countryman Adam Smith (*Theory of Moral Sentiments,* 1759), whose teachings moreover show, in combining an ethics of sympathy with the economic doctrine of laissez faire, free action in the economic world for individual profit (*The Wealth of Nations,* 1776), that the basic assumption of the age is "that true self-love and social are the same."

E. Albee, *History of English Utilitarianism* (London, 1902); A. W. Benn, *History of English Rationalism in the Nineteenth Century,* I (London, 1906); C. Becker, *The Heavenly City of the Eighteenth Century Philosophers* (New Haven, 1932); Berkeley, *Works,* ed. A. C. Fraser (4v, Oxford, 1901); E. Bréhier, *Histoire de la philosophie,* II, ii (Paris, 1930); *English Philosophers from Bacon to Mill,* ed. E. A. Burtt (New York, 1939); E. C. Mossner, *Bishop Butler and the Age of Reason* (New York, 1936); W. J. Norton, Jr., *Bishop Butler: Moralist and Divine* (New Brunswick, 1940); E. Cassirer, *Die Philosophie der Aufklärung* (Tübingen. 1932); J. M. Creed and J. S. B. Smith, *Religious Thought in the Eighteenth Century* (Cambridge, 1934); P. Hazard, *La crise de la conscience européenne, 1680-1715* (3v, Paris, 1935); Hume, *Works,* eds. T. H. Green and T. H. Grose (4v, London, 1874-75); J. Laird, *Hume's Philosophy of Human Nature* (London, 1932); N. K. Smith, *The Philosophy of David Hume* (London, 1941); Locke, *Essay,* ed. A. C. Fraser (2v, Oxford, 1894); *Selections,* ed. S. P. Lamprecht (New York, 1938); T. Fowler, *Locke* (New York, 1906; English Men of Letters); K. MacLean, *John Locke and English Literature of the Eighteenth Century* (New Haven, 1936); A. O. Lovejoy, *The Great Chain of Being* (Cambridge, Mass., 1936); "The Parallel of Deism and Classicism," *Modern Philology,* XXIX (1932). 281-99; Mandeville, *The Fable of the Bees,* ed. F. B. Kaye (2v, Oxford, 1924); H. M. Morais, *Deism in Eighteenth Century America* (New York, 1934); *The Classical Moralists,* ed. B. Rand (Boston, 1909); Marjorie Nicolson, *Newton Demands the Muse* (Princeton, 1946); C. W. Hendel, *Jean Jacques Rousseau, Moralist* (2v, London, 1934); E. H. Wright, *The Meaning of Rousseau* (New York, 1929); L. A. Selby-Bigge, *British Moralists* (2v, Oxford, 1897); J. Seth, *English Philosophers and Schools of Philosophy* (London, 1912); Shaftesbury, *Characteristics,* ed. J. M. Robertson (2v, London, 1900); T. Fowler, *Shaftesbury and Hutcheson* (New York, 1883); C. A. Moore, "Shaftesbury and the Ethical Poets in England," *Publications of the Modern Language Association,* XXXI (1916). 264-325; E. Tiffany, "Shaftesbury as Stoic," *ibid.,* XXXVIII (1923). 642-84; Preserved Smith, *A History of Modern Culture,* II (New York, 1934); T. V. Smith and M. Grene, *From Descartes to Kant* (Chicago, 1940); W. R. Sorley, *History of English Philosophy* (Cambridge, 1920); Leslie Stephen, *History of English Thought in the Eighteenth Century* (3rd ed., 2v, New York, 1902); R. A. Tsanoff, *The Moral Ideals of our Civilization* (New York, 1942); Voltaire, *Selections,* ed. G. R. Havens (New York, 1925); N. L. Torrey, *Voltaire and the English Deists* (New Haven, 1930); *The Spirit of Voltaire* (New York, 1938); Basil Willey, *The Eighteenth Century Background* (London, 1940); A. Wolf, *History of Science, Technology and Philosophy in the Eighteenth Century* (New York, 1939).

JONATHAN SWIFT (1667-1745)
>>>

Swift is perhaps the most interesting and puzzling personality of his age. Like all the major Augustans, he was deeply involved in contemporary politics, society, and thought, yet his pride and scorn detach him from his contemporaries and force us to reckon with a powerful and enigmatic individuality. In estimating Swift we must balance the Augustan against the lonely genius; the biographer and the student must not go too far in either direction.

Swift was born in Dublin of English parents and was educated at Kilkenny Grammar School and at Trinity College, Dublin. His connection with the Anglo-Irish

SWIFT

minority that governed Ireland fostered his allegiance to the Church of England, strengthened his attachment to the policies of William and at the same time led him to view both England and Ireland with a certain detachment. Even more important than his Irish background and his formal education was the decade (1689-1699) which he spent as secretary and assistant to Sir William Temple at Moor Park, Surrey (see p. 53). He was proud, sensitive, and discontented, though we must not exaggerate his unhappiness in these early years. Temple initiated him in scholarship and literature, and gave him the distrust of pedantry, scholastic and scientific, expressed in *A Tale of a Tub* and *The Battle of the Books,* though the powerful satire is, of course, Swift's own. He was not happy or at ease because he had more than the conventional satirist's scorn of human folly, and because, dependent on favor from the great like other young men in humble place, he was ambitious for power. Temple did not get great things for him; after he took holy orders in 1694, he held the Prebend of Kilroot in Ireland, and later had other unimportant Irish livings and was Chaplain and Secretary to Lord Berkeley (1699). It was during the Moor Park period that he formed his lifelong attachment to Esther or Hester Johnson, known as "Stella." Whether he married her or not—scholars still debate the question—she meant more to him than any other human being.

Swift's genius thus matured in semi-retirement in the 1690's; during the reign of Queen Anne he entered English politics, spending much time in London and forming friendships with literary and political leaders, notably Addison and Steele. He sided with the Whigs (*A Discourse of the Contests and Dissensions in Athens and Rome,* 1701), but was largely interested in defending the prerogatives of the Church, as in the brilliantly ironical *Argument Against Abolishing Christianity* (written 1708, published 1711), *Sentiments of a Church of England Man* (1708), *A Project for the Advancement of Religion and the Reformation of Manners* (1709) . He vehemently opposed deists, Dissenters, and Whigs who wanted to repeal the Test Act. In lighter vein was his humorous campaign against the astrological quack Partridge, whose death he predicted and duly described in spite of the protests of his victim. Here Swift first used the famous pen name "Isaac Bickerstaff."

Swift went over to the Tory government of 1710, and soon became their principal writer, editing the *Examiner* (1710-11) and arguing against the continuance of the war in one of his most powerful and influential pamphlets, *The*

Conduct of the Allies (1711, dated 1712). The famous *Journal to Stella* (written 1710-13, published 1765), set down day by day in playful, even childish style for Stella and her companion Rebecca Dingley in Ireland, gives a minute record of the time when Swift felt himself to be at the height of his political power in London. Politics colored his literary friendships; he felt that he was partly estranged from Addison, and he became a bitter opponent of Steele, whom

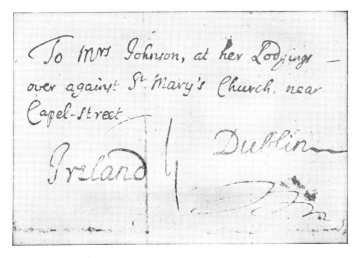

SWIFT WRITES TO STELLA
Address of a letter written in March, 1712.

he attacked in *The Importance of the Guardian Considered* (1713) and *The Public Spirit of the Whigs* (1714). The formation of Tory clubs at this time shows shifting personal relationships: Swift belonged to the Saturday Club, which centered about Harley, and to the Brothers, often called by Swift "our Society," founded by Bolingbroke in opposition to the Whig Kit-Cats. He drew closer to Pope, and was admitted to the Scriblerus Club, including, besides Swift and Pope, Gay, Parnell, and Arbuthnot. Scriblerus represented the best Tory genius of the time, but did not engage as a club in politics; its literary pastimes were directed against pedantry, always a favorite target, and eventually had some connection with *Gulliver* and the *Dunciad*. As to politics, Swift was not in Harley's complete confidence, nor did he ever abandon his attitude of proud independence, hard though he labored for the Tory cause. The Tories did not seem to be much more anxious to reward him than the Whigs had been; he did not get the bishopric he wanted, only an appointment as Dean of St. Patrick's Cathedral, Dublin, where he was inducted in June, 1713.

After the collapse of Tory hopes at Queen Anne's death in 1714, Swift made Dublin his permanent residence. He was embittered and disappointed, and to some extent thrown back upon himself and a small circle of Irish intimates. His strange friendship or love affair with Hester Vanhomrigh, who had followed him from London to Dublin—an affair marked by ardent love on her side and puzzling aloofness on his—complicated his private life and came to some sort of crisis before her death in 1723. The poem *Cadenus and Vanessa* (begun about 1713, published 1726) records this relationship. At times he turned his energy to mature and intense writings—*Gulliver* in the early 1720's, important poems in the early 1730's; these are creative periods scarcely second to the early months of inspiration which had produced *A Tale of a Tub* and *The Battle of the Books*. Swift did his best work in a state of irritated semi-detachment rather than in the depths of savage despair. His power also appears in his brilliant correspondence with such friends as Pope and Bolingbroke. In the political field he conducted a fierce and effective opposition to the policies of the English government in Ireland, and here his achievements surpass anything he did in the last years of Queen Anne. His first loyalty was to the Anglican Church in Ireland, his chief hostility to the Irish Presbyterians; he was far from being in complete sympathy with the oppressed Irish Catholics. Yet his interest in Irish social and economic problems and his indignation at the exploitation of Ireland by the English made him in a sense the spokesman for the whole nation, as in his *Proposal for the Universal Use of Irish Manufactures* (1720), in his *Modest Proposal* (1729), with its bitterly ironical suggestion that the children of the Irish poor be used for food, and in the famous *Drapier's Letters* (1724-25), the principal part of a brilliant campaign against the English government's issuance of a patent for a new copper coinage in Ireland. Swift rose to heights of indignation about the inferior currency with which the patentee Wood might flood the country. The excitement was rather artificial, but Swift won the fight and became a national hero. The Dublin populace kindled bonfires on the birthday of the misanthropic Dean.

During visits to England in 1726 and 1727 he renewed his friendships and saw to the publication of *Gulliver*. After the death of Stella in 1728 his life became more and more lonely, and he suffered from serious attacks of giddiness and deafness, "that old vertigo in my head." He continued to develop his vein of playfulness in verse and prose, notably in the marvellous record of inane everyday talk called *A Complete Collection of Genteel and Ingenious Conversation* (1738). In his latest years he sank into utter gloom and despair. He was declared insane in 1742 and died in 1745. But we must not fix our attention too exclusively on the final tragedy.

Swift always asserted that the good life was the life of reason, by which he meant a life controlled not by hard and daring thought but by plain common sense. Man's failure to realize this moderate ideal is due to his passions, his unbridled desire for sensual power, pleasure, and success, and worst of all his senseless pride. He has enough reason to see that he is wrong, but does he have enough reason to improve himself? Is he always the dupe of pride and passion? This is the familiar issue raised by Shaftesbury and Mandeville, and by Pope's *Essay on Man.* Does Swift despair of mankind altogether, or does he hope that his satire will correct as well as castigate? Of course, like all satirists, he professes to correct. But when we say this we miss something characteristic of Swift, the unmatched intensity with which he attacks the actual ways of mankind. His most famous strokes seem to step up the attack so as to include all human activities. In the "Digression on Madness" in *A Tale of a Tub,* happiness is the perpetual pleasure "of being well deceived," human action is based on illusion, to live is to play the lunatic. This is a vision of a world without reason. An ambiguity remains: Is this man as such, or man at his worst? In the fourth voyage of *Gulliver,* the Yahoos represent the irrational or animal side of man, but Gulliver, not necessarily Swift, identifies them with humanity, and sets them below well-conducted animals, the horses of Houyhnhnmland, who make a reasonable and normal use of their natural powers and thus attain "the perfection of nature." The theme is echoed in the poem called *The Beasts' Confession.*

A famous passage in a letter to Pope, September 29, 1725, connects *Gulliver* with Swift's general satiric purpose:

> The chief end I propose to myself in all my labours is to vex the world rather than divert it, and if I could compass that design without hurting my own person or fortune, I would be the most indefatigable writer you have ever seen. . . . When you think of the world give it one lash the more at my request. I have ever hated all nations, professions, and communities, and all my love is toward individuals; for instance, I hate the tribe of lawyers, but I love Counseller Such-a-one and Judge Such-a-one; so with physicians—I will not speak of my own trade—soldiers, English, Scotch, French, and the rest. But principally I hate and detest

that animal called man, although I heartily love John, Peter, Thomas, and so forth. This is the system upon which I have governed myself many years, but do not tell, and so I shall go on till I have done with them. I have got materials toward a treatise proving the falsity of that definition *animal rationale,* and to show it would be only *rationis capax* [capable of reason]. Upon this great foundation of misanthropy, though not in Timon's manner, the whole building of my *Travels* is erected; and I never will have peace of mind, till all honest men are of my opinion.[1]

Man is then capable of reason, and there are honest men, but human life in general, particularly collective action and the working of institutions, justifies a realistic misanthropy. This covers Swift's attitude pretty well, though it does not account for his disgust at the human body and the ferocity of his attack. Swift was after all committed to a party and a church, and was a reformer and a laborer in public causes. This is the comparatively genial view we get in the *Verses on the Death of Doctor Swift* (written 1731, published 1739), lines which every student should compare with the fourth voyage of *Gulliver,* though the exact truth about Swift is not to be found in either place. It is hard to get a balanced estimate of Swift because his attack on unreason has much greater force than his defence of reason.

While Swift's verse is secondary to his prose, it has been underestimated, possibly because of the notoriety of a few coarse pieces. In general he works with the octosyllabic couplet of Butler and Prior, and attains memorable plainness and point. Of all eighteenth-century writers he is most hostile to the romantic imagination (*Of Poetry—A Rhapsody*), but this does not keep him from exercising his remarkable powers of statement in verse. His style always conforms to his own standard of simplicity; his prose and verse both keep clear of rhetorical ornament and are intensified by humor and scorn.

[1] *Correspondence,* ed. Ball, III. 276-78.

A TALE OF A TUB

This first masterpiece is Swift's most exuberant, resource-
ful, and brilliant work. It was probably written in 1696
and 1697, with additions made in and after 1698, but not
published until 1704. The tale itself is a simple parable of
a father who leaves coats to three sons, Peter (the Catholic
Church), Martin (the Church of England), and Jack (the
Dissenters). They change their coats to follow the fashion,
finding in their father's will pretexts for everything they
do. Peter becomes arrogant and denounces ferociously those
who will not accept his dogmas; Jack in a frenzy of reformation tears his coat to tatters and views his father's will with
superstitious reverence. Swift's purpose was to defend the
Church of England, but it seemed to many readers that his
caricature of ritual and dogma was irreverent. The allegory
of the coats suggests Selden's sardonic remark in his *Table
Talk* (1689): "Religion is like the fashion; one man wears
his doublet slashed, another laced, another plain, but every
man has a doublet. So every man has his religion. We differ
about trimming."

The Digressions in the *Tale* are brilliant and ingenious
burlesques on the absurdities of learning and literature—
the vanity of authors, the labor of scholars, the pretensions
of critics. Swift's method is to provide grotesque and ignoble
physical symbols for the abstract and the spiritual: the pulpit is a wooden device which elevates the preacher, and
stands for claims to learning and inspiration; inspiration
itself is so much wind. The coats of Peter, Martin, and
Jack, the judge's wig, the soldier's uniform, are identified
with the institutions and callings they represent. In the
same way the process of earning a college degree might be
represented as a long period of sitting in uncomfortable
chairs for the sake of wearing a cap and gown and getting
a piece of parchment. The method is that of Butler's *Hu-*

dibras. The hollow symbols are then taken to be the only reality, and it follows that men spend their lives in pursuit of meaningless shams. This leads to the culminating "Digression on Madness." It should be remembered, however, that Swift here presents, not the universe as seen by a philosopher, but the side of human life which the satirist sees.

Closely related is *The Battle of the Books* (written about 1698, published 1704), Swift's contribution to the famous controversy between the Ancients and the Moderns. Temple had been drawn into this dispute on the side of the Ancients (see p. 53), and Wotton and Bentley were on the other side. Swift, without making any direct contribution to the controversy, represents the two factions joining battle in St. James's Library, and thus presents another satire on literary pretensions and pedantry by a skilful application of the formula of the mock-epic.

GULLIVER'S TRAVELS

Gulliver probably originated in the projects of the Scriblerus Club, particularly in burlesque of travel literature and satire of scientific pedantry. The four parts were substantially written between 1721 and 1725 and published in 1726. The countries Gulliver visits are situated in parts of the Pacific imperfectly known at that time; the South Pacific region of the first and fourth voyages and the North Pacific area of the second were not really put on the map until the second half of the century. *Gulliver* belongs to the familiar type of the imaginary voyage, but instead of a mere recital of travelers' wonders, Swift made it a plain chronicle which is at the same time a sweeping satirical estimate of human nature and society. The first part, Gulliver's sojourn among the tiny Lilliputians, offers an elaborate political allegory, reflecting in some detail the experiences of Swift's fellow Tories at the end of Queen

Anne's reign, and also Swift's hostile attitude toward the
government of George I; man is here shown in his political pretensions, which carry him from mere selfishness and
triviality to bitter malevolence and heartless intrigue.
Among the giant Brobdingnagians Gulliver finds magnified
the physical grossness of man, but he also finds an admirably simple state superior to the European system. The
political satire is centered in Gulliver's professed defense
of European civilization against the criticisms of the king
of Brobdingnag. Throughout the first two voyages, and
especially in the first, Swift's ingenuity and humor have free
play, and make the first half of this powerful satire a universally known children's book. The fourth voyage, to the
land of the Houyhnhnms, was written next, and finally the
voyage to Laputa and other countries which was published
as the third. This is a somewhat scattering satire on the
follies of science and scholarship, of economists and projectors ("promoters"). The scorn for speculation is characteristic of Swift, and continues the theme of *A Tale of a Tub*.
There are also many allusions to public affairs of the 1720's,
especially to Wood's halfpence. But the third voyage lacks
the effective unity which the others gain from a simple
central action. Gulliver is here a passive observer, not an
active participant. The climax of the voyages, though not
Swift's last word on human life, comes in the famous visit
to the land of the reasonable horses, the Houyhnhnms, who
live a simple sensible life in sharp contrast to the ape-like
Yahoos, filthy and degraded creatures with whom Gulliver
must reluctantly admit kinship. The misanthropy of this
narrative has been discussed above. Gulliver is progressively
disillusioned: in the first voyage he discovers social and
political malice; in the second, man's full measure of cruelty and wickedness; in the third, the emptiness of the life
of the mind; in the fourth, the repulsive effect of man's
failure to attain his status as a rational animal—man as a

signal illustration of the truth that the corruption of the best is the worst. It is important to remember that Gulliver is not the whole of Swift; he represents only one aspect of a complex personality; but it is a mistake to separate the two completely, to say that Swift has no share in Gulliver's final disgust and bitterness and that he is moved only by reasonable desire for political and moral reform. There is a utopian element in *Gulliver*—the chapter on education in Lilliput, the peacefulness and simplicity of the Brobdingnagians, and the "horse sense" of the Houyhnhnms; but Swift's ideals, his orthodox views of Church and State and his admiration of colorless good sense, lack the emotional, intellectual, and imaginative power of his satire.

H. Teerink, *Bibliography* (The Hague, 1937); L. A. Landa and J. E. Tobin, *Jonathan Swift: A List of Critical Studies Published from 1895 to 1945* (New York, 1945); *Prose Works*, ed. Temple Scott (12v, London, 1897-1908); *Prose Works*, ed. Herbert Davis (Oxford, 1939-); *Poems*, ed. Harold Williams (3v, Oxford, 1937); *A Tale of a Tub and The Battle of the Books*, ed. A. C. Guthkelch and D. Nichol Smith (Oxford, 1920); *Gulliver's Travels*, ed. H. Williams (London, 1926); ed. A. E. Case (New York, 1938); *Drapier's Letters,* ed. H. Davis (Oxford, 1935); *Journal to Stella,* ed. H. Williams (2v, Oxford, 1948); *Correspondence,* ed. F. E. Ball (6v, London, 1910-14); *Letters to Charles Ford,* ed. D. Nichol Smith (Oxford, 1935); Sir Henry Craik, *Life* (2v, London, 1882); Émile Pons, *Swift: les années de jeunesse* (Strasbourg, 1925); Carl Van Doren, *Swift* (New York, 1930); W. D. Taylor, *Jonathan Swift* (London, 1933); Ricardo Quintana, *The Mind and Art of Jonathan Swift* (New York, 1936); Bernard Acworth, *Swift* (London, 1946); George Sherburn, "Methods in Books about Swift," *Studies in Philology,* xxxv (1938). 635-56; Herbert Davis, "Swift's View of Poetry," in *Studies in English by Members of University College* (Toronto, 1931); "Recent Studies of Swift: A Survey," *University of Toronto Quarterly,* vii (1938). 273-88; "The Poetry of Jonathan Swift," *College English,* ii (1940). 102-15; *Stella* (New York, 1942); "The Conciseness of Swift," in *Essays on the Eighteenth Century Presented to David Nichol Smith* (Oxford, 1945); *The Satire of Jonathan Swift* (New York, 1947); W. A. Eddy, *Gulliver's Travels: A Critical Study* (Princeton, 1923); Marjorie Nicolson and Nora M. Mohler, "The Scientific Background of Swift's Voyage to Laputa," *Annals of Science,* II (1937). 299-334, 405-30; A. E. Case, *Four Essays on Gulliver's Travels* (Princeton, 1945); G. R. Potter, "Swift and Natural Science," *Philological Quarterly,* XX (1941). 97-118; L. A. Landa, *"A Modest Proposal* and Populousness," *Modern Philology,* XL (1942). 161-70; "Swift's Economic Views and Mercantilism," *ELH,* X (1943). 310-35; "Jonathan Swift and Charity," *Journal of English and Germanic Philology,* XLIV (1945). 337-50; "Swift, the Mysteries, and Deism," *University of Texas Studies in English* (1944). pp. 239-56; G. Wittkowsky, "Swift's *Modest Proposal," Journal of the History of Ideas,* IV (1943). 75-104.

DANIEL DEFOE (1660-1731)
>>

Defoe has the outlook and the style of the plain middle-class Englishman, with a few strong basic religious and social beliefs; in another light he appears as a clever and unscruplous journalist and propagandist, too clever for his own good; and then at last he appears to be beyond all else a man of genius, the author of one of the world's most famous books. His complex career still baffles biographers at many points; the list of his authenticated works now runs to over four hundred titles, and even this figure does not tell the whole story.

Defoe was the son of a pious dissenting tradesman, James Foe, in the parish of St. Giles Cripplegate. He got a sound practical education at the famous dissenting academy kept at Newington Green by the Reverend Charles Morton, later vice-president of Harvard. His early years were no doubt colored by the austerity, the religious gloom, and the political sufferings of the Dissenters. We know that he fought in Monmouth's rebellion in 1685, and he was always a loyal supporter of the Revolution settlement and William III. He was probably intended for the ministry, but instead went into business. Always a speculator and trader rather than a cautious and thrifty shop-keeper, he was involved in many lawsuits, went bankrupt in 1692, and was saddled with heavy debts. His wide ranging interests appear in his *Essay upon Projects* (1697), a series of suggestions for improvements and reforms in finance, public works, law, education, and other matters, expressing the new interest in social and economic policy which had begun to appear in such a work as Andrew Yarranton's *England's Improvement by Sea and Land* (1677-81).

As a staunch defender of William, Defoe answered a satire by one John Tutchin against the "foreign" king with his famous verses, *The True-Born Englishman* (1701). Who are the mongrel English to complain about being governed by foreigners? He further followed the Whig party line by defending the people's right to petition Parliament (*Legion's Memorial,* 1701), and in *The Mock-Mourners* (1702) he rebuked the Tory partisans who were exulting over William's death. But he wrote with such pungency and dash that he soon got into trouble. The accession of Anne led the extreme Tories to intensify their attacks against Dissent, particularly against the practice of occasional conformity (the taking of communion according to the Anglican form by Dissenters who thereby qualified for public office under the Test Act). Defoe himself denounced the practice, but he also suspected the motives of the Tories who were bringing in a bill against it, and in his famous *The Shortest Way with the Dissenters* (1702) he tried to reduce their position to an absurdity by ironically arguing that Dissent should be extirpated altogether. His irony was at first misunderstood, but soon he felt the full rage of the Tories; he was arrested and sentenced to stand in the pillory, an extremely severe punishment. The Whigs cheered him, but the affair damaged his reputation and, indeed, his character. When he was freed from prison in November,

1703, through the somewhat tardy assistance of Robert Harley, he became the secret political agent of his deliverer.
His chief purpose was to keep Whig and dissenting opinion
in line for the government. To a certain extent he could
rightly disregard party and say that the policy of a moderate Tory like Harley was not far from his own views, but
his position was unsound because his secret connection
with the government forced him to be evasive and un-
truthful.

Single handed he went on to write the *Review* (1704-13),
one of the most important journals of the day, notable not
only for Defoe's political writing but for his sound discussions of business and trade, and of some importance also
for the development of the essay-periodical (see p. 154).
Much of Defoe's work was done in the form of anonymous
pamphlets which cannot always be identified with certainty.
As an agent for Harley, he resided for some time in Scotland and had a part in the complicated moves which preceded the union of England and Scotland (1707). When
Harley resigned in 1708 Defoe continued to work for the
minister Godolphin, and when the Tories came to power
in 1710 he went back to work for Harley. Both master and
man were compromisers or "trimmers," but Defoe was at
least sincere in his support of the Hanoverian succession.
Ironical pamphlets against the Jacobites (*A Seasonable
Warning*, 1712; *Reasons against the Succession of the
House of Hanover*, 1713; *And What if the Pretender Should
Come?*, 1713; *What if the Queen Should Die?*, 1713) got him
into trouble and into jail again. At the accession of George I
Defoe turned his hand to secret work for the new Whig
ministry; his devious course cannot be fully followed, but
he evidently took government pay for collaborating as editor on Tory journals (*Mist's Journal* and others) with the
secret intention of toning down their attacks so as to make
them ineffective.

Though his journalistic work continued in the 1720's, his interests now turned in a different direction. In five years (1719-1724) he proceeded to earn for himself a key position in the history of European fiction. The beginnings of his work in prose fiction are obscure; his characteristic interest in specific detail and his plain objective style counted for much. As early as *The Apparition of Mrs. Veal* (1706) his power of manipulating detail had appeared; this famous narrative is not a fabrication of Defoe's, but the effective presentation of a received report. Another important component of his fiction was his didactic purpose, the heavy vein of Puritan middle-class moralizing which appeared in his *Family Instructor* (1715; 1718) and *Religious Courtship* (1722). A familiar form of popular literature at the time was the biographical narrative, whether of the criminal, the adventurer, the traveler, or all these at once. Defoe makes a composite of autobiographical detail, that is, detail said to have been experienced or observed at first hand, for the ostensible purpose of offering useful examples and inculcating morals and warnings. Such a formula covers all his prose fiction—*Robinson Crusoe* (I, II, 1719; III, 1720), *Memoirs of a Cavalier* (1720), *Captain Singleton* (1720), *Moll Flanders* (1722), *Journal of the Plague Year* (1722), *Colonel Jack* (1722), *Roxana* (1724). At the time this amazing series of works was considered popular trash for the humble and the semi-literate. Several were of topical interest: thus Crusoe connects with the recent rescue of Alexander Selkirk, the *Plague Year* with the plague scare of 1720, and *Singleton* with African exploration and piracy. All of them keep to the plain, canny, factual tone, and yet range widely from the piety of Crusoe to the scandalous career of Moll Flanders, and from the familiar life of the London streets to adventure in the heart of Africa or on the high seas. Defoe's travel-and-adventure formula is regularly applied to unscrupulous or vicious people, and owes something to the picaresque, the literature of roguery. But Defoe radically alters picaresque fiction and criminal biography by his sobriety of tone, his middle-class practicality, and his insistence on ways and means and bargains. Whether the story is of low life, or deals, as in *Roxana,* with aristocratic vice, the central characters nonetheless show thrift and moderation, and a certain degree of humane feeling; Defoe's assumed attitude always is that crime, trickery, greed, and recklessness do not pay, however interesting the details may be.

Apparently without realizing the value of his stories, Defoe turned away from this kind of work. *A General History of the Pirates* (1724; enlarged 1726), which has been attributed to him with virtual certainty by Professor John Robert Moore, shows the interest in sea adventure which lies back of some of his fiction; and another probable attribution is *Memoirs of Captain Carleton* (1728). His interest in economics appears in his remarkable *Tour thro' Great Britain* (1724-27), his *Complete English Tradesman* (1725-27), and *Plan of the English Commerce* (1728); his curious interest in the occult in his works *On the History and Reality of Apparitions, Political History of the Devil,* and *History of Magic*; his abiding zeal for projects and municipal improvements in *Augusta Triumphans.* One of Defoe's chief merits is his firm grasp of social and economic problems, based on sound and careful observation. Here he rose superior to the polite Augustans who despised him. During the last months of his life he evidently went into hiding to escape a creditor; he died in 1731, and was buried in Bunhill Fields.

ROBINSON CRUSOE

This is one of the most famous books in the world, and has been read in innumerable languages by millions of people who never heard of Defoe. Part 1 gives the island

ROBINSON CRUSOE, FRONTISPIECE OF THE FIRST EDITION.

story, Part II Crusoe's further travels in the Orient and
Russia, and Part III is merely a collection of devotional and
moral essays. The title-page suggests that the island story
was from the beginning, as it has remained, the absorbing
center of interest. The theme of shipwreck on a desert
island was already familiar, and the case of Alexander Selkirk's solitary life on Juan Fernandez had just attracted
attention. Many of the details were assembled from travel
books. The unparalleled success of the story is due to the
complete harmony between Defoe's point of view, the
island story itself, and the basic interests of humanity. On
the island Defoe's utilitarianism can cover the whole field—
his interest in how man manipulates things and gets along
as best he can. Defoe does not simply accumulate details
for their own sake; though often prolix and trivial, they are
such as the central character would be interested in noting
under the circumstances. Thus in *Crusoe* we get back to a
situation in which the ordinary physical details of life take
on a renewed and dramatic significance. At the same time
Crusoe's life is not primitive; civilization gives him his
ideas and standards as well as the material he salvaged from
the wreck; he is man against nature, but he is also a British
settler making his way, and also, in thought and action, a
plain middle class dissenter. His is a record of progress, a
success story couched in universally intelligible terms.

Romances and Narratives, ed. G. A. Aitken (16v, London, 1895);
Novels and Selected Writings (14v, Oxford, 1927-28; Shake-
speare Head edition); *Journal of the Plague Year and Other
Pieces*, ed. A. W. Secord (Garden City, 1935); *Review,* ed. A. W.
Secord (22v, New York, 1938; Facsimile Text); Thomas Wright,
Life (rev. ed., London, 1931); W. P. Trent, *Daniel Defoe: How to
Know Him* (Indianapolis, 1916); P. Dottin, *Daniel DeFoe et ses
romans* (Paris, 1924), trans. L. Ragan (New York, 1929); J. R.
Sutherland, *Defoe* (London, 1937); A. W. Secord, *Studies in the
Narrative Method of Defoe* (Urbana, 1924); John Robert Moore,
"Daniel Defoe and Modern Economic Theory," *Indiana Univer-*

sity Studies, XXI (1935). 1-28; *Defoe in the Pillory and Other
Studies* (Bloomington, 1939); *Defoe's Sources for 'Robert Drury's
Journal'* (Bloomington, 1943); W. T. Morgan, "Defoe's *Review*
as a Historical Source," *Journal of Modern History*, XII (1940).
221-32; J. F. Ross, *Swift and Defoe* (Berkeley, 1941): G. A. Aitken,
"Defoe's Apparition of Mrs. Veal," *Nineteenth Century*, XXXVII
(1895). 95-100; Sir Charles Firth, "Defoe's True Relation of the
Apparition of Mrs. Veal," *Review of English Studies*, VII (1931).
1-6; Dorothy Gardiner, "What Canterbury Knew of Mrs. Veal
and Her Friends," *ibid.*, 188-97.

EARLY PERIODICALS

>>

The *Tatler* was a special type of periodical evolved to
meet contemporary tastes and requirements, and the *Spectator* was the consummate realization of this type. To
understand their success we must consider not only the
talents of Addison and Steele, but also the history of English periodicals in the preceding generation. There was
comparative freedom of the press after the Licensing Act
lapsed in 1695, and a great increase in the publication of
small units, such as newspapers and other periodicals,
pamphlets, fugitive verse, and small miscellanies. The coffee houses kept a supply of such reading matter for their
customers. Much of the political discussion in early newspapers was in dialogue form.[1] But the provision of periodical entertainment was separable from the news, and here
we have a main line of origin for the *Tatler*. John Dunton
in his *Athenian Gazette* or *Athenian Mercury* (1691-97)
used the device of question and answer, queries of all kinds,
serious and absurd, being answered by a supposed editorial
board called the "Athenian Society," and thus giving rise
to an endless series of odd items and brief essays. This peri-

[1] L'Estrange's *Tory Observator, in Question and Answer* (1681-87),
Tutchin's Whig *Observator* (1702-12), Leslie's Tory *Rehearsal* (1704-09).

odical was very popular; it combined commonplace moralizing with an appeal to curiosity. In his *Pegasus* (1696) Dunton offered, along with news, an "Observator" or "Observation," a brief essay on some topic of current interest. The step from the editorial dialogue of the political papers and the question-and-answer box of the Athenians to the essay was natural and important. Other minor periodicals, such as the *Weekly Entertainment* (1700), seem to have realized the single-essay-per-number principle which was to become highly important, but which remained incidental and obscure for a few years. Decidedly literary was Peter Anthony Motteux' *Gentleman's Journal* (1692-94), with book reviews, verse, essays, popular science, short tales, riddles, even music. Motteux wanted to appeal to the ladies. His project was important, but he scattered his fire too much.

Defoe's famous *Review* (1704-13) was largely devoted to editorials on politics and economics, but gave a secondary place to entertaining and moralizing comment on manners. Defoe began by appending to his main article a collection of answers to correspondents called for a time "Advice from the Scandalous Club; being a Weekly History of Nonsense, Impertinence, Vice, and Debauchery." The Scandalous Club, combining miscellaneous comment with moral censorship, derives from Dunton's Athenian Society, though some credit may be due to Henry Care's *Pacquet of Advice from Rome,* to which Defoe acknowledges a debt. The transactions of the Club were put into a supplement, and then for a time in 1705 published separately as the *Little Review*. Defoe was not primarily interested in polite entertainment, but he made the important transition from question-and-answer and dialogue form to essay, and a specific contribution of his was the use of the fictitious letter to the editor. The *British Apollo* (1708-11), the last important example of the question-and-answer type, had considerable success under the guidance of a "society of gentlemen" which included Aaron Hill and John Gay. The idea that literary matter was a necessary part of an entertaining periodical was handed on from Motteux' *Gentleman's Journal* to the *Muses Mercury* (1707-08) and the *Monthly Miscellany* (1707-10). What was now necessary was that topics directly related to the contemporary scene should be treated from a definite point of view in such a way as to give both continuity and variety of interest.

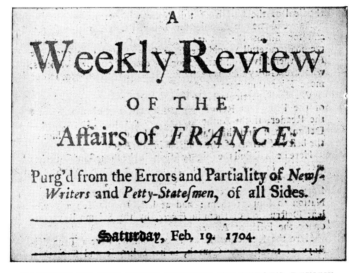

A

Weekly Review,

OF THE

Affairs of *FRANCE*:

Purg'd from the Errors and Partiality of *News-Writers* and *Petty-Statesmen*, of all Sides.

Saturday, Feb. 19. 1704.

CAPTION OF THE FIRST NUMBER OF DEFOE'S *REVIEW*

Steele published the *Tatler* three times a week from April 12, 1709, to January 2, 1711. "I own myself of the Society for Reformation of Manners," he wrote in No. 3, but moral reproof was to be part of an entertaining variety.

All accounts of gallantry, pleasure, and entertainment shall be under the article of White's Chocolate-house; Poetry, under that of Will's Coffee-house; Learning, under the title of Grecian;

foreign and domestic news you will have from Saint James's Coffee-house; and what else I have to offer on any other subject shall be dated from my own apartment. (No. 1)

My chief scenes of action are coffee-houses, play-houses, and my own apartment. (No. 18)

At first a single number had news and comment under several of these headings, but eventually news items dropped out, and a single short essay developed from the miscellaneous section headed "From my own apartment" comes to occupy an entire number. The topics are varied so as to maintain much of the appeal of the multiple departments. Steele took from Swift's pamphlets against Partridge the pen-name Isaac Bickerstaff, and a Bickerstaff family group is sketched, though this scheme does not dominate the paper. Addison came in early, and contributed about one quarter of the papers, but was never in control of the *Tatler*. Various literary forms are used—character sketches (satirically pointed at individuals in the early numbers), letters with comment, dialogues, allegories, short tales. The novelty lies in the ingenious slight variations together with the maintenance of an even tone. Extremes were excluded, particularly the extremes of political controversy, though Steele was sometimes partisan in the *Tatler,* and this was perhaps the reason why the paper was rather suddenly dropped and a new start made in the *Spectator.*

The rival *British Apollo* admired the grace and good humor of the *Tatler.* Defoe too admired, though he favored harsher methods and asked doubtfully, "Are we to be laughed out of our follies?" Gay in *The Present State of Wit* (1711) praised Bickerstaff for correcting "false sentiments" and "vicious tastes" and presenting "learning" (we should say "good reading") in a form acceptable to town and court. "Lastly, his writings have set all our wits and men of letters upon a new way of thinking." Gay thus forecast the wide and enduring influence of the periodical essay,

an appeal which was due to a reconciliation of morals and
manners worked out within the actual framework of society. The courtier was to become virtuous and the solid
citizen polite. "The courtier, the trader, and the scholar
should all have an equal pretension to the denomination
of a gentleman" (No. 207).

The *Spectator* was published six times a week from
March 1, 1711, to December 6, 1712, and was revived briefly
by Addison in 1714. Addison played a much more prominent part here, though Steele sketched the famous Club
and was the creator of Sir Roger de Coverley. Previous periodicals had developed the idea of a club both as a board
of editors (Athenian Society or Scandalous Club) and as a
fictitious group satirically or humorously described. In the
Tatler the Bickerstaffs combined the two; the Spectator
Club is primarily literary portraiture, though it is occa-
sonally represented as engaging in editorial discussion.
Except for Sir Roger, the characters are not highly developed. At times the *Spectator* approaches the novel of manners, but its chief purpose is to formulate in a persuasive
and good humored way the matters on which men and
women of good sense and good taste can agree. Addison
gives a touch of elegance; he is less sentimental and less
uneven than Steele, and the famous essays on literary criticism, such as the papers on *Paradise Lost*, the pleasures of
the imagination, and the popular ballads, are entirely his.
He prided himself on the success of a periodical which was
free from political controversy, cynicism, infidelity, or personal animus (No. 262). Early critics, convinced that Addison had more dignity and weight than Steele, gave him
most of the credit for the success of this program; recent
students have been inclined to exalt the frankness, charm,
and originality of Steele at the expense of the more sedate,
reserved, and conventional Addison. At any rate, Steele was
justified in saying as the *Spectator* drew to a close: "I claim

STEELE   ADDISON

NUMB. I.

The SPECTATOR.

Non fumum ex fulgore, fed ex fumo dare lucem
Cogitat, ut fpeciofa dehinc miracula promat.   Hor.

To be Continued every Day.

Thurfday, March 1. 1711.

CAPTION OF THE FIRST NUMBER OF THE *SPECTATOR*

to myself the merit of having extorted excellent productions from a person of the greatest abilities, who would not
have let them appear by any other means" (No. 532). In the
Guardian (1713) Addison and Steele continued their alliance.

The influence of the periodical essay was important
throughout the century. It persisted as an independent
periodical, as a unit in a larger periodical, as a collection
of essays in book form, and as a formative influence in the
development of the novel. In the generation after Steele
and Addison periodicals like Fielding's *Champion* centered
about a principal essay. In the mid-century there was a
revival of the independent series expressing the point of
view of an individual or a small group of contributors—
Johnson's *Rambler* (1750-52), Hawkesworth's *Adventurer*
(1752-54), with aid from Joseph Warton, Johnson, and
Bathurst, Fielding's *Covent-Garden Journal* (1752), Edward
Moore's *World* (1753-56), with important contributions
from Chesterfield, Walpole, and others, Colman and Thornton's *Connoisseur* (1754-56). Goldsmith wrote the short-
lived *Bee* and contributed *The Citizen of the World* to the
Public Ledger (1760-61). Henry Mackenzie gave considerable individuality to the *Mirror* (1779-80) and the *Lounger*
(1785-87). The form was extensively imitated on the Continent. Meanwhile the *Tatler* and the *Spectator* themselves
went through innumerable editions, and the periodical
essay became the staple content of readers and anthologies,
and influenced the early reading and writing of generations
of schoolchildren in England and America.

Katherine K. Weed and Richmond P. Bond, *Studies of British
Newspapers and Periodicals from their Beginning to 1800: A
Bibliography* (Chapel Hill, 1946); W. J. Graham, *The Beginnings
of English Literary Periodicals* (New York, 1926); *English Literary
Periodicals* (New York, 1930); G. S. Marr, *The Periodical Essayists
of the Eighteenth Century* (New York, 1924); R. S. Crane and F.
B. Kaye, *Census of British Newspapers and Periodicals, 1620-1800*

(Chapel Hill, 1927); Stanley Morison, *The English Newspaper* (Cambridge, 1932); Laurence Hanson, *Government and the Press, 1695-1763* (London, 1936); *Tatler,* ed. G. A. Aitken (4v, London, 1898-99); *Spectator,* ed. G. G. Smith (8v, London, 1897-98) (4v, London, 1907; Everyman's Library); *Spectator,* ed. G. A. Aitken (8v, Edinburgh, 1898); *Selections from the Tatler, Spectator, and Guardian,* ed. Austin Dobson (Oxford, 1896).

RICHARD STEELE (1672-1729)

>>>

Though Addison and Steele are inseparably connected in life and literature, they exhibit wide personal differences. We are sometimes tempted to think that all the Augustan worthies look alike in their periwigs, but Steele's broad good-natured features are in obvious contrast to the conventional oval face of Addison. Steele was born in Dublin; his father was English, his mother possibly Irish. At any rate he shows an impulsiveness and warmth which we may fairly call Irish, and these traits give a touch of pathos and charm to some of his best writing. Thus his personality and work remind us at times of another Anglo-Irishman, Oliver Goldsmith. Steele was educated in London at the Charterhouse, where his lifelong friendship with Addison began. He proceeded to Oxford, being a member first of Christ Church and then of Merton College. Instead of taking a degree, however, he entered the army, where he spent several obscure years as ensign (lieutenant) in one regiment and captain in another. Soon he had also entered into the literary life of the town and was known as a member of the group at Will's. He was probably extravagant and dissipated, though we need not magnify his sins.

His first important publication combines didactic purpose with a naïve personal touch. He had been forced, against his conscience, to fight a duel; and in general he found it hard to be a Christian and a soldier at the same time, so he wrote *The Christian Hero* (1701), "with a design," he tells us, "to fix upon his own mind a strong impression of virtue and religion, in opposition to a stronger propensity towards unwarrantable pleasures." Socially this is a step in the post-Restoration "reformation of manners"; philosophically the tract sets Christian piety above the ideal of pagan and stoical virtue exalted by the admirers of classical antiquity. Steele's early plays, *The Funeral* (1701), *The Lying Lover* (1703), and *The Tender Husband* (1705) illustrate more clearly than those of his contemporary Cibber the movement toward reform of the English stage by avoidance of gross indecency, by the use of gentler and more playful ridicule, and by an appeal to the tender emotions (pp. 82-84). Steele's interest in the theater was lifelong, but he was soon absorbed in politics. He was always a staunch supporter of Marlborough and the Godolphin ministry, and under that government he held the position of gazeteer (editor of the official newspaper). In 1707 he married Mary Scurlock, the "Prue" to whom he addressed the famous letters which help to confirm the impression that he was always in trouble, involved in debt and given to the careless life of the tavern.

The fall of the Whigs in 1710 put a strain on his relations with Swift. He never withdrew from party strife, but the *Tatler* was largely non-partisan, the *Spectator* almost completely so. It is significant that the success of these two papers came when Steele and Addison were out of office during the Tory régime. Steele had a main hand in several other periodicals, but usually with some controversial purpose. Of these the most important was the *Guardian,* which had many of the qualities of the *Spectator* but took the Whig side and came into conflict with Swift and the *Examiner.* For a political pamphlet called *The Crisis* the Tories expelled Steele from the House of Commons, though he rightly declared that all he had done was to assert his devotion to the principles of 1688 and his opposition to the Jacobite cause. With the accession of George I and the Whig triumph, Steele was once more in favor; he was knighted, resumed his seat in Parliament, and was given among other things a share in the patent of Drury Lane Theater. Theatrical business complicated Steele's finances and got him into trouble with the Duke of Newcastle, the Lord Chamberlain, who tried to punish him by suspending his patent. In 1722 Steele produced his most successful play, *The Conscious Lovers,* a more markedly sentimental piece than his early plays and one of the most characteristic and influential dramas of the century. Meanwhile he had become partly estranged from Addison for political reasons, but after the death of the latter in 1719 Steele paid generous tribute to his memory and convincingly showed the sincerity of his friendship. His health broke in 1723, and he spent the last six years of his life as a semi-invalid in retirement in Wales.

Tracts and Pamphlets, ed. Rae Blanchard (Baltimore, 1944); *Correspondence,* ed. Rae Blanchard (London, 1941); *The Christian Hero,* ed. Rae Blanchard (London, 1932); Austin Dobson, *Richard Steele* (London, 1886); G. A. Aitken, *Life* (2v, London, 1889); Willard Connely, *Sir Richard Steele* (New York, 1934); Bonamy Dobrée, *Variety of Ways* (Oxford, 1932).

JOSEPH ADDISON (1672-1719)
>>

Joseph Addison was the son of a distinguished clergyman, Lancelot Addison, rector of Milston, near Amesbury, Wiltshire, and later Dean of Lichfield. Thus the son inherited a tradition of piety and learning. He was educated at the Charterhouse, where he met Steele, and then went

up to Queen's College, Oxford. Later his Latin verses won
him an appointment as a demy (scholar) of Magdalen. His
literary interests appear also in his juvenile piece of verse,
An Account of the Greatest English Poets, and in the editorial matter which he supplied for Dryden's *Virgil.* He
seemed destined to be a scholarly churchman like his father.
At this point his promise attracted the attention of Lord
Somers and Charles Montagu, later Earl of Halifax, two
Whig magnates noted for their literary friendships and
their patronage of men of letters. The latter got for Addison a pension (what we should call a "traveling fellowship")
to enable him to make the grand tour on the Continent in
preparation for the diplomatic service. He spent four years
abroad (1699-1703), mostly in Italy, and wrote of his travels
in his verse *Letter from Italy to Lord Halifax* (1704) and
in his prose *Remarks on Italy* (1705). As a scholar he
thought of Italy as classic ground, but not as the great
treasury of Renaissance art; as a Whig he dwelt on the
contrast between English liberty and continental tyranny.

On returning to England he was not immediately given
political patronage, though by his election to the Kit Cat
Club he was taken into the inner circle of the Whigs. But
soon the government wanted a poet to celebrate Marlborough's great victory at Blenheim. Several versifiers tried
the subject, but Addison's poem *The Campaign* (1705)
scored by far the greatest success and established him as a
leading writer for the Whigs. His friendship with Steele
was thus confirmed, and his friendship with Swift, based
on sincere esteem, developed rapidly. His opera *Rosamond*
(1707) was a failure, but during these early years of political and literary activity in the coffee houses Addison made
secure his position among the wits. He held government
office, and during 1709 resided in Ireland as secretary to
Lord Wharton. On his return to London he was drawn
into the *Tatler* and had a main hand in the *Spectator.*

The periodical essay was an ideal medium for the reserved and sedate personality of Addison, who resembles the grave "Mr. Spectator" himself. His wide though not profound scholarship, his amused and playful observation of contemporary life, his mild piety and moralism, all find definitive expression here. His skilful manipulation of the various themes of the *Spectator* is carried on in an easy familiar prose style perfectly adapted to his purpose. If the *Spectator* at times seems tame and trite to us, we must remember that this work represents a newly attained moral equilibrium after the license of the Restoration, and that the reformation of manners and the popularization of knowledge and good taste were still novelties. A success of this kind must be won by a sacrifice of intensity and an avoidance of extremes.

Meanwhile there was a great deal going on in town and in Addison's own life which showed how precarious was the equilibrium attained by the *Spectator*. Swift was now a political opponent, and wrote against the Whigs in the *Examiner*. Pope was estranged from Addison for complicated personal reasons in which politics had a share (see p. 167). Pope's grievance was largely against the little coterie of Whig writers which Addison, seceding from Will's, had gathered around him at Button's nearby. Addison and Steele turned to political writing again, the former in the *Freeholder* and the latter in the *Guardian*. Addison's drama *Cato,* produced in 1713, was a bipartisan political event, and Whig and Tory vied with one another in cheering Cato's devotion to liberty. *Cato* is a formal piece, one of the few important English plays written in strict observance of the unities. Its patriotic sentiments and somewhat arid stoicism won general admiration throughout the century, and an age which looked for sententious utterance in serious drama found many noble lines in *Cato,* wooden though the verse and the characters are. The play represents the scholastic Addison. In 1716 he married the Dowager Countess of Warwick. He was, of course, in high political favor after George I came to the throne, and held the position of Secretary of State for some time before his death in 1719.

The eighteenth century and the Victorians united in exalting Addison; even Pope later paid his tribute—"No whiter page than Addison remains"—and Johnson and Macaulay agreed in praise of his virtues and his literary power. A close study of the period has shown later scholars that Addison was too deeply involved in personal and political intrigue to be set up as the paragon of his age, but there is no denying the importance and centrality of his position. To adapt the familiar words of Dr. Johnson, whether we wish "to attain an English style, familiar but not coarse, and elegant but not ostentatious," or whether we wish merely to understand the eighteenth century better, we "must give our days and nights to the volumes of Addison."

Works, ed. H. G. Bohn (6v, London, 1882-83); *Miscellaneous Works*, ed. A. C. Guthkelch (2v, London, 1914); *Letters*, ed. Walter Graham (Oxford, 1941); *Selections*, ed. B. Wendell and C. N. Greenough (Boston, 1905); Lucy Aikin, *Life* (2v, London, 1843); W. J. Courthope, *Joseph Addison* (New York, 1903; English Men of Letters); Bonamy Dobrée, *Essays in Biography* (London, 1925); C. S. Lewis, "Addison," in *Essays on the Eighteenth Century Presented to David Nichol Smith* (Oxford, 1945).

ALEXANDER POPE (1688-1744)

>>>>>>>>>>>>>>>>>>>>>>>>:>>>>>>>>>>>>>>>>>>>>>>>>>>>>>>>>>

In the Revolution year 1688 was born the poet who was destined to perfect the formal style developed in the late seventeenth century and to dominate English verse for two generations. Alexander Pope was of Catholic parentage and therefore could not get his education at public school and university. Moreover, he was a sickly and deformed boy, and was denied a normal physical and social life. He was for the most part privately educated in his parents' country house at Binfield, on the edge of Windsor Forest. He read widely if not exactly, with the imitativeness and docility often found in bookish and precocious youth. From his study of Latin and English poetry and the neo-classical principles transmitted through Dryden and the French critics he developed a literary code and program which would pass as orthodox in any London coffee house or coterie of wits. He accepted what had become the official neo-classical view of the history of English poetry—that modern English verse began with Waller's smooth couplets and reached its greatest glory in Dryden; yet it should be remembered that he knew and appreciated in his own way Shakespeare and Milton, to a less degree Chaucer and Spenser, and that he responded to the picturesque and the romantic. He was a sensitive young poet, not a mere rationalist or formalist. As to style, however, he accepted the advice which the minor poet and critic Walsh gave him: "He used to encourage me much, and used to tell me that there was one way left of excelling; for though we had several great poets, we never had any one great poet that was correct; and he desired me to make that my study and aim." [1] The correctness here recommended perhaps meant a rigorous choice of

POPE

[1] Joseph Spence, *Anecdotes* (London, 1820), p. 280.

words and nice adjustment of meter to get what Pope calls "sense" and "sweetness."

Pope's *Pastorals* (perhaps written 1704, published 1709), and the greater part of *Windsor Forest* (completed and published 1713) were composed with the encouragement of his literary advisers, Sir William Trumbull, William Walsh, George Granville (later Lord Lansdowne), and William Wycherley. As descriptions of external nature these pieces can be judged too conventional and formal, but they are primarily exercises in style. Even before publication these early verses were Pope's passport to the literary circles of London, and he continued to make important friendships. At an early age he appeared at Will's, and by 1711 he was on friendly terms with Congreve, Addison, and Steele. After the appearance of the *Essay on Criticism* (1711) and the first version of *The Rape of the Lock* (1712) it seemed that he had already won first place among the poets of the time. Yet his supremacy was not ungrudgingly recognized. The irascible John Dennis answered Pope's unfavorable allusion to him as "Appius" in the *Essay* by publishing a furious personal attack. Moreover, jealousies and political differences estranged him from the Whig group centering about Addison, and his closest associates were eventually to be found among the Tories—Gay, Swift, Arbuthnot, and Parnell. In 1713 he was still trying to be neutral, with the praise of the Tory peace at the end of *Windsor Forest* counterbalanced by his Prologue to Addison's Whig tragedy *Cato* and his contributions to Steele's *Guardian*. Yet Pope resented the support which Addison's group gave to the pastorals of Ambrose Philips (see p. 411), he professed to believe that Addison was acting in bad faith when he urged him not to revise *The Rape of the Lock*, he found that Addison would not stand by him when he attacked Dennis, with good reason he suspected Addison of countenancing or even encouraging attacks upon him, and finally proposals by Tickell to translate the *Iliad* were, he thought, really instigated by Addison in opposition to his own prior proposals. The climax of this complicated series of episodes was the writing of the famous "Atticus" lines, perhaps about 1716, first printed in a newspaper in 1722 and later inserted in the *Epistle to Arbuthnot*. Here the vein of personal and literary jealousy in Addison is pitilessly analyzed.

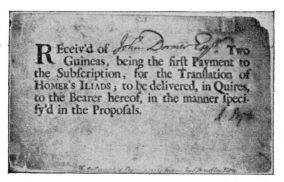

RECEIPT FOR SUBSCRIPTION TO POPE'S *ILIAD*
By courtesy of Goodspeed's Book Shop, Boston.

Meanwhile he was trying work in various kinds—the *Messiah* (a Virgilian paraphrase of Isaiah first published in the *Spectator* in 1712), the artificial *Ode for Music on St. Cecilia's Day,* and the passionate though rhetorical poems, *An Elegy to the Memory of an Unfortunate Lady* and *Eloisa to Abelard.* The collected edition of 1717 contains all his important work up to that time and shows a comparatively wide and experimental range of subject and style.

By his translation of the *Iliad* (proposed 1713, published 1715-1720) Pope established his position as the foremost professional writer of the day, and attained financial security at a time when it was almost a unique thing for an author to be independent both of the caprices of patronage and of the booksellers. In the translation of the *Odyssey*, carried out with the partly unacknowledged aid of two minor versifiers Broome and Fenton, he did task-work of a somewhat less distinguished kind. The Homer as a whole became a sort of poetic model for the age, a treasury of spirited verse and elegant diction. Another project of this period was his edition of Shakespeare (1725). In 1718 he moved to his villa at Twickenham, on the Thames just out-

POPE'S VILLA AT TWICKENHAM

side London and opposite Richmond. Here he enjoyed a gentlemanly rural retirement, entertained his friends, nursed his grudges against his enemies, and busied himself with his gardening and his grotto. His gardening was in the picturesque and irregular English style.

After this period of translating and editing, the course of his career was again deeply affected by personal feuds. He paid off his accumulated grudges in the *Dunciad,* pro-

jected as a sweeping rejoinder to his enemies and slander-
ers, and as a general attack on the scribblers of Grub
Street. Pope's malevolence and coarseness cannot obscure
the brilliance of his satire and the just cause of good sense
which he defends. A more serious blot on his character was
the amazing and devious series of intrigues he carried on
in the 1730's to trick the rascally bookseller Curll, an old
enemy, into publishing a spurious version of his correspondence in order that he himself might publish his own version with cries of injured innocence. Nineteenth-century
biographers, confronted with the fact that Pope unscrupulously doctored the evidence in his letters, were only too
ready to echo an elegy of November, 1744:

> Dan Pope, this character be thine:
> Thy soul was mean, thy verse divine.

To counterbalance all this, we have the picture of Pope in
his Twickenham villa living a life of lettered ease if not of
happiness, and capable of sincere friendship with men like
Swift and Bolingbroke. He was so intensely self-conscious
that he always played a rôle, but it was a brilliant rôle, and
fundamentally he believed in it. Accepting the standards
of the enlightened society which neo-classicism presupposes,
he set up as the witty, trenchant commentator on life and
as the defender of good sense in society and morals. He
vaguely planned a great "ethic work in four books," and
part of this scheme is represented by the *Essay on Man,*
published in four successive epistles in 1733 and 1734, and
intended as a serious contribution to philosophy in contrast
to his vein of personal satire. Other fragments of the "ethic
work" are now gathered as the group called *Moral Essays,
or Epistles*; but there is no essential difference between this
and the other group of pieces called *Satires, or Imitations
of Horace.* Both Pope and Dryden in their mature work
attain a facile alternation of verse-essay and satire, passing

easily "from grave to gay, from lively to severe." Pope
gives Bolingbroke credit for advising him to amuse himself
by adapting Horace's Satires and Epistles to the modern
English scene, but the same device had been used by
Rochester and Oldham. From 1730 the Horatian satire or
epistle was Pope's favorite form. Here, often adapting his
Latin original with great skill, but following casual asso-
ciations of ideas rather than any systematic plan, he develops his favorite themes: man, he teaches, forsakes reason to
follow the "ruling passion" which warps his life; this is
particularly clear in the lives of the great and fashionable.
But some few there are, Pope's friends, who keep their lives
in rational balance, and one there is, the poet himself, who
sees and speaks the truth without fear or favor. This highly
affected version of his own personality is best set forth in
Pope's elaborate piece of self-defence, the *Epistle to Arbuthnot* (1735), or *Prologue to the Satires,* an adaptation of the
traditional *apologia* of Roman satire. There is much sagac-
ity, shrewdness, and urbane wit in these superbly finished
pieces, but there is also much personal satire, sometimes
concentrated, as in the Atticus lines and the portrait of
the Duchess of Marlborough as Atossa and of Hervey as
Sporus, but often conveyed with deft and subtle touch, as
in the ironical tribute to George II as Augustus. Personal
attacks were discovered by Pope's enemies even when he
declared there were none, as in the portrait of Timon in the
epistle *Of the Use of Riches* (1733), often taken to be a
satire on the Duke of Chandos. In the 1730's Pope was
drawn into the opposition to Walpole, and much of his
later satire shows political coloring in its denunciation of
folly and corruption. The poem *One Thousand Seven
Hundred and Thirty-eight,* later made the *Epilogue to the
Satires,* is markedly political in purpose. If we set aside
the undue pretense to superior virtue, we find the wit and
sense of these later poems incomparable. Pope's art is often

called formal, and his lines are indeed phrased and
weighted with high precision; nevertheless they bend in
response to his thought and mood like well tempered steel,
and they often have the easy modulation of ideally intelligent conversation. The *Moral Essays* and *Satires* at their
best have the elegance of *The Rape of the Lock* and the
sense of the *Essay on Man*. They give Pope's final shrewd
estimate of art, literature, society, and human nature.

Pope's reputation suffered in later generations which set
a particularly high value on qualities not to be found in
his work. Joseph Warton, though by no means hostile,
argued in his *Essay on the Writings and Genius of Pope*
(1756) that Pope's claims to greatness were limited by his
cultivation of wit and ethics rather than sublimity and
pathos. Later romantic critics underestimated Pope because
they insisted on judging him by their own standards, which
laid perhaps exaggerated emphasis on the description of
external nature. But Pope's art should be considered in its
social context. He inherited the standards of the elegant
and aristocratic amateur of letters, but modified this ideal
by his exacting professional attitude; no pains were too
great when it was a question of clarifying his thought,
polishing his lines, and harmonizing his numbers. In this
endless labor he was not flippant or frivolous; here he
showed an artistic conscientiousness which was more con-
vincing than his profession of high moral aims. He was,
therefore, somewhat out of touch with the sobriety and
utilitarianism of the rising middle-class spirit of his time.
He built with the greatest skill on a rather narrow foundation. At its best his poetry is a manifestation of high technical competence in detail, rather than the execution of plans
on a large scale. In massiveness, indeed, Pope is outweighed
by the other great English representatives of the neo-classic
tradition, Dryden and Johnson. But though they were able

to put greater personal power behind their work, Pope is their superior in poise, adequacy, and finish.

AN ESSAY ON CRITICISM

Perhaps begun in 1704 and considerably revised before publication in 1711, the *Essay* sums up Pope's early literary studies and at the same time establishes his final position. He works here in the tradition of the Renaissance verse-essays on poetry, such as Vida's *De Arte Poetica* and Boileau's *Art Poétique,* which go back to Horace's Epistle to the Pisos or *Ars Poetica.* Preceding Pope in English were the *Essay on Poetry* (1682) by John Sheffield, Earl of Mulgrave, later Duke of Buckingham, the *Essay on Translated Verse* (1684) by Roscommon, and Lansdowne's *Essay upon Unnatural Flights in Poetry* (1701). In all these works principles of poetry taken as agreed upon by men of intelligence and taste are neatly and briefly set forth without formal argument. Pope is giving advice to the critic rather than the poet, but this makes little difference, for according to Pope the poet consciously uses the same standards which the critic will apply. These standards are said to be given or discovered in the order found in nature, which is also the order of reason. John Dennis put it thus: "As Nature is order and rule and harmony in the visible world, so Reason is the very same throughout the invisible creation." [1] The great ancients, such as Homer, followed or imitated this order, and then the great critics, Aristotle, Horace, Quintilian, Longinus, described this order as found in the works of the poets, and so formulated the Rules, which are "Nature still, but Nature methodized." The theory is thus a series of identities—Nature-Reason-the Classics-the Rules. The whole sequence is thought of as congenial to man's mind, or, as it is sometimes put, Pope's Nature is

[1] *Advancement and Reformation of Modern Poetry,* in *Critical Works,* ed. E. N. Hooker, I, 202.

identified with the permanent or universal elements in
human nature. The Rules are right not simply because the
Ancients presented them; the Ancients presented them because they are right. In practice, however, the best way to
get at the Rules is to study and imitate the Ancients. The
poet at work is not exactly in the position of a philosopher
dealing directly with Reason and Nature; he learns as
every one else learns, by imitation; he is brought up in a
tradition which reverences ancient authors, and he writes
for a public which accepts that tradition. One great error
of criticism is to become peremptory in formulating rules
without regard to the practice of great writers, and thus to
become dull and mechanical (ll. 104-117). In theory the
critics whom Pope largely followed, Boileau and Dryden,
handed on a moderate and liberal creed which reconciled
free imitation of classical models with the imitation of
Nature essential to all poetry. But in practice the example
of the Ancients often came to have the weight usually attached to legal or religious authority. When Pope praises
the unlicensed beauties not covered by the Rules, he hastens
to add the warning:

> But tho' the ancients thus their rules invade,
> (As Kings dispense with laws themselves have made)
> Moderns, beware! or if you must offend
> Against the precept, ne'er transgress its end;
> Let it be seldom, and compell'd by need;
> And have at least their precedent to plead.   (ll. 161-166)

Because of the primacy of the Ancients, the later history of
literature is a history of decline.

But how does the poet deal with Nature? Obviously not
by an exact and indiscriminate imitation, a mirror-image.
The Rules are "Nature methodized." This process of meth-
odizing, of getting at the essential Nature, involves the
exercise of Wit and Invention. Both terms are used in different senses by Pope, but in their most significant use

they cover the initiative the poet takes in creative work: they denote the faculty that discovers and selects themes for the poet and makes new combinations of ideas. Wit and Invention are distinguished from Judgment, a faculty which separates ideas and excludes the irrelevant and the irregular. Thus Nature is to be sought both through the daring operations of Wit and Invention, duly tempered by Judgment, and through close study of the Ancients who found her long ago. Though Nature is "divinely bright" (l. 70), the light at times is but glimmering (l. 21); though Reason is unchanging and universal, it is not easily found by all; on the contrary, "true genius" and "true taste" are rare (ll. 11-12). It is not quite clear on Pope's premises why it is so difficult to be a poet or a critic, why Nature should not be obvious and irresistible, or why "pride, malice, folly" should always come in to bedevil poets and critics (ll. 458-59). There is an unsolved problem of error here, just as there is an unsolved problem of evil in the *Essay on Man* (see p. 180). On the other hand, artistic success is also a mystery, whether we have in mind the actual production or the appreciation of a poem. The Rules do not do it all. Pope falls back at times on a long-run social standard; true Wit is sure to make its way at last. But the taste of the town at a given time is not definitive. Moreover, even adequate criticism, a fully enlightened application of the Rules, will find something which cannot be accounted for, the "grace beyond the reach of art," otherwise called the *je ne sais quoi,* which may often be the essential thing. This quality, not covered by the Rules, is nevertheless attained by "true genius" and apprehended by "true taste." An underlying belief in the harmony of things leads Pope and others, such as Shaftesbury, to assert a harmony between the "nameless grace" and good sense. Thus the subjectivity of the school of taste is avoided. Obviously the *je ne sais quoi* is not something that can be taught a young

poet, who, Pope warns, had better curb his wit. If the
Essay concedes freedom of operation in theory, its admonitions check rather than spur the poet, and deal largely with
correctness of style and meter. Here belong the famous passages on conceit, language, and numbers in Part II. Pope is
not really qualified to grapple with the philosophical foundations of criticism, though he gives a brilliant restatement
of current doctrine: his real interest is in his shrewd and
sometimes satiric view of poet, critic, and public, and in
the clear aphoristic expression of familiar ideas. In this
respect the Essay on Criticism teaches both by precept and
example.

THE RAPE OF THE LOCK

   (Original version in two cantos in Lintot's Miscellany, 1712;
revised and enlarged version in five cantos, 1714.)

Robert Lord Petre had cut off a lock of Miss Arabella
Fermor's hair, and this trifling episode had caused ill-will
between their kinsfolk. Both families were prominent in
Roman Catholic circles, and a common friend John Caryll
asked Pope to help matters by turning the whole affair into
a joke. Accordingly Pope wrote the first version of The
Rape of the Lock in the summer or autumn of 1711. In
the revised and final version Pope more than doubled the
length of the poem by adding the machinery of the sylphs,
which he took from a contemporary Rosicrucian romance
in French. To the original episode, the tempest in a tea-
pot, Pope applies the mock-heroic method; that is, he
treats trifling matters in an elaborate and elevated style
full of echoes from classical epic: the supernatural machinery, the set speeches, the description of the card-game
(ombre) as a battle, the final combat between beaux and
belles, the journey to the Cave of Spleen, all connect with
traditional epic devices. In general method Pope follows
Boileau's Lutrin, which deals with the quarrels of the

priests of the Sainte Chapelle, and Garth's *Dispensary,*
which deals with the quarrels of physicians. But Pope's
subject, the contemporary world of fashion, entailed certain
differences in method. The earlier burlesques often dealt
with the low and ugly, and used the mock-heroic style
chiefly to give a heavy caricature. Pope's theme is trivial
rather than low; his mock-heroic elevation enlarges and illustrates it without distorting it; though he takes some
specific hints for his satire of fashionable life from Garth,
he avoids the ponderousness that usually appears in the
employment of epic devices for humorous effect, and attains playful brilliance and elegance. His style is related to
the graceful treatment of feminine fashions and ways in
the *Tatler* and the *Spectator,* and it suggests some com-
parisons with the playful devices which Swift later used in
the voyage to Lilliput. There are some touches of the grotesque, as in the caricature of Sir Plume and the details of
the Cave of Spleen, but throughout there is a systematic
use of idealized and heightened decoration, as in the description of the toilet table, the progress of the heroine
Belinda up the Thames, and the party at Hampton Court.
The mocking overstatements and elaborate style in the
hands of a less skilful artist would be clumsy exaggeration,
but here form an essential part of the decorative pattern,
and are kept in place by Pope's systematic use of the device
of anticlimax. This artificial society is not rejected or denounced; it is accepted as a fascinating spectacle, yet there
is a didactic note—vanity, folly, spite are censured, and
good sense and good humor are recommended. Such control of cynicism and satire, except for a few lines in which
the underlying theme of sex is too grossly expressed, shows
the great change in manners as we pass from Restoration
comedy to Pope and Addison. For all these reasons, *The
Rape of the Lock* has been Pope's most popular poem, not
only in its day of publication but in later periods which

looked back on the eighteenth century as a kind of costume
piece.

THE DUNCIAD

(Books I-III, 1728; *Dunciad Variorum,* with satirical notes and
much introductory and appended matter, 1729; *New Dunciad*
(Book IV), 1742; complete edition in four books, 1743.)

Pope developed from about 1725 to 1727, with the help
and advice of Swift, a comprehensive satire in which he
might take revenge on his literary enemies and deride the
whole tribe of dull and mercenary scribblers. Behind the
whole project, along with personal animus, was the contempt felt by the inner circle of great writers for what they
took to be the cheapening of authorship in an age of journalism, pamphleteering, and hackwork. A specific purpose
of the *Dunciad* of 1728 and 1729 was to attack pedantry in
the person of Lewis Theobald, whose *Shakespeare Restored*
(1726) had effectively attacked Pope's work as an editor of
Shakespeare, and who was continuing his campaign in the
newspapers. The notes in the variorum edition serve this
purpose. This is an extension of a device used in *A Tale
of a Tub* and in earlier skits on pedantry by the Scriblerus
Club. The plan of the poem is mock-epic, though it does
not have the skilfully unified structure of *The Rape of the
Lock*. In Book I the Goddess of Dulness chooses Theobald
for her own—Cibber was substituted later. The basic scheme
here is from *Mac Flecknoe*. Elaborating the idea of a contest
among the dunces for supremacy, Book II burlesques the
account of the funeral games for Anchises in *Æneid* v; the
dunces run races, dive in filth, and so forth. In Book III
the hero has an epic vision of the Progress of Dulness (the
original title of the piece) from the most remote past to
the final triumph of Chaos and Night. The tone throughout is often broad and jocular rather than malicious and
bitter. The *New Dunciad* of 1742, written with the advice

of Warburton, gives a sweeping view of defective education and of the follies of pedantry, antiquarianism, scientific virtuosity, and free thought. The book is less personal than the first three, and relatively grave, decent, and elegant. The general scheme is that of a court reception at which the Goddess of Dulness bestows honors or favors upon groups of her followers and subjects; Professor Sherburn has suggested that Pope may have taken this device from Fielding's popular farces of the 1730's.[1] When Cibber is substituted for Theobald in the version of 1743 we see that the term *dunce* is made to cover a good deal; a dunce may be pedantic, as Pope said Theobald was, or "lively," like Cibber, but always wrong-headed. Against all varieties of folly and error the true wit must break a lance; it follows, as Pope said, that "the life of a wit is a warfare upon earth."

AN ESSAY ON MAN

The four epistles that make up the *Essay* were published anonymously from February 1733 to January 1734. The work strikes the moral or didactic note which is prominent in Pope's work after the *Dunciad*. It is his most ambitious philosophic effort, and indeed the most familiar and frequently quoted piece of popular philosophy in the eighteenth century. "Essay" does not seem to mean here something merely tentative, but a fairly systematic treatise. Although Pope talks much about man's weakness and blindness, and his presumption in aspiring to understand the whole, the poet nevertheless undertakes to set forth a coherent scheme of the universe, and thus to "vindicate the ways of God to man." An ancient conception, widely popularized and generally accepted in Pope's day, was that God in his overflowing goodness must create the best of all possible worlds, that is, a world in which all possible

[1] *University of Texas Studies in English* (1944), pp. 179-82.

forms of being, low and high, simple and complex, are actually realized: the universe is thus an unbroken chain, scale, or continuum, and everything must be just what it is and where it is in order that the great scheme may be realized. The history of this idea is fully told in Lovejoy's classic study *The Great Chain of Being* (1936), and to the exposition of such a scheme of things Pope devotes a large part of the first epistle. He has been much censured for this hasty leap into metaphysics. Bolingbroke was his philosophic guide; it is uncertain how definite Bolingbroke's actual contributions to the *Essay* were, but it seems that they were probably made orally rather than in writing. In any case both men were rather beyond their depth and showed no original philosophic power. We should not underestimate, however, the power of general ideas, particularly the vision of the chain of being, to touch the poet's imagination and to inspire brilliant aphoristic verse.

The one thing needful is to know one's place in the chain—"Order is Heaven's first law." This means acceptance of and resignation to the world order, avoidance of the cardinal sin and error of Pride. But obviously man falls short here. In Epistle II Pope finds that human nature does not fit easily into the perfect scheme expounded in Epistle I. Man's reason is at war with his passions ("modes of self-love"), and competing passions themselves may be, usually are, overmastered by the ruling passion. Now a thorough-going optimism might argue that since partial evil becomes universal good, the passions, like everything else, work for good. It is also possible to view the spectacle of contending passions as a dramatic or aesthetic pattern. But Pope easily slips back into his rôle of satirist, and emphasizes the irrational element in man and man's responsibility for keeping that element under control. "Whatever is, is right," and yet sin, error, and folly keep preachers and satirists busy. Popular philosophy is often a matter of basic images or metaphors; for the image of the perfect and static chain in Epistle I Pope here substitutes the image of strong conflicting forces which it is man's duty to keep in equilibrium. The conflict of reason and passion in the *Essay on Man* is exactly parallel to the conflict of wit and judgment in the *Essay on Criticism*.

In the account of the development of human society in Epistle III, Pope again expounds a divinely ordered scheme, in which the operations of the lower animals are determined by God-given instinct, and the relations between men in the state of nature by God-given benevolence. The familiar primitivistic idea of the Golden Age appears here. The basic conception is that of divine design, or what Pope's contemporaries called physico-theology. Of course the whole scheme of the chain of being might be thought of in terms of design, but the arguments of contemporary physico-theology concerned themselves not so much with metaphysics as with the evidences of design which appeared in the new findings of science. Man should not be encouraged to think of himself as the center of the universe, but nothing is more salutary than to observe how exquisitely all things have been planned by the Creator. As we contemplate this grand scheme, it appears that even the conflicts and stresses of human nature are divinely arranged, for "true self-love and social are the same." In Epistle IV Pope considers the good life, the way to happiness, and thus shows how the *Essay* connects with the *Moral Essays* and *Satires* to follow. The general connection between the system of the *Essay* and contemporary satire is seen in *Spectator* No. 404:

The Creator of the universe has appointed everything to a certain use and purpose, and determined it to a settled course and sphere of action, from which if it in the least deviates, it becomes unfit to answer those ends for which it was designed. . . . The civil economy is formed in a chain as well as the natural;

and in either case the breach but of one link puts the whole in
some disorder.... Most of the absurdity and ridicule we meet
with in the world is generally owing to the impertinent affectation of excelling in characters men are not fit for, and for which
Nature never designed them.

The *Essay* deals with natural, not revealed, religion. It
is not Christian but deistic, though most of the ideas it expresses were the common property of freethinkers and
orthodox in Pope's day. The system is largely that of
Shaftesbury, who was definitely hostile to Christianity.
When we come across ideas which can be labeled deistic,
it is often hard to tell whether they are thought of as co-
existing with and supporting orthodox Christianity, or as
constituting a natural religion sufficient in itself. Pope
would never say that he was setting forth the ideas of the
Essay in opposition to the Roman Catholic faith which he
nominally professed. His *Universal Prayer,* published in
1738, was also taken as deistic, his orthodoxy was seriously
attacked, and he was very grateful to his new friend and
champion Bishop Warburton for undertaking to demonstrate in opposition to his critic Crousaz that the *Essay on
Man* was really the utterance of a Christian.

R. H. Griffith, *Alexander Pope: A Bibliography,* I, i and ii
(Austin, 1922-27); J. E. Tobin, *Alexander Pope: A List of Critical
Studies Published from 1895 to 1944* (New York, 1945); *Works,*
ed. W. Elwin and W. J. Courthope (10v, London, 1871-89);
Poetical Works, ed. H. W. Boynton (Boston, 1903; Cambridge
edition); *Poems* (London, 1939- ; Twickenham edition, in prog-
ress); II: *The Rape of the Lock,* etc., ed. G. Tillotson; IV: *Imita-
tions of Horace,* etc., ed. J. Butt; V: *Dunciad,* ed. J. Sutherland;
Prose Works, ed. N. Ault, I (Oxford, 1936- ; in progress); *Selec-
tions,* ed. G. Sherburn (New York, 1929); *Poetry and Prose,* ed.
H. V. D. Dyson (Oxford, 1933); *Dunciad Variorum,* ed. R. K.
Root (Princeton, 1929); Joseph Spence, *Anecdotes,* ed. S. W.
Singer (London, 1820); Leslie Stephen, *Alexander Pope* (London,
1880; English Men of Letters); G. Sherburn, *The Early Career of
Alexander Pope* (Oxford, 1934); J. Warton, *Essay on the Genius*

and Writings of Pope (2v, London, 1756-82); Austin Warren, *Alexander Pope as Critic and Humanist* (Princeton, 1929); E. Audra, *L'Influence française dans l'oeuvre de Pope* (Paris, 1931); F. R. Leavis, "Pope," in *Revaluation* (London, 1936); G. Tillotson, *On the Poetry of Pope* (Oxford, 1938); R. K. Root, *The Poetical Career of Alexander Pope* (Princeton, 1938); G. Sherburn, "'Timon's Villa' and Cannons," *Huntington Library Bulletin*, no. 8 (1935). 131-52; *University of Texas Studies in English* (1944) [several important articles on Pope, including variorum texts of *Essay on Criticism, Essay on Man*, Epistles I and II, and *Rape of the Lock*]; G. Sherburn, "Pope at Work," and J. Butt, "The Inspiration of Pope's Poetry," in *Essays on the Eighteenth Century Presented to David Nichol Smith* (Oxford, 1945).

HENRY ST. JOHN, VISCOUNT BOLINGBROKE
(1678-1751)
>>

Bolingbroke's is the great vanished reputation of the eighteenth century. He was the most brilliant of the young men who came to the fore in politics at the end of the seventeenth century, and, as we have seen (p. 88) shared with Harley the leadership of the Tories under Queen Anne, made the Peace of Utrecht, undoubtedly engaged in Jacobite intrigue, and at the accession of George I fled to the Pretender's court in France. Soon after his pardon and return to England in 1723, he formulated the ideology of the opposition to Walpole in his papers in the *Craftsman* from 1726. In the two brilliant series called *Remarks on the History of England* and *A Dissertation upon Parties* he rejected the old Tory doctrine of the divine right of kings and expounded the conception of a monarch taking the leadership in the preservation of a balanced government and thus maintaining the traditional liberties of England. His new Toryism professed to be a return to the true

Whig doctrine of the Revolution as against the Whig oligarchs of the Walpole faction, who would disturb the balance in favor of special interests. The final expression of this doctrine was the famous *Idea of a Patriot King* (1749). Whether or not this pamphlet was actually the political gospel of George III, it anticipated his program, gave classic expression to the ideal of government without party which fascinated many in the eighteenth century, and influenced the later Toryism of Disraeli in the nineteenth century. Bolingbroke's futility in practical politics has somewhat obscured the significance of his political ideas; by 1735 he felt that his campaign against Walpole was a failure, and retired once more to France, though his ideas still colored the attitude of the opposition centered around Prince Frederick.

In his famous literary friendships with Swift, Pope, Atterbury, Gay, and Arbuthnot, Bolingbroke represented a new style of patronage, with the patron no longer a condescending grandee but a personal friend and intellectual equal of the writer. Thus he became Pope's "guide, philosopher, and friend," and furnished philosophic hints and jottings for the groundwork of the *Essay on Man*. This contribution was important, yet it is as a philosopher that Bolingbroke's reputation has collapsed most completely. He believed in the simple natural religion common to all reasonable men, but emphasized the aberrations from right reason to be found in the various customs and religions of the world, including, by insinuation, Christianity. Like other eighteenth-century devotees of reason, he was disposed to emphasize its limitations and its ineffectual rôle in the actual life of man. His posthumous collected works, published in 1754 by David Mallet, first made the public aware of his underlying hostility to Christianity, and prompted Johnson's savage verdict: "Sir, he was a scoundrel and a coward: a scoundrel, for charging a blunderbuss

against religion and morality; a coward, because he had
not resolution to fire it off himself, but left half a crown
to a beggarly Scotchman to draw the trigger after his
death!" This ferocity goes too far, but there has always been
an uneasy feeling that Bolingbroke's fine prose expresses the
facile workings of an insincere and shallow mind, that he
is more interested in making a good showing for himself
than in seeking political or philosophic truth; and such
an impression or prejudice has led later readers to neglect
even his most truly brilliant writings.

*Letters on the Spirit of Patriotism and the Idea of a Patriot
King* (Oxford, 1926); W. S. Sichel, *Bolingbroke and His Times*
(2v, London, 1901–02); Sir Charles Petrie, *Bolingbroke* (London,
1937); Fannie Ratchford, "Pope and the Patriot King," *University
of Texas Studies in English*, VI (1926).

JOHN DENNIS (1657-1734)
>>

Dennis' career is important for the history of neo-classical
criticism and for the personal feuds of men of letters in the
Augustan period. He figured as a critic at Will's in the 1690's,
a literary associate of Dryden, Congreve, and Wycherley. It
must be remembered that the professional critic about town
was a new phenomenon in this age, and would almost inevitably lay himself open to accusations of pedantry and personal malice. Though Dennis failed as dramatist and poet, he
did important critical work at the turn of the century—*The
Impartial Critick* (1693), *The Usefulness of the Stage* (1698,
a reply to Collier), *The Advancement and Reformation of
Modern Poetry* (1701), *The Grounds of Criticism in Poetry*
(1704). He held a strictly neo-classical doctrine of the eternal validity of rules and literary types, but from Longinus'
conception of the sublime and Milton's poetry he devel-

oped a theory which identified poetic inspiration with passion and the highest poetry with the expression of religious enthusiasm. Though the emphasis on religious inspiration naturally connects Dennis with the poets who were cultivating the Christian sublime, Watts, Blackmore, and Hill, he is far superior intellectually to this group. After the attack on Dennis as "Appius" in the *Essay on Criticism,* the unfortunate critic was constantly embroiled in personal feuds with Pope, Addison, Steele, and others. He found serious fault with the *Essay on Criticism,* the *Tatler,* the *Spectator, Cato,* and *The Conscious Lovers,* appealing to critical principles but obviously moved in part by private grievances. He was never at ease in the Augustan period, and became for his age the incarnation of the malevolent and snarling critic. His personal defects and his lack of urbanity obscured the real vigor and intelligence of his best work.

H. G. Paul, *John Dennis, His Life and Criticism* (New York, 1911); *Critical Works,* ed. E. N. Hooker (2v, Baltimore, 1939-43).

MARY WORTLEY MONTAGU (1689-1762)
>>>

The clever daughter of Evelyn Pierrepont, later Duke of Kingston, was brought up in the Whig aristocracy, but led a studious and bookish girlhood. Somewhat against her father's wishes, she married Edward Wortley Montagu, the man of her choice, but he turned out to be dull and mediocre. He was sent as ambassador to Turkey in 1716, and in the following two years she wrote the travel-journal from which were drawn her famous Turkish letters. She brought back to England the Turkish practice of inoculation for smallpox. Her *Town Eclogues* (1716), pirated by the bookseller Curll as

Court Poems by a Lady of Quality, contains some of the
verses by which she earned her reputation as a wit and illustrate her friendship with Pope. But the poet's curious
admiration or infatuation turned within a few years to
bitter enmity, for reasons not fully understood; his attacks
were nothing short of libelous, and she retaliated. The famous phrase "the wicked wasp of Twickenham," attributed
to her, occurs in a letter of doubtful authenticity. In 1739
she went to the Continent to live, and finally settled at
Lovere, in Lombardy, where she lived in retirement and
whence many of her best letters were addressed to her
daughter, Lady Bute. Boxes of books, particularly novels,
were sent out to her, and her lively comments make her
one of the most interesting novel-readers in literary history.
She has the free utterance and easy play of opinion which
mark the best letter-writers; she has too the true letter-
writer's talent of being particularly interesting when she is
prejudiced, unscrupulous, or indiscreet. Though she writes
from the head rather than the heart, and can at times be
called harsh, unromantic, and malicious, she is also shrewd,
sensible, and courageous. She returned to England shortly
before her death in 1762. Her daughter burned the volumes
containing her diary in 1794, but her letters have won her
a place as the best feminine correspondent of the English
eighteenth century.

Letters and Works, ed. Lord Wharncliffe, rev. Moy Thomas (2v,
London, 1861); George Paston, *Lady Mary Wortley Montagu and
her Times* (New York, 1907); P. E. More, *Shelburne Essays,* Series
Ten (New York, 1911); Lewis Melville, *Lady Mary Wortley
Montagu* (London, 1925).

MATTHEW PRIOR (1664-1721)
>>>

Prior was known to his contemporaries as an office-holder and diplomat and as an associate of the Tory wits. He is remembered now for some charming light verse. His poetic skill has on the whole been undervalued, though we may not feel that it deserves the elaborate monument which was set up for him in the Poets' Corner in Westminster Abbey. He came of a humble Dorsetshire family, but was born and brought up in London. As a boy he worked in his uncle's tavern, and here, so the story goes, the Earl of Dorset found him reading Horace and sent him to Westminster School. He proceeded to St. John's College, Cambridge. With his school friend Charles Montagu, later Earl of Halifax, he wrote a clever attack on Dryden, *The Hind and the Panther Transversed* (1687). From 1690 he was secretary of the English legation at The Hague, and took part in the negotiations leading to the Peace of Ryswick (1697). He sought political patronage wherever it could be found, and courted Marlborough rather unsuccessfully. In 1710 he was an associate of Harley, St. John, and Swift in the Tory "Brothers." As a diplomat he specialized in French affairs, and did important work in Paris preliminary to the Peace of Utrecht in 1713. After the accession of George I, Prior was arrested and severely examined while the Whigs were trying to get evidence against his superior Harley. He was now out of office and in financial straits. His occasional and scattered verses had been collected in 1709, but now his influential friends arranged for the publication by subscription of his *Poems on Several Occasions,* a sumptuous folio which appeared in 1719 (dated 1718). He made much money by this project and lived out his Epicurean life comfortably, enjoying the friendship of the Earl of Oxford to the last.

In the Preface to the poems of 1709 Prior describes the contents as "amorous odes, serious reflections, or idle tales, the product of his leisure hours, who had business enough upon his hands, and was only a poet by accident." Among "serious reflections" he would later include the heavy didactic poem *Solomon,* and perhaps *Alma,* a piece of rather flippant philosophizing in Hudibrastic couplets, inspired by the skepticism of Montaigne. His "idle tales," such as *An English Padlock* and *Hans Carvel,* are witty and sometimes coarse. The once admired *Henry and Emma,* an artificial paraphrase of the sixteenth-century *Nut-Brown Maid,* now fails to please. His "amorous odes" have the imagery of Anacreontic verse (flames, myrtles, Cupid and his bow, Venus and her doves), but this highly conventional mode is skilfully transformed into familiar verse of high quality. Prior is one of the most successful English adapters of the Horatian style, and thus he celebrates his light amours with Cloe (perhaps Anne Durham) and her jealousy of Lisetta (perhaps Elizabeth Cox). The result is often a subtle or playful burlesque of lyric forms. Prior's adroit versification appears in his octosyllabic couplets, adapted from Butler, and also in some highly original pieces in long anapestic lines—*Lines Written at the Hague in 1696, Down Hall* (1723), and the epitaph, not published until 1907, called *Jinny the Just.* Prior's triviality should not lead us to overlook his versatile talent and the distinctive personal quality of his best work.

Writings, ed. A. R. Waller (2v, Cambridge, 1905-07); L. G. Wickham Legg, *Matthew Prior* (Cambridge, 1921); Francis Bickley, *Life of Matthew Prior* (London, 1914); C. K. Eves, *Matthew Prior: Poet and Diplomatist* (New York, 1939); H. B. Wright, "Matthew Prior: A Supplement to his Biography," *Northwestern University Summaries of Doctoral Dissertations,* v (1937). 34-38.

JOHN GAY (1685-1732)
>>

Gay had a fresh individual talent for verse which operated naturally and freely within the limits set by current poetical forms. Born and educated at Barnstaple, north Devon, he was left an orphan and apprenticed to a mercer in London, but a small inheritance evidently gave him a chance to become a literary free-lance. Never a struggling hack writer, he was not servile, but came to depend on friendly patrons, and his life is to be written largely in terms of his relations with contemporary noblemen, politicians, and authors. By 1712 he was a friend of Pope's, and though not deeply involved in politics he drifted away from the Whigs and was drawn into the famous Scriblerus Club. The spirit of Scriblerus no doubt stimulated Gay's interest in burlesque and in literary impromptus and *jeux d'esprit*.

By the end of Anne's reign he had published *Wine* (1708) —an insipid imitation of John Philips' *Cyder—Rural Sports* (1713), another georgic exercise; *The Fan* (1713, dated 1714) in imitation of *The Rape of the Lock,* and best of all *The Shepherd's Week* (1714), a delightful series of burlesque pastorals following Virgil's *Eclogues* and marked by keen and playful observation of the details of country life. All these poems follow leads given by contemporary literature; *The Shepherd's Week* develops from the interest in the pastoral form stimulated by the rivalry between Pope's *Pastorals* and those of Ambrose Philips (see 167, 411), and ridicule of Philips is probably one of Gay's motives, though it cannot be shown that Pope incited him to the project.

Despite the imitative and conventional nature of much of Gay's work, he was a careful writer, and resisted the

temptation which overcame many secondary poets of the
time to turn out reams of mechanical verse. He rapidly
extended his work in burlesque: *The What D'ye Call It*
(1715) is a successful take-off of the high flown absurdities
of tragedy, in the tradition of *The Rehearsal*; *Trivia, or,
The Art of Walking the Streets of London* (1716) is the
greatest of burlesque georgics, and also, as Gay's biographer
Professor Irving says, "the greatest of all poems on London
life." The abundant details are vivid and objective; the
use of the literary formula is occasionally stiff and mechanical. The immediate model was furnished by Swift's city-
pieces in the *Tatler, A Description of the Morning* and
A Description of a City Shower. Parallel is Gay's development of the "town eclogue," an application of the pastoral
form to city life; he published examples of this kind of
work in 1720. He also collaborated with Arbuthnot and
Pope in the farce *Three Hours after Marriage* (1717), which
created a disturbance in town not so much because of its
absurdity as because of the activities of Pope's enemies.
A more attractive memorial of his friendship with Pope is
the delightful set of verses, *Mr. Pope's Welcome from
Greece,* celebrating the completion of the translation of
the *Iliad.*

The Whig magnates in power did little to help Gay,
and his friends put through a highly successful subscription
for his *Poems* (1720). This brought a thousand pounds
which he soon lost in South Sea stock. He was on good
terms with the dissident Whig leader Pulteney, Lord Burlington, the Duke and Duchess of Queensberry, and the
family of the Prince of Wales. For the little prince William
Augustus he began to write the *Fables* (I, 1727; II, 1738)
which became one of the most widely read books of the
century. Meanwhile his estrangement from Walpole and
the Whigs became complete. This political background
largely explains the origin of *The Beggar's Opera.* In this

A SCENE FROM *THE BEGGAR'S OPERA*, ACT III

From an engraving by Blake, after Hogarth.

brilliant piece Gay exploits the familiar parallel between high and low life, between the man in great place and the criminal. His hero-highwayman Macheath was usually taken for Walpole. Swift's suggestion of a "Newgate pastoral" as far back as 1716 may have counted for something, but since 1724 the current interest in famous criminals like Jonathan Wild, Jack Sheppard, and "Blueskin" had brought forth various Newgate pieces on the stage. Gay's turn for burlesque reaches its height in the brilliant take-off of Italian opera. His talent for song writing had already appeared in the familiar pieces *Sweet William's Farewell* and *'Twas when the seas were roaring,* and now in the arias of *The Beggar's Opera* it produced a series of cynical little lyrics acceptable alike to the man on the street and the sophisticated. Produced at Lincoln's Inn Fields in January 1728 with Lavinia Fenton as Polly, Tom Walker as Macheath, and Hippisley as Peachum, *The Beggar's Opera* took the town by storm and had an unprecedented run. It established a type of ballad-opera, with the prose dialogue of comedy frequently interspersed with ballad airs, and many imitations appeared on the London stage, though Gay's success was never repeated. Here Hogarthian realism and lyric lightness combine to unique effect; clear of serious didactic purpose, *The Beggar's Opera* represents the frivolous side of the eighteenth century in a way to delight the twentieth, as appeared in its long run (1919-1923) when revived by Nigel Playfair at the Lyric Theater, Hammersmith. The sequel *Polly* was denied production by the censorship of the Lord Chamberlain, but its publication brought Gay a thousand pounds. During the last years of his life he lived most of the time with his devoted friends, the Duke and Duchess of Queensberry. Although Gay and his loyal friends used to complain that he was too naïve to make his way in the world, we need not take these complaints too seriously. He reminds us in some respects of

Goldsmith. Though he lacked the solidity and power of his greater contemporaries, his use of accepted literary forms has an ingenuity and charm that were freely enjoyed and amply rewarded.

Poetical Works, ed. G. C. Faber (London, 1926); *Trivia,* ed. W. H. Williams (London, 1922); *The Shepherd's Week,* ed. H. F. B. Brett-Smith (Oxford, 1924); W. H. Irving, *John Gay, Favorite of the Wits* (Durham, 1940); C. E. Pearce, *Polly Peachum and the Beggar's Opera* (London, 1913); W. E. Schultz, *Gay's Beggar's Opera: Its Content, History, and Influence* (New Haven, 1923); W. H. Irving, *John Gay's London* (Cambridge, Mass., 1928).

JOHN ARBUTHNOT (1667-1735)
>>

Arbuthnot was a genial Scot who was educated at Aberdeen, Oxford, and St. Andrews and practiced medicine in London. His appointment as personal physician to Queen Anne and his membership in the Tory Brothers Club marked his professional and social success. He was the central figure of the Scriblerus Club and his most important literary work is somewhat vaguely connected with the literary projects of the Tory wits. From March to July 1712 appeared his series of pamphlets in favor of the Tory peace policy, setting forth a political allegory: John Bull (England) and Nicholas Frog (Holland) go to law against Lewis Baboon (Louis XIV), with Hocus (Marlborough) as their lawyer. The scheme of allusion suggests the method of *A Tale of a Tub,* and Teerink has unsuccessfully argued that Swift had a large share in the project. The series, originally known by the title of the first pamphlet, *Law is a Bottomless Pit,* was reprinted at Edinburgh in 1712 as *The History of John Bull,* and was included in the second volume of the Pope-Swift *Miscellanies* (1727). Arbuthnot's figure of John Bull, elaborated

later in political cartoons, has been to Great Britain what
Uncle Sam is to the United States. His principal contribution to the projects of the Scriblerus Club was the burlesque of pedantry in *Memoirs of Martinus Scriblerus,* first
published in the second volume of Pope's *Works* (1741).
But the exact attribution of shares in the Scriblerus projects
must remain uncertain. Arbuthnot contributed to the notes
of the *Dunciad Variorum* (1729). Pope's tribute in the
Epistle to Arbuthnot is familiar, and Swift in his ironical
way compliments the good physician in *Verses on the Death
of Dr. Swift,* and is said to have remarked that if there were
a dozen more men like Arbuthnot he would burn *Gulliver's Travels.* Later American imitations of *The History
of John Bull* are Francis Hopkinson's *Pretty Story* (1774)
and Jeremy Belknap's *The Foresters* (1792).

A Miscellany of the Wits, ed. K. N. Colvile (London, 1920);
History of John Bull, ed. H. Teerink (Amsterdam, 1925); G. A.
Aitken, *Life and Works of John Arbuthnot* (Oxford, 1892); L. M.
Beattie, *John Arbuthnot, Mathematician and Satirist* (Cambridge,
Mass., 1935).

JAMES THOMSON (1700-1748)
>>

Thomson is the greatest of modern poets born in Scotland
before Burns, and, except for Pope, the most celebrated British poet of the first half of the eighteenth century—in the long
run, indeed, his popularity was greater than Pope's. He was
born at Ednam, Roxburghshire, but spent his boyhood at
Southdean, in the valley of the Jed, a tributary of the Tweed.
The local color and the history of this famous region were
later immortalized by Scott. Thomson's earliest memories
were of the Border landscape and of simple country life, and
this background counted for much in his work, though he

makes little direct use of the specific Scottish scene. His father, who died in 1716, was a Presbyterian clergyman, and Thomson was originally intended for the ministry when he entered the University of Edinburgh. His work as a student of arts and divinity gave much of the literary and philosophical background for his poetry. The Presbyterian faith was being softened and liberalized in Scottish university circles. The Bible, Milton, and Virgil set literary themes, and Locke and Shaftesbury gave a framework of ideas. Science too was studied, especially in the popular form of physico-theology, the use of new scientific detail to demonstrate the work of God in the creation. Such a union of religious, scientific, and literary motives had been made by Richard Blackmore, especially in his *Creation* and *Paraphrase of Job,* mediocre work which is nevertheless historically important. All this may sound more formidable than it actually was; Thomson wrote juvenile verse in an undergraduate club at Edinburgh without being fully conscious of the forces at work upon him.

In 1725 he went to London, and soon decided to become a poet, not a preacher. His first important poem, *Winter,* was published in the spring of 1726; *Summer* followed in 1727, *Spring* in 1728, and *Autumn* and the concluding *Hymn* with the collected *Seasons* published by subscription in 1730. Thomson worked rapidly in these years, publishing also *A Poem Sacred to the Memory of Sir Isaac Newton* (1727) and *Britannia* (1729). His tragedy *Sophonisba* was successfully produced at Drury Lane in 1730, though in general his dramas have added nothing to his after-fame. At the end of 1730 he went abroad as tutor to Charles Talbot, son of the Solicitor General, and traveled in France and Italy. His next literary project was the long and overambitious poem *Liberty* (1735-36), elaborately setting forth the familiar view that political liberty was attained in ancient Greece and Rome, lost in the Middle Ages and again

in the degenerate Italian culture of modern times, preserved and renewed in the northern Germanic tradition
most completely exemplified in Great Britain. The poem
disappointed admirers of *The Seasons*. Its ideas are characteristic of the Whig opposition. As early as *Britannia* Thomson had been dissatisfied with the peace policy of Walpole
and had paid tribute to the Prince of Wales, about whom
the opposition was beginning to
center. This allegiance is expressed in the dedications of *Liberty,* the dramas *Agamemnon*
(1738) and *Edward and Eleonora*
(prohibited under the terms of
the new Licensing Act but published in 1739), and the masque
Alfred (1740), in which he collaborated with David Mallet.
This piece is famous for the song
Rule Britannia; Thomson's authorship seems certain, though it
has been questioned.

From about 1738 George Lord
Lyttelton became one of Thomson's closest friends, giving him
both political aid and literary advice. On the whole, however,

PROPOSALS

For Printing by SUBSCRIPTION

THE

FOUR SEASONS,

With a Hymn on their Succession.

To which will be added a POEM sacred to the
Memory of Sir ISAAC NEWTON. And an
Essay on Descriptive Poetry will be prefixed to
the Whole.

By Mr. *THOMSON.*

I. THIS Work is proposed to be printed in one Volume in Quarto, on a Superfine Royal Paper,
and adorned with Copper-Plates, adapted to the Subject.

II. The Price of the Book in Sheets to Subscribers is
One Guinea, to be paid at the time of Subscribing.

III. The Names of Subscribers to be printed before
the Work, which is in great Forwardness, and will be
published with all possible speed.

N. B. The Pieces already published, *viz.* Winter,
Summer, and a Poem on the Death of Sir *Isaac
Newton,* will be corrected and enlarged in several
Places.

Subscriptions are taken in by the Author, at the *Smyrna* Coffee-
House in *Pall-Mall,* and by G. STRAHAN, at the Golden Ball
in *Cornhill,* A. MILLAR, at *Buchanan's Head,* over-against St. *Clement's*
Church in the *Strand,* J. MILLAN at the Blue Anchor in *Pall-Mall,*
and by A. RAMSAY, at *Edinburgh.*

PROPOSALS FOR
THE SEASONS
Issued with *Spring,* 1728.

Thomson remained a detached spectator of life, living mod-
estly in a small cottage in Kew Lane, near Richmond and
just across the river from Pope at Twickenham. Though he
said he preferred "the Muses of the great simple country, not
the little fine-lady Muses of Richmond Hill," and complained that there were too many villas nearby, he delighted
in the rich and ordered English landscape. After 1743 he was
an annual visitor at Lyttelton's country seat, Hagley, Wor-
cestershire. At this time he made an elaborate revision of

The Seasons (1744, final version 1746). In 1748 he published his most charming poem, *The Castle of Indolence*. This piece, the most successful Spenserian imitation of the eighteenth century, began as "little more than a few detached stanzas in the way of raillery on himself, and on some of his friends, who would reproach him with indolence, while he thought them at least as indolent as himself." The poem is nominally on the side of progress, and

VIEW UP THE THAMES VALLEY FROM RICHMOND HILL

in Canto II the Knight of Arts and Industry breaks the spell cast by the wizard Indolence, but the best stanzas are those that present the delights of reverie, relaxation, and the refined pleasures of the senses. The less serious side of Thomson's personality, the playfulness characteristic of one side of eighteenth-century art, and the example of Spenser's rich verse combine to form one of the most pleasing poems of the age. Thomson died at the age of forty-eight, and William Collins wrote a poem to his memory.

THE SEASONS

Thomson, it is often said, "returned to nature" in the artificial age of Pope. His fine descriptions of landscape and atmospheric effect and his genre pictures have always given pleasure. But contemporaries thought of *The Seasons* as not merely descriptive but didactic and reflective. They accepted in Thomson the conception of the poet as a seer, like Virgil and Milton, a virtuoso and patriot, like Shaftesbury and Addison; his mind was open alike to the inspiration of literary models, the new findings of science, and the ideals of patriotism and philanthropy. It is in this spirit that Thomson writes in the Preface to the second edition of *Winter:* "I know no subject more elevating, more amusing, more ready to awake the poetical enthusiasm, the philosophical reflection, and the moral sentiment, than the works of Nature." Such, he goes on to say, are the themes of the greatest poets, Virgil, Milton, and the author of Job. *Winter* was originally a short meditative-descriptive poem somewhat on the plan of *Il Penseroso*. The success of this piece encouraged him not only to extend it but to proceed to describe "the various appearance of Nature ... in the other Seasons," as he says in the Preface to the second edition. This led to the full development of the long descriptive-didactic poem, with a loose structure which admits easy transitions and digressions. The influence of the georgic form and of Miltonic style is always marked. Thomson's interest in science and in natural religion was evidently at its height in the years 1726-30. The lines on Newton express the same interest. The scheme of a universe ordered by divine Harmony and Reason, expounded in Thomson's day not only by Shaftesbury but by more orthodox authorities, is filled up to some extent with scientific detail. This practice may be called Newtonian, but in a poet like Thomson it has no scientific rigor, and can easily be combined with the benevolism of Shaftesbury and Hutcheson. Ethical, philanthropic, and patriotic themes appear frequently. The later version shows elaborate additions drawn from the literature of geography and travel, particularly the descriptions of the Far North in *Winter* and of the Tropics in *Summer*. Set topographical descriptions of English scenes, such as Lyttelton's Hagley and the view from Richmond Hill, are also added. The common opinion that these additions are inferior is hardly justified; Thomson is uneven, but he shows no marked decline of poetic power. It is true, however, that his greatest success is in exact and delicate notation of sense effects in a setting planned on a fairly large scale, and for this combination the scenes inspired by English and Scottish landscapes are of course the best.

Thomson's diction is often a handicap; his Miltonic phrases and Latinized vocabulary exemplify to a far greater degree than Pope the poetic diction which Wordsworth was to attack. His opinions show inconsistencies which need not trouble us much. In the spirit of Whig panegyric he is a believer in progress, and yet, like many others, he is at times fascinated by the ideal of the Golden Age, by the virtues of simple Laplanders and Indians, and uses such themes in a polemic against luxury and sophistication (see p. 361). His religious views are deistic. His quiet substitution of the God of Nature for the God of Revelation is characteristic of the time. There can be no doubt that he was a Shaftesburian freethinker, not, like most of the Newtonians, an orthodox Christian. But the average reader of *The Seasons* troubled himself as little about Thomson's theology as about Milton's; the poem was read for pleasure and for edification in countless families and schools in Great Britain and America for over a century after the poet's death.

Complete Poetical Works, ed. J. Logie Robertson (Oxford, 1908); *The Seasons*, ed. O. Zippel (Berlin, 1908); Léon Morel,

James Thomson, sa vie et ses oeuvres (Paris, 1895); G. C. Macaulay,
Thomson (London, 1908; English Men of Letters); Herbert
Drennon, [studies of Thomson and Newtonianism], *University
of Chicago Abstracts of Theses,* Humanistic Series, VII (1930).
523-28; *Publications of the Modern Language Association,* XLIX
(1934). 71-80; *ibid.,* LIII (1938). 1094-1101; *Studies in Philology,*
XXXI (1934). 453-71; *Englische Studien,* LXVIII (1934). 397-409;
ibid., LXX (1936). 358-72; *Philological Quarterly,* XIV (1935). 70-82;
A. D. McKillop, *The Background of Thomson's 'Seasons'* (Minneapolis, 1942); J. E. Wells, "Thomson's *Seasons* Corrected and
Amended," *Journal of English and Germanic Philology,* XLII
(1943). 104-14; Marjorie Nicolson, *Newton Demands the Muse*
(Princeton, 1946).

MARK AKENSIDE (1721-1770)
>>>

Philosophic poetry blends with the didactic-descriptive
in the 1730's and 1740's. The popularity of Thomson's *Seasons* and Pope's *Essay on Man* encouraged this fusion; other
secondary poems are more exclusively concerned with expounding the world-order which had been described by
Shaftesbury as a harmony of the true, the good, and the
beautiful. Henry Brooke's *Universal Beauty* (1735-36), Akenside's *Pleasures of Imagination* (1744), and John Gilbert
Cooper's *The Power of Harmony* (1745) all belong here,
and all are worth reading, but Akenside's work is perhaps
the best of the group. The blank-verse pieces of the Wartons are more purely descriptive.

Born at Newcastle-upon-Tyne and educated as a Dissenter, Akenside was a precocious boy destined for the
ministry, but he chose medicine instead, and completed his
education at Edinburgh and Leyden. His real interests however were in philosophy and aesthetics, in the cult of ancient heroism and freedom found in Thomson's *Liberty,*
and in the revival of supposedly Greek forms of lyric. His

Odes on Several Subjects (1745) fall far short of Collins, but belong to the same movement. His philosophical and aesthetic ideas are set forth in *Pleasures of Imagination*. The title and some of the ideas come from Addison's series in the *Spectator* (Nos. 411-421), which, following Locke, derived aesthetic pleasure from the senses, particularly from sight. Like Addison, Akenside finds that man is naturally inclined to take pleasure in "greatness, novelty, and beauty," but a full account of these pleasures, Akenside finds, is impossible if we merely follow the empirical philosophy of Locke. Through Shaftesbury he goes back to those authorities, Plato, the Stoics, Longinus, who emphasize man's innate powers and their harmony with or correspondence to an ordered universe. Like Shaftesbury, too, he sets up the supposedly rational ideas of the ancients in art, politics, and religion, and has an unconcealed dislike for the medieval, and, we may say, the Christian. He has in common with Thomson and other contemporary poets and popular philosophers the ideas of world-harmony and of a chain or scale of being, but he expounds them more elaborately. He wrote no great poetry, but gives a dignified exposition of a system of ideas which was very important for his time.

Poetical Works, ed. A. Dyce (London, 1894; Aldine edition); Charles Bucke, *On the Life, Writings, and Genius of Akenside* (London, 1832); A. O. Aldridge, "The Eclecticism of Mark Akenside," *Journal of the History of Ideas,* v (1944). 292-314; "Akenside and Imagination," *Studies in Philology,* XLII (1945). 769-92; Marjorie Nicolson, *Newton Demands the Muse* (Princeton, 1946); C. T. Houpt, *Mark Akenside* (Philadelphia, 1944).

EDWARD YOUNG (1683-1765)
>>

Young's best-known works, the *Night Thoughts* and *Conjectures on Original Composition*, were published toward the end of a long career marked by varied literary and social experiences, in the light of which the poet appears to be an Augustan wit and man of the world turned pious and enthusiastic. After his education at Winchester and Corpus Christi College, Oxford, he sought literary success and political favor, and was soon widely acquainted with important writers and potential patrons, but does not seem to have caught on; he scored no great literary triumph in this early period and got no important patronage. His early writings show a coarse energy of style and a marked tendency to take ideas and opinions from his surroundings: *The Last Day* (1713) and *A Paraphrase on Part of the Book of Job* (1719) are bombastic pieces of religious verse; *Busiris* (1719) and *The Revenge* (1721) are stilted tragedies; the series of satires published under the general title *Love of Fame, the Universal Passion* (1725-28) shows high literary competence, sharpness of phrase, and neatness of wit, and may be said to establish a standard for the Horatian satire of the age, but these pieces lack the personal conviction which is necessary to animate important satire. They precede Pope's satire by a few years, and take a place next to his. Young took holy orders in 1724, and was later made a royal chaplain, but never got a bishopric. In 1730 he was given the living of Welwyn, Hertfordshire, where he lived the rest of his life. From about 1740 we have abundant information about Young in his correspondence with the Duchess of Portland and with the novelist Samuel Richardson, the closest literary friend of his later years.

The Complaint: or, Night Thoughts on Life, Death and Immortality, published in nine *Nights* from 1742 to 1746, made Young one of the most widely known poets of the time. His work, like that of his friend Richardson, was very popular on the Continent, and modern readers are likely to wonder why. Young's poem is colored by melancholy and is the most specifically theological of the major literary works of the age. Its main purpose is the defense of Christian orthodoxy against freethinkers and libertines, and Young sets up an erring youth Lorenzo against whom he levels the arguments of contemporary English apologetics. But he also tells us that the occasion of the work was "real, not fictitious," and in the poem itself he refers to the successive deaths of Lucia (his wife), Narcissa (his step-daughter, Elizabeth Lee), and Philander (her husband, Henry Temple). In particular he tells of Narcissa's secret burial in a foreign land, and this has been taken to refer to the burial of Elizabeth Lee at Montpelier. There are other hints of personal experience in the poem, which is thus related to the elegy and more remotely to sentimental fiction; readers were moved by the figure of the solitary mourner. Yet Young does not luxuriate in grief, paint the horrors of the tomb, or describe landscapes suffused in melancholy. His real theme is the mixed nature of man, the eternal alternation of triumph and defeat, of hope and despair. He gives an exaggerated and satirical view of man's plight on earth, only to point him forward. Man finds himself after all the center of the great world drama, and he may anticipate a career in which experience is infinitely extended and enriched and his own possibilities more and more fully realized. This is Young's interpretation of the cardinal doctrine of immortality. He uses other arguments for orthodoxy, such as those based on the new evidences of design in the universe, but his characteristic theme is upward progress through endless gradations of being:

> Nature revolves, but man advances; both
> Eternal; that a circle, this a line.

The doctrine had been expounded by Addison, Blackmore, and many others, and with less interest in orthodoxy by James Thomson. The chief attraction in Young's presentation was his energetic, staccato blank verse—at once declamatory and epigrammatic, preserving much of the point, ingenuity, and paradox of the heroic couplet. He was one of the most quoted of eighteenth-century poets, and, of course, he was read for Christian edification by many people who paid little or no attention to the exact bearing of his ideas.

These ideas came over without a break into his last and most brilliant work, *Conjectures on Original Composition, in a Letter to the Author of Sir Charles Grandison* (1759). This essay undertakes to defend originality against slavish imitation, and its basis is clearly to be found in Young's religious thought. The original writer, as contrasted with the imitator, is thought of both as one who travels far afield in search of new experiences and new material, and as a daring individual who independently realizes and expresses the infinite possibilities of human nature. Thus Young enthusiastically restates many of the arguments which had been developed in the old controversy between the Ancients and the Moderns. If the Moderns are inferior, it is no necessary inferiority; in the long run it is of the nature of man and the universe that the future shall surpass the past. The original should imitate the great originals, both ancient and modern, by being like them free, creative, and independent. In science, who knows what discoveries remain to be made? In religious terms, God reveals himself progressively to man, a doctrine which had already been expounded by Anglican divines. Thus Young's unflagging energy and enthusiasm gave new impetus to familiar ideas, especially in Germany, where, rather than in

England, the *Conjectures* became an important manifesto for the cult of original genius.

Complete Works, ed. John Doran (2v, London, 1854); *Conjectures on Original Composition,* ed. Edith Morley (Manchester, 1918); W. Thomas, *Le Poète Edward Young* (Paris, 1901); H. C. Shelley, *Life and Letters of Edward Young* (London, 1914); H. H. Clark, "The Romanticism of Edward Young," *Transactions of the Wisconsin Academy,* XXIV (1929). 1-45; A. D. McKillop, "Richardson, Young, and the *Conjectures,*" *Modern Philology,* XXII (1925). 391-404; Isabel St. John Bliss, "Young's *Night Thoughts* in Relation to Contemporary Christian Apologetics," *Publications of the Modern Language Association,* XLIX (1934). 37-70; R. S. Crane, "Anglican Apologetics and the Idea of Progress," *Modern Philology,* XXXI (1934). 273-306, 349-82; H. Pettit, "Preface to a Bibliography of Young's *Night Thoughts,*" *University of Colorado Studies in the Humanities,* II (1945). 215-22.

THE CHURCH

>>

Theology was no longer "the queen of the sciences." The Church had to meet the demands of secular thought by adjusting theology to the supposed norm of reason; in politics the settlement of 1688 gave the Church a definite but limited place in the State. Some extreme defenders of the High Church doctrine became Non-jurors, that is, refused to take the oath of allegiance to William and Mary, and so removed themselves from active politics. There still remained the theoretical claim of independence or autonomy for the Church; but this was a position urged by powerful controversialists like Swift and Johnson, or by mere agitators like Sacheverell, rather than a practical policy to be seriously considered. After the Revolution the bishops took the political coloring of the government, Whig under William, Tory during the reign of Anne, and markedly

Whig under Walpole. Bishop Hoadly, arguing against High
Church prerogative, was an extreme Erastian, denying virtually all independent political power to the established
Church, and his writings precipitated the noisy and complex Bangorian controversy in and after 1717. Convocation,
the assembly of the bishops and lower clergy, was suspended from that time until 1852. Walpole subordinated
the strong dissenting element in the Whig party, and made
his political alliance with moderate Anglicanism. Thus the
bishops and others of the clergy who got high preferment
were mostly Whigs; the rank and file of the lesser clergy in
the country were Tories.

In spite of all we hear about the worldliness of the eighteenth-century Church, it was still an important part of the
fabric of society. At the top were the bishops and the other
dignitaries of cathedral chapters (deans, prebends, and so
forth), and the chaplains attached to the royal household
and the nobility. These men might hope to become bishops,
or at least to get several good livings, and many of them
received large unearned incomes. Though they did not all
neglect their ecclesiastical duties, they were not consumed
with devotion. Some of them were learned, and some indeed won their success by skill in apologetics, the argu-
mentative defense of orthodoxy. Favors from the great were
constantly sought by the middle professional class to which
the upper part of the clergy belonged; younger sons of the
gentry and even of the nobility were also given preferment.
The social position of the parson would depend on his
income and social class; too often, however, he would be
despised as a beggarly underling. Early in the century
domestic chaplains were common in great houses; we hear
of their withdrawing from table before dessert and marrying one of the servants. But the clergyman attached to a
family might be a tutor, or a confidential adviser, agent,
and friend. In general the lower clergy were in an unhappy

THE SLEEPING CONGREGATION, AFTER HOGARTH

position. Curacies might pay thirty or forty pounds a year, sometimes less. The poor parson might combine several curacies; he might farm a little, or teach the village school. He was often of humble origin, and had an opportunity for the unlimited exercise of the Christian virtues of patience and humility. We think of Fielding's Parson Adams, Goldsmith's Vicar of Wakefield, and the saintly clergyman of *The Deserted Village*. As the century advanced, the incomes of many livings were somewhat increased, and the country clergymen were drawn from somewhat higher social levels. Thus the clergymen in Jane Austen's novels are allied by blood and interest with middle-class property and the squires rather than with their humbler parishioners. There was little new building of churches in town or country after the reign of Anne. Church attendance was large, and the galleries of the City churches were crowded. Sermons were important, at least in London, and besides the regular Sunday services there were "lectures" and even daily prayers. Church interiors were bare and whitewashed. A glance at some of Hogarth's pictures (e.g., *The Sleeping Congregation*) will show the high pulpit, the square pews, and the large galleries.

METHODISM

The older dissenting groups, especially the Presbyterians and Independents (Congregationalists) were becoming complacently middle-class and losing their religious zeal (see *Isaac Watts*, p. 416). But against sluggish convention and cool common sense came as always a fervent reassertion of religion as a personal experience of God's power. The intense individualization of the religious life, culminating in mysticism, might be expected to appear in scattered enthusiasts or religious geniuses, and as a movement to be supported largely by the lower classes in whom a sense of spiritual need had not been stifled by worldly success. Such

had been the "inner light" of the Quaker, but Quaker influence did not spread in the eighteenth century because
of intense prejudice against the peculiarities of that sect.
From Germany came the influence of the Moravians, with
their emphasis on individual salvation by saving faith. The
non-juring high churchman William Law, under the influence of the German mystic Jakob Böhme (1575-1624), dwelt
on the essential unworldliness of Christianity in his classic
Serious Call to a Devout and Holy Life (1728) (see p. 407).

JOHN WESLEY

From 1729 a small group
of students at Oxford began
to meet regularly for intensive religious exercises and
were nicknamed "Metho-
dists." Two principal members, John and Charles
Wesley, were the sons of
Samuel Wesley, the high
church rector of Epworth,
Lincolnshire. There were,
however, nonconformist elements in the background of
the Wesleys. On leaving Oxford John Wesley went to
Georgia with Oglethorpe, but at this time he was still a high
churchman and his preaching was not popular in America.
The actual beginning of his great career was on May 24,
1738, when, under Moravian influence, "assurance" of salvation came to him in the meeting in Aldersgate Street, London. Thereafter the Methodist program was simply to preach
saving faith directly to the people. The Methodists still
thought of themselves as members of the Church of England, but, excluded from Anglican pulpits, they founded
societies and built chapels, and under the leadership of the
greatest pulpit orator of the time, George Whitefield, took

to preaching in the open air. Thus they reached countless thousands in England and Wales who had never come near the parish churches. Indeed, the established Church was making no attempt to serve new centers of population. The Methodists used lay-preachers and spread the gospel everywhere, at races, executions, or wherever a crowd might be gathered. They employed the methods of the revival, which soon became an important part of religious life on both sides of the Atlantic; they wrought on the emotions and the nerves, and sinners were smitten with "the arrows of the Lord." Whitefield was their most eloquent orator, but John Wesley was the real leader, with his unflagging zeal, his unbending will, and his power of organization. He was capable of preaching eight hundred sermons a year. He kept Methodism clear of fanatical extremes, and fitted it into the fabric of English society. Though he continued to think of himself as a priest of the Church of England, his great emphasis on conversion and his practice of "setting apart" (ordaining) lay-preachers practically separated him from Anglicanism.

In making his direct appeal to the uneducated masses Wesley sacrificed much: he taught that salvation was the one thing necessary, and that anything not bearing on salvation was worse than useless; art, amusement, the life of the mind were crassly condemned; such superstitions as witchcraft and an almost equally superstitious reverence for the literal words of the Bible were encouraged. Yet Methodism was the most important religious and social movement of eighteenth-century England. Like the Protestant Reformation itself, it had a dynamic power which came from the unsatisfied religious needs of the humbler classes. It spread morality and piety; it represented the most serious assault that had yet been made on eighteenth-century complacency, on the supremacy of "reason" over "enthusiasm." As a cultural force, however, Methodism did not get into literature directly. It was viewed unsympathetically by such writers as Fielding and often satirized (e.g., Richard Graves, *The Spiritual Quixote,* 1773). Wesley's superb command of plain English makes literature of his *Journals.* The numerous hymns of Charles Wesley are a direct Methodist contribution to literature. James Hervey's once popular *Meditations and Contemplations* (1746-47) and other inferior works of that kind represent evangelicalism acting on belles lettres, and on a much higher level the poetry of William Cowper occupies an analogous position.

C. J. Abbey, *The English Church and Its Bishops, 1700-1800* (2v, London, 1887); C. J. Abbey and J. H. Overton, *The English Church in the Eighteenth Century* (2v, London, 1878); J. H. Overton and T. Relton, *The English Church from the Accession of George I to the End of the Eighteenth Century* (London, 1906); A. Plummer, *The Church of England in the Eighteenth Century* (London, 1910); N. Sykes, *Church and State in England in the Eighteenth Century* (Cambridge, 1934); *Edmund Gibson, Bishop of London, 1669-1748* (Oxford, 1926); H. W. Clark, *History of English Non-Conformity,* II (London, 1913); John Wesley, *Journal,* ed. N. Curnock (8v, London, 1909-16); W. H. Hutton, *John Wesley* (London, 1927); A. Lunn, *John Wesley* (London, 1929); J. D. Wade, *John Wesley* (New York, 1930); M. Piette, *John Wesley in the Evolution of Protestantism* (New York, 1937); T. W. Herbert, *John Wesley as Editor and Author* (Princeton, 1940); U. Lee, *The Historical Backgrounds of Early Methodist Enthusiasm* (New York, 1931); R. Green, *The Works of John and Charles Wesley: A Bibliography* (London, 1896); H. Bett, *The Hymns of Methodism* (3rd ed., London, 1945); R. F. Wearmouth, *Methodism and the Common People of the Eighteenth Century* (London, 1945)

ROMANTICISM AND CHANGING TASTE
>>

Earlier sections (pp. 26-33, 173-76) have already given a brief statement of the neo-classical position. That position set up a central fixed standard, based at once on the uniformity of nature, the workings of the rational mind, and the coherence of organized society. It did not exclude diversity or spontaneity from art or life, but it looked on them as secondary and limited; it preferred the stable, the normal, the continuous, and the predictable to the unstable, the abnormal, the discontinuous, and the unpredictable. This is often stated in terms of a "just balance or equilibrium of the faculties," a control of feeling and imagination by reason, and is thus taken to involve the deepest issues of religion, philosophy, and ethics. When mechanically applied, this doctrine makes an over-sharp division between reason and feeling; this division corresponds to the contrast between the simple optimistic view of neo-classicism that reason is as a matter of fact clearly embodied in the world-order, and the actual complexity and intricacy of the facts of life. These evil or irrational elements were admitted to literature in satire, drama, and realistic fiction, but they were presented as bad examples. Thus neo-classical standards led to a high and indeed an excessive degree of abstraction or generality in art.

The changes in literary art and criticism that appear during the eighteenth century are naturally in the direction of relaxing these rigorous demands for unity and rational control. Variety is more freely admitted in various forms— fluctuations in mood or feeling, differences of taste in individuals or societies, novelty, surprise, and variety in the manner or content of a work of art, originality (unique

individuality) in the artist. Criticism comes to be deeply
influenced by psychological studies of aesthetic experience;
the work of art is viewed not as a product to be considered by objective rules, but, in relation to the artist, as
a process, and, in relation to the reader or observer, as an
experience. There is analysis of such terms as *sublime,
beautiful, pathetic, sentimental, picturesque, romantic.*
Whatever interests, moves, or attracts spontaneously is taken
to be important in advance of any other critical test.
Because of this assumption of the priority of spontaneous
appeal over abstract rule, doctrines of natural goodness,
which, as we have seen, had been elaborated in ethical and
religious thought, come to be associated with these aesthetic
doctrines. The various -isms of which we speak so much,
primitivism, sentimentalism, humanitarianism, are consistent and partly identical with the same assumption of the
immediate and direct emotional validation of natural goodness. So are the other phenomena which we have learned
to call romantic, such as the cult of original genius and
the rebellion against social convention.

These tendencies were not organized into a consistent
and consecutive romantic movement or revolt in the eight
eenth century. They are a complicated outgrowth and reaction from the neo-classical position and the conditions
and situations which this over-simplified position could not
fully control. But eighteenth-century English art was not
moved by violent reaction or rebellion. Mr. W. J. Bate has
brilliantly demonstrated how much compromise and balancing there was in the most characteristically English criticism: empirical confidence in sensation and feeling did
not mean abandonment of judgment and reason, nor was
the imagination turned loose without rational guidance.
On the other hand, neo-classical critics were not bigots. In
the name of general nature itself Johnson repudiates some
of the stricter neo-classical rules; Reynolds, holding to gen-

eral nature, admits more and more intense feeling into art.
Elsewhere it has been remarked that the sentimentalist was
not ready to forego allegiance to a rational system (see p.
258), nor was the primitivist ready to abandon all the advantages of progress (pp. 362-63).

The student therefore should no more consider the English romantic movement as a complete abandonment of
classical values than he should think of the English neo-
classical movement as "unpoetical." At the other extreme,
he should avoid thinking of the eighteenth-century change
in attitude merely in terms of superficial earmarks or symptoms, a mere variation of subject matter, a mere shift in
styles and manners or a casual adoption of new literary
fads. Unsatisfactory tests for eighteenth-century romanticism are Miltonic blank verse, Spenserian stanza, ballad
form, description of rural landscape and humble life, interest in the Middle Ages (especially Scandinavian and
Celtic antiquities) and the Elizabethan period, use of remote and exotic geographical settings. Romanticism should
not be completely broken up into "romanticisms," a bundle
of tendencies that just happen to appear in the same period.
The term has been so much used and abused that scholars
seek to avoid it. But unless they are content to say that the
various changes have nothing at all to do with one another,
they have to bring them together under some one term, and
the definition or description of this term may still be considered a definition or description of romanticism. Perhaps,
as has been suggested above, the most practical way to center the discussion of the various phases of romanticism is
to say that a doctrine of natural goodness and conceptions
of natural and spontaneous interest come together, and
that moral and aesthetic ideas thus reënforce one another.
It is not the idea of natural goodness as such that makes
romanticism; classicism, as we have seen in the discussion
of the *Essay on Criticism,* assumes that right reason is in

some sense natural to man. Romanticism associates natural goodness more immediately with direct experience and spontaneous expression. This is more nearly basic than a contrast between romantic emphasis on the faculty of "imagination" and classical emphasis on the faculty of "reason." But it is not a sharp line of cleavage, for the compromising Englishman found reason or form involved as a guiding principle in the experience itself. There was no complete escape from sanity or rule, not even in the Gothic extravagances of William Beckford. The delights of pure reverie were considered as dangerous as the delights of unbridled feeling. The program of connecting romantic imagery and sentiment with ethical, social, and rational values was handed on by the eighteenth century to Scott, Coleridge, and Wordsworth.

This account presents the romantic and the classical as compensatory and balancing tendencies in human experience. The facts of literary history seem to warrant emphasis on such a balance or interplay of forces. Though at a given period one may be preferred to the other, both enter in varying degrees into great literature. The student will find, however, a constant tendency in modern literary criticism to take sides in a controversy between the two schools. If nineteenth-century critics underestimated Pope, Swift, and Johnson, and if English readers have always underestimated the French classical drama, romanticism has also been subjected to severe attack, especially in the powerful writings of Irving Babbitt and in the less effective utterances of those who are consciously or unconsciously influenced by him. When all concessions have been made, the "new humanism" of the school of Babbitt is anti-romantic; using religious and philosophical ideas drawn from classical and Christian sources it finds in and above man an "ethical reason" or "intuition" which connects him with ultimate supernatural reality and disciplines him in the flux of feeling and sensation in which, according to this doctrine, the romanticist is ultimately swamped. True classicism, it is said, is the expression of this "ethical reason," and is, of course, wider than the neo-classicist's dependence on abstract reason. In practice this leads to an evaluation of writers in didactic terms, according to the supposed ethical correctness of the ideas they express, and it often seems to lead to a lack of sympathy with the richness, complexity, and variety of artistic forms and techniques.

J. Barzun, *Romanticism and the Modern Ego* (Boston, 1943); W. J. Bate, *From Classic to Romantic* (Cambridge, Mass., 1946); B. I. Evans, *Tradition and Romanticism* (London, 1940); P. H. Frye, "The Terms Classic and Romantic," in *Romance and Tragedy* (Boston, 1922); *Longinus on the Sublime*, trans. B. Einarson, and Reynolds, *Discourses*, introd. E. Olson (Chicago, 1945); A. O. Lovejoy, "The First Gothic Revival and the Return to Nature," *Modern Language Notes*, XLVII (1932). 419-46; " 'Nature' as Aesthetic Norm," *ibid.*, XLII (1927). 444-50; "On the Discrimination of Romanticisms," *Publications of the Modern Language Association*, XXXIX (1924). 229-53; "Optimism and Romanticism," *ibid.*, XLII (1927). 921-45; Mario Praz, *The Romantic Agony* (New York, 1933); Herbert Read, *Reason and Romanticism* (London, 1926).

See also under Literary Types and Standards (p. 33-34), Baldensperger, Crane, Vines; under General Literary History and Criticism (pp. 420-22), Babbitt, Beers, Bernbaum, Draper, Fairchild, Folkierski, Havens, de Maar, Monk, Moore, Phelps, Robertson, Van Tieghem, Williams; and also references given under Sentimentalism (p. 258), Medieval Revival (p. 367), and Primitivism (p. 365).

WILLIAM COLLINS (1721-1759)

>>

In the 1740's some important young writers turned away from satirical and didactic poetry to the cultivation of formal lyric—the elegy, the Pindaric, and a new type, centering about a personified abstraction and largely indebted to Milton's minor poems, which came to be called the "descriptive and allegorical ode." With very different degrees of literary power, Akenside, the Wartons, Shenstone, Gray, and Collins all take this new direction. Collins, like Gray, wrote only a few supremely important lyrics, yet at his best he is the greatest English lyrist of the mid-century. His career was brief and unfortunate. He was the son of a prosperous citizen in the cathedral town of Chichester, Sussex, and was educated at Winchester, where he was a school-fellow of Joseph Warton, and at Queen's and later at Magdalen College, Oxford. He began to write verses in his school-days, and early published his *Persian Eclogues* (1742) and an epistle to Sir Thomas Hanmer on his edition of Shakespeare (1743), then went up to London, frequented literary and theatrical circles, and made various literary plans without settling down to the hard and steady work required of a Grub Street writer. He projected a *History of the Revival of Learning,* a commentary on Aristotle's *Poetics,* a periodical to be called the *Clarendon Review,* and no doubt other things. His financial troubles were eased by legacies from two uncles in 1745 and 1749. Joseph Warton and he planned to collaborate on a volume of odes, but eventually each published separately in December 1746—Warton his *Odes on Various Subjects,* Collins his *Odes on Several Descriptive and Allegoric Subjects.* Collins's work, though far superior, was less successful than Warton's; he is said to have destroyed the remainder copies, but there is little evidence for

the familiar statement that the failure of the *Odes* embittered his life.

In Collins's slender sheaf of odes the reader will find
much conventional diction and rhetoric, but closer attention will reveal high artistic versatility and skilful lyric
effects unmatched in their time. The unrimed *Ode to
Evening* is of unique beauty, and "How sleep the brave"
is perhaps the finest short dirge in the language outside of
Shakespeare. The *Ode on the Poetical Character* represents
Collins's preoccupation with the idea of poetry, his quest
for true enthusiasm and inspiration. *Simplicity* and *Liberty* express the familiar idea of the union of political
liberty and artistic inspiration. The *Passions,* in the "power
of music" tradition familiar in Dryden's *Alexander's Feast,*
was the most popular of these pieces in the eighteenth century and was often declaimed and set to music. *Pity* and
Terror show Collins's interest in the theory of Greek tragedy. Like Gray, Collins often versifies trite ideas which
seem somewhat arid to us; but his poems at their best express exquisite sensitiveness and enthusiastic scholarship;
they reflect his interest in Greek poetry, and in Spenser,
Shakespeare, and Milton. His recurring references to these
themes center about the idea of a lost inspiration which the
modern enthusiast seeks to recover.

In 1749 Collins published his *Ode Occasioned by the
Death of Mr. Thomson,* commemorating a significant literary friendship. Johnson was also a personal friend,
though incapable of admiring his work wholeheartedly.
The Thomson ode was apparently the last piece published
during his lifetime. Shortly after 1750 he became insane,
or at least suffered a complete nervous breakdown, and
was thus lost to his friends and to English literature long
before his death at Chichester in 1759. The loss may be
partly estimated from his *Ode on the Popular Superstitions
of the Highlands of Scotland, Considered as the Subject of*

Poetry, addressed to John Home in 1749, eventually re-discovered and published at Edinburgh in 1788. Here Collins turns to a richly romantic vein of poetry which would have given further scope to his literary enthusiasms, and shows that he was on the verge of a new and significant period in his work. Other pieces unpublished and now lost, an *Ode on the Music of the Grecian Theatre* and *An Epistle to the Editor of Fairfax his Translation of Tasso,* would also probably attest the increasing range of his power. During his lifetime his work was appreciated chiefly by a small circle of friends, but after the publication of Langhorne's edition of his poems in 1765 he was more and more highly esteemed until finally the romantic poets exalted him above Gray.

Poems, ed. W. C. Bronson (Boston, 1898); ed. E. Blunden (London, 1929); P. L. Carver, "Notes on the Life of William Collins," *Notes and Queries,* CLXXVII (1939). 128-32, 146-50, 167-71, 182-85, 201-04, 220-23, 240-43, 258-61, 272-74; H. W. Garrod, *Collins* (Oxford, 1928); A. S. P. Woodhouse, "Collins in the Eighteenth Century," (London) *Times Literary Supplement,* Oct. 16, 1930, p. 838; "Collins and the Creative Imagination," in *Studies in English by Members of University College, Toronto* (Toronto, 1931); E. G. Ainsworth, *Poor Collins* (Ithaca, 1937).

THOMAS GRAY (1716-1771)

>>

Thomas Gray was born in London; he had a brutal father and a long suffering mother to whom he was devotedly attached. He was the only survivor of a large family of children, and at his mother's expense was sent to Eton, where two of her brothers were tutors. Here he was one of a "Quadruple Alliance" of friends, along with Horace Walpole, the unfortunate young scholar Richard West, and Thomas Ashton. He matriculated at Peterhouse,

Cambridge, in 1734. The course of his life was largely determined by his private studies and by the friendships
which called forth from this shy, fastidious recluse some of
the best letters ever written in English. He traveled in
France and Italy with Walpole (1739-1741); after a quarrel
with his friend he returned to England and lived for a
time with his mother and her two sisters in the parish of
Stoke Poges, Buckinghamshire, near Eton and Windsor.
Here he wrote his first important poems in English and
here is the famous churchyard associated with the *Elegy*.
In 1742 he took up residence at Peterhouse, and Cambridge
was his home for the rest of his life; he moved to Pembroke
College across the way in 1756. The University as such
meant little to him; until he received an honorary profes-
sorship of history in 1768 he had no official status there,
but at least this way of life gave him the leisure and retirement which he preferred. There is no reason to believe with
Matthew Arnold that an uncongenial age drove the genius
and scholar Gray into a retreat where "he never spoke out."
Like other writers and scholars in other times, he deliberately preferred seclusion. He was under little external
pressure, and like many another virtuoso, to use the old
word, he loved technical detail for its own sake. His varied
studies in the classics, medieval antiquities and literature,
modern literature, especially English, French, and Italian,
music, the fine arts, and natural science are recorded only
in collections of notes and fragments. He had too much
taste and scholarship to be a mere dilettante, but he had
no professional zeal and little incentive to self-expression
except privately in his brilliant letters to his friends. His
most important correspondents were Walpole, with whom
he was reconciled in 1745, Dr. Thomas Wharton of Pembroke (to be distinguished from the poet Thomas Warton
of Oxford), and the minor poet William Mason. In the
jargon of our time, Gray was not "productive." Yet the

impression he gives of fine taste, learning, and personal power has always led readers to scrutinize with intense interest the slender sheaf of poems that practically make up his complete works.

Gray shows how the changing taste of the mid-century was bound up with literary culture and serious scholarship. The same may be said of Collins and the Wartons. These poets were less interested in wit, analysis, and exposition than many of their contemporaries, and turned in the 1740's to the intensive cultivation of certain lyric forms in which description and meditative moralizing are fused. Gray's beginnings were scholarly and traditional: his first important poem was the fine set of Latin Alcaics written in the album of the monastery at the Grande Chartreuse (1741). The poems written at Stoke Poges in 1742, *Ode on the Spring, Ode on a Distant Prospect of Eton College, Hymn to Adversity,* and the sonnet on the death of West are conventional in diction, Christian-Stoic in thought, pensive and melancholy in mood. They are colored by Gray's personal experiences, his temporary estrangement from Walpole and his grief at the death of West, but they are not planned as a direct expression of personal feeling. Nor did he make his chronic low spirits, his "white melancholy or rather leucocholy," into a lyric theme. The *Elegy Written in a Country Churchyard,* perhaps begun in 1742 or more probably in 1746, likewise subdues personal feeling to meditation on the common lot of humanity. It deals in Augustan commonplace but heightens pathos; the familiar theme of rural retirement and obscurity, slightly tinged by pastoral idealization, is combined with a sense of the inherent tragic dignity of man. But the tone becomes more subjective and self-conscious with the figure of the pensive poet and his epitaph at the end; the last nine stanzas or so seem to have been composed in a different spirit and at a different time. The *Elegy* should not be closely associated with such meditations on death as Young's *Night Thoughts* and Blair's *Grave*; it is much less concerned with specifically theological matter. Nor is it directly in the *Penseroso* line. Yet it owes much to moral didacticism and to literary tradition. Working with conventional diction and imagery, Gray here connects literature with life so successfully as to write the best-known piece of verse in the language.

STOKE POGES CHURCHYARD
The churchyard of the *Elegy*. Gray's tomb is in the background.

Of 1748 is the fragment of a didactic poem called *The Alliance of Education and Government* which would have been more admired by Gray's age than ours. The historian Gibbon later asked, "Instead of compiling tables of chronology and natural history, why did not Mr. Gray apply the powers of his genius to finish the philosophic poem of which he has left such an exquisite specimen?" [1] But Gray

[1] *Decline and Fall of the Roman Empire,* ed. J. B. Bury (London, 1912), III, 332, Chap. xxxi, note 131.

completed even short poems with difficulty, and published reluctantly, usually under pressure from Walpole. The Eton ode appeared in 1747, and again, along with *Spring* and the *Ode on the Death of a Favorite Cat* in the second volume of Dodsley's *Collection* (1748). The *Elegy* was completed in 1750 and brought out in 1751 to forestall unauthorized publication in magazines, and won Gray instant literary fame. In 1753 Walpole arranged for the elaborately illustrated work called, at Gray's insistence, *Designs by Mr. R. Bentley for Six Poems by Mr. T. Gray.* In 1757 from Walpole's Strawberry Hill Press appeared the two famous odes which impressed and puzzled Gray's contemporaries, *The Progress of Poesy* and *The Bard.* Here the level moralizing style of the early pieces is abandoned for the Pindaric model considered appropriate for lofty verse, and into this elaborate form he puts themes and images drawn from his wide reading and especially from his historical studies. *The Progress of Poesy* was at first called *The Power of Poetry,* and this indicates the theme of the power of music, in the tradition of the odes for St. Cecilia's Day. This power is primordial or primitive, and Gray holds the balance between its early and universal manifestations and its progress in the western tradition from Greece to Britain. In *The Bard* the same exaltation of poetry and the balance between earlier and later manifestations are presented in more dramatic form and in a richer historical context. Gray uses as a framework the tradition of the slaughter of the Welsh bards by Edward I, and puts into the mouth of the last surviving bard a prophetic survey of English history. Both odes are connected with Gray's elaborate studies for a projected history of English poetry. His only important poems of the 1760's, translated specimens of Norse and Welsh verse (*The Fatal Sisters, The Descent of Odin, The Triumphs of Owen*), were written as part of this same plan. These fragments were published in 1768. Gray

had been disappointed that the public found the two Pindaric odes obscure, and thereafter he made no ambitious
attempts in verse, but continued his miscellaneous antiquarian and scientific studies. The Ossianic poems interested him keenly, though he had doubts about their
authenticity. He made many summer tours, and his records
of journeys in Scotland (1765) and in the Lake Country
(1769) show his discriminating response to natural beauties.
He died in 1771 and was buried at Stoke Poges. The biography published by his friend and correspondent William
Mason in 1775 is an important part of his literary record,
containing, though in garbled form, the text of many of
his famous letters.

C. S. Northup, *A Bibliography of Thomas Gray* (New Haven,
1917); *Works*, ed. E. Gosse (revised ed., 4v, London, 1902-06);
Selections, ed. W. L. Phelps (Boston, 1894); *English Poems*, ed.
D. C. Tovey (Cambridge, 1898); *Poetry and Prose*, ed. J. Crofts
(Oxford, 1926); *Elegy*, ed. F. G. Stokes (Oxford, 1929); *Corres-
pondence*, ed. P. Toynbee and L. Whibley (3v, Oxford, 1935);
E. Gosse, *Gray* (London, 1882; English Men of Letters); R. Mar-
tin, *Chronologie de la vie et de l'oeuvre de Thomas Gray* (Lon-
don, 1931); *Essai sur Thomas Gray* (London, 1934); R. W. Ketton-
Cremer, *Thomas Gray* (London, 1935); W. P. Jones, *Thomas
Gray, Scholar* (Cambridge, Mass., 1937); H. W. Starr, *Gray as a
Literary Critic* (Philadelphia, 1941); Lord David Cecil, *The Poetry
of Thomas Gray, Proceedings of the British Academy*, xxxi (1945)
(Warton Lecture on English Poetry); Odell Shepard, "A Youth to
Fortune and to Fame Unknown," *Modern Philology*, xx (1923).
347-73; Amy L. Reed, *The Background of Gray's Elegy* (New
York, 1924); H. W. Garrod, "Note on the Composition of Gray's
Elegy," in *Essays on the Eighteenth Century Presented to David
Nichol Smith* (Oxford, 1945); W. P. Jones, "The Contemporary
Reception of Gray's Odes," *Modern Philology*, xxviii (1930).
61-82.

THOMAS WARTON THE ELDER (1688?-1745)
JOSEPH WARTON (1722-1800)
THOMAS WARTON THE YOUNGER (1728-1790)

The Wartons were a poetical family: father and sons
wrote verse which illustrates and in some respects anticipates the changes in English literary taste throughout the
century. They were pioneers not because they planned to
initiate a romantic revolution, but because the leisurely life
of church and university enabled them to indulge their
tastes and to carry on the literary and antiquarian studies
of their choice. Their poetry was a natural product of these
tastes and studies.

The life-span of the father coincides almost exactly with
that of Pope. He was educated at Magdalen College, Oxford, was professor of Poetry at that university from 1718
to 1728, and vicar of Basingstoke, Hampshire, for the last
twenty-two years of his life, holding other church livings
also. At the university he was noted for strong Tory and
Jacobite views; he had in many respects the opinions of a
typical Oxford don, but his prejudices and preferences evidently freshened and stimulated his literary tastes. Almost
none of his verse was published in his lifetime; his *Poems
on Several Occasions* was brought out by his son Joseph in
1748. Little known at the time except to the Wartons themselves and a few friends such as William Collins, his pieces
have been brought to light again by students who have
sought evidence for romantic tastes in the age of Pope.
Amid much conventional work, the elder Warton shows
himself in a few pieces remarkably sensitive to the charm
of Milton's minor poems, imitates Milton and Chaucer,
and even, following Sir William Temple, writes a paraphrase of a Scandinavian death-song. Whether this be called

romanticism or not, it represents a widening of historical perspective. Greater than these slender contributions was his unquestionable influence on his sons.

Joseph Warton was educated in his father's school at Basingstoke and at Winchester, where he and William Collins wrote verses together. He then matriculated at Oriel College, Oxford. After taking holy orders he spent about thirty-five years as headmaster at Winchester. Thomas the younger was educated at the Basingstoke school and at Trinity College, Oxford, and spent his long life at the university, as fellow of Trinity, professor of Poetry like his father (1757-67), and professor of Ancient History (1785-90). The two brothers began at the same point and developed long academic and literary careers in parallel. Joseph's blank verse poem, *The Enthusiast,* written about 1740 and published in 1744, is very much like Thomas's *Pleasures of Melancholy,* written about 1745 and published in 1747. Both pieces are inventories of the new themes which were interesting the young descriptive and lyrical poets of the decade—Shakespeare and Spenser, a cult of melancholy based on *Il Penseroso* but with more emphasis on the somber and the solitary, the preference for wild and even savage and desolate scenes, the cult of primitive man, the use of varied geographical material in connection with all these themes. Many of these motifs had appeared in Thomson's *Seasons,* but here undergo melodramatic and sentimental heightening. The advertisement to Joseph Warton's *Odes on Various Subjects* (1746) deliberately proclaims a new program:

The public has been so much accustomed of late to didactic poetry alone, and essays on moral subjects, that any work where the imagination is much indulged, will perhaps not be relished or regarded. The author therefore of these pieces is in some pain lest certain austere critics should think them too fanciful or descriptive. But as he is convinced that the fashion of moralizing in verse has been carried too far, and as he looks upon Invention and Imagination to be the chief faculties of a poet, so he will be happy if the following odes may be looked upon as an attempt to bring back poetry into its right channel.

Collins came closer to realizing this program than Joseph Warton, whose best work was done in criticism. His famous *Essay on the Writings and Genius of Pope* (I, 1756; II, 1782) belittles Pope only in the sense that it describes the best of Augustan ethical verse as essentially inferior to the work of a "creative and glowing imagination," the sublime and the pathetic in Spenser, Shakespeare, and Milton. By the time of the publication of the second volume and still more in his edition of Pope (1797) this view becomes a defense of "the great poet of Reason, the *first* of *ethical* authors in verse ... a writer fit for universal perusal." The breadth of Joseph Warton's scholarly interests is also indicated by his commentary on Virgil and by his tentative plan for a *History of Grecian, Roman, Italian, and French Poetry*.[1]

Another shift in critical opinion appears in the altered view of the history of English poetry presented by Thomas Warton in his *Observations on the Fairie Queene of Spenser* (1754) and his great *History of English Poetry* (I, 1774; II, 1778; III, 1781). Like others of his generation, Thomas Warton felt the fascination of medieval poetry and Gothic architecture. The question which had exercised the critics of the Italian Renaissance again arose: How far were the standards of neo-classical criticism to be applied to irregular or "Gothic" writers like Ariosto and Spenser? Warton's mind is divided; he does not rebel against the rational standards of his age, but extends his sympathies and interests to the great field of pre-Elizabethan English literature and makes an important though, of course, imperfect survey of that area. He is an accumulator of materials, an

[1] *Correspondence of Percy and Malone,* ed. A. Tillotson (Baton Rouge, 1944), p. 12, n.

antiquarian, but he does not altogether lose sight of large historical issues. His work, like Sir Walter Scott's, shows the intimate connection between scholarship and the romantic movement. The best of his later poems, *The Crusade, The Grave of King Arthur, Verses on Sir Joshua Reynolds's Painted Window,* are an expression of his interest in medieval themes. The position of the Wartons was prominent, though it remains uncertain how far they affected or how far they merely represented the tastes and opinions of their times. But at least a clear line of influence can be traced through Joseph Warton to a group of minor poets educated at Winchester, Thomas Russell, Henry Headley, F. N. C. Mundy, and William Lisle Bowles, who count for something in the romantic movement at the end of the century.

The Three Wartons, ed. E. Partridge (London, 1927); Thomas Warton the Elder, *Poems on Several Occasions* (New York, 1930; Facsimile Text); D. H. Bishop, "The Father of the Wartons," *South Atlantic Quarterly,* XVI (1917). 357-68; John Wooll, *Biographical Memoirs of Joseph Warton* (London, 1806); Thomas Warton the Younger, *History of English Poetry,* ed. W. C. Hazlitt (4v, London, 1871); *Poetical Works with Memoirs,* ed. R. Mant (2v, Oxford, 1802); Clarissa Rinaker, *Thomas Warton, a Biographical and Critical Study* (Urbana, 1916); R. D. Havens, "Thomas Warton and the Eighteenth-Century Dilemma," *Studies in Philology,* XXV (1928). 36-50; René Wellek, *The Rise of English Literary History* (Chapel Hill, 1941).

WILLIAM SHENSTONE (1714-1763)
>>>

From the work of William Shenstone we can learn some of the weaknesses and limitations of the eighteenth century, but we can also approach the secret of some of its attainments. His life was passed under restrictions imposed

by his own personality and circumstances; he wrote graceful minor verse, practiced landscape gardening on a small
scale, was a dilettante or minor virtuoso who played a
rather small game in a secure retreat, and sometimes ended
by being tired of it all. In a quest for affected simplicity he
often approaches triviality. Yet within these limits he is a
finished artist in the "rococo" style which is often contrasted with the more massively ornate "baroque." His
poetry has the lighter artificiality found in some of the
architecture, decoration, and landscaping of the time.
Moreover his letters and miscellaneous prose show considerable power of self-criticism, a fairly wide range of taste
and interest, and a pleasant wit.

Shenstone was born at Halesowen, Shropshire, near Birmingham, and was educated at Pembroke College, Oxford.
He published poems in 1737, including the first version of
his Spenserian *Schoolmistress*, which he expanded in 1742
and still further in the version published in Dodsley's
Collection (1748). This is a skilful exercise in style, combining sympathy and humor. From 1745 he resided at the
farm at Halesowen, the Leasowes, which he made into a
famous small landscaped estate or *ferme ornée* in the natural style of English gardening. Here he carried out his
projects and wrote his poems, letters, and essays. His *Essays
on Men and Manners, pensées* in the manner of La Rochefoucauld, have been undeservedly forgotten. There is an
obvious connection between his verse and the planning of
the Leasowes, with its carefully arranged pattern of shrubbery, water, walks, and vistas. Among his friends and correspondents in the "Warwickshire coterie" were Lady
Luxborough, Richard Jago, and Richard Graves. He exchanged many letters with Bishop Percy, and gave substantial aid in editing the *Reliques of Ancient English
Poetry*. Dodsley the bookseller was another correspondent,
and many of his poems appear in the successive editions

of Dodsley's *Collection,* including his sentimental and pensive elegies and the once famous *Pastoral Ballad,* a piece which irritated Doctor Johnson but which shows Shenstone's skill in playing with a literary form.

Works in Verse and Prose (3v, 1764-69); *Poetical Works,* ed. C. C. Clarke (London, 1880); *Letters,* ed. D. Mallam (Minneapolis, 1939); ed. Marjorie Williams (Oxford, 1939); A. I. Hazeltine, *A Study of William Shenstone and of his Critics* (Menasha, 1918); E. M. Purkis, *William Shenstone: Poet and Landscape Gardener* (Wolverhampton, 1931); Marjorie Williams, *William Shenstone* (Birmingham, 1935); A. R. Humphreys, *William Shenstone* (Cambridge, 1937).

ROBERT DODSLEY (1703-1764)

>>>

Dodsley, only a minor poet and playwright, was the most important bookseller of the second and third quarters of the eighteenth century, and thus played an important part in literary history. He first appears as a versifying footman, a talented writer in humble life like the thresher Stephen Duck, and in 1732 attracted attention by a miscellany called *The Muse in Livery.* With the aid of Pope he opened his bookshop at the sign of Tully's Head in Pall Mall. He was soon publishing Pope's later works, and brought out Johnson's *London* (1738). His alliance with the anti-administration writers appears with his publication of Glover's *Leonidas* (1737) and Brooke's *Gustavus Vasa* (1739) and in his friendship with Chesterfield. He succeeded in getting much of the important poetry of the time on his list; in 1742, with the publication of *The Schoolmistress,* his long personal and literary friendship with Shenstone began. From 1742 Dodsley published the first six parts of Young's *Night Thoughts,* in 1744 Akenside's *Pleasures*

of Imagination, in 1745 the same writer's *Odes* and
Cooper's *Power of Harmony,* in 1746 Joseph Warton's *Odes.*
He had less success at first with periodicals, but his *Museum*
(1746-47) had literary distinction. His relations with Johnson continued to be cordial; he published *The Vanity of
Human Wishes* and *Irene* in 1749 and *Rasselas* ten years
later, and had an important part in getting the *Dictionary*
under way. With the Eton ode (1747), the *Elegy* (1751),
and the *Six Poems* (1753) he added the great name of Gray
to his list. His publication of poetry culminated in the
famous collection known by his name, three volumes in
1748, a fourth in 1755, two more in 1758. Aided by the
advice of Walpole, Spence, Shenstone, and others, Dodsley
made this series a chief repository of the shorter poems of
his generation, and through it the work of writers like
Collins, Dyer, and Green got wide and continuous currency. By his *Collection of Old Plays* (1744-45) he helped
to further knowledge of earlier English literature. His chief
connection with English fiction was the London edition of
Tristram Shandy. The new men Goldsmith and Burke published with him; from 1758 Burke conducted for him the
Annual Register, one of the most successful periodicals of
the century. Though Dodsley quarreled with Garrick about
his tragedy *Cleone,* he usually succeeded, as the pages of
Boswell show, in combining the practical work of a publisher with personal friendship and sound literary judgment.

Ralph Straus, *Robert Dodsley, Poet, Publisher, and Playwright*
(London, 1910).

NEWSPAPERS, MAGAZINES, AND REVIEWS
≫≫≫

The Stamp Tax of 1712 imposed a half-penny duty on pamphlets or papers printed on a half-sheet, a penny on those using a half to a whole sheet. This encouraged a six-page weekly usually called a "journal," using one and a half sheets and thus avoiding the tax. The typical daily was a half-sheet printed in double columns and carrying only news and a few advertisements, but the journal regularly admitted a political editorial or an essay on the *Spectator* model, and other miscellaneous matter. Though evasion of the tax became impossible, the most influential papers continued to be of this type. They were deeply involved in politics: *Mist's Weekly Journal, or Saturday's Post*, changed to "Fog's" after a prosecution, was the most extreme Tory organ, but from 1726 the *Craftsman* was the principal opposition paper. Walpole subsidized various papers, including the *Daily Gazetteer*. As the century advances, most of the features of the modern newspaper develop—an increase in advertising (notably in the *Daily Advertiser* from 1730), control by proprietors who were not printers, and later the regular reporting of parliamentary debates, and the "leader" (editorial) under a masthead on an inner page. Almon in the *London Evening Post* and William Woodfall in the *Morning Chronicle* were prominent in political reporting in the age of Wilkes and the American Revolution. The London *Chronicle* from 1757 extended its content to include varied material, such as book reviews. The size and circulation of newspapers continued to be very small by modern standards, even though they were prominent and influential. Surviving files often give important evidence in their advertisements for the

publication of books and the production of plays. Familiar
names such as the *Times* and the *Morning Post* appear late
in the period, though the *Times* did not get its command-
ing position until early in the next century.

In 1731 Edward Cave, a printer at St. John's Gate, Clerk-
enwell, began his famous *Gentleman's Magazine*. By "magazine," a new use of the word, he meant a collection or
miscellany made up of essays extracted from the weekly
journals together with a systematic chronicle of the events
of the month. Secondarily he reprinted poetry and began
to list new books. While the weekly journals of the 1730's
were largely political, they appealed to literary interests
also, as has been said; in this group were the *Universal
Spectator,* the *Weekly Miscellany,* and the *Grub-street
Journal,* and Cave owed more to them than to more distant precedents for literary entertainment. For a systematic
monthly record of the news, Cave's model was a type of
monthly publication which gave a comprehensive but dry
report of current events, such as Abel Boyer's *Political
State of Great Britain* (1711-40), and the *Historical Register* (1716-38). The early *Gentleman's* had much political
matter. Like other journalists, Cave undertook to print the
debates in Parliament, and after 1738 this was largely done
for him by Samuel Johnson under the title of "Debates in
the Senate of Magna Lilliputia." But Cave always gave
space to miscellaneous matter, and interest shifted from
public affairs to literature, science, biography, and antiquities. The amount of poetry was increased, though the
Gentleman's verse was never very high in quality, so that
the subscriber got the equivalent of a poetical miscellany.
The listing of books was expanded to include brief reviews
and notices. The contents were on the level of the well
informed though superficial reader, and a bound set of the
Gentleman's came to be, as the name implies, a necessary

part of the gentleman's library in town or country. Cave's success soon called forth many imitators, most important the *London Magazine* from 1732, put out by a syndicate of booksellers, and the *Scots Magazine* at Edinburgh from 1739. The *Universal Magazine* from 1747 was also early and successful, and many others could be named.

From the seventeenth century a well defined type of periodical was devoted to the summarizing and abstracting of books, on the model of the *Journal des Sçavans*. This became standard for the voluminous French periodicals with *Bibliothèque*-titles. Somewhat similarly, though not on the same scale, we have English periodicals variously called *Memoirs of Literature, Present State of the Republic of Letters,* and *History of the Works of the Learned.* The last title is accurate, for the tendency was to make long extracts from learned or technical works. A somewhat similar method was applied by the bookseller Ralph Griffiths to the general field of belles lettres in the *Monthly Review* from 1749; the policy at first was not to write reviews in our sense, but to list every book published, with extracts from or summaries of the most important. In 1756 Archibald Hamilton started the *Critical Review* with Smollett as principal editor. The Tory bias of the *Critical Review* and Smollett's harsh methods provoked much controversy. But there was general resentment of the reviewer in this period, whether he was discussing a play or an art-exhibition in the newspaper, or doing a notice of a book in the *Monthly* or the *Critical.* These two reviews never attained the prestige and power of their early nineteenth-century descendants, the *Edinburgh* and the *Quarterly.* They contained much hack work, but they were widely read, they recorded literary opinion as more fugitive notices did not, and they enlisted the services of some important men, not only Smollett in the *Critical,* but Goldsmith in the *Monthly* (with some contributions to the *Critical* also), and Johnson in the short-lived *Literary Magazine or Universal Review* (1756-58).

H. R. Fox Bourne, *English Newspapers*, I (London, 1887); D. H. Stevens, *Party Politics and English Journalism, 1702-1742* (Chicago, 1916); J. T. Hillhouse, *The Grub-street Journal* (Durham, 1928); C. L. Carlson, *The First Magazine: A History of the Gentleman's Magazine* (Providence, 1938); B. C. Nangle, *The Monthly Review: First Series, 1749-1789: Indexes of Contributors and Articles* (Oxford, 1934).

See also above, pp. 159-60.

THE FINE ARTS

▶▶

A full consideration of the fine arts in eighteenth-century England is not possible here, but the student of literature will find in painting, architecture, and landscape gardening an invaluable guide for the interpretation of critical standards, a rich commentary on changing tastes, and a vivid introduction to the actual daily life of the age.

PAINTING

Seventeenth-century critics had put historical painting first, then portraiture, then landscape and still life. Tasteless historical allegories continued to be used for the decoration of great houses, the work of Sir James Thornhill and others. The English upper classes, though they freely bought Italian and Dutch pictures of various kinds, especially encouraged portraits painted by foreigners working in England. The elegant aristocrats of the Fleming Van Dyke in the age of Charles I and the voluptuous Restoration beauties of the Hollander Peter Lely were succeeded by the stiff formal portraits produced in quantity by the studio of the German Sir Godfrey Kneller. The first art school in

England was opened by Kneller; one of its important successors was the academy in St. Martin's Lane where Hogarth studied. A native English tradition was thus fostered, but the development of portraiture was limited by the customers' demand for conventional and flattering pieces. Hogarth, the first great English painter, did not meet this requirement and went his own way (see p. 252). After Kneller important portrait painters were Jonathan Richardson, who wrote on art and gave Pope lessons in painting, Charles Jervas, Thomas Hudson, Allan Ramsay, son of the poet, and Joseph Highmore. Highmore and others also practiced the popular form of the conversation piece, a portrait group in an intimate setting. Though few masterpieces were produced in this form, save by Hogarth and Gainsborough, it is of great documentary value to the student of the times, and had important effects on the history of book illustration, as in Highmore's admirable twelve plates telling the story of Richardson's *Pamela*. A minor but characteristic vein, the painting of horses and dogs and hunting and racing scenes, as by George Stubbs and John Wootton, testifies to the interests of English squires. From this developed the English sporting print which has had such a large place in popular art. Meanwhile the interest in native landscape painting developed rather slowly—surprisingly so when we consider the new and important developments in landscape gardening. A distinction can be made between the simple rendering of English scenes, somewhat in the Dutch picturesque-genre manner, and the elaborate romantic landscapes in the manner of Salvator Rosa, Poussin, and Claude Lorraine. The latter school dominated taste in the mid-century, but the work of the first important British landscapist Richard Wilson (1714-1782) shows a compromise between the two tendencies. Wilson never got the recognition he deserved.

In the second half of the century the public interest in

RICHARD WILSON. "CICERO'S VILLA"
Engraved by Timothy Cole. Reproduced by permission of *The Century Magazine.*

painting increased greatly. Regular exhibitions were held by organized artists from 1760; after quarrels and secessions the Royal Academy was founded in 1768 and flourished under the presidency of Reynolds and the patronage of the King. Reviews and discussions of paintings multiplied; the public crowded to see popular pictures and bought innumerable prints. Reynolds, on his return from Italy in 1752, had become the great exponent of a dignified traditional style. The discourses which he delivered annually as President of the Royal Academy apply to painting the neo-classical doctrine of imitation of the best masters and uphold truth to nature in the sense of elevated generality as opposed to extreme particularity. Reynolds, an extremely ambitious man and a seeker after social success, is known to students of literature as an eminent associate of Johnson, Goldsmith, and Burke. His tremendous popularity in portrait painting brought out his weaknesses, idealization and sometimes facile sentiment, but at his best he could interpret and dramatize character admirably. The portrait painter had to give the patron what he wanted, and only Reynolds and his great contemporary Gainsborough transcend this difficulty. In general the later portraiture of the century is marked by greater variety of costume, setting (interior and exterior), color, and mood. The same holds true of the ever popular conversation piece.

Gainsborough (1727-1788), born in Sudbury, Suffolk, served his apprenticeship in London, then lived in Ipswich for many years until he reached a late period of success as a fashionable painter in Bath and London. Yet he stood comparatively clear of fashion, drew always on the local impressions and what may be called the Dutch art traditions of his native East Anglia, relied on temperament rather than on academic code, and so produced portraits, conversation pieces, and landscapes of unsurpassed spirit, charm, and refinement. In landscape the East Anglian tradition

SIR JOSHUA REYNOLDS, GEORGIANA, DUCHESS
OF DEVONSHIRE
Engraved by Timothy Cole. Reproduced by permission of *The Century
Magazine*.

continues down into the nineteenth century in John Crome of Norwich (1768-1821), John Sell Cotman (1782-1842), and the far greater John Constable (1776-1837). George Morland, a popular painter of the English rural scene, tended to the trivially picturesque and sentimental. A successful portraitist was the prolific and conventional John Zoffany (1733-1810), who painted gentry and bourgeois in domestic settings, and thus recorded much realistic detail. Sentimental weakness appears in the work of John Hoppner (1758-1810) and George Romney (1734-1802), the indefatigable portrayer of the alluring Lady Hamilton, and also in Sir Thomas Lawrence (1769-1830). The Scot Sir Henry Raeburn was more vigorous, and has left us a fine survey of the compatriots and contemporaries of Sir Walter Scott. The American Gilbert Stuart did excellent work on both sides of the Atlantic.

Historical painting, still considered the highest form, took a prominent place in the age of the American Revolution and the wars against France. Here several Americans won great success—Benjamin West with his *Death of General Wolfe* in 1771, John Singleton Copley with the *Death of Chatham* in 1781, both Copley and John Trumbull with pictures of the siege of Gibraltar in 1787 and 1789. Unimportant as paintings, these great stretches of canvas are not to be despised by the student; they were widely circulated in popular prints, and every schoolboy still visualizes eighteenth-century warfare in their terms.

ARCHITECTURE

The term *neo-classical,* hard to explain when applied to poetry and painting, fits the architecture of the age exactly. The neo-classical style most conspicuously illustrated by Palladio in sixteenth-century Italy—a style of round arches, domes, long straight perspectives, simple forms—was brought to seventeenth-century England by Inigo Jones.

Examples of his work were the Banqueting House at Whitehall, a portico added to the west front of old St. Paul's
Cathedral, and the church of St. Paul's, Covent Garden,
the last referred to in Gay's *Trivia:*

> Where Covent Garden's famous temple stands,
> That boasts the work of Jones' immortal hands;
> Columns with plain magnificence appear,
> And graceful porches lead along the square.

In the rebuilding of London after the Great Fire of 1666,
the new style was applied by Christopher Wren. He combined the simple Palladian style with some elements drawn
from the medieval and also from the heavy ornate style
called "baroque," and showed great originality and re-
sourcefulness in his numerous City churches. His spires
still mark the London skyline, though many of the churches
have been seriously damaged by German bombs; his masterpiece St. Paul's, a great cruciform building with the second
largest dome in Europe, still dominates the City. An act
of Queen Anne authorized fifty more city churches in 1711;
only thirteen were built, but some of them are excellent
examples of the work of James Gibbs—St. Martin's in the
Fields and St. Mary-le-Strand. Gibbs left his mark on Cambridge with the fine Senate House, and Nicholas Hawks-
moor on Oxford with Queen's College.

The great new mansions of the Whig aristocracy rose in
town and country. Sir John Vanbrugh's baroque buildings,
notably Blenheim, built by the nation for Marlborough,
and Castle Howard, Yorkshire, were impressive and almost
notorious in their extravagant massiveness. Such town mansions as Devonshire House and Chesterfield House were in
a style more suitable for public buildings than for residences. A movement toward stricter Palladian simplicity
was encouraged by Richard Boyle, Earl of Burlington, who
was an amateur architect himself and fostered the work of

INTERIOR OF ST. STEPHEN'S WALBROOK

The dome is supported by Corinthian pillars. One of the finest interiors
among Wren's City churches. From *London and its Environs*, 1761.

William Kent and Colin Campbell. Campbell's Burlington House was strictly Palladian; the famous Chiswick House, in which Burlington and Kent were associated, a copy of an admired villa by Palladio at Vicenza, represents the application of classical forms on a more modest scale.

In the second half of the century classical influences were reënforced by renewed interest in ancient art. We should remember the excavations of Herculaneum and Pompeii,

THE CIRCUS, BATH
Designed by the elder Wood.

explorers' reports of Palmyra, Piranesi's great plates. The brothers Adam, especially Robert, developed from classical models a lighter, more graceful and decorative style expressive of the increasing amenities and elegance of social life. But they should be considered as decorators rather than as architects.

Smaller town houses came to be built in blocks, terraces, squares, and circles; the result was dignified though somewhat monotonous. Bath was the model town of this order, the work of the elder and the younger Wood. Much greater variety appears in small country houses, which varied somewhat according to local material and terrain but almost always showed good taste and dignity. Formal styles in architecture held their own very well, even while the informal garden prevailed. The new styles were often added to older work, to Elizabethan manors and even to medi-

PINE-PANELLED GEORGIAN ROOM, 1740
From Stanwick Park, Yorkshire. In the Minneapolis Art Institute.

eval remains. But on the whole the eighteenth century gave many localities the appearance which they still preserve in spite of nineteenth-century industrialism and twentieth-century war. Meanwhile innumerable churches, castles, and monastic ruins kept medieval styles before English eyes. Still the new Gothicism remained a fad, as in Walpole's Strawberry Hill and Beckford's Fonthill Abbey, as well as in the Gothic cottages, villas, and farm buildings which began to appear.

While styles in decoration and furniture fluctuated somewhat, the interiors of the great mansions admitted elaborate and ornate styles, relieving classical severity and adding intricacy and richness to a simple formal scheme. The magnificent wood carvings of Grinling Gibbons were a great individual achievement, but there was an infinite amount of good work by nameless artists in wood, stucco, stone, and iron. Most of the architects, notably William Kent, designed furniture and interior decorations, with waves of influence from the Dutch and French, and later Gothic and Chinese elements. The Adam style in the second half of the century marks a great change from the massive and ornate to the light and elegant. The diverse styles associated with the name of Chippendale illustrate this change, and the influence of Adam is also marked in the elegant furniture of Hepplewhite and Sheraton. The work of the silversmiths, always showing variety in style, manifests the same shift.

From the late seventeenth century and the reign of Anne there was a craze for oriental porcelain, lacquered and japanned work, and other rich and decorative objects sold in "China houses," "India houses," and "toyshops." There was another wave of "chinoiserie" in the mid-century. Imported China, oriental or European, was very expensive, as was the early English porcelain made at Chelsea and Bow. Wedgwood's famous Staffordshire potteries in the latter part of the century produced fine work at a low cost, designed in strict and elegant classical styles.

The English sculpture of the period shows no vigorous native growth. The sculptor was a craftsman engaged in the decoration of tombs and public buildings, and the best work was done by foreigners—Gabriel Cibber, father of the dramatist, and Rysbrack and Roubiliac, notable for their fine portrait busts.

LANDSCAPE GARDENING

In 1754 a writer remarked that England, "if it is not already one great and complete garden, contains at least more sumptuous country houses, parks, gardens, temples, and buildings, than all the rest of Europe" (*World,* No. 59). Landscaping had become a fashionable and popular art, practiced on a grand scale by the magnates, on a smaller scale by men of good taste and moderate means—an art which is fully recorded in literature. In gardening as in architecture seventeenth-century style in Italy and then in France had favored formal geometrical designs, prolonging and elaborating the design of the house itself by developing perspectives along a main axis. Le Nôtre, the great landscape architect of Louis XIV, applied this style to the flat terrain of France and developed it on a vast scale at Versailles, which became for all Europe the archetype of the formal garden. Characteristic of Versailles are the avenues radiating to form secondary axes, the lavish use of water in fountains and canals, the great terraces and parterres (level flower beds in formal patterns), symmetrically arranged statues and shrubbery. Princes and nobles all over Europe copied the style; an excellent English example is Wren's addition to Hampton Court, made for William III. The same principles in simpler form were applied to town planning through the whole period.

Within the magnificence, formality, and glaring publicity of the French style compensating elements were introduced—intricate labyrinths, surprising designs with boskets (clumps or small groves of trees), hermitages or rural retreats. But whether complicated or simple the style might be interpreted as a deviation from nature. England became the exponent of the natural garden—nature, a word of many meanings, indicating here about the degree of irregularity actually found in the countryside unmodified by the hand of the gardener. Milton sets forth this ideal in his description of the Garden of Eden (*Paradise Lost,* IV). Sir William Temple wrote in his essay on gardens that he hears that the Chinese practice a way of planting which has no order or symmetry, and have a special word for this principle, *sharawadgi.* There were practical reasons why the Englishman who thought of his garden as a pleasant

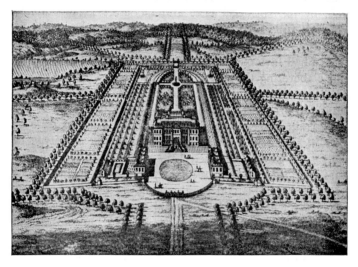

A FORMALLY LANDSCAPED ESTATE—RAGLEY, WARWICKSHIRE
From Beeverel, *Les Dèlices de la Grande Bretagne,* 1727.

place to walk in might seek relief from French formality, why the squire or citizen might welcome a style suited to the moderately varied topography of the English country-side. Literary and aesthetic models came in to reënforce such a preference. Addison's praise of nature over art was very influential (*Tatler,* Nos. 161, 218; *Spectator,* Nos. 414, 417). The discussion was parallel to the praise of Shake-speare as a "natural genius" in poetry. Pope's comments

(*Guardian*, No. 173 and *Epistle IV: Of the Use of Riches*) and his own gardening at Twickenham mark him as an opponent of the formal style. However, the smaller gardens and grottoes (Pope's own garden, Burlington's at Chiswick, Queen Caroline's Hermitage and Merlin's Cave at Richmond) seek variety by winding paths and shell and rock-work, following the decorative style called "rococo" rather than unadorned nature. Important developments took place at some of the great estates in the hands of eminent designers like Bridgman, Kent, and "Capability" Brown. Bridgman developed the "ha-ha," a sunken ditch or hedge which concealed the boundary between the park and the surrounding countryside. Winding walks, irregularly placed shrubbery and statues, concealed retreats and suddenly opening views mark the most famous places—Temple's Stowe, in Buckinghamshire, Leicester's Holkham, Hoare's Stourhead, Lyttelton's Hagley, and the neighboring small-scale *ferme ornée* of the poet Shenstone, called the Leasowes.

During the second half of the century the ideal of the English garden came to be denoted by the words "picturesque landscape." The landscape should form such a design as may be found in a picture—especially in the school of landscape painting developed in seventeenth-century Italy by the French artists Poussin and Claude Lorraine and in more rugged and romantic style by the Neapolitan Salvator Rosa. This tradition stimulated, though of course it did not create, the taste for landscape of wide perspectives and irregular variety, and in particular for ancient ruins (as in Poussin), and wild mountain scenery (as in Salvator). Such tastes appear in the poets James Thomson and John Dyer, though at first the preference is merely for the wide and varied prospect rather than for the wild and rugged, later called the "sublime." A secondary wave of Chinese influence about 1750, based on the Jesuit Attiret's account of Chinese gardens, made for odd and grotesque rather than sublime effects; Sir William Chambers was an exponent of this style, which principally influenced decorative detail. The main line of English tradition encourages the idea of the gardener as an artist composing an ideal landscape.

We have in England added another to the elegant sister arts. . . . Gardening may now join itself to poetry, music, and painting. . . . It is, indeed, nearly allied to the latter, though, in my opinion, far superior to it: it is the creating a real landscape, instead of painting an imaginary one.[1]

Sentimentalism interprets this theory to mean that the gardener should put feeling into the landscape; thus Shenstone remarks in his *Thoughts on Gardening* that scenes are to be conceived as sublime, beautiful, melancholy, etc., and that the prevailing emotion should be heightened. Hence the "natural" garden is studded with hermitages, temples of friendship and death, and artificial ruins. Movements in other arts than painting—chinoiserie in decoration, the cult of melancholy in poetry, renewed interest in both classical and medieval architecture and archaeology— all blend in this popular composite. Novels, essays, and poems are full of references to gardening and landscaping. The large specific literature of the subject may be illustrated by Mason's long poem, *The English Garden,* and by discussions of the theory of the picturesque by Richard Payne Knight and Uvedale Price. The formal theory, stated by Gilpin and Price, was that "the picturesque is rougher than the beautiful, but not so overwhelming as the sublime." Tourists sought the picturesque both in natural landscape and in the innumerable estates of England, and recorded their impressions in a new literature of travel, as in the writings of William Gilpin.

[1] William Combe, *Original Love Letters* (London, 1784), II, 99.

B. S. Allen, *Tides in English Taste, 1619-1800* (2v, Cambridge, Mass., 1937); R. A. Aubin, *Topographical Poetry in Eighteenth Century England* (New York, 1936); "Grottoes, Geology, and the Gothic Revival," *Studies in Philology*, XXXI (1934). 408-16; T. Borenius, *English Painting in the Eighteenth Century* (London, 1938); K. Clark, *The Gothic Revival* (London, 1928); J. W. Draper, *Eighteenth Century English Aesthetics* (Heidelberg, 1931); R. Edwards and M. Jourdain, *Georgian Cabinet Makers* (London, 1944); Roger Fry, *Georgian Art (1760-1820)* (New York, 1929); W. Gaunt, *Bandits in a Landscape: A Study of Romantic Painting from Caravaggio to Delacroix* (London, 1937); J. A. Gotch, *The Growth of the English House* (London, 1928); M. L. Gothein, *A History of Garden Art* (2v, London, 1928); C. R. Grundy, *English Art in the XVIII Century* (London, 1928); C. Hussey, *The Picturesque* (London, 1927); M. Jourdain, *English Decoration and Furniture of the Later XVIIIth Century (1760-1820)* (London, 1922); *English Interiors in Smaller Houses, 1660-1830* (London, 1933); F. Lenygon, *Decoration in England, 1640 to 1760* (London, 1928); *Furniture in England from 1660 to 1760* (London, 1914); E. W. Manwaring, *Italian Landscape in Eighteenth Century England* (New York, 1925); A. Graves and W. V. Cronin, *A History of the Works of Sir Joshua Reynolds* (4v, London, 1899-1901); Sir W. Armstrong, *Sir Joshua Reynolds* (New York, 1900); Reynolds, *Discourses*, ed. A. Dobson (Oxford, 1907); F. W. Hilles, *The Literary Career of Sir Joshua Reynolds* (Cambridge, 1936); S. Sitwell, *British Architects and Craftsmen* (London, 1945); *Narrative Pictures* (London, 1937); *Conversation Pieces* (London, 1936); J. Summerson, *Georgian London* (London, 1946); J. Swarbrick, *Robert Adam and His Brothers* (London, 1915); W. D. Templeman, *Life and Work of William Gilpin* (Urbana, 1939); C. B. Tinker, *Painter and Poet* (Cambridge, Mass., 1938); *Johnson's England*, ed. A. S. Turberville (2v, Oxford, 1933); W. T. Whitley, *Artists and Their Friends in England, 1700-1799* (2v, London, 1928); G. C. Williamson, *English Conversation Pictures* (London, 1932).

WILLIAM HOGARTH (1697-1764)

In the history of English painting William Hogarth stands for an honest, independent, and realistic native art in contrast to the pretentious performances of historical painters and the routine work of commercialized portrait painting. In the history of English literature he takes his place with the writers who use realistic caricature for didactic purposes. Our theory of art is hostile to pictures that tell stories; Hogarth had no scruples about making his pictures documentary.

Born in 1697 in St. Bartholemew's Close, Hogarth was apprenticed to an engraver. His early works included tradesman's cards, shop-keepers' signs, and illustrations for *Don Quixote* and *Hudibras*. As an artist he was largely self-taught, and this fostered his independence, and his scorn for the academic in art and for the patrons and collectors who sought antique rubbish and third-rate pictures from the Continent. He tried some things in the elevated and grand style without success. He showed great power in portraits and in informal family and social groups, but was too honest to be successful in this field.

His most characteristic pictures reflect an age of satire and a tradition of caricature. Caricature, in line with the old comedy of humors, used heavily emphasized or exaggerated detail symbolic of an idea or situation. Its method was that of the political cartoon, and it had become common during the political struggles of the eighteenth century, but it could, of course, be applied to the whole social scene. Beside caricatures satirizing masquerades, operas, and the virtuosi, Hogarth's early works include dramatic and anecdotal pieces, such as a scene from *The Beggar's Opera* (see p. 192) and an elaborate *Southwark Fair*. The type of picture known as the "conversation piece," in which a family or other group appears in a characteristic setting or pose, helped Hogarth to work out his own method, and there were probably lines of influence from French caricaturists and Dutch painters. Dutch and Flemish art was a standard for low realism in the criticism of the day.

Thus about 1730 Hogarth got the idea of "composing

pictures on canvas similar to representations on the stage.'
This carried with it the plan of a series presenting a story
with a plain moral, first realized in *A Harlot's Progress*
(1732). The country girl Moll Hackabout comes up to
London, is ensnared by a procuress, after brief prosperity
sinks into poverty and misery, is sent to Bridewell and dies
a miserable death. This sordid story, told with no softening
touches, had great success. It was a concentrated dose of
didactic narrative, vivid and homely, as graphic and moralistic as Defoe, and sometimes as grotesque as Smollett.

Hogarth's method was to paint his pictures, then to sell
sets of engravings at popular prices. His work was constantly pirated, and in 1735 he sought a remedy through
a bill giving designers and engravers exclusive rights in
their own work. In that year appeared *A Rake's Progress,*
telling how the young heir succeeds to his miserly father's
fortune, surrounds himself with flunkeys and parasites and
squanders his money, makes a mercenary marriage, gambles
and loses, is sent to the Fleet Prison for debt, and dies in
Bedlam. The third important series and probably the best,
Marriage à la Mode, appeared in 1745: the son of a haughty
peer marries a rich alderman's daughter for her money;
their life of fashionable dissipation is joyless and loveless;
the husband is killed by the wife's lover, and the woman
commits suicide. *Industry and Idleness* (1747) contrasts the
careers of two apprentices: the industrious Francis Good-
child marries his master's daughter and eventually becomes
Lord Mayor; Tommy Idle goes from bad to worse, and is
at last hanged at Tyburn. This tradesman's morality in the
vein of Defoe and Richardson is set forth with marvelous
realism and humor. *Four Times of Day* (1738) gives Hogarth's most elaborate street scenes; his contrast of the
bloated prosperity of *Beer Street* with the ghastly horrors of
Gin Lane (1751) is his contribution to current discussion
of the liquor problem. The *Election Prints* (1755-58), de-

HOGARTH'S MARRIAGE A LA MODE—THE CONTRACT

In a pompously furnished room the gouty peer points to his family tree; the bride's
father examines the marriage settlement; the bride listens to the flattery of a suave
lawyer; the foolish youth takes snuff and admires himself in the glass.

scriptive and anecedotal rather than dramatic, make up Hogarth's last great documentary series.

Hogarth's full merits as an artist, particularly his fine portraits, cannot be discussed here. He was long underrated, and his reputation suffered because he was considered "low." About 1745 a French observer, the Abbé Le Blanc, said that his moral prints were in every house; probably this was true for the next hundred years. His monotonous moralism and his heavy poetic justice are on the crude level of the chapbook, but are of the greatest interest for the history of the society in which he lived. Contemporary comment often put him among the satirists; later in the century an increasingly sentimental and fastidious generation found him indelicate. But without laboring too hard the analogies between painting and literature, the student will find Hogarth to be a faithful and often an inspired interpreter of eighteenth-century life.

F. Weitenkampf, *A Bibliography of William Hogarth* (Cambridge, Mass., 1890); S. E. Read, *A Bibliography of Hogarth Books and Studies* (Chicago, 1941); *Genuine Works,* ed. G. Steevens and J. Nichols (London, 1808); J. Nichols, *Biographical Anecdotes of William Hogarth* (London, 1785); J. Ireland, *Hogarth Illustrated* (2nd ed., 3v, London, 1793-1804); Austin Dobson, *William Hogarth* (London, 1891); H. B. Wheatley, *Hogarth's London* (London, 1909); Marjorie Bowen, *William Hogarth, The Cockney's Mirror* (New York, 1936); F. D. Klingender, *Hogarth and English Caricature* (New York, 1944).

SENTIMENTALISM

>>

Sentimentalism, like certain other words in *-ism,* is one of the indispensable terms used to denote underlying ideas and attitudes which color and change various aspects of life. But the ideas and attitudes may not be very clearly defined in the minds of the people who are supposed to hold them, and the changes in question may seem to be merely in feeling, in taste, or in fashion. The historian risks something when he connects the phenomena of style or taste with important ideas or philosophies. If he starts with what he thinks is an underlying idea, it may distort his selection and interpretation of the facts. In sentimentalism, however, we have a deliberate didactic program, not merely implied but expressed in formulas or sentiments; it is no play on words to say that sentimentalism is "sententious." In the minds of many people who admired edifying sentiments in plays, essays, sermons, poems, and novels the literature of sentiment may have meant little more than this, as far as conscious definition is concerned.

But strictly speaking we have to do here not merely with overt moralizing but with moralizing on a certain system. The system assumes that its idea of goodness will be recognized or admitted on sight; that is, that there is something in man which immediately identifies and responds to the good. In opposition to Hobbes's theory of the selfishness of human nature, and to the doctrine of original sin as expounded by orthodox Christianity, English divines of the seventeenth century had emphasized man's natural aptitude to recognize and accept religious and moral truth. Man gets the truth by the light of nature and reason; in parallel fashion he enters into social relations through his innate feelings of sympathy and benevolence. Without fully developed philosophic interests, Cibber and Steele suggested this view of human nature in the drama as opposed to Restoration cynicism, and Addison and Steele in the *Tatler* and the *Spectator* expounded a similar doctrine. There may, of course, be different degrees of emphasis on natural goodness; man may still go wrong through natural defect or through the fault of society; his goodness may be conceived of as potential rather than actual, but there remains "a very solid respect for human nature, however it is distorted from its natural make by affectation, humor, custom, misfortune, or vice" (*Tatler,* No. 29). The presumption in favor of natural goodness became so strong that it largely determined the course of British ethical thought (see p. 133). Though different moralists inclined to emphasize reason, or feeling, or a special faculty called the moral sense, a natural compromise was to include reason, feeling, and the sense of beauty in one harmonious process which recognized, felt, and aesthetically approved the good. This is what Shaftesbury did, and though his philosophy is not to be considered by any means the source of sentimentalism, he offered an inclusive scheme which appealed to various interests and was adapted in various ways. As yet sentimentalism was not felt as a radical doctrine; it was eclectic and conciliatory. Its continued emphasis on reason and morals made it congenial to eighteenth-century minds. It was opposed by some tough-minded thinkers, notably Mandeville and Swift, who, admitting the desirability of an ideal of simple reason accepted by all men, denied in the light of the harsh facts about human nature that man was capable of living up to such an ideal. But very few pushed this anti-rational idea of man to an extreme; the satirist, who viewed many human actions with disapproval, and the sentimental optimist, who put the best construction on man's powers and inclinations, co-existed in this period, sometimes within the same individual.

Two tendencies appear about the mid-century: the satirist loses ground, and sentimentalism tends to give wider play to feeling, still professing to keep within the framework of the rational. In the work of Richardson, who is sometimes thought of as an arch-sentimentalist, the feelings are approved as far as they ratify a fairly rigorous code, which is thought of as rational, Christian, and conventional. Fielding objected to Pamela, not because she believed in the goodness of her own feelings, but because he thought she was insincere and hypocritical. He would have her trust to her unspoiled sense of right and wrong. Natural goodness, whether naïve as with Parson Adams, impulsive as with Tom Jones, or pathetic and long suffering as with Amelia, commands Fielding's admiration and sympathy. His broad and hearty humor should not be allowed to obscure his basic sympathy with sentimental doctrine.

The later development of sentimentalism is often described as an unbridled release of the tender feelings—sensibility or *sensiblerie* or *Empfindsamkeit*. In its increasing extravagance it divorces feeling from action, or else turns feeling loose in real life as a disruptive force. Sterne and Rousseau and Mackenzie are cited as classic examples. Yet the old pattern, the harmony of the moral, the aesthetic, and the rational, still remains. In the first place, the typical state of sensibility is self-conscious and self-approving; it is not overwhelming emotion or passion; it is indeed the endorsement of the doctrine that tender feelings are beautiful and good and that one ought to feel rather than sheer feeling itself. In the second place, even extreme sentimentalists indulge in considerable self-criticism; many would agree that the unrestrained delights of feeling are dangerous to the individual and to society. Hannah More in the verses called *Sensibility* expounds the orthodox doctrine that feeling is not in itself virtue, but given wisdom, reason, and true religion, "then Sensibility exalts the whole."

E. Bernbaum, *The Drama of Sensibility* (Boston, 1915); I. Babbitt, *Rousseau and Romanticism* (Boston, 1919); C. A. Moore, "Shaftesbury and the Ethical Poets in England, 1700-1760," *Publications of the Modern Language Association,* xxxi (1916). 264-325; R. S. Crane, "Suggestions toward a Genealogy of the Man of Feeling," *ELH,* 1 (1934). 205-30; W. F. Wright, *Sensibility in English Prose Fiction 1760-1814* (Urbana, 1937); G. G. Williams, "On Sentimentality," in *Readings for Creative Writers* (New York, 1938).

THE APPROACH TO THE NOVEL

>>

The most important development in English prose of the eighteenth century was the emergence of the modern novel. This is to be explained partly in terms of numerous antecedent and contributory literary forms, and partly also in terms of the new reading public created by the growing influence and literacy of the middle class. People whose grandparents had read little or nothing except a few religious works and popular chapbooks were now ready to buy and read prose fiction.

The antecedent forms may be roughly divided into *romantic* and *realistic*. Prose romance, derived ultimately from the medieval code of chivalry and courtly love, was still accessible to readers; Sidney's *Arcadia* and the French heroic romances of the seventeenth century (the works of Gomberville, La Calprenède, and Scudéry) were familiar before and after 1700. But such works were out of line with the tastes of an unheroic and increasingly bourgeois age. Shorter romances, purporting to be closer to real life and high life, were written by Mrs. Behn, Mrs. Aubin, and others. Mrs. Behn's famous *History of the Royal Slave, or Oroonoko* (1688) is an heroic and exotic piece of this kind. Stories on this scale were called "novels," and were often mere pieces of complicated intrigue and scandal. The reaction against over-artificial romance often leads writers into burlesque and anti-romance, one of the commonest roads to realism. There was some work of this kind at the end of the seventeenth century, but, falling far short of *Don Quixote,* it was too clumsy to lead far. Again, one might expect the refined analysis of motive and conduct in the romantic tradition to lead to psychological realism, and this actually happens in Mme de Lafayette's famous *Prin-cesse de Clèves* (1678), but England shows no such turn toward fiction at once analytic and aristocratic.

At the other end of the scale, realistic fiction, associated with the life of the lower classes, tended to remain coarse and sub-literary. An exception must be made of the intensely vivid realism of Bunyan's great allegories (see p. 56), yet Bunyan's work is in part an anticipation of rather than an influence on the later novel. Allied with anti-romance, the Spanish picaresque tradition, the fiction of roguery, was coherent and well established, but English imitation of this form (Kirkman and Head, *The English Rogue,* 1665-71) lacks humor and humanity. About on the same level were the criminal biographies so popular during this period. The central picaresque theme had undergone developments on the Continent which were to be of great importance for English fiction; the original scheme setting forth the adventures of a *picaro* (servant-rogue) might be modified to present the travel experiences of a young man, perhaps of good family, seeking his fortune, and this brings us close to Fielding and Smollett.

Without undertaking a formal definition of the novel, we can say that it entails a critical or analytical attitude toward characters represented under actual or conceivable social conditions. The critical attitude is directed toward both individual character and the social situation. As it appears in eighteenth-century fiction, it does not derive simply from the commentary on life to be found either in earlier romance or in low-life realism; it does not have the artificiality and fastidiousness of the one or the social irre-sponsibility of the other, but the sober practical outlook of the middle class. This outlook had a religious tinge and a strongly moral turn, but it was not daringly imaginative or intensely pious, as we see when we pass from Bunyan to Defoe. In other words, eighteenth-century fiction had to

be didactic and secular, not only to win the approval of
middle-class readers but to develop its own characteristic
criticism of life. For the development of this criticism, the
methods afforded by other literary forms were of great
importance. Tragedy and comedy offered an analysis of
character in action more powerful and penetrating than
almost anything earlier fiction had to show. The eighteenth-
century novel took the predominant place occupied by the
drama in earlier periods. The character-sketch extensively
practised in the seventeenth century, the new type of
periodical essay perfected by Steele and Addison, the letter-
form applied to fiction—all afforded means of combining
a formulation of social and moral standards with an analysis of character in action. This combination yields the
novel. It is perhaps unprofitable to argue just when the
type appears. If Defoe does not seem to us to be writing
novels, it is perhaps because he does not develop an elaborate analysis by means of the contributory forms. The
origins of Defoe's fiction are not entirely clear, but evidently he works on the model of fictional biography, the
"life and adventures" formula, with some indebtedness to
the picaresque, the criminal biography, and the travel
narrative, at the same time substituting for other possible
points of view (the irresponsibility of the picaresque, the
wonder and excitement of the travel story) a sober moralizing attitude derived from bourgeois conduct-books. He
does not seem to take lessons from drama, essay, or character-sketch in developing his characters. The greater preoccupation with the inner life of the characters, the finer
shades of personality, and the personal and social overtones
of episode to be found in Richardson and Fielding twenty
years later marks a step of crucial importance.

For fiction before 1740: F. M. Warren, *A History of the Novel
Previous to the Seventeenth Century* (New York, 1895); T. P.
Haviland, *The Roman de Longue Haleine on English Soil*

(Philadelphia, 1931); Charlotte Morgan, *The Rise of the Novel of Manners* (New York, 1911); A. J. Tieje, *The Theory of Characterization in Prose Fiction Prior to 1740* (Minneapolis, 1916); E. Bernbaum, *The Mary Carleton Narratives, 1663-1673* (Cambridge, Mass., 1914).

See also Defoe, pp. 152-53, and general references on the history of English fiction, p. 285.

SAMUEL RICHARDSON (1689-1761)

>>

Though Richardson happened to be born in Derbyshire, he was apprenticed to a London printer at the age of seventeen and spent the rest of his life as an industrious and prosperous city tradesman. His immediate background was much like Defoe's, but unlike Defoe he never sought material for fiction in travel and low life, but took as a starting point the life of the gentry, their servants, and the urban middle class. His literary beginnings were humble and, it may seem, drearily didactic. As early as 1733 he brought out a letter of advice which he had written to his nephew on taking him apprentice, along with other admonitions of the same kind, in a little book called *The Apprentice's Vade Mecum*. In 1739 he continued this kind of work, at the request of the booksellers Osborn and Rivington, by providing a volume of model letters. It was usual for letter-manuals to contain realistic sketches and much moralistic advice. One situation treated in these *Familiar Letters* was that of the servant girl "under temptation from her master," and so Richardson turned aside to complete the story of *Pamela, or Virtue Rewarded* (1740), which records in "letters written to the moment" how a virtuous serving maid is subjected to the outrageous advances of the clumsy Mr. B——, and is finally rewarded with his hand in marriage. The great success of *Pamela* was due to the com-

CLARISSA.

OR, THE

HISTORY

OF A

YOUNG LADY:

Comprehending

The most Important Concerns *of* Private LIFE.

And particularly shewing,

The D I S T R E S S E S that may attend the Misconduct
Both of P A R E N T S and C H I L D R E N,

In Relation to M A R R I A G E.

Published by the EDITOR *of* PAMELA.

V O L. I.

L O N D O N:

Printed for S. Richardson:

And Sold by A. MILLAR, over-against *Catharine-street* in the *Strand;*
J. and JA. RIVINGTON, in *St. Paul's Church-yard;*
JOHN OSBORN, in *Pater-noster Row;*
And by J. LEAKE, at *Bath.*

M.DCC.XLVIII.

TITLE-PAGE OF *CLARISSA,* FIRST EDITION

bination of a crudely familiar theme and a conventional code with a new technique which treated the thoughts and actions of the principal characters on an unprecedentedly elaborate scale, keeping at the same time to a simple central situation.

Pamela's moral code was justly criticized by other contemporaries beside Fielding, but Richardson's power of creating and analyzing character outlived the furor caused by his best seller in the early 1740's, and appeared to much greater advantage in his second and greatest novel *Clarissa* (1747-48), the somber story of a girl driven by the tyranny of her family into the power of the libertine Lovelace, who amid protracted intrigue and negotiation drugs and violates her, and then sues in vain for the privilege of redressing the wrong by marriage. Clarissa is a partly though not completely idealized character; her tragedy is somewhat weakened by monotonous pathos and religiosity, but the novel has strict unity, cumulative force, and high intensity; in his elaborate use of the letter form in the seven volumes of *Clarissa* Richardson records complexities and fluctuations of character and mood operating within the limits of the domestic code and the social system he knew. The character of Lovelace is relatively theatrical and artificial, but is conceived and executed with amazing energy. *Clarissa* was widely read as a melodramatic tale of active evil and injured innocence, and was enjoyed indiscriminately by the sentimental and the pious, but readers and critics of taste were right when they put the work, along with *Tom Jones,* at the head of eighteenth-century fiction.

Richardson's third novel, *Sir Charles Grandison* (1753-54), though much admired to the end of the century, has since been neglected and indeed underrated. He thought that his female readers were admiring Lovelace and Tom Jones too much, and wanted to set up a hero in opposition. The plan of presenting an ideal English gentleman, of high

birth, varied accomplishments, infinite tact, and flawless
character, discourages us at the outset. Instead of con-
centrating on this theme, however, Richardson diffuses
interest over varied groups of characters; if *Grandison* fails
as a drama, it is a skilful and at times brilliant narrative
of society on the drawing-room and country house level.
It seeks romantic variety also in the story of the Italian
heroine Clementina who finally, for religious reasons, gives
up Sir Charles to the English heroine Harriet Byron. The
aristocratic scene is at times handled awkwardly; Richardson has the middle-class impulse to climb, and by this time
is too far from the social setting he knew best. But *Grandison*
was a principal model for two generations of feminine
novelists, and can fairly be considered the ultimate source
of Jane Austen's art.

Richardson died in 1761, flattered to the last by his
admiring feminine coterie and aware of his growing fame
in France and Germany. His complacency and vanity,
especially his jealousy of his rival Fielding, show to poor
advantage in his voluminous correspondence. But we
should not allow his failings as a man to obscure his importance as a writer. When he began his work it might
seem that he would be hopelessly weighed down by his
prosaic mind and his didactic purpose. But didacticism led
him into psychology; he soon showed himself capable of
remarkably subtle analysis of character and manners, and
his moral and religious intentions did not cramp his style
as much as might be expected. He was capable of losing
himself in the exacting technical problems that confront
the artist. For two generations he was the most popular
English author on the Continent, and his influence fell in
with though it was not entirely identical with the sentimentalism of the age. The great epistolary novels of sentiment, Rousseau's *Nouvelle Héloïse* (1761) and Goethe's
Werther (1774) owe something, though not everything, to

SIR CHARLES GRANDISON RESCUES MISS BYRON
FROM HER ABDUCTOR
Drawn and engraved by Isaac Taylor, 1778.

Richardson. The elaborate scale of *Clarissa* and *Grandison* was not practicable for his followers, and one of the main problems of English fiction was to preserve some of the values of Richardson's work on a smaller scale by combining a lighter comedy of manners with his serious interest in character.

W. M. Sale, Jr., *Samuel Richardson: A Bibliographical Record* (New Haven, 1936); *Novels* (18v, Oxford, 1929-31; Shakespeare Head edition); *Correspondence*, ed. A. L. Barbauld (6v, London, 1804); *Familiar Letters on Important Occasions*, ed. B. W. Downs (London, 1928); A. Dobson, *Samuel Richardson* (London, 1902; English Men of Letters); B. W. Downs, *Richardson* (London, 1928); Paul Dottin, *Samuel Richardson, 1689-1761, imprimeur de Londres* (Paris, 1931); A. D. McKillop, *Samuel Richardson, Printer and Novelist* (Chapel Hill, 1936); "Samuel Richardson's Advice to an Apprentice," *Journal of English and Germanic Philology*, XLII (1943). 40-54; Erich Schmidt, *Richardson, Rousseau, und Goethe* (repr. Jena, 1924); J. Texte, *Jean Jacques Rousseau et les origines du cosmopolitisme littéraire* (Paris, 1895); F. H. Wilcox, "Prévost's Translations of Richardson's Novels," *University of California Publications in Modern Philology*, XII (1927), 341-411.

HENRY FIELDING (1707-1754)
>>

Fielding was a younger son in an aristocratic family, was educated at Eton and Leyden, and from 1728 to 1737 was one of the most active playwrights in London (see pp. 296-97). His birth, education, and knowledge of contemporary London literary and stage life contrast with the background of his great contemporary and rival Samuel Richardson. His early plays are only fair routine comedy, save for his lively vein of dramatic burlesque; he attracted much attention by his political satires at the Haymarket in the 1730's, and the Walpole government deliberately silenced

him by the Licensing Act of 1737. Hard pressed to make
a living, he turned to the study of law, conducted a periodical called the *Champion,* and then half by accident became
a great pioneer realist. As Bernard Shaw puts it with
pleasant exaggeration, "Fielding, driven out of the trade
of Molière and Aristophanes, took to that of Cervantes,
and since then the English novel has been one of the
glories of literature." The success of Richardson's *Pamela*
called forth censure and satire as well as indiscriminate
praise, and Fielding, who had already shown a strong turn
for burlesque, hit off the weakness of Richardson's moral
code, first in the broad satire called *Shamela* (1741, published anonymously, but certainly his), and then in the
incomparable *History of the Adventures of Joseph Andrews
and of His Friend Mr. Abraham Adams, Written in Imitation of the Manner of Cervantes* (1742). This story begins
with a burlesque account of the virtuous serving man Joseph
Andrews, who under temptation from Lady Booby, aunt
of Richardson's Mr. B——, emulates his chaste sister Pamela.
But with the entrance of the great comic character Parson
Adams the story takes a different turn; in a genial account
of adventures on the road Fielding shows the naïveté of the
guileless and pedantic Adams in contrast with a coarse and
selfish world. Widely versed in the works of Cervantes, Le
Sage, Scarron, and others, Fielding undertakes to construct
what he calls in his preface a "comic epic in prose." This
form, he explains, may be at times burlesque in manner
but not in content and purpose, which is to show human
nature in its actual operation in society, flawed by affectation (which derives from vanity and hypocrisy) and re-
claimed by generous and spontaneous impulse. The theory
of the comic epic would suggest a broad picture of the life
of the time, such as we have in *Don Quixote,* and Fielding
is capable of painting such a picture, but he usually con-
centrates on a satirical and analytical portrayal of human

nature. The broad humor and realism of *Joseph Andrews* should not conceal the seriousness of the novelist's underlying moral purpose. His satire is exceptionally bitter in *Jonathan Wild* (1743), an ironical portrayal of a heartless criminal as a "great man."

His program is at length fully realized in his masterpiece *Tom Jones* (1749). Here he is critical and self-conscious, and accompanies his story with interpolated essays, themselves masterpieces of prose, which furnish a running commentary on his methods and principles. Tom Jones, of supposedly mean birth, is loyal and manly, but imprudent and sensual; his errors give his hypocritical enemies a good chance to attack him. After he loses the favor of his generous benefactor Allworthy, he travels from Somersetshire to London, where his good name and his fortunes are endangered, and he is drawn into corrupt intrigue, but he regains the favor of Allworthy and wins the hand of the heroine Sophia Western. Thus Fielding rewards virtue. Richardson's conception of virtue is formal and calculating; Fielding's is based on the conception of a natural goodness which expresses itself imperfectly but spontaneously in the active life of the world. This notion of goodness would include such diverse characters as Parson Adams and Tom Jones; it would not include Pamela and would hardly apply to Clarissa, the victim of a tragic and insoluble dilemma. Richardson's work is often thought of as feminine, pathetic, and serious, Fielding's as masculine and comic. His invocation to Genius in *Tom Jones* shows

THE

HISTORY

OF

TOM JONES,

A

FOUNDLING.

In SIX VOLUMES.

By HENRY FIELDING, Esq;

——*Mores hominum multorum vidit.*——

L O N D O N:
Printed for A. MILLAR, over-against
Catherine-street in the *Strand.*
MDCCXLIX.

TITLE-PAGE OF
TOM JONES,
FIRST EDITION

that he aspires to work in the tradition of the great humorists: [1]

> Come thou that hast inspired thy Aristophanes, thy Lucian,
> thy Cervantes, thy Rabelais, thy Molière, thy Shakespeare, thy
> Swift, thy Marivaux, fill my pages with humor, till mankind
> learn the good nature to laugh only at the follies of others, and
> the humility to grieve at their own.

The best remembered character in *Tom Jones* is Squire Western, the incomparable portrait of a coarse, hard drinking Tory squire. Though Richardson had considerable realistic humor, he was incapable of creating such a character. Yet Richardson and Fielding have much more in common than would appear from a comparison which emphasizes the differences between *Clarissa* and *Tom Jones.* Both novelists present and test moral principles by showing characters under the stress and strain of difficult situations. Fielding admired *Clarissa,* and praised the book in the *Jacobite's Journal.* His last novel *Amelia* (1751, dated 1752) shows him moving toward Richardsonian pathos. To understand this change, it must be noted that Fielding, once a robust man of the town, had become a sober-minded magistrate and reformer, having been appointed Justice of the Peace for Westminster in 1748. He was seriously concerned with such matters as the crime wave of 1750, the liquor problem, legal aid for the poor, and the reorganization of the London police. His high spirits and humor subside, without being completely subdued; his genuine interest in religion and ethics becomes more prominent. Amelia, the heroine of his last novel, is married to a young lieutenant named Booth, as sensual as Tom Jones but less loyal and generous. His infidelities and follies subject her to a martyrdom which ends only with his conversion; the principal theme is the contrast between her saintly patience and the

[1] *Tom Jones,* Book XIII, Chap. i.

ugly vices of contemporary life. On the fly-leaf of her copy
Lady Mary Wortley Montagu wrote, "Inferior to himself,
superior to most others." The last of his periodicals was
the *Covent-Garden Journal* (1752). Fielding now suffered
a complete physical breakdown; he undertook a voyage to
Lisbon for his health and died there in 1754. He left a
record of this journey in the *Journal of a Voyage to Lisbon*
(1755).

Works (16v, London, 1903); (10v, Oxford, 1926; Shakespeare
Head edition); *Joseph Andrews,* ed. J. P. deCastro (London,
1929); *Covent-Garden Journal,* ed. G. E. Jensen (New Haven,
1915); *Selected Essays,* ed. G. H. Gerould (Boston, 1905); Austin
Dobson, *Fielding* (London, 1889; English Men of Letters); W. L.
Cross, *The History of Henry Fielding* (3v, New Haven, 1918); H.
K. Banerji, *Henry Fielding* (Oxford, 1929); B. M. Jones, *Henry
Fielding, Novelist and Magistrate* (London, 1933); A. Digeon, *Les
Romans de Fielding* (Paris, 1923), trans. *The Novels of Henry
Fielding* (London, 1925); F. T. Blanchard, *Fielding the Novelist*
(New Haven, 1926); E. M. Thornbury, *Henry Fielding's Theory
of the Comic Prose Epic* (Madison, 1931); F. O. Bissell, *Fielding's
Theory of the Novel* (Ithaca, 1933); G. Sherburn, "Fielding's
Amelia: An Interpretation," *ELH,* III (1937). 1-14; W. R. Irwin,
The Making of "Jonathan Wild" (New York, 1941).

TOBIAS GEORGE SMOLLETT (1721-1771)
>>

Smollett, the younger son of a Scottish laird, was born
in the valley of the river Leven, Dumbartonshire (between
Glasgow and Loch Lomond), and studied medicine at the
University of Glasgow. In 1739 he came to London, got a
post as surgeon's mate aboard the *Chichester,* and took
part in the disastrous Carthagena expedition (1741-42). He
returned for a time to Jamaica and married there, but soon
began the practice of medicine in London. Literature came
to be his chief interest and occupation, however, and after

publishing some conventional satires and trying in vain to get his tragedy *The Regicide* produced, he made an important place for himself among the pioneer novelists by publishing *Roderick Random* (January, 1748). A much younger man than Richardson and Fielding, he was thus in the field with them in the same decade. *Random* falls short of the power of structure and characterization shown in *Tom Jones* and *Clarissa,* but it reflects a shrewd, harsh, and forceful personality, and shows Smollett's grotesque humor and his turn for making literary copy of his experiences. He carries his Scottish hero and his man Strap through a series of adventures which go somewhat like his own early life in Scotland and the Navy, though, as he afterwards wrote, "the low situations in which I have exhibited Roderick, I never experienced in my own person." [1] He reverts to the loose structure of the picaresque, with Le Sage's *Gil Blas* as his model, though he is not content with the easy-going geniality of the picaresque tradition, because it "prevents that generous indignation which ought to animate the reader against the sordid and vicious disposition of the world." A succession of vivid scenes, often violent and brutal, present the seamy side of eighteenth-century life with characters drawn in the manner ·of the comedy of humors, that is, by sharp delineation of oddities and eccentricities. His method is swift and graphic, not analytical, and he deals largely with national, social, or vocational peculiarities (Scot, Irishman, sailor, lawyer, physician, old maid).

Peregrine Pickle (1751) follows the same method, carrying the grotesque to its height in the great portrait of Commodore Trunnion and his crew, adding personal satire and contemporary scandal, and using travel material drawn from one or more tours on the Continent. In *Ferdinand Count Fathom* (1753) the rascality of the hero shades into

[1] To Richard Smith, May 8, 1763. *Letters,* ed. Noyes, p. 80.

villainy, and the novelist seeks variety by extending adventure to include the sentimental and what was later called the "Gothic" (the appeal to terror).

At this point Smollett's work in the strictly picaresque form came to an end, and he turned for a time from fiction to multifarious literary hackwork. He had already translated *Gil Blas* (1749), and went on to translate *Don Quixote* (1755). From 1756 he was a principal editor of the *Critical Review,* a Tory periodical established in opposition to the Whig *Monthly Review;* his supposed responsibility for certain articles in the *Critical* involved him in serious personal quarrels, as did his editorship of the *Briton* (1762-63), an organ of Bute's Tory administration. Single-handed he wrote a once famous *Complete History of England* (1757-58) from the Tory point of view, and he was co-editor of a *Compendium of Voyages* (1756), the modern part of the huge *Universal History,* and the *Present State of All Nations* (1768-69). He also supervised an English translation of Voltaire. Except for *Sir Launcelot Greaves* (1760-61), an inferior imitation of *Don Quixote,* he wrote no fiction during this period. Much of this work was thankless, and left Smollett a disappointed man, though it did not break his spirit, as we may see from one of his letters: [1]

The public has been always a liberal patron to me since I commenced author. My difficulties have arisen from my own indiscretion, from a warm temper easily provoked to rashness, from a want of courage to refuse what I could not grant without doing injustice to my own family; from indolence, bashfulness, and want of economy.

In failing health, Smollett resided in France and Italy from 1763 to 1765, and recorded his experiences in his *Travels* (1766), curiously combining guide-book material with his own harsh and shrewd opinions and observations.

[1] To Dr. John Moore, August 19, 1762. Laing MSS, University of Edinburgh, II, 263. Cf. *Modern Language Notes,* XLII (1927), 231-35.

The Adventures of an Atom (1769) is a somewhat gross political allegory. From 1768 he took up permanent residence in Italy, and there he completed *Humphry Clinker* (1771). This is a landmark in English fiction, a masterpiece of humor and the last work published by one of the four major novelists of the age. The travels through England and Scotland of a family group centering about the humorous and eccentric Welshman Matthew Bramble are recorded in letters by various members of the party. As usual Smollett constructs the story not by analyzing a central situation but by accumulating vivid sketches, episodes, and miscellaneous bits of material. The travel-theme in *Clinker* owes much to his own travel experiences and use of travel-books, and, when he reaches Scotland, to the growing interest in local color and picturesque landscape, and to his patriotic enthusiasm. He still uses caricature, as in the sour spinster Tabitha and the grotesque Scot Lismahago, but his humor is softened by sheer fun and even by a playful and sentimental vein remarkable in a battered veteran of letters. In the dedication to *Fathom,* Smollett had defined the novel as "a large diffused picture, comprehending the characters of life, disposed in different groups, and exhibited in various attitudes, for the purposes of an uniform plan, and general occurrence, to which every individual figure is subservient." But in practice he treated the "uniform plan" in a perfunctory way, and emphasized the "diffused picture," the "different groups" and "various attitudes." He is largely responsible for the tendency in English fiction to shift the interest from the main plot to the incidental detail and comic relief. Thus his influence appears clearly in such major writers as Scott, Cooper, Marryat, and Dickens.

Novels (11v, Oxford, 1925-26; Shakespeare Head edition); David Hannay, *Life* (London, 1887; Great Writers); Oliphant Smeaton, *Tobias Smollett* (Edinburgh, 1897; Famous Scots Series); *Letters,* ed. E. S. Noyes (Cambridge, Mass., 1926); H. S. Buck, *A Study in*

Smollett (New Haven, 1925); L. L. Martz, *The Later Career of Tobias Smollett* (New Haven, 1942); C. E. Jones, *Smollett Studies* (Berkeley, 1942); G. M. Kahrl, *Tobias Smollett: Traveler-Novelist* (Chicago, 1945). [Biography in preparation by Lewis M. Knapp.]

LAURENCE STERNE (1713-1768)
>>>

Sterne was of an old Yorkshire family, the great-grandson of an archbishop of York. He was born at Clonmel, Ireland, where the regiment of his father, an ensign, was stationed, and his earliest experiences were of army life and of school-days in Yorkshire. After attending Jesus College, Cambridge, he took holy orders, held several small livings near York, and was also a prebend of the Cathedral. His uncle Jaques involved him in local politics and journalism on the Whig side, but for the most part he led a leisurely and aimless life in these early years, following his own whims and indulging a desultory interest in farming, hunting, painting, music, and books. His literary pursuits might be described by a word of his own, as "hobbies" rather than serious studies. Under the guidance of his college friend John Hall-Stevenson, whom he often met at "Crazy Castle," his reading turned toward the quaint and eccentric learning to be found in Burton's *Anatomy of Melancholy* and other more obscure works. In 1759 he published a satirical pamphlet called *A Political Romance,* later *A Good Warm Watchcoat,* in the manner of Swift, and the local success of this piece led him to begin *Tristram Shandy,* a work which occupied the rest of his life and into which he put all his literary skill, whimsical genius, and multifarious reading. *Shandy* was published in a series of nine volumes over a period of eight years (I-II, 1760; III-IV, 1761; V-VI, 1762; VII-VIII, 1765; IX, 1767). It was the literary sensation of

1760, and Sterne came up to London and became a literary
lion, following up his success with the publication of *Sermons of Mr. Yorick.* The years of his literary fame were
also years of increasingly serious illness, for Sterne was a
consumptive; for almost four years he resided and traveled
in France and Italy, partly for pleasure and partly in quest
of health. His travels yielded material for Volume VII of
Shandy and for the charming *Sentimental Journey through
France and Italy,* published in the year of his death, 1768.

The Life and Opinions of Tristram Shandy appealed to
the eighteenth-century interest in the burlesque and the eccentric by its erratic, unpredictable, whimsical movement, its
flouting of the conventions of orderly narrative and even
of decency. At first sight it seems to be a deliberate attempt
to turn all the rules topsy-turvy; Sterne declares that his
one rule is to be spontaneous and untrammeled. Thus we
never get to an ordered account of the life of the hero; he
is begotten but not born in the first volume; the narrative
proceeds by "progressive digressions," and the writer calculates that since it takes him a year to write four volumes
covering a day of his life, there is no reason why the book
should ever come to an end. But if we look more closely,
we find that Sterne is not merely breaking down the carefully planned models of Richardson and Fielding, but
making ingenious constructive use of current psychology
and ethics. Under the influence of Locke's psychology, he
studies the workings of the mind and takes an inventory of
its contents. To him the actual content of consciousness,
what passes through the mind of the character at a given
moment, and the accompanying reactions and gestures, are
of primary importance. Thus he changes the scale of his
narrative even more radically than Richardson had done
by his epistolary method, and lays even more stress on
"writing to the moment." Yet the fleeting impulses and
gestures are often organized into little episodes of formal

TRISTRAM PITIES THE POOR ASS

Tristram Shandy, Book VII. From *Beaulies of Sterne*, 1787.

pattern, with counterbalancing moods and skilful repetition of words and gestures to advance the action ("incremental repetition"). He is didactic in his sentimental emphasis on natural benevolence and philanthropy, but he does not dwell systematically on principles; he is much less abstract than Richardson and Fielding, and moralizes in such a light and playful way as almost to give a delicate caricature of moralizing. The eighteenth century would find his benevolism familiar, and also the group of humorous and grotesque characters who surround Tristram—Walter Shandy his father, with his pedantic ideas and systems, Uncle Toby, the old soldier who plays at military engineering and is full of naïve and quixotic benevolence, seconded by his faithful Corporal Trim. But the humor is irradiated with sympathy; the humorous character is regarded not as a ridiculous creature who departs from the standard of right reason but as a quaint exponent of natural goodness who moves us to sympathetic smiles and tears. Sterne carries farther than any writer before him the idea of mixed feelings. The whole paradox of man as a rational animal, which had aroused Swift's indignation and disgust, produces in Sterne various modes of mixed feeling, notably a vein of playful obscenity. There is some affectation, but great subtlety also, in his discovery of the proximity of the comic to the tearful, and the grotesque to the pathetic. These complex feelings fill his characteristic episodes, the famous sketches which are the best known parts of *Tristram Shandy* and the *Sentimental Journey*. No one, except perhaps Dickens, has succeeded fully in recapturing his special effects, but he has had a surprisingly great influence on later English novelists.

Works (7v, Oxford, 1926-27; Shakespeare Head edition); *Tristram Shandy*, ed. J. A. Work (New York, 1940); W. L. Cross, *Life and Times of Laurence Sterne* (3rd ed., New Haven, 1929); *Letters*, ed. L. P. Curtis (Oxford, 1935); L. P. Curtis, *The*

Politicks of Laurence Sterne (London, 1929); H. Read, *The Sense of Glory* (Cambridge, 1929); W. C. Watkins, "Yorick Revisited," in *Perilous Balance* (Princeton, 1939); T. Baird, "The Time Scheme of *Tristram Shandy,* and a Source," *Publications of the Modern Language Association,* LI (1936). 803-20; L. Hartley, *This is Lorence* (Chapel Hill, 1943).

THE LATER NOVEL

>>

Though the minor fiction of the second half of the century can be roughly classified as epistolary, feminine, and sentimental, of the school of Richardson, or robust and humorous, of the school of Fielding and Smollett, there was much interweaving and combination. A dominantly Richardsonian novel of merit, such as Frances Sheridan's *Sidney Bidulph* (1761, revised and expanded 1767) is exceptional. *Tom Jones* and *Clarissa* were too long and complex to serve as practicable models. Stereotyped characters and situations were presented in more facile style and were expected to call forth stock responses; the reader could instantly identify the suffering heroine, the seducer, the harsh parent, the selfish rich man, the deserving poor man, the faithful servant. Plots and devices from Richardson and Fielding were repeated on a smaller scale. The influence of Marivaux' *Marianne* was especially clear in the minor feminine novel. Prévost's pervasive influence will be considered later. Most of this fiction was written by obscure hackwriters or sometimes by mediocre amateurs, read indiscriminately by patrons of circulating libraries, and viewed with contempt by the critics.

Fanny Burney (1752-1840). In the 1770's Fanny Burney succeeded in blending the Richardson and the Fielding traditions, adding a special quality of feminine sensitiveness and cleverness. The daughter of a prominent musician, she set down her varied observation of manners both in her diary and her novels. After secretly writing *The History of Carolyn Evelyn* and destroying the manuscript, she won great success with the story of that heroine's daughter, *Evelina,* published anonymously in 1778. This highly readable story combines devices drawn from the great novelists with the freshness of a young girl's point of view. The plot is negligible; the best parts are those in which the heroine makes the rounds of London places of amusement and is embarrassed by vulgar relatives and presuming fops. *Evelina* was much admired by Dr. Johnson, Mrs. Thrale, and their associates. *Cecilia* (1782) is much longer and more serious; it heaps misfortunes on the devoted heroine, and while it shows more power has far less spontaneity and playfulness. Miss Burney became a keeper of robes in the Queen's household, married a French refugee named d'Arblay, and published two more novels, *Camilla* (1796) and *The Wanderer* (1814). Historically she stands as a representative of the best qualities in the innumerable obscure feminine novelists of the late eighteenth century, and she may be regarded as a link between Richardson and Jane Austen. Her *Diary and Letters 1778-1840,* first published 1842-46, and her *Early Diary 1768-1778,* first published 1889, are biographical and social records of the greatest interest.

THE NOVEL OF SENTIMENT

Sentimentalism, we have seen, was closely tied up with the moral purpose which was necessary to get analytical fiction under way. The novel gave a fuller opportunity for this analysis than the drama, and in the hands of great writers like Richardson, Fielding, and Sterne, sentimentalism led to a subtler psychology, but no sooner were sentimental views widely diffused than they encouraged novelists, dramatists, and poets to take short cuts to quick

and easy effects. As has been said, it was not generally felt
that social and rational controls could be abandoned for
the charms of sensibility. Sterne's position is extreme, and
yet his playful exaltation of impulse and feeling is an artistic device rather than a program for life; we get the impression that sensibility is a mood or tone which colors the
mind and society. The system is given, and then sensibility
plays over it. Though Goldsmith did not admire Sterne,
we may say the same thing of the free play of humor and
sentiment in *The Vicar of Wakefield* (1766). The novels of
the young Scottish advocate Henry Mackenzie (*The Man
of Feeling*, 1771; *The Man of the World*, 1773; *Julia de
Roubigné*, 1777) are considered the most sentimental in
the language, a reputation which he earned by his first and
most successful book. Though he imitates Sterne's methods,
he swings from delicately sentimental effects to violent
melodrama. Yet Mackenzie is capable of pointing out the
dangers of an over-sensible heart. This ambiguity of sentimentalism, its disposition to dwell on both the dangers
and delights of feeling, is one of its most characteristic
features. It appears in the great continental novels of sensibility, in Rousseau's *Nouvelle Héloïse* (1761), which begins
by presenting sympathetically the claims of passion in the
account of the love affair of Julie and her tutor St. Preux,
and then, after marrying Julie to the philosophic Wolmar,
dwells on the merit of restraint and renunciation; and in
Goethe's *Werther* (1774), which describes sympathetically
the hopeless passion of the hero and his suicide, but which
could be interpreted also as an example of the evils of
excessive sensibility.

The various applications of the sentimental doctrine of
natural goodness to the problems of education (Rousseau,
Emile, 1762; Henry Brooke, *The Fool of Quality*, 1765-
1770; Thomas Day, *Sandford and Merton*, 1783-1789) criti-
cize the rich and fashionable, and develop natural piety

and altruism by carefully planned devices. To assert in earnest the rights of the sentimental rebel, the man who pits his intuitions against tradition, is to be a revolutionary. A few English novelists, notably William Godwin and Thomas Holcroft, came close to this point in the last decade of the century, in the heated atmosphere created by the French Revolution, but underlying English conservatism checked this development, and English sentiment did not find its outlet in political action.

GOTHIC AND HISTORICAL ROMANCE

The new vein of Gothic and historical romance is also connected with sentimentalism in the broad sense of an appeal to the feelings. It tried to get its effects by an appeal to the sense of the sublime and the picturesque, as well as to the softer feelings of pity and sympathy. The theory of the appeal to terror as a source of the sublime had already been formulated in Burke's *Enquiry into the Origin of our Ideas of the Sublime and Beautiful* (1757); the association of the marvelous and the supernatural with the Middle Ages was enthusiastically recognized in Hurd's *Letters on Chivalry and Romance* (1762) (see p. 366). In Thomas Leland's *Longsword, Earl of Salisbury* (1762), a historical romance of the time of the Crusades, and in Horace Walpole's *Castle of Otranto* (printed 1764, published 1765), which presents supernatural events in a medieval setting in southern Italy, we have examples classified respectively as historical and Gothic. The sub-title of *Otranto* is *A Gothic Story,* and later "Gothic romance" was taken to denote a narrative devised to arouse terror by suggestion or presentation of the supernatural, but this aspect can scarcely be separated from the historical side of Gothic, and it is not profitable to keep a sharp distinction between two kinds of fiction here. The movement does not begin with *Otranto,* a curious and somewhat special manifestation

Garrick's first appearance on the London stage. The Licensing Act of 1737, intended to restrict the production of plays to Drury Lane and Covent Garden, was not completely enforced, but no doubt narrowed the field. Provincial theaters and strolling companies became more common in the second half of the century.

The physical theater and the methods of production changed very slowly. What has been said of the structure of the Restoration theater largely holds good for the following century. Characters were often "discovered" by opening flat sets, but the curtain was not regularly used between acts. The fashionable members of the audience sat in the boxes, side or front, on the stage itself, or even at times in the orchestra-pit ("music room"), and the gallants went behind the scenes into the "green room." Garrick finally succeeded in getting the spectators off the stage in 1763, except for benefit performances. After-money, reduced admission for the last two acts, was taken until the 1780's, and stimulated the development of the after-piece. The audiences slowly grew better behaved. Attempts were made to exclude masked prostitutes early in the century. There were the usual complaints about the behavior of the fashionable part of the audience, but more serious trouble usually started among the occupants of the pit and among the servants in the upper gallery. Garrick's importation of French dancers for his unsuccessful Chinese Festival led to bad disturbances in 1755, and the attempt to abolish after-money in 1763 led to one of the worst outbreaks of the century (see illustration, p. 291). The pit gradually became more fashionable, and was thought to contain the most discriminating part of the audience. In the middle gallery (pit balcony) were average middle-class citizens, in the upper gallery the unruly rabble and the servants. Prologues and epilogues sometimes addressed the different parts of the house:

You relish satire [to the pit]; *you* ragouts of wit [the boxes];
Your taste is humor, and high season'd joke [first gallery];
You call for hornpipes, and for Hearts of Oak [second gallery]!
  (Garrick's Epilogue to Murphy's *All in the Wrong*, 1761)

Performances regularly began at six; since places were not reserved in advance, the gentry and well-to-do citizens sent footmen early to hold their seats. Others came early themselves and scrambled for places. Both theaters were remodeled near the end of the century to accommodate larger audiences.

London eighteenth-century life would be unthinkable without the theater, yet it was chiefly an age of prominent actors, not of creative dramatic genius. Controversies about the immorality of the stage died down, though evangelical prejudice against the theater persisted. But after 1700 the drama no longer consistently enlisted the best writers. Nevertheless, competent playwrights were fairly well paid, and a successful play could get a writer fame and money. Aspiring dramatists, even if rank amateurs, found it not very hard to get their plays produced, though there was much complaint against Garrick and other managers on that score. The dramatist's profit came from the benefit performance on the third night, and with luck the sixth and ninth nights; he had to guarantee expenses on these occasions, and even at times to hawk tickets. Plays were popular reading matter, and publication rights of successful pieces were of considerable value—apparently about £100 in the 1730's. But many favorite entertainments, such as operas and pantomimes, were non-literary or sub-literary. The dramatists often complained that spectacular scenic effects were what the public really wanted.

The emergence of great actors, their careers and their rivalries, largely determined dramatic history and stimulated dramatic criticism. The stage inherited from the Restoration a heavy and declamatory style of acting in tragedy,

and a genteel and sophisticated or else broadly farcical
style in comedy. Different styles seem to be indicated for
actors and actresses; the most popular serious plays called
for gravity and pomp in the masculine rôles, for elevated
pathos in the feminine. Betterton was the great exponent
of the established style for the tragic actor at the beginning
of the century, and Booth and Quin carried on the tradition. But a more natural and realistic style came to be
favored. Thus Aaron Hill's *Prompter* (1734) attacked Quin's
formality, and called for a more delicate and sensitive expression of the passions; and similarly Churchill's *Rosciad*
(1761) satirically described Quin:

> His eyes, in gloomy socket taught to roll,
> Proclaimed the sullen habit of his soul.
> Heavy and phlegmatic he trod the stage,
> Too proud for tenderness, too dull for rage.

Garrick brilliantly realized the new style and applied it to
both tragedy and comedy, ranging from a new interpretation of the serious rôles in the Elizabethan and Restoration
repertory to polite comedy and broad farce. An admiring
contemporary remarked that other actors were much the
same in all their parts: Booth was always the philosopher,
Cibber always the fop, but Garrick realized a different
personality in each rôle. Macklin's Shylock and Garrick's
Richard III marked the advent of this imitation of nature
by the actor. This meant emphasis on gesture and impersonation rather than declamation. Yet interest in declamation persisted, indicated in the mid-century by Thomas
Sheridan's teaching of rhetoric and elocution, and eventually a more formal grand style was favored, exemplified
in the late eighteenth century by John Philip Kemble and
his sister Mrs. Siddons.

As to costume, the traditional plume of feathers and full
wig for tragic heroes, the truncheon for kings and generals,

the black wigs and chalked faces for murderers and con-
spirators were retained. Tragedy queens swept the stage in
black velvet gowns with a train carried by a page. For the
rest, actors donned such second-hand finery as they could
get, much of it taken from the theater's stock wardrobe.
Costume was more sumptuous during the age of Garrick,
but there was still no consistent effort to dress characters
with historical correctness. Characters in plays with classical, medieval, or oriental settings might appear in strange
robes or inappropriate armor. Yet Cato or Hotspur might
wear a wig, Macbeth a fashionable waistcoat and breeches.
Macklin's Scottish costume in *Macbeth* (1773) and Garrick's
"old English" costumes in *Lear* (1776) marked a period in
which greater verisimilitude in costume was developing,
along with an interest in more elaborate pictorial effects.
The stage finally responded to the new romantic interest
in landscape, local color, and antiquities.

While there were no drastic changes in the structure of
the stage, important developments came after the first third
of the century. In addition to flat scenes, drop-scenes and
later box-scenes came to be used. An act-drop (painted
curtain dropped between acts) was in use by 1760. Doors
in the back scenes now made possible entries otherwise than
through the proscenium doors. The lighting had been
mainly by large chandeliers above the stage, which could
be raised or lowered, but footlights were in use by 1735.
In 1765 Garrick brought over from France a new system
of lighting, in which strong illumination from the wings
made it possible to do away with the chandeliers. This just
preceded a development of elaborate settings by the Alsa-
tian Philippe Jacques de Loutherbourg, who did important
work for Garrick in the 1770's. The elaborate effects of
opera and pantomime had long been dear to London play-
goers, but changing taste called for detailed realism and
at the same time for romantic, picturesque, and grandiose

effects. De Loutherbourg showed new possibilities in perspective and lighting, and now for the first time producers offered elaborate representations of exotic and wild landscapes, ruins, and magnificent buildings. The two principal

THE STAGE OF COVENT GARDEN

Note the stage boxes, behind them the proscenium doors with balconies above, the chandeliers above the stage, the musicians' pit, the allegorical statues of Comedy and Tragedy. From a print representing a scene in the half-price riots of 1763. A performance of Arne's *Artaxerxes* is being interrupted by the rioters.

theaters were enlarged at the end of the century so as to accommodate about 3500 spectators each, and this encouraged the spectacular in setting and the declamatory in acting.

Bibliography, see below.

TRAGEDY

The theory of tragedy was a principal part of the neo-classical critical heritage, but tragedy, like the other grand form epic, failed in practice. The swelling rhetoric of the heroic play established a strong tradition: "Declamation roared while passion slept." Young's *Busiris* (1719) and *The Revenge* (1721) show how far a respectable poet could go in this direction, which easily lent itself to the burlesque of Carey and Fielding (see p. 296). Nor could tragedy be saved by the disciplinary power of neo-classical controls. Ambrose Philips's *Distrest Mother* (1712), adapted from Racine's *Andromaque,* and Addison's *Cato* have more dignity than vitality. *Cato* observes the classical rules, though not with extreme strictness; its regularity makes it almost unique among successful English plays. Thomson's *Sophonisba* (1730), following *Cato,* reduces a love and honor theme to a somewhat tame interplay of reason and passion.

The pathetic vein of Otway and Rowe was associated with Shakespearean imitation and with developing sentimentalism. Tragedy fostered sentimentalism when it put a stronger emphasis on the appeal to pity and on the response to such an appeal as a test of virtue. As Pope's prologue to *Cato* puts it, the tragic muse commands "tears to stream through every age," and Britons are adjured to "show you have the virtue to be moved." Sentimentalism found a less exacting mode of expression in comedy, yet it did produce an important innovation in serious drama, the prose bourgeois tragedy of Lillo, Johnson, and Moore, with later important results on the Continent in the work of Lessing and Diderot.

Nicholas Rowe (1674-1718). Rowe, a young barrister of the Middle Temple, appeared in 1700 as a likely successor to Dryden and Otway in tragedy. He was not a needy bohemian playwright but a dignified man of letters, a friend of the Augustan wits. His *Tamerlane* (produced 1701, published 1702) was a vehicle of Whig sentiment, and was long played on the anniversary of William's landing. Rowe's politics won him patronage under George I, and he was made poet laureate in 1715. He wrote only one unsuccessful comedy; all his important contributions are in serious drama. Heroic trappings were being exchanged for domestic themes and rhetorical moralizing, a more direct appeal to the sympathies of a middle-class audience, and sentimental moods and effects found their way at first more easily into tragedy than into comedy. In the dedication to his first play, *The Ambitious Step-Mother* (1700), Rowe argues that tragedy, while it should arouse terror, should make its chief appeal to pity, "a sort of regret proceeding from good nature," and adds, "It was this passion that the famous Mr. Otway succeeded so well in touching." In *The Fair Penitent* (1703), an adaptation of Massinger and Field's *Fatal Dowry,* he scored his first great success. Like Otway's *Orphan,* this play deals with the woes of a private family instead of "the fate of kings and empires"; in the seduction of the fair Calista by the "gay Lothario," whose name became proverbial, he presented the first of his "she-tragedies." This play and its most important successor *Jane Shore* (1714), "written in imitation of Shakespeare's style," provided favorite rôles for eighteenth-century actresses, and remained in the standard repertory. A less important she-tragedy was his *Jane Gray* (1715). Dr. Johnson explains that Rowe's popularity came from "the reasonableness and propriety of some of his scenes, from the elegance of his diction, and the suavity of his verse." Rowe was also the first modern editor of Shakespeare (see below, p. 310) and his translation of Lucan's *Pharsalia* (1718) was widely read.

George Lillo (1693-1739). Lillo was a London jeweller of Dutch extraction who had some small part of the gift of Defoe and Richardson for putting pedestrian bourgeois matter into significant literary form. He evidently acquired some literary background; he had considerable familiarity with earlier English drama, and an adaptation of *Arden of Feversham* shows that he was interested in Elizabethan domestic tragedy. After a trivial ballad-opera *Silvia* (1730), he scored a great success with *The London Merchant, or The History of George Barnwell* (1731). In stiff prose dialogue which still shows the influence of blank verse Lillo here tells the story of the apprentice who was driven by his infatuation for the harlot Millwood to rob his master and kill his uncle, and was finally led repentant to the gallows. He took this traditional city theme from a broadside ballad. Hogarth's *Industry and Idleness* tells a parallel story, and not long afterwards a contemporary moralist, almost certainly Samuel Richardson, praised the play as the only instance "where the stage has condescended to make itself useful to the City youth." [1] For many years *The London Merchant* was regularly acted at Christmas or Easter as a warning to the young. Lillo's middle-class setting and his clumsy moralizing went straight to the heart of his public. With no poetry or subtle psychology, he made a sentimental appeal by dwelling on Barnwell's youthful innocence and edifying repentance. His crude originality appears also in his remarkable verse-tragedy *Fatal Curiosity* (1736), the story of the return of young Wilmot, who is entertained as an unrecognized guest by his poverty-stricken parents, and murdered by them for his money. The bitterness of poverty and the somber pride of the elder Wilmot are well portrayed; the atmosphere is gloomy and fatalistic, Stoic rather than Christian. Lillo was admired by Richardson and Fielding, and imitated on the Continent by Diderot (*Le Père de Famille*), Lessing (*Miss Sara Sampson*), and others. Though he had followers in England (Charles Johnson, *Caelia*, 1732), and Edward Moore (*The Foundling*, 1748; *The Gamester*, 1753), his influence tends either to revert to the sub-literary level of the chapbook and broadside ballad, or to be taken up into the more elaborate sentimental effects of the novel.

[1] *The Apprentice's Vade Mecum* (London, 1734), p. 16.

References for tragedy: C. C. Green, *The Neo-Classic Theory of Tragedy in England during the Eighteenth Century* (Cambridge, Mass., 1934); Rowe, *The Fair Penitent and Jane Shore*, ed. S. C. Hart (Boston, 1907); *Three Plays: Tamerlane, Fair Penitent, Jane Shore*, ed. J. R. Sutherland (London, 1929); A. Jackson, "Rowe's Historical Tragedies," *Anglia*, LIV (1930). 307-30; E. Bernbaum, *The Drama of Sensibility* (Boston, 1915); F. O. Nolte, *The Early Middle Class Drama, 1696-1774* (Lancaster, 1935); Lillo, *The London Merchant and Fatal Curiosity*, ed. A. W. Ward (Boston, 1906).

COMEDY

The age was disposed to view man, not in his ultimate struggle with the world as presented by the imagination and the will, but in his transaction of everyday affairs in a social context. When a great writer like Swift takes both points of view, the result is puzzling. The effect was to favor comedy, and to further the attempt to make comedy edifying. At the same time stage tradition was strong; Restoration modes persisted; rakes continued to swagger and fine ladies to coquet; much of the surface play of life in town encouraged at least the affectation of cynicism and flippancy. Under these conditions, the rate of progress of the reformation of manners in comedy is stated differently by different historians. If we classify Farquhar as a Restoration dramatist, we find that his work is softened by moral scruples (see above, p. 81). If we call Cibber a moral reformer, we find that his attitude toward sex relations is often flippant. Mrs. Susanna Centlivre's comedies of intrigue (*The Busy Body*, 1709; *A Bold Stroke for a Wife*, 1718) set forth farcical complications with Restoration irresponsibility, though not with intellectual keenness. Thus Belair exclaims in her *Love at a Venture* (1706): "Oh, the pleasure of intrigue; it finds employment for every sense, sharpens the wit, and gives a life to all our faculties." Even when she writes about the evil of gambling (*The Gamester*,

1705; *The Basset Table,* produced 1705, published 1706) she deals with a situation, not a moral. She may be taken as illustrative of the interest in varied, realistic, and amusing episode which appears strongly in Vanbrugh, Farquhar, and Steele. The devices of humors, complicated intrigue, broad farce (with abundant gags by popular comedians), satirically exaggerated comment on the life of the town—all could still be used. But in seeking pure entertainment, "making an audience merry," comedy lost a controlling idea or purpose. In the long run the chief form of control came to be the moralizing and sentimental. To get a balanced view, however, we should consider all the current entertainments, and avoid the idea that the stage was given over mainly to the triumph of sentiment.

Fielding's dramatic career is interesting in this connection. He was the most active writer of comedy from 1728 to 1737; he did pieces in the man-about-town Restoration style (*Love in Several Masques,* 1728; *The Temple Beau,* 1730; *The Modern Husband,* 1732; *The Universal Gallant,* 1735), but also turned to farce from Molière (*The Mock Doctor,* 1732; *The Miser,* 1733), and to plays of specific satiric purpose (*The Coffee House Politician,* 1730; *The Old Debauchees,* 1732). His most characteristic work, however, was in the short piece devoted to burlesque of current drama and to political satire. Such were *The Author's Farce* (1730), the popular *Tom Thumb* (1730), and *The Covent-Garden Tragedy* (1732). For the three-act enlargement of *Tom Thumb* as *The Tragedy of Tragedies* (1731), Fielding added elaborate annotation, a device taken from Swift and Pope. The tradition of Buckingham's *Rehearsal* lies back of this work, and, in the foreground, the success of *The Beggar's Opera* had stimulated burlesque. Henry Carey's *Chrononhotonthologos* (1734) is another amusing burlesque of pompous tragedy. From 1736 Fielding had his own company at the Haymarket, and here appeared his daring anti-Walpole burlesques, *Pasquin* (1736) and *The Historical Register* (1737). The government then passed the Licensing Act of 1737; Fielding's company was put out of business, and he had to turn to law, journalism, and prose fiction. No one can tell whether Fielding's unwritten comedies would have gained in depth and significance, but his career as it stands shows the divergence between popular dramatic entertainment and serious literature. His work is also important for the history of the after-piece: there was an increasing demand for short pieces to end the evening's entertainment—pantomime, satirical burlesque, or farce. In the next generation Samuel Foote's after-pieces and David Garrick's were notable. James Townley's *High Life below Stairs* (1759) is an excellent example. In Garrick's programs a still shorter piece, the interlude, might come between the principal play and the after-piece. From 1728, the year of *The Beggar's Opera* and Fielding's first piece, ballad opera, burlesque, farce, and pantomime threw regular comedy into the shade. But the chief reason for the decline of the comic spirit is usually said to be the rise of the drama of sentiment or sensibility. Here Cibber and Steele occupy key positions.

Colley Cibber (1671-1757). Colley Cibber was the son of Caius Gabriel Cibber, a sculptor of some importance (see *Dunciad*, I, 31-32). He began as an actor in the Drury Lane company, and heralded the reform of comedy with his successful *Love's Last Shift* (1696). Cibber was not a consistent moralist, though the drift was in the direction of the reformation of manners. He was interested in pleasing the audience and providing good acting parts. In *Love's Last Shift* he took the part of Sir Novelty Fashion, a ridiculous fop derived from Etherege's Sir Fopling Flutter and Crowne's Sir Courtly Nice. When Vanbrugh wrote his amusing and cynical *Relapse,* describing how the reformed Loveless of *Love's Last Shift* goes back to his old ways,

Cibber played the rôle of Lord Foppington, which became traditionally his own. Of this period he wrote in characteristic sprightly fashion: "It may be observable too that my muse and my spouse were equally prolific, that the one was seldom the mother of a child but in the same year the other made me the father of a play." [1] His most important play is *The Careless Husband* (1704). Here his favorite theme of the unfaithful husband is treated with a more

subtle blending of genteel dialogue and virtuous sentiment; Sir Charles Easy's natural virtue is brought out when the infinitely patient Lady Easy forgives his infidelities. A famous scene is that in which Lady Easy finds Sir Charles and her maid asleep in two chairs, and silently withdraws, leaving her "steinkirk" (neckcloth) as a gentle reproach. The duel of the sexes in Restoration comedy is here turned into semi-serious discussion of the problems of married life, and the middle-

CIBBER AS LORD FOPPINGTON

class domestic theme appears, yet the play did not have the stuffy didacticism of the bourgeois, but was considered for a century a classic of polite comedy. Cibber took up the theme again in *The Lady's Last Stake* (1707) ; here the main plot deals with the reconciliation of an incompatible couple by the good offices of one Sir Friendly Moral. Cibber had a long and varied career as actor-manager, and for a generation took a prominent part in the direction of Drury Lane. Other historically important pieces of his were an adaptation of *Richard III* (1700) which after initial failure

[1] *Apology* (2nd ed., London, 1740), Chap. viii, p. 217.

held the stage for over a century, and the Whig *Non-Juror* (1717). *The Provoked Husband* (1728), a completion of Vanbrugh's unfinished *Journey to London,* shows in Cibber's additions the increasing seriousness of stage moralizing.

Cibber's Whig connections got him the laureateship in 1730, and he was much derided in that office. But despite the ill-will of dissatisfied actors and dramatists, the accumulation of literary, political, and personal jealousies, and the misdeeds of his notorious children Charlotte and Theophilus he was unabashed to the last. From the time when he had 	ade fun of *Three Hours after Marriage,* an ill-starred far. by Pope and Gay, he was regarded as an enemy by Pope and was attacked again and again, though he did not answer in kind until shortly before the appearance of the final version of the *Dunciad* (October, 1743), in which Cibber inappropriately replaced Theobald as the hero. Theatrical feuds dating from the 1730's also made Fielding his enemy. Cibber set down a personal record and preserved much important theatrical history in his *Apology* (1740), which Fielding thereupon derided (along with *Pamela,* of course) in *Shamela* and *Joseph Andrews.* Long after Cibber retired from Drury Lane he continued to take an active part in the life of the town.

STEELE'S PLAYS

Steele's contribution to sentimental comedy was more characteristic and decisive than Cibber's. He put much of his personality into his plays. *The Funeral* (1701) is clear of indecency, and shows Steele to be a reformer of manners; it shows too his interest in a fresh sympathetic presentation of character, and in odd and amusing situations. This, as has been noted, parallels changes manifest in the atmosphere and spirit of Farquhar and Mrs. Centlivre. *The Lying Lover* (1703) was intended to "show just regard to a reforming age"; Steele presents an amusing rake, from Corneille's *Le Menteur,* who reforms after a duel in the last act.

Though the pattern is much like Cibber's, the morality is more pervasive; decency and virtue are exalted without cynicism, and there is a more radical appeal to "generous pity." The pleasant *Tender Husband* (1705), though it bestows easy forgiveness on a repentant rake and recommends domestic morality, is best remembered for its fresh and natural humors, as in the romance-reading Biddy Tipkin and the yokel Humphry. This proves to be an important development; throughout the century, from Sir Roger de Coverley to Sterne's Uncle Toby and beyond, it will be seen that sympathetic coloring can be used to vivify and vary the comedy of humors. Long afterwards Steele produced in his *Conscious Lovers* (1722) his most important though not most enjoyable play. His natural humorous bent is here checked by pervasive moralizing, by the idealization of delicacy in conduct. The central character Bevil is a fine gentleman who exemplifies virtue and utters noble sentiments throughout the play, and who attains moral heights in his refusal to fight a duel. Here at last is the full display in social relations of man's natural goodness, the exact counterpoise of eighteenth-century satire. *The Conscious Lovers* was the archetype of comedy turned to formal moralizing; Parson Adams in Joseph Andrews approved *Cato* and *The Conscious Lovers* because each was as good as a sermon.

English comedy, 1700-1750: F. W. Bateson, *English Comic Drama, 1700-1750* (Oxford, 1929); Henry Fielding, *Tragedy of Tragedies,* ed. J. T. Hillhouse (New Haven, 1918); D. F. Smith, *Plays about the Theatre in England* (New York, 1936); D. M. E. Habbema, *An Appreciation of Colley Cibber* (Amsterdam, 1928); D. Senior, *Life and Times of Colley Cibber* (New York, 1928); R. H. Barker, *Mr. Cibber of Drury Lane* (New York, 1939); Cibber, *Apology,* ed. R. W. Lowe (2v, London, 1889); Steele, *Plays,* ed. G. A. Aitken (London, 1894); Leo Hughes, "The Influence of Fielding's Milieu upon his Humor," *University of Texas Studies in English (1944).*

PANTOMIME AND OPERA

The favor of the public was easily won by entertainments other than dramatic—by opera, ballad-opera, pantomime, ballet, sub-literary farce, and other performances as miscellaneous as vaudeville acts. The Restoration had enjoyed productions in which song, dance, and scenic effect overshadowed dramatic interest, and called these pieces "operas." But from the time of Queen Anne Italian opera took the taste of the town, and singers and composers (Handel and Buononcini) were serious rivals of actors and dramatists. There are many contemptuous references to Italian opera by such writers as Dennis, Addison, and Steele. Handel's *Rinaldo* (1711) made him the leading figure in the field. Grand opera did not occupy so important a place later in the century, though Arne's *Artaxerxes* (1762) was a great success, and the operas of Metastasio, from whom Arne took this piece, were very popular. It would be almost impossible to exaggerate the effect of *The Beggar's Opera* (1728). For ten years numerous imitations appeared, checking the production of regular ·drama, but no one repeated Gay's success. Isaac Bickerstaffe, however, inaugurated a new period of light opera in the 1760's with *Love in a Village, The Maid of the Mill,* and *Lionel and Clarissa.* Sheridan's *Duenna* (1775) was a last great hit of this kind, but that quarter of the century saw innumerable operettas, burlettas, and the like, with varied combinations of comedy, music, dancing, and scenery. Charles Dibdin's popular songs were an important part of this chapter in the history of musical entertainment.

The public enjoyed "turns" between the acts and afterpieces following the regular play. We have noted that the demand for after-pieces put a premium on burlesque and farce, and thus modified the development of comedy. A similar demand stimulated the development of pantomime.

This was the specialty of John Rich at Lincoln's Inn Fields from 1724 and at Covent Garden from 1732. The vogue began in 1723, when Thurmond produced *Harlequin Dr. Faustus* at Drury Lane, and Rich a rival *Necromancer, or Harlequin Dr. Faustus*. A typical pantomime was in two parts, one treating a historical or mythological theme, the other centering about the comic pranks of Harlequin. Both parts had dancing, music, and spectacular scenic effects, especially "transformations," sudden changes wrought by Harlequin as magician. This kind of entertainment was so popular that admission prices were raised on pantomime nights. Arthur Murphy gives a good brief description of the pantomime: [1]

A Gothic taste has taken possession of the public. Nature is banished. We give credit to the magician's wand, and harlequin's wooden sword. The seasons are confounded together.... all climates are presented before us; heaven and hell appear; good angels and evil demons meet; the trap doors open; Pluto rises in flame-colored stockings; and this monstrous chaos makes the supreme delight of an enlightened nation.

Charles Burney, *General History of Music* (2v, repr. New York, 1935), Book IV, Chap. vi, "Italian Opera in England"; N. Flower, *George Frederic Handel* (Boston, 1923); H. Langley, *Doctor Arne* (Cambridge, 1939); E. M. Gagey, *Ballad Opera* (New York, 1937); E. L. Avery, "Dancing and Pantomime on the English Stage, 1700-1737," *Studies in Philology*, XXXI (1934). 417-52; "The Defense and Criticism of Pantomimic Entertainments in the Early Eighteenth Century," *ELH*, v (1938). 127-45.

LATER TRAGEDY

In tragedy dull formal plays were accepted and produced by both houses, no doubt because they were thought to give actors important opportunities in serious parts. Voltaire's tragedies were popular, especially as translated by

[1] *Gray's Inn Journal*, No. 76, March 30, 1754. Cf. *Rape of the Lock*, IV, 42-45; *Dunciad*, III, 233-48; *Tom Jones*, v, i.

Aaron Hill (*Zara*, 1736; *Alzira*, 1736; *Merope*, 1749). Remote classical and foreign themes prevailed; in spite of the example of Lillo and Moore, a direct treatment of contemporary life did not develop in tragedy. Moore's *Gamester* (1753) has a somber power superior to Lillo, but is crude in its contrast of villainy and virtue. The treatment of the somewhat similar situation of erring husband and forgiving wife in Fielding's *Amelia* shows how the novel was coming to surpass the drama. Middle-class tragedy could go no farther than Richardson's *Clarissa*. The fine acting of Shakespearean rôles by Garrick and some of his best contemporaries no doubt gave the mid-century its truest experience of stage tragedy.

John Home's *Douglas* (produced at Edinburgh 1756, at London 1757, published 1757) aroused much excitement because it was written by a Scottish Presbyterian clergyman; historically it marks the point where tragedy is directly affected by pre-romantic poetry; the ballad source (*Child Maurice*), the localized setting, the pervasive pathos and sentimental treatment of fate give this play some poetic as well as dramatic value. But the romantic coloring of the serious play was later connected with the growing interest in spectacular scenery and in what was called the "Gothic": here we may put Walpole's *Mysterious Mother* (1768), Jephson's *Count of Narbonne* (1781, a dramatization of *The Castle of Otranto*), and numerous other stage versions of the Gothic novels in the 1790's. This kind of play, combined with music and scenic effects, came to be called *melodrama* or *melodrame* from about 1802. It was of more theatrical than literary importance.

LATER COMEDY

Comedy failed to amuse and to offer important characterization at the same time. This appears even in the successful comic pieces of Fielding and Garrick. Serious characterization in comedy came to be the province of the sentimentalists. As we have seen, the drama of sensibility had a mixed inheritance from Cibber and Steele. In Cibber there was an attempt to blend virtue with the genteel and the witty; in Steele virtue was blended with the humane, the pathetic, and the bourgeois. The Cibberian blend persisted, and was important both for comedy and prose fiction, but there is deeper significance in what Steele had to offer. As Mr. F. W. Bateson puts it, the real center of gravity in this movement is humanitarian, a new interest in a sympathetic and vivid presentation of character.[1] This was fully realized in the *Spectator* essay and the novel rather than in comedy. The novel accustomed the public to more vivid characterization and more elaborate moralizing, and then exerted a reflex influence on the drama, eventually producing extreme examples of sensibility on the stage. Meanwhile, under English influence, the work of Destouches appeared in France in the 1720's and the fully developed *comédie larmoyante* of La Chaussée in the 1730's. The genial treatment of character as it appears in eighteenth-century literature at its best was here sacrificed to a didactic cult, as it had before been sacrificed to the cynical Restoration code.

There were almost no important new English comedies from the middle 1730's to about 1760; most notable were Hoadly's *Suspicious Husband* (1747), with the rake Ranger as one of Garrick's principal parts, and Moore's *Foundling* (1748), directly influenced by Richardson. The dominant comic type was a refined or softened play on the Restoration model, or else a short piece dependent for its effect on mimicry and farce. Aside from Garrick, Samuel Foote and Arthur Murphy were chief exponents of the short piece. Foote was a remarkable mimic who unscrupulously caricatured individuals on the stage. His farces are of little

[1] *English Comic Drama, 1700-1750*, pp. 9-11.

literary value, but they hit many current fads and modes
(*Taste,* 1752; *The Author,* 1757; *The Patron,* 1764; *The
Englishman in Paris,* 1753; *The Minor,* 1760; *The Mayor
of Garratt,* 1763). Important full-length comedies, not
serious, appear about 1760: Macklin's *Love à la Mode*
(1759), and *The True-Born Scotchman* (produced at Dublin
1764, prohibited at that time in England, later produced
as *The Man of the World,* 1781), and two admirable comedies by George Colman, *The Jealous Wife* (1761) and *The
Clandestine Marriage* (1766, in collaboration with Garrick),
the latter one of the great hits of the period. Colman's
short pieces, beginning with *Polly Honeycombe* (1760), are
often fresh and effective. The workmanlike Arthur Murphy
showed competence both in short pieces (*The Apprentice,*
1756; *The Upholsterer,* 1758; *The Citizen,* produced 1761,
published 1763), and in full-length comedies (*The Way to
Keep Him,* 1760; *Know Your Own Mind,* 1777). Evidently
the public was not insisting on the tearful and the edifying,
but a turn in that direction appeared in the 1760's, when
we have Whitehead's *School for Lovers* (1762), a superior
comedy which owes something to Richardson's novels and
to the refined analysis of sentiment in French drama, and
Mrs. Sheridan's *The Discovery* (1763). These markedly
sentimental plays were produced by Garrick, even though
he protested against the mode. Hugh Kelly's *False Delicacy*
(1768), which Garrick brought out in opposition to Goldsmith's *Good Natured Man,* shows the movement reaching
its peak; the play has the ambiguity of much sentimental
moralizing; false delicacy or sentimental over-refinement
is dangerous, and characters are introduced to warn against
it, but the charms of true delicacy are also presented. Here,
as in Kelly's *School for Wives* (1773), sentimentalism criti-
cizes itself. Its influence is felt in the cultivation of scrupulous and fastidious characters, "self-tormentors," even in
plays not classed as sentimental, notably Beverley in

Murphy's *All in the Wrong* (1761) and Faulkland in Sheridan's *Rivals* (1775).

In the drama, however, sentimentalism did not lead to sustained analysis, but to facile emotionalism and the quest for quick and easy effects. Richard Cumberland's first comedy, *The Brothers* (1769), combines this vein of sentiment (extreme benevolence versus foiled and finally repentant villainy) with a tangled plot. In *The West Indian* (1771) he presents a good rake or corrigible libertine in connection with a varied presentation of social types. He undertook to show the good side of the nabob, and later of the Scot (in *The Fashionable Lover*) and the Jew, in the play of that name. In Cumberland the analytical power of sentimentalism is lost; he goes in for emotional short-cuts and rapid action; hence a type of play develops which we should now call melodrama, in Holcroft's pieces and the translations from the German of Kotzebue—*The Stranger, Lovers' Vows,* and Sheridan's *Pizarro*. The true comedy of manners was thus eclipsed.

It is against this background that the brilliant comedies of Goldsmith and Sheridan should be considered. It had long been Goldsmith's view that nature and humor, unjustly stigmatized as "low," should override the refinements of sensibility; his was the humane realism of Steele. This did not exclude a touch of sentimental sympathy for the errors of a generous heart, as in *The Good Natured Man* (1768). In 1773 Goldsmith gave his views in the *Essay on the Theatre; or, a Comparison between Laughing and Sentimental Comedy,* and put them into practice in *She Stoops to Conquer.* If Goldsmith is opposed to sentimental excess he also keeps clear of the Restoration vein of satire and drawing-room wit; like Steele, he shows a personal enjoyment of his own fun and a preference for homely circumstance. Goldsmith's great contemporary in comedy, Richard Brinsley Sheridan, is much closer to the Restoration; indeed, in his brilliant early years (*The Rivals,* 1775; *The School for Scandal,* 1777) he moved rapidly toward the ideal of a Restoration comedy purged of offense. This program is further illustrated by his remaking of Vanbrugh's *Relapse* as *A Trip to Scarborough* (1777) and his brilliant reapplication of the methods of *The Rehearsal* in *The Critic* (1779). His work can be described in terms of the Cibberian ideal, not hitherto fully realized on the stage, of polite virtue and triumphant wit reconciled with the reformation of manners. He was also affected though not infected by the mode of extreme delicacy and *sensiblerie,* especially in the Faulkland-Julia plot of *The Rivals.* By the end of the decade he dominated Drury Lane and the London stage. His success was unchallenged, yet the forces allied with sentimentalism were too strong to make a prolongation of this triumph possible. The social poise represented by the comedies of Goldsmith and Sheridan could not be maintained, and the framework of the best eighteenth-century comedy could not sustain the strains and stresses of the age of the French and the American revolutions.

For later comedy: M. M. Belden, *The Dramatic Works of Samuel Foote* (New Haven, 1929); H. L. Bruce, *Voltaire on the English Stage* (Berkeley, 1918); J. P. Emery, *Arthur Murphy* (Philadelphia, 1946); H. H. Dunbar, *The Dramatic Career of Arthur Murphy* (New York, 1946); E. R. Page, *George Colman the Elder, 1732-1794* (New York, 1935); J. F. Bagster-Collins, *George Colman the Younger, 1762-1836* (New York, 1946); W. A. Kinne, *Revivals and Importations of French Comedies in England, 1749-1800* (New York, 1939); S. T. Williams, *Richard Cumberland, his Life and Dramatic Works* (New Haven, 1917); Sheridan, *Plays and Poems,* ed. R. C. Rhodes (3v, Oxford, 1928); *Plays,* ed. I. A. Williams (London, 1926); *Major Dramas,* ed. G. H. Nettleton (Boston, 1906); *The Rivals,* ed. R. L. Purdy (Oxford, 1935); W. S. Sichel, *Sheridan* (2v, London, 1909); R. C. Rhodes, *Harlequin Sheridan* (Oxford, 1933).

See also Goldsmith, p. 340.

David Garrick (1717-1779). Garrick's early days are associated with Samuel Johnson's career; he was one of Johnson's few pupils in the school at Edial, and together they came from Lichfield to London in 1737. Garrick made his first stage appearance at Ipswich in 1741, and in that same year scored a great triumph in *Richard III* at Goodman's Fields. His new and natural mode of acting and his versatility marked an epoch in stage history. After seasons at Dublin and Covent Garden he became co-manager at Drury Lane in 1747, and was thereafter for a generation the domi-

GARRICK

nant figure of the English theater. No great new dramatists were appearing, and Garrick depended largely on a repertory based on the work of Elizabethan and later generations. Shakespeare was his mainstay, and he became the great interpreter of the tragic rôles of Macbeth, Lear, and Hamlet. His Shakespearean productions were far from faithful to the originals: thus he adapted Tate's notorious version of *King Lear*, and while he added some of the comedies and tragicomedies to the standard repertory (e.g., *Much Ado, The Taming of the Shrew, The Winter's Tale*), they were drastically altered. He was not a pioneer in the mid-century Shakespearean revival, though he was its most brilliant representative.

Space fails to record Garrick's triumphs in tragic and comic parts. His was an art of impersonation, and he was endlessly praised for "that truth of imitation, which he had displayed in the higher characters of tragedy, and in the

lower personages of comedy; as well in Lear, Macbeth, and
Hamlet, as in Sir John Brute, Kitely, and Abel Drugger." [1]
He produced many mediocre plays, and had to comply with
the current taste for sentimental comedies and miscellaneous entertainments. Of the last the most notable example
was the Shakespeare Jubilee of 1769. As a manager he incurred the ill-will of certain authors and actors, and he had
some of the egotism and sensitiveness of the man who lives
on praise and publicity; but in general his wit and intelligence won him the friendship of his great contemporaries.
He is, of course, one of the principal figures in Boswell's
Life of Johnson; his correspondence, not yet fully collected
and edited, is of great interest; he was a facile writer of
prologues, epilogues, and impromptu verse. As an author
his importance is secondary, but he did good work in short
farces and after-pieces, some of them adapted from the
French (*Lethe,* 1740; *The Lying Valet,* 1741; *The Guardian,*
1759; *Bon Ton,* 1775), and he collaborated with Colman in
one excellent comedy, *The Clandestine Marriage* (1766).

Private Correspondence, ed. J. Boaden (2v, London, 1831-32);
Pineapples of Finest Flavour [unpublished letters], ed. D. M.
Little (Cambridge, Mass., 1930); P. Fitzgerald, *Life of David
Garrick* (rev. ed., London, 1899); F. A. Hedgcock, *A Cosmopoli-
tan Actor, David Garrick and His French Friends* (New York,
1912); *Three Farces,* ed. L. B. Osborn (New Haven, 1925); *Three
Plays,* ed. E. P. Stein (New York, 1926); E. P. Stein, *David Gar-
rick, Dramatist* (New York, 1938).

SHAKESPEARE IN THE RESTORATION AND THE EIGHTEENTH CENTURY

Ever since Shakespeare's own day his fame and influence
have been of high importance for the English stage, English
poetry, and English criticism. He was always admired and
enjoyed, though changes in literary taste, especially dislike
of the extravagant Elizabethan poetic style, led great critics

[1] *Gray's Inn Journal,* No. 65, Jan. 12, 1754.

like Dryden to make reservations. The neo-classical insistence on the rules, pushed to an extreme in Thomas
Rymer's violent attacks on Shakespeare (*The Tragedies of
the Last Age Considered,* 1678; *A Short View of Tragedy,*
1693) seems to have been of little practical importance. Yet
the neo-classical idea that literature should be scholarly,
rational, and formal kept up Ben Jonson's reputation
among the literati, partly at the expense of Shakespeare.
In their influence on the Restoration drama, Jonson and
Beaumont and Fletcher were more obviously effective than
Shakespeare. It should be remembered that until the eighteenth century Shakespeare's plays were often produced
in mangled form. Among the more notorious of these
versions were the Davenant-Dryden *Tempest* (1667), a
distorted operatic piece; Otway's *Caius Marius* (produced
1679, published 1680), a remaking of *Romeo and Juliet;*
Tate's atrocious *King Lear* (1681), omitting the Fool and
adding a love affair between Edgar and Cordelia and a
happy ending. Shakespeare truly lived in the rôles of the
great actors, notably in Betterton's Hamlet and later in
Garrick's performances. Faulty though some of the acting
versions were, Shakespeare was acted more often in the
eighteenth century than in later times. When Garrick began
his career, some twenty to twenty-five of the plays were in
repertory, more than half in unaltered versions.

The eighteenth century supplied practicable editions of
Shakespeare to a larger and larger reading public. Rowe's
edition (1709) provided a biographical sketch, indicated
places of scenes as well as scene divisions, added stage direc-
tions, and gave lists of dramatis personae. Pope's rival Lewis
Theobald was the first to pay attention to the readings of
old editions, though his collations were not full. Pope and
Warburton played the old game of emending and improving. Johnson showed scholarship and good judgment, col-
lated texts, and wrote sensible and sometimes definitive

notes. By this time the new interest in antiquarian studies and in English literary history was bringing a vast amount of material to bear on Shakespeare, and we finally reach the learned editors of the end of the century, George Steevens and Edmond Malone. The old question about Shakespeare's learning, long debated in terms of the stock contrast between the untutored Shakespeare and the bookish Jonson, was now discussed with a greater knowledge of the Elizabethan background and of his actual sources (Richard Farmer, *Essay on the Learning of Shakespeare,* 1767).

The stock neo-classical objections, that Shakespeare violated the unities, confused the genres by mixing tragedy and comedy, committed breaches of decorum in characterization and diction—these never seriously impaired his great reputation in England. He remained the supreme example of natural genius. Many echoed Dryden's praise of his fidelity to nature, his infinite variety in sentiment and characterization, his power over the passions. His diction and his power of dramatic construction were in general underrated. But, in the critical tradition of Longinus *On the Sublime,* the beauties were judged to outweigh the faults. The famous prefaces of Pope and Johnson are both in this tradition. But with the advance of pre-romantic ideas Shakespeare often becomes the archetype of the romantic poet. His supernatural beings are particularly admired as "Gothic"; thus Mrs. Montagu says of *Macbeth,* "Here are opened new sources of terror, new creatures of fancy." Voltaire's attacks on the barbaric Shakespeare called forth patriotic defence (Mrs. Elizabeth Montagu, *Essay on the Writings and Genius of Shakespeare,* 1769). When his faithfulness to nature is praised, it is traced in more detail. The critics of the mid-century, like Joseph Warton in his *Adventurer* papers, want to get away from "general criticism" and to examine characters and motives more closely. Johnson's praise described Shakespeare's command of character as a presentation of types. The newer criticism, as in William Richardson's *Philosophical Analysis and Illustration of Some of Shakespeare's Remarkable Characters* (1774 and later editions) began with the familiar principle of the "ruling passion," by which individuals can be subsumed under types—Richard III, for example, under "lust for power." But, psychology goes on to point out, the ruling passion is complicated by subordinate passions. The character in Shakespeare is then studied as if he were a complex individual in real life. The idea of the character as a unique individual and an objective reality is reënforced by the idea of the dramatist as a creative genius. Thus the new psychological criticism is not merely analytical; it is closely connected with ideas of original genius and creative imagination. It reached a new high point in Maurice Morgann's *Essay on the Character of Falstaff* (1777), but continued to extend itself and to make larger philosophical claims in the criticism of the romantic period, notably in the famous pronouncements of Coleridge.

Hazelton Spencer, *Shakespeare Improved* (Cambridge, Mass., 1927); G. C. D. Odell, *Shakespeare from Betterton to Irving* (2v, New York, 1920); T. R. Lounsbury, *Shakespeare as a Dramatic Artist* (New York, 1901); A. Ralli, *History of Shakespearian Criticism* (2v, London, 1932); D. N. Smith, ed., *Eighteenth Century Essays on Shakespeare* (Glasgow, 1903); *Shakespeare in the Eighteenth Century* (Oxford, 1928); R. B. McKerrow, *The Treatment of Shakespeare's Text by His Earlier Editors, 1709-1768* (London, 1933); R. W. Babcock, *The Genesis of Shakespeare Idolatry, 1766-1799* (Chapel Hill, 1931); H. S. Robinson, *English Shakespearean Criticism in the Eighteenth Century* (New York, 1932); D. Lovett, *Shakespeare's Characters in Eighteenth Century Criticism* (Baltimore, 1935); A. C. Sprague, *Shakespeare and the Actors* (Cambridge, Mass., 1944); Herschel Baker, *John Philip Kemble* (Cambridge, Mass., 1942).

General references for eighteenth-century drama: A. Nicoll, *A History of Early Eighteenth Century Drama, 1700-1750* (Cambridge, 1925); *A History of Late Eighteenth Century Drama, 1750-1800* (Cambridge, 1927); Ernest Bernbaum, *The Drama of Sensibility* (Boston, 1915); F. O. Nolte, *The Early Middle Class Drama 1696-1774* (Lancaster, 1935); H. S. Wyndham, *The Annals of Covent Garden Theatre* (2v, London, 1906); D. MacMillan, ed., *Drury Lane Calendar, 1747-1776* (Oxford, 1938); *Larpent Plays in the Huntington Library* (San Marino, 1939); C. H. Gray, *Theatrical Criticism in London to 1795* (New York, 1931); A. S. Downer, "Nature to Advantage Dressed: Eighteenth-Century Acting," *Publications of the Modern Language Association*, LVIII (1943). 1002-37; L. B. Campbell, "The Rise of a Theory of Stage Presentation in England during the Eighteenth Century," *Publications of the Modern Language Association*, XXXII (1917). 163-200; P. J. Crean, "The Stage Licensing Act of 1737," *Modern Philology*, XXXV (1938). 239-55.

General references for drama, 1660-1789: G. H. Nettleton, *English Drama of the Restoration and Eighteenth Century 1642-1780* (New York, 1914); J. Doran, *Annals of the English Stage*, rev. R. W. Lowe (3v, London, 1888); K. Mantzius, *A History of Theatrical Art*, trans. von Cossel, v (London, 1909); J. Genest, *Some Account of the English Stage ... 1660-1830* (10v, Bath, 1832); A. Thaler, *Shakespeare to Sheridan* (Cambridge, Mass., 1922); A. H. Thorndike, *English Comedy* (New York, 1929); *Tragedy* (Boston, 1908); S. Rosenfeld, *Strolling Players and Drama in the Provinces, 1660-1765* (Cambridge, 1939); Dorothy Canfield (Fisher), *Corneille and Racine in England* (New York, 1904); R. G. Noyes, *Ben Jonson on the English Stage, 1660-1776* (Cambridge, Mass., 1935); La Tourette Stockwell, *Dublin Theatres and Theatre Customs* (Kingsport, Tenn., 1938).

POLITICAL HISTORY (1760-1789)
>>>

With the first ministry of Pitt and the accession of George III the English eighteenth century becomes less inert and stable; new successes and failures in imperial policy abroad, violent political excitement at home, far-reaching changes in industry and agriculture which transform the national economy give a new and more dramatic color to the age.

At the beginning of his long reign (1760-1820) George III tried to govern in person, by the exercise of his royal prerogative; he wanted ministers and a Parliament that would do his bidding. This can be called Tory doctrine, the attempted realization of Bolingbroke's conception of a "patriot king" who should really lead his people; it was a program theoretically possible under the constitution, as long as the King did not force a completely unacceptable government upon the nation. George II had delegated his powers to Whig ministers who produced parliamentary majorities by patronage and bribery; the King was now to be his own first minister. Many Englishmen were ready, in Goldsmith's words, to "flee from petty tyrants to the throne." Jacobite Tories like Johnson were now disposed to accept the exercise of the royal prerogative by a Hanoverian monarch. But in real life the King's government, whether called Whig or Tory, still had to use ministers to create parliamentary majorities. Furthermore, George did not have the imagination and political intuition to lead his country, even though he said that he "gloried in the name of Briton" [or Britain]. For the great leader Pitt he substituted the unpopular Scotsman Lord Bute (1762), and later, after a series of ministerial failures, the subservient Lord North (1770-1782). In the 1760's the political crisis was dramatized by the unscrupulous demagogue John Wilkes. His campaign against Bute, culminating in an attack on the King in his periodical the *North Briton* (1763), led to his expulsion from the House of Commons and his repeated reëlections by his Middlesex constituency. He was opposed by Smollett, Hogarth, Johnson, supported by the satirist Churchill and by other more responsible men like Pitt and Burke. At the height of the excitement about Wilkes and the new Toryism, the writer "Junius" attacked the government and the King in the most famous series of political invectives in English history (see p. 351).

The British colonization of America had been tremendously successful; the fringe of colonies along the Atlantic coast had been growing rapidly, prospering in trade, and developing the traditions of English liberty to such a point as to make difficult further economic and political subservience to the mother country. At this point the Tory ministry precipitated a crisis with America which undid the work of Pitt and threatened to break up the Empire. The Grenville ministry, by passing the Stamp Act (1765), raised the issue of "taxation without representation"; though the Act was soon repealed, the right of Parliament to tax the colonies was reaffirmed, and the Townshend Act (1767) imposed a tax on tea, paper, glass, and paints. Both Burke and Pitt opposed this unwise policy, though on different grounds. But the opposition during these crucial years was never able to organize for effective political action; Pitt could never coöperate with Burke's group, the Rockingham Whigs. The American War of Independence (1775-1783) ran its course; the intervention of France made the situation difficult and finally impossible for Britain. In 1778 Pitt, now Earl of Chatham, still called in his dying words for a policy that would consolidate the colonies within the framework of the Empire. As far as we can speak in terms of parties, Tory opinion was against America, Whig and dissenting opinion in favor of America. The effect of Cornwallis's surrender at Yorktown was to undermine the King's political position.

A government headed by Rockingham was succeeded by the Shelburne government in 1782. But the various Whig factions, though they all professed to hold to the principles of 1688 (liberty, toleration, parliamentary rule) could not pass from lofty generalities to concerted action. This was true even of the greatest Whig of all, Edmund Burke. In 1783 occurred the famous coalition of Lord North, identified with George III's discredited system, and Charles James Fox, who had been the most aggressive of opposition Whigs. This cynical piece of politics led by reaction to the great ministry of William Pitt the Younger, who became prime minister in his twenty-fifth year. Party lines and responsible cabinet government had now taken shape, with prime minister and cabinet acting as a single political unit. Pitt was the head of a new Tory party, conservative, nationalistic, interested in efficient government and in guaranteeing constitutional rights and liberties, but not primarily in social reform. A student of Adam Smith's *Wealth of Nations,* Pitt was a firm believer in individual enterprise and free trade. Given a free hand, he would have put through a series of moderate liberal reforms: he was disposed to correct such abuses as the slave trade, the archaic and unjust system of parliamentary representation, and the injustices imposed by law on the Irish and the Catholics. But his party took shape in opposition to the new democratic movements represented by and stimulated by the French Revolution. Liberals turned reactionary, and reform in England was postponed until the nineteenth century. Burke, without any violent change, now found himself in

TRIAL OF WARREN HASTINGS IN WESTMINSTER HALL

the Tory rather than the Whig camp. Charles James Fox as naturally found himself committed to opposition, that is, to an ardent defense of revolutionary principles. In spite of his factious and irresponsible behavior, much modern English liberal tradition stems from Fox. But popular rule was still far distant; the populace could express its views only by mob violence, as in the anti-Catholic Gordon riots of 1780.

On the eve of the French Revolution England was principally excited by the impeachment of Warren Hastings for graft and cruelty in his administration of Indian affairs. This was a last spectacular outburst of political oratory in the grand style, with Burke, Fox, and Sheridan taking leading parts. The temporary insanity of George III in 1789 raised the question of a regency; the Prince of Wales, the future George IV, was as usual in opposition, and Fox was his political colleague and champion. The opposition maintained that the Prince should automatically succeed to the regency; Pitt argued for the power of Parliament to appoint the regent. George III recovered, to find himself more popular than ever before despite his personal peculiarities, and thus the great body of English sentiment and opinion may be described as predominantly conservative and Tory to the end of the century.

Leo Gershoy, *From Despotism to Revolution, 1763-1789* (New York, 1944); L. B. Namier, *The Structure of Politics at the Accession of George III* (2v, New York, 1929); *England in the Age of the American Revolution* (London, 1930); G. O. Trevelyan, *The Early History of Charles James Fox* (London, 1881); *The American Revolution* (3v, in 4, New York, 1899-1907); *George III and Charles Fox* (2v, London, 1912-14); B. Williams, *The Life of William Pitt, Earl of Chatham* (2v, New York, 1913); B. Tunstall, *William Pitt, Earl of Chatham* (London, 1939); Lord Rosebery, *Pitt* (London, 1891); J. H. Rose, *Life of William Pitt* (2v, London, 1934); D. G. Barnes, *George III and William Pitt* (Stanford University, 1939); R. Coupland, *The American Revolution and the British Empire* (London, 1930); O. A. Sherrard, *Life of John Wilkes* (London, 1930); G. Nobbe, *The North Briton* (New York, 1939).

See also above, p. 93, references to Robertson, Petrie, Feiling.

General references for the history of the period 1660-1789:

Cambridge History of the British Empire, I: *The Old Empire from the Beginnings to 1783* (Cambridge, 1929); *Cambridge Modern History* (12v, New York, 1909-10), V-IX; *Catalogue of Prints and Drawings in the British Museum*, Division I: *Political and Personal Satires* (6v, in 7 parts, London, 1870-1938); C. R. Cheney ed., *Handbook of Dates for Students of English History* (London, 1945); B. Dobrée and others, *From Anne to Victoria* (London, 1937); Hans Kohn, *The Idea of Nationalism* (New York, 1944); Louis Kronenberger, *Kings and Desperate Men* (New York, 1942); W. E. H. Lecky, *History of England in the Eighteenth Century* (7v, repr. New York, 1921); A. T. Mahan, *The Influence of Sea Power upon History, 1660-1783* (Boston, 1890); R. B. Mowat, *England in the Eighteenth Century* (London, 1932); E. Malcolm-Smith, *British Diplomacy in the Eighteenth Century, 1700-1789* (London, 1937); M. A. Thompson, *Constitutional History of England, 1642-1801* (London, 1938); T. Wright, *Caricature History of the Georges* (London, 1904).

AUTHORS, PATRONS, AND PUBLIC
>>

There were important changes in the relation of authors to patrons and public during the century after 1660. We may distinguish three types of author at the beginning of the period: (*a*) the gentlemanly or aristocratic amateur; (*b*) the humble hack writer without literary or social pretensions; (*c*) the able man of letters who depended on the approval of powerful patrons and a discriminating public. Class (*a*) declines in importance. Class (*b*) becomes more important with the further development of journalism and pamphleteering and a general increase in the demand for edifying and entertaining reading. It evolves into a large group of professional writers who still carry the stigma of being needy scribblers. It peoples the lines of Pope's *Dunciad*, and is the basis for stories about starving writers in Grub Street garrets (see Hogarth's *Distressed Poet* and illustration, below). But too much has been made of the accounts of the struggles of Johnson, Savage, Goldsmith, and others.

A GRUB-STREET WRITER IN HIS GARRET
From John Bancks, *Miscellaneous Works*, 1739.

The demand in Grub Street was not merely for political pamphlets and timely satires. Religious works predominated in the booksellers' lists, and to this extent many of the clergy were professional writers. To didactic manuals the eighteenth century added compilations (cyclopedias, histories, travel collections, dictionaries) as among the most profitable projects, and a large group of writers, from Smollett and Goldsmith down, were engaged in such works. Such men were also likely to write for magazines and reviews. An act of 1710 gave copyright to the author of a new work, or his assignee, for a period of fourteen years, renewable for fourteen more. This seems to have worked to the advantage of the bookseller (as publisher) rather than the literary journeyman, but talent could nevertheless lift men out of the rank and file.

Class (c) represents an aristocracy of talent on which the attention of the literary historian is concentrated. Here belong most of the great names up to the middle of the eighteenth century—Dryden, Swift, Pope, Addison, Steele. These men wrote for the élite, and they sought not merely the gifts and perquisites of patronage, but an association with the magnates of the age on friendly terms. They were professionals in varying degrees, but did not wish to be considered mere authors. Publication by subscription instead of by sale of copy (that is, copyright) to a bookseller became common from the late seventeenth century on. Though the device was used by literary beggars, it was also used by prominent writers seeking a broader basis for patronage, e.g., in the publication of Prior's *Poems* of 1718 and Pope's Homer.

After the Revolution patronage combined personal and political motives, and came largely from the great Whig lords: thus Dorset befriended Prior and Addison; Somers, Locke and Addison; Halifax, Addison and Congreve. The alignment of the writers of the age of Queen Anne with Whig and Tory is well known (see pp. 87-88). Walpole's lack of interest in the literary élite has been mentioned, and his policy of subsidizing obscure journalists. This put the rising generation of writers into the Opposition, and patronage in the second quarter of the century came mostly from Tories and dissident Whigs. Pope's friends, Burlington, Cobham, Bathurst, Bolingbroke, Lyttelton, were also the friends and patrons of the new writers. Specific acts of patronage became more sporadic. Some authors, like **Gay** and Young, complained of insufficient patronage; others, like Thomson, picked up what they could get.

The change was not entirely to the discredit of the upper classes; it meant that the basis of literary success had been broadened. Patronage atrophied in a larger reading public. Able men could more surely make their way from Class (*b*) to Class (*c*), though Defoe had not been able to do so; under varying circumstances, this is what Richardson, Fielding, Smollett, Johnson, and Goldsmith did. Johnson's famous letter to Chesterfield was described by Macaulay as the author's declaration of independence; perhaps a remark of Goldsmith's in 1760 gives a fairer statement:

> At present, the few poets of England no longer depend on the great for subsistence; they have now no other patrons but the public, and the public, collectively considered, is a good and a generous master.... A man of letters, at present, whose works are valuable, is perfectly sensible of their value. Every polite member of the community, by buying what he writes, contributes to reward him. (*Citizen of the World*, Letter LXXXIV.)

With the wider diffusion of books and ideas, an author often came to be thought of, not as appealing merely to gentlemen of taste, but as a leader of opinion and taste in the large. The participation of writers in politics in the age of Queen Anne may be considered not merely as a stage in the history of patronage, but as a new rapprochement between the author and the national life. This could lead, as Professor Preserved Smith remarks, to "a sort of graph-ocracy, or rule of writers." The literature of ideas so characteristic of the eighteenth century is not directed to aristocrats as patrons, nor to the great mass of the populace, but to a large literate group composed of the upper middle and professional classes and the gentry, often buttressed, of course, by wider popular support.

A. Beljame, *Le public et les hommes de lettres en Angleterre au dix-huitième siecle* (Paris, 1883); A. S. Collins, *Authorship in the Days of Johnson* (London, 1927); *The Profession of Letters* (London, 1928); G. E. Beauchamp, "The Profession of Writing in England from 1660 to 1740," *Northwestern University Summaries of Doctoral Dissertations,* x (1942), 12-15; Harry Ransom, "The Rewards of Authorship in the Eighteenth Century," *University of Texas Studies in English* (1938), pp. 47-66.

SAMUEL JOHNSON (1709-1784)

>>

Samuel Johnson was the subject and James Boswell the author of the greatest biography in the language and one of the most interesting books in the world. The reader who has fallen under the spell of Boswell will inevitably think of Johnson's life and personality as greater than the sum of his literary work. This judgment is correct, yet it should be our purpose to find the true Johnson both in the life and the works. And this, as we shall see, involves a just estimate of Boswell also. If we say that Boswell merely reported Johnson, we underestimate Boswell's skill and art. If we say that Johnson lives in Boswell's work, we should understand that Johnson is much more than a fascinating, humorous, and eccentric character in a book.

The Johnson we know in Reynolds's familiar portraits and in the pages of Boswell is a veteran man of letters who has won his place in the world but who keeps to the last the dogged resolution, intellectual honesty, and masculine power that carried him all the way. He had always followed his early bent and his inherited loyalties. His father Michael Johnson was a bookseller in the cathedral town of Lichfield, Staffordshire. (When Johnson mentions Lichfield in his *Dictionary* he adds a phrase from Virgil, "Salve, magna parens,"—"Hail, great mother.") In his father's shop

JOHNSON   GOLDSMITH

BURKE

he became a glutton of books, and like his father he was
always a Tory and a High Churchman. He entered Pembroke College, Oxford, but was in residence only a little
more than a year, and left at the end of 1729 because he
did not have enough money to carry him through. In later
years he always looked on Oxford with pride and affection.

He spent the next few years in the neighborhood of Lichfield and Birmingham, teaching school and tutoring, and doing for a Birmingham bookseller his first piece of hackwork, a translation of Lobo's *Voyage to Abyssinia* (1735).

JOHNSON'S BIRTHPLACE AND MEMORIAL STATUE, LICHFIELD

He then married a widow, Mrs. Elizabeth Porter, some twenty years older than he was, and in 1736 tried to start a school at Edial, near Lichfield. The next year, in company with one of his pupils, David Garrick, he came up to London bringing his unfinished tragedy *Irene*. He attracted attention almost immediately by his impressive though academic satire *London* (1738). But he made his way by resolute routine work, not by the leisurely production of finished masterpieces. With his own career in mind, he names the ills that assail the aspirant to literary fame— "Toil, envy, want, the garret [later 'the patron'], and the jail" (*The Vanity of Human Wishes*). A more moderate statement would be that he spent his early years in London in the garret, the bookshop, and the tavern. He was soon doing miscellaneous work for Edward Cave, the publisher of the *Gentleman's Magazine,* of which Johnson might be considered in the early 40's as the editor. In 1744 he published his *Life of Richard Savage,* a remarkable account of a disreputable literary adventurer who had been one of his earliest London associates. In 1747 he issued the plan for his *Dictionary,* for which he had already contracted with Dodsley and other booksellers and which took most of his time and energy for eight years. Thus he continued to live the life of a hack-writer, though he was no longer desperately poor. During this period he was living in the house in Gough Square, north of Fleet Street, now a Johnsonian shrine, though badly damaged by German bombs. The *Dictionary* (1755) established his reputation as an authority on language and literature. The age sought a norm in language as in other fields, and welcomed one who undertook to regularize English usage. The basis for the work was a wide and discriminating reading of English writers of the seventeenth and eighteenth centuries; the definitions are for the most part clear and sound, and the illustrative quotations are of rich and varied interest. The famous humorous definitions, as for oats, lexicographer, Whig, etc., should not cause us to overlook the real importance of the *Dictionary*. Meanwhile Johnson had published his second great Juvenalian satire, *The Vanity of Human*

Wishes (1749), and in the same year Garrick had produced his tragedy *Irene* with indifferent success. His *Rambler* (1750-52) was one of the most important of essay-periodicals; though Johnson does not have the varied appeal and the light touch of Addison and Steele at their best, he sets forth impressive moralizings in his heavy balanced style. The height of his moralistic work is reached in the famous tale of *Rasselas* (1759), written in the month of his mother's death. A new series of periodical essays in somewhat lighter vein, the *Idler,* appeared in the *Universal Chronicle,* 1758-60.

In 1762 the Tory government of George III gave Johnson a pension of £300, and thus enabled him to live and talk at leisure. A long delayed project was the edition of Shakespeare which he brought out at last in 1765. But he no longer felt it necessary to take on big jobs. He met Boswell in 1763, the famous Club was founded in 1764, and in the next year began his famous friendship with the Thrales. Thus the immortal circle dominated by Johnson and recorded by Boswell was formed within this decade. Burke and Goldsmith and Garrick are in the foreground, and the vivacious Mrs. Thrale is the principal feminine figure; we know the group like old friends, and yet the scene is endlessly varied by new visitors and new topics of conversation. The characteristic situation is the gathering of a group about Johnson in coffee house or chambers or at the Thrale's villa at Streatham, and the fluctuating but always vigorous reactions of Johnson himself give dramatic quality to the most trivial episode. The spirit of these meetings is well expressed in Johnson's own words: "As soon as I enter the door of a tavern, I experience an oblivion of care, and a freedom from solicitude. . . . I dogmatize and am contradicted, and in this conflict of opinions and sentiments I find delight."

Johnson defended traditional and authoritarian views in

an age which was soon to see the unsettling of many of the principles in which he believed. He opposed the formula of the Whigs, the ideal of "liberty" or "independence" which was being used in America and was soon to be used in France for revolutionary ends. He opposed the changing literary tastes of his time, and looked with suspicion on all those fads which have been considered symptoms of romanticism, such as the Ossianic poems and the Spenserian, Miltonic, and ballad revivals. He defended luxury and progress against primitivism and the affected cult of simplicity. He had no inkling of the Industrial Revolution or of the crying need for political and social reform. In his bitter opposition to the American cause, his uncompromising Tory view of Church and State, his indiscriminate contempt for the liberal ideas diffused by such important writers as Rousseau and Voltaire, he seems to us to be in the wrong. But we should not assume that there is nothing to be said for Toryism. Johnson's honest acceptance of things as they are enables him to identify himself with institutions and with the ways of the world, and goes with a positive enjoyment of life, an endless gusto and rich humor which are combined in his personality with deep seriousness. We expect the reactionary to say in changing times that the world is going to the dogs, and we expect the devout man to say that the world is desperately wicked; yet Johnson never cut himself off from his own times, was never embittered by the whole spectacle of a changing world, and met old age with dignity and fortitude. The death of friends, the estrangement from Mrs. Thrale because of her marriage with the Italian Piozzi, his own growing infirmities do not throw a deep shadow over the last pages of his life. In these latter years Johnson expressed himself by the spoken rather than the written word. His pamphlets on the American crisis (1770-75) are of merely historical interest, and his *Journey to the Western Islands of Scotland* (1775) is overshadowed by Boswell's account of the same journey, *The Journal of a Tour to the Hebrides* (1785); but the preface and notes to his Shakespeare, and above all his *Lives of the English Poets* (1781) show the full weight of his personality and intelligence applied to literary criticism.

RASSELAS

Rasselas is a philosophic tale with a nominally oriental setting, though the geographical color is confined to a few details drawn from Lobo's *Abyssinia* and perhaps from Baratti's *Travels* (English translation 1670), and Lockman's translation of *Travels of the Jesuits* (1743). The plan of the story seems to have been developed from two papers in the *Rambler* (Nos. 204, 205) which describe a vain quest for pleasure by "Seged, Lord of Ethiopia." In *Rasselas,* Johnson begins by describing the confinement of the Abyssinian princes in the Happy Valley, whence the hero escapes, suffering from the boredom of pleasure and security, and goes to see the world in the company of the sage Imlac, while he ponders "the choice of life" or "the pursuit of happiness." Rasselas is warned by one example after another that romantic reverie, romantic love, the flights of the imagination, the daring speculations of philosophy, the great discoveries of science—all do harm to man by giving him an inaccurate estimate of what life has to offer and encouraging false hopes. The demands of real life are best met not by seeking actual perfection, but by calculating what may be the lesser evil. Man has to act, not merely to speculate and hope; but even in choosing among good things one excludes the other, and further limits on happiness are imposed by incalculable fatalities. The attack is partly directed against the optimism of the eighteenth century, or more generally against all simple formulas which profess to lead man to happiness, against all glib generalizations about the goodness of nature and the satisfactions of solitude, of learning, or of social life. To be sure, man should make the most of what order and reason he can find, but it is folly to stake one's hopes on a facile discovery of divine order in the world we see. Johnson is interested in ethics, not in physico-theology, and he warns the sensible man out of the area occupied in common by deism and liberal Christianity. *Rasselas* has often been compared with Voltaire's *Candide;* the two works were published only a few weeks apart. Voltaire's work is also an attack on optimism, but is more exclusively concerned than Johnson with an attack on philosophical optimism, the Leibnizian conception of the best of all possible worlds, and is of course more purely satirical.

Johnson teaches that life is to be accepted on these terms with Christian resignation. "Happiness is to be placed only in virtue, which is always to be obtained," he had said in the *Life of Savage.* His praise of resolution and patience approaches Christian Stoicism, though he repeatedly says that the ideal Stoic indifference is impracticable (*Rambler* No. 32). *Rasselas* is a formal statement of the ethical position to be found in Johnson's satires and essays, and to be assumed as underlying his innumerable pungent comments in Boswell and the *Lives of the Poets.* Paraphrased and reported, his views seem commonplace to the last degree, but as he utters them they gain significance. The style is pompous and polysyllabic at times, but at its best simple and forceful, and the thought is always clear. Johnson does not try to be ingratiating or picturesque; *Rasselas* strikes us as hardly a work of imaginative fiction at all, but Johnson's claim would be that he is true to the general human situation which is his theme. As he said at the end of the *Rambler* (No. 208) , "In the pictures of life I have never been so studious of novelty or surprise, as to depart wholly from all resemblance."

THE LIVES OF THE ENGLISH POETS

This is the last and the most important of Johnson's large-scale literary tasks. In opposition to an Edinburgh publisher, a syndicate of London booksellers undertook to bring out a collected edition of the English poets, and Johnson hastily agreed to write introductory notices for the series. But the accounts of the individual poets grew on his hands; he put into the work the fruits of a lifetime of reading and of his long familiarity with the London literary scene. His opinions are at times prejudiced and erroneous, but they are seldom perfunctory or languid. They do not represent mere eighteenth-century convention, but convention as experienced and interpreted anew by Samuel Johnson. His unsympathetic treatment of Milton and Gray is notorious. His estimates of Dryden and Pope and his praise of Addison are from the eighteenth-century point of view definitive. Other lives make famous contributions to criticism, e.g., the description of metaphysical poetry in the life of Cowley, the account of Collins's romanticism, and the argument that the mysteries of the Christian religion are not suitable for poetry. Johnson did not trouble himself, like Boswell, to unearth new biographical material; he used what was at hand, and inserted at full length his earlier life of Savage; but the *Lives* abound in shrewd comment on the personalities of the poets, and on the actual operations of literary ambitions and rivalries, and the unique quality of the work is due to the combination and fusion of biography and criticism.

W. P. Courtney and D. Nichol Smith, *Bibliography* (rev. ed., Oxford, 1925); R. W. Chapman and A. T. Hazen, "Johnsonian Bibliography; A Supplement to Courtney," *Oxford Bibliographical Society*, v, iii (1938). 119-66; *The R. B. Adam Library Relating to Dr. Samuel Johnson and His Era* (3v, London, 1929); *Works*, ed. Sir John Hawkins (15v, London, 1787-89); (11v, Oxford, 1825); *Rasselas*, ed. O. F. Emerson (New York, 1895); ed. R. W.

Chapman (Oxford, 1927); *Journey to the Western Islands of Scotland*, ed. R. W. Chapman (London, 1924) (with Boswell's *Journal of a Tour to the Hebrides*); *Lives of the English Poets*, ed. G. B. Hill (3v, Oxford, 1905); *Poems*, ed. D. Nichol Smith and E. L. McAdam (Oxford, 1941); *Prefaces and Dedications*, ed. A. T. Hazen (New Haven, 1937); *Letters*, ed. G. B. Hill (2v, Oxford, 1892); *Critical Opinions*, ed. J. E. Brown (Princeton, 1926); *Life*, see Boswell, p. 336; Mrs. Piozzi, *Anecdotes of Samuel Johnson*, ed. S. C. Roberts (Cambridge, 1925); *Johnsonian Miscellanies*, ed. G. B. Hill (2v, Oxford, 1897); A. L. Reade, *Johnsonian Gleanings* (10 parts, London, 1909-46); W. Raleigh, *Six Essays on Johnson* (Oxford, 1910); P. H. Houston, *Dr. Johnson: A Study in Eighteenth-Century Humanism* (Cambridge, Mass., 1923); W. B. C. Watkins, *Johnson and English Poetry before 1660* (Princeton, 1936); W. K. Wimsatt, Jr., *The Prose Style of Samuel Johnson* (New Haven, 1941); J. W. Krutch, *Samuel Johnson* (New York, 1944); F. R. Leavis, "Johnson as Critic," *Scrutiny*, XII (1944). 187-204; B. H. Bronson, *Johnson and Boswell: Three Essays* (Berkeley, 1944); R. W. Chapman, *Two Centuries of Johnsonian Scholarship* (Glasgow, 1945).

JAMES BOSWELL (1740-1795)
>>

Boswell's relation to Johnson and his supreme achievement in biography must be considered in the light of his remarkable career and personality. The son of a harsh Scottish laird, Alexander Boswell of Auchinleck, Ayrshire, he was destined for the law, but his chief ambitions were to associate with the great and win literary fame. His meeting with Johnson and admission to friendship with the great man in 1763 meant the ultimate realization of these ambitions. Other interests claimed much of his attention in the 1760's: he studied law at Utrecht, visited Voltaire and Rousseau in Switzerland, and associated with the exiled John Wilkes in Italy. He also visited Corsica, gained the confidence of the leader of the Corsican patriots, Pasquale

Paoli, and on his return to England published his *Account of Corsica* (1768) and appeared in Corsican costume at the Shakespeare Jubilee at Stratford in 1769. Despite a certain tendency to make a fool of himself in public and in private, he was at last admitted to the Club in 1773 and succeeded in getting Johnson to tour the Highlands with him. Thus his more intensive Johnsonian period began. The *Journal of a Tour to the Hebrides* (1785) was a preliminary sample of the methods and materials Boswell used in the great *Life of Samuel Johnson, LL.D.* (1791). The standard text is that of the third edition (1799) revised by Malone. This work completely outdistanced the other first-hand biographical works in the field—Mrs. Piozzi's *Anecdotes* (1786) and Sir John Hawkins's *Life* (1787).

BOSWELL IN CORSICAN
COSTUME
From the *London Magazine*, 1769.

By this time Boswell had had much literary experience of one kind and another and had by his curiosity, sociability, and industry got command of an unrivaled body of material and information about Johnson and his circle. Though not infallible or unprejudiced, his work stands the keenest scrutiny. Not only is the *Life* one of the most thoroughly studied books in English literature, but we can now go far into the pre-history of the work and examine it in the light of Boswell's private papers—notes, journals, and letters recently

THE

L I F E

OF

SAMUEL JOHNSON, LL.D.

COMPREHENDING

AN ACCOUNT OF HIS STUDIES
AND NUMEROUS WORKS,

IN CHRONOLOGICAL ORDER;

A SERIES OF HIS EPISTOLARY CORRESPONDENCE
AND CONVERSATIONS WITH MANY EMINENT PERSONS;

AND

VARIOUS ORIGINAL PIECES OF HIS COMPOSITION,
NEVER BEFORE PUBLISHED.

THE WHOLE EXHIBITING A VIEW OF LITERATURE AND LITERARY MEN
IN GREAT-BRITAIN, FOR NEAR HALF A CENTURY,
DURING WHICH HE FLOURISHED.

IN TWO VOLUMES.

BY JAMES BOSWELL, ESQ.

———— *Quò fit ut* OMNIS
Votiva pateat veluti deſcripta tabella
VITA SENIS,————   HORAT.

VOLUME THE FIRST.

LONDON:
PRINTED BY HENRY BALDWIN,
FOR CHARLES DILLY, IN THE POULTRY.
M DCC XCI.

TITLE-PAGE OF BOSWELL'S *LIFE OF JOHNSON*, FIRST EDITION

brought to light at Malahide Castle, near Dublin. A first mass of these papers was acquired by an American collector, Colonel Isham, in 1927 and 1928. More material, including the original manuscript of the *Tour to the Hebrides,* was found in an old croquet box at Malahide in 1930, and in 1936 other valuable papers, including Johnson's diary, in an iron chest in the castle strong room. The earlier finds have been edited by Geoffrey Scott and Frederick Pottle. Still more Boswell papers have been discovered at Fetter-cairn Castle, but these have as yet merely been indexed. All this material will eventually be published by Colonel Isham.

Boswell's general method was to make rough notes at the end of the day (seldom or never on the spot) and then to write them up in his journals, which in turn formed the immediate basis of the *Life.* Successive installments of new evidence vindicate his scrupulous care and accuracy in detail, and show his skill in pointing up and organizing his material while remaining true to the facts. Boswell's weaknesses as a man are obvious and notorious. He was sensual and unstable, harassed by melancholia and morbid sensibility and vanity, and at last fell a victim to strong drink. He characteristically called a series of essays he wrote *The Hypochondriack* (1777-1783). He stands in strange con-trast to the rough old laird his father, and to the sturdy moralist and dogmatist Samuel Johnson. There is some-thing volatile and subtle about Boswell's personality and talents, and something inspired too in the tenacity, sure sense of direction, and artistic self-discipline by which, even in the midst of personal failure and disaster, he carried out the great project of his life. While his work was under way he wrote with confidence: "I am absolutely certain that *my* mode of biography, which gives not only a *history* of Johnson's visible progress through the world, and of his publications, but a *view* of his mind, in his letters and con-versations, is the most perfect that can be conceived, and

JOHNSON AND BOSWELL
Caricatured by Rowlandson.

will be *more* of a *Life* than any work that has ever yet appeared."

F. A. Pottle, *The Literary Career of James Boswell* (Oxford, 1929); *Private Papers of James Boswell from Malahide Castle,* ed. G. Scott and F. A. Pottle (18v, Mount Vernon, N.Y., 1928-34); F. A. Pottle and others, *Index to the Private Papers* (London, 1937); C. C. Abbott, *A Catalogue of Papers relating to Boswell, Johnson, and Sir William Forbes* (Oxford, 1936); *Journal of a Tour to Corsica,* ed. S. C. Roberts (Cambridge, 1923); *Journal of a Tour to the Hebrides,* ed. F. A. Pottle and C. H. Bennett (New York, 1936); *The Hypochondriack,* ed. Margery Bailey (2v, Stanford University, 1928); *Life of Samuel Johnson,* ed. G. B. Hill, rev. L. F. Powell (4v, Oxford, 1934); ed. C. B. Tinker (New York, 1933); *Letters,* ed. C. B. Tinker (2v, Oxford, 1924); C. B. Tinker, *Young Boswell* (Boston, 1922); F. A. Pottle, "The Power of Memory in Boswell and Scott," in *Essays on the Eighteenth Century Presented to David Nichol Smith* (Oxford, 1945); "The Life of Boswell," *Yale Review,* xxxv (1946), 445-60.

MRS. PIOZZI (HESTER LYNCH SALUSBURY THRALE) (1741-1821)

>>

Hester Salusbury was a clever Welsh girl, dependent on the uncertain favors of rich kinsfolk, who made a loveless marriage with the wealthy brewer Henry Thrale. The residences of the Thrales at Streatham and Southwark were virtually Dr. Johnson's home from 1766 to 1781. From 1778 Fanny Burney was also an intimate of the household. But all this was changed by Thrale's death in 1781. Mrs. Thrale's love for the Italian musician Piozzi and her marriage to him in 1784 alienated her from Dr. Johnson. He had been, as she said, "friend, father, guardian, confidant," but pride, prejudice, and jealousy made it impossible for him to accept this change. Mrs. Thrale entered the competition among Johnson's biographers with her *Anecdotes of the Late Samuel Johnson* (1786) and *Letters to and from the Late Samuel Johnson* (1788), and of course gives first-hand information of great importance, but the text of the letters she prints is even more untrustworthy than is usual with eighteenth-century editors, and her desire to justify herself distorts her picture of Dr. Johnson. Her account of Johnson is livelier than the heavy work of Sir John Hawkins, but is far less accurate and balanced than Boswell's. As her authoritative biographer Professor Clifford says, she was "an inveterate diarist and commentator." A sprightly account of her travels called *Observations and Reflections* (1789), is but a sample of the great mass of autobiographical material which she left, and which has only recently been evaluated and in part edited.

J. L. Clifford, *Hester Lynch Piozzi (Mrs. Thrale)* (Oxford, 1941); *Thraliana*, ed. K. C. Balderston (2v, Oxford, 1942); F. A. Pottle and C. H. Bennett, "Boswell and Mrs. Piozzi," *Modern*

Philology, xxxix (1942). 421-30; *Autobiography, Letters, and Literary Remains,* ed. A. Hayward (2v, London, 1861); *The Queeney Letters,* ed. Lord Lansdowne (London, 1934).

OLIVER GOLDSMITH (1730?-1774)
>>>

   Goldsmith's contemporaries were much interested in his personality and career, and there are many autobiographical touches in his writings, yet, except for the last fifteen years of his life, when he was a prominent man of letters in London, we have to trust to a bare outline of fact filled in with tradition and hearsay. He was born in Pallas, County Longford, Ireland, the son of the Reverend Charles Goldsmith. He was a scapegrace undergraduate at Trinity College, Dublin, failed of ordination to the Church, and made abortive plans for studying law and sailing to America. Then he studied medicine in a desultory way at Edinburgh and Leyden, wandered on foot in France and Italy for a year or more, and returned to England, a "philosophic vagabond," in 1756. After trying his hand at medicine, school teaching, and proofreading, he began to work for Griffiths on the *Monthly Review,* contributed to the *Critical* also, and soon became one of the most versatile professional writers in London. His *Enquiry into the Present State of Polite Learning in Europe* (1759) has the formal and judicial attitude which the age expected of its critics; but Goldsmith did better when he went on to combine the critic's themes and comments with the personal touch of the familiar essay, and thus produced, when he was at his best, fresh and delightful variants on the periodical-essay formula of Addison and Steele. Many of his early essays, published anonymously in various journals, were reprinted again and again in other periodicals, and collected only in part by the author in 1765. Best known were the pieces in the short-lived *Bee* (1759) and the *British Magazine* (1760). "If there be a pride in multiplied editions," he remarked, "I have seen some of my labors sixteen times reprinted, and claimed by different parents as their own." He takes hints and materials from the Encyclopedists and other French writers, but even his most hasty and meager bits of work have a touch of distinction. He had a real though not a profound interest in ideas.

His most extensive prose work in this period is the series of *Chinese Letters* contributed to the *Public Ledger* in 1760-61 and collected as *The Citizen of the World* in 1762, based on the familiar scheme of a commentary by a philosophic oriental on the manners of western Europe, a device already used by Montesquieu, d'Argens, and others. He had already developed his felicitous prose style, unsurpassed for ease and clarity in an age of good prose. On some of his favorite ideas he based his first important and successful poem, *The Traveller* (1764). The principal themes are man's natural attachment to his home and country (later elaborated in *The Deserted Village*), the varying characteristics of the nations of western Europe, the defects and compensating advantages of natural environment and national character. His one novel, *The Vicar of Wakefield,* was written in the early 1760's, hastily sold by Johnson to a bookseller when Goldsmith needed money to pay his landlady, and published in 1766. The idyllic country scenes in this story and the quaint character of the Vicar, Dr. Primrose, show Goldsmith at his best, though he did not take his plot very seriously.

Johnson was always Goldsmith's friend and sponsor, and saw to it that he was admitted to the famous Club in 1764. We should not take too seriously Boswell's account of Goldsmith's harmless follies and blunders in conversation. Though he may at times have been the butt of his circle and though he was always careless about money, he was a better man than most of those who condescended to him. In the witty lines called *Retaliation* (1774) he retorted pleasantly upon his friends and associates. Always hard pressed for cash, he continued to do hack compilations such as his histories of Rome and Britain and his *History of Animated Nature*. In his comedy *The Good Natured Man* (1768) he treats a favorite and personal theme; his good natured man is helpless in a selfish world; the very qualities recommended by the sentimental creed threaten to ruin him. After the success of this play he went on to write *She Stoops to Conquer* (1773), one of the chief triumphs of the anti-sentimental drama and ever since a perennial favorite.

But the greatest favorite of all is *The Deserted Village* (1770). Professor R. S. Crane has brought to light an essay of Goldsmith's published in 1762, "The Revolution in Low Life," which laments the depopulation of the countryside to make way for the luxurious estates of the rich. English rural life was being transformed in the eighteenth century. But Goldsmith is not thinking primarily of enclosure (the change from the medieval open-field system of cultivation to the enclosure of arable land, meadow and pasture), though he does refer to the poor man's loss of rights in common land. The grandee sometimes tore down cottages simply because they brought little rent and because he wanted to improve the landscaping of his estate. The ruin of sweet Auburn was due to the luxury which has ruined states ever since the days of ancient Rome. Elsewhere (e.g., *Citizen of the World,* Letter XI), Goldsmith praises material progress and the increase of reasonable enjoyment, and even reduces the doctrine of the simple life to an absurdity (*Asem, An Eastern Tale*); but he opposes the excessive luxury that comes, he thinks, with the extension of commerce and the extravagance of the new plutocracy. Goldsmith undoubtedly idealizes the life of the village, interweaving reminiscences of his early days in Lissoy; he is rather sentimental about the plight of the inhabitants of Auburn, though he rightly claims for his poem a foundation in fact. After all, the poem is closer to the facts of human nature, if not to actuality, than Crabbe's anti-pastoral *Village,* planned as an answer to Goldsmith. Johnson said the last word about Goldsmith in his famous Latin epitaph, part of which reads in translation: "He undertook almost every kind of writing, and he undertook nothing that he did not adorn."

Temple Scott, *Oliver Goldsmith, Bibliographically and Biographically Considered* (London, 1928); *Works,* ed. J. W. M. Gibbs (5v. London, 1884-86); ed. P. Cunningham (10v, New York, 1908); *New Essays,* ed. R. S. Crane (Chicago, 1927); *Complete Poetical Works,* ed. A. Dobson (London, 1906); John Forster, *Life* (London, 1877); A. Dobson, *Life* (London, 1888); K. C. Balderston, *History and Sources of Percy's Memoir of Goldsmith* (Cambridge, 1926); *Collected Letters,* ed. K. C. Balderston (Cambridge, 1928); *Plays,* ed. C. E. Doble and G. Ostler (Oxford, 1928); Stephen Gwynn, *Oliver Goldsmith* (New York, 1935); A. L. Sells, *Les Sources françaises de Goldsmith* (Paris, 1924); H. J. Smith, *Oliver Goldsmith's The Citizen of the World* (New Haven, 1926); R. W. Seitz, "Goldsmith and the *Literary Magazine,*" *Review of English Studies,* v (1929). 410-30; Arthur Friedman, "Goldsmith and the *Weekly Magazine,*" *Modern Philology,* xxxii (1935). 281-99; "Goldsmith's Contributions to the *Critical Review,*" *ibid.,* xliv (1946). 23-52; H. J. Bell, "*The Deserted Village* and Goldsmith's Social Doctrines," *Publications of the Modern Language Association,* lix (1944). 747-72.

THE WRITING OF HISTORY
>>

A historian should control the facts, interpret the facts, and tell a good story. The classical historians had emphasized the interpretation of public events and the careers of

great men. In modern historiography the accumulation of
materials had outrun interpretation, and the staggering
industry of collectors of documents and texts continued in
such vast compilations as Muratori's *Rerum Italicarum
Scriptores* (1723-1751) and Rymer's *Foedera* (1704-1735). A
critical attitude developed in Mabillon's new science of
diplomatics, the study of the authenticity of documents
(*De Re Diplomatica,* 1681), in Bayle's ruthless scrutiny of
evidence in his *Dictionnaire critique et historique* (1697),
and in Leibniz's remarkable historical studies.

The Enlightenment wanted to trace a law of progress in
the complex phenomena of history and thus to simplify
them and give them meaning. The assumption usually
made was that human reason is uniform, but has had to
make its way against error and tyranny. This situation or
process was to be studied in the whole social and cultural
history of man, not merely in the political and military
history of the great nations. In his *Siècle de Louis XIV*
(1751, dated 1752), Voltaire set a new standard of compre-
hensiveness and accuracy in the treatment of a period of
history, though he did not really unify his subject. His
Essai sur les moeurs (1753-1758) is the first general cultural
history. The French *philosophe* was a drastic critic and
reformer; England lagged behind in interpretative history
because political complacency bred intellectual inertia. The
first respectable study of the historical development of the
English nation was made by the Huguenot refugee Paul
de Rapin-Thoyras, whose work had wide currency in England. The coöperative *Universal History* published in
England in the middle of the century represents accumulated information rather than critical interpretation, though
its scope is impressive. Like other large-scale publishing
projects of the time, it was an attempt to make encyclo-
paedic learning available to a wider public.

David Hume wrote his *History of England* (1754-1762)

in the belief that certain "constant and universal principles of human nature" can be found operating in all history, but this is not accompanied by an ardent belief in reason and progress. Since he refused to endorse Whig dogma, he was counted as a Tory. He tries to take a detached position and to stand clear of party strife, but he is still preoccupied with politics, and falls short in cultural history. Gibbon was likewise wary and disillusioned, but far more imaginative, comprehensive, and scholarly. Meanwhile the Scottish clergyman William Robertson wrote sound works in a variety of fields (*The History of Scotland during the Reigns of Queen Mary and of King James VI,* 1759; *Charles V,* 1769; *History of America,* 1777). Though he succeeded in being both readable and accurate by organizing a direct narrative and massing his evidence and technical discussion in separate sections, he has fallen into neglect. The historians of the Enlightenment at their best seek to put human life into a general social and cultural frame of reference, but their formulas are too simple, and rationalistic dogma keeps them from an adequate understanding of large areas of history, notably the Middle Ages. These considerations help to explain why literary history lagged even behind other forms of historical writing, and did not get far beyond the stage of accumulating materials, even in Thomas Warton's *History of English Poetry* (1774-1781).

J. B. Bury, *The Idea of Progress* (London, 1920); J. B. Black, *The Art of History* (London, 1926); H. E. Barnes, *A History of Historical Writing* (Norman, Okla., 1937); J. W. Thompson and B. J. Holm, *A History of Historical Writing,* II (New York, 1942); T. P. Peardon, *The Transition in English Historical Writing, 1760-1830* (New York, 1933); René Wellek, *The Rise of English Literary History* (Chapel Hill, 1941); Gladys Bryson, *Man and Society: The Scottish Inquiry of the Eighteenth Century* (Princeton, 1945).

EDWARD GIBBON (1737-1794)
>>

The eighteenth century did not stifle individuality, but allowed it to develop within a framework of convention and in relative peace and security. It was thus that Gibbon was enabled to write the greatest historical work in English, *The Decline and Fall of the Roman Empire.* Born of a prosperous family, he owed his training to self-discipline and eager independent study rather than to his tutors or to his unprofitable residence at Magdalen College, Oxford. His *Memoirs* (edited by Lord Sheffield, 1796; variant texts edited by Murray, 1896) record all this in one of the best of all English autobiographies. As a boy he was converted to Catholicism; he was thereupon exiled to Switzerland, where he returned to a nominal Protestantism, continued his studies, and fell in love with Suzanne Curchod. But he was more of an enthusiast for books than for people, and broke off his engagement at his father's command. "I sighed as a lover; I obeyed as a son." He did some of his early writing in French, but was soon taking pains to perfect his English style. For two years he served in the militia, and later remarked, "The captain of the Hampshire Grenadiers has not been useless to the historian of the Roman Empire." Though he spent much time in the salons of Paris and of Italy, he was never in danger of becoming an expatriate. His master-passion was always history. Unlike a modern scholar, who must choose a limited field and stay within it, Gibbon ranged far and wide and considered diverse subjects; he even began in French a history of Swiss liberty. A famous passage in the *Memoirs* tells how and when the decisive impulse came: "It was at Rome, on the fifteenth of October, 1764, as I sat musing amidst the ruins of the Capitol, while the barefooted friars were singing vespers in the temple of Jupiter, that the idea of writing the decline and fall of the city first started to my mind." Gibbon never became a recluse; he mingled in society, had a seat in Parliament, and belonged to the famous Club, but he always followed his main bent and worked quietly and steadily. *The Decline and Fall of the Roman Empire* began to appear in 1776; the sixth and last volume was finished at Lausanne in 1787.

Gibbon's scholarship stands modern tests, despite the enormous accumulation of materials since his day and the exacting standards now imposed on the historian. But Gibbon is likewise an artist, and seeks to keep his facts under control: "A minute accumulation of circumstances must destroy the light and effect of those general pictures which compose the use and ornament of a remote history" (Chap. xlviii). He presents a great pageant or drama, and commands a stately style adequate to the dignity, color, and excitement of his theme. Oftentimes it is enough to watch this great procession go by, but eventually we ask what it means. Does Gibbon have a philosophy of history? Much controversy centers about this question, because it involves the other question of Gibbon's attitude toward Christianity. He tells us that his theme is "the triumph of religion and barbarism"; if there is a great cycle in history, his part is to tell of a decline and fall, not of progress upward and onward. He accepts the rational standards of the Enlightenment, but not its optimism. He is after all very much in the position of the philosophic satirist who sees that man can be pronounced a rational animal only if we add that he does not act rationally. Destructive forces in history may outweigh constructive forces; "the power of kings is most effectual to destroy" (Chap. xliii). He relates "the progress, the persecutions, the establishment, the divisions, the final triumph, and the gradual corruption of Christianity" (Chap. xxxvii). Though he professes to believe in progress, sees a

decrease of fanaticism in modern times, and thinks it safe
to assume that Western man will not relapse into barbarism, he does not dwell enthusiastically on the present or
the future. But he has the artistic skill to transform this
attitude into a pervasive irony which adds flavor and color
to his whole work. He gives play to all the motives that
may animate a historian, though the attractions of his
theme and the demands of his art have the right of way
over any speculative or doctrinaire purpose. He falls short
of making a great synthesis by grasping underlying causes
and the operation of social forces, but his feeling for the
pageant of history gives his work color, resonance, and
depth. In our own day Gibbon's elevated style and imaginative sweep have had a marked effect on the thought and
style of Winston Churchill.

J. E. Norton, *A Bibliography of the Works of Edward Gibbon*
(London, 1940); *Decline and Fall of the Roman Empire,* ed. J.
B. Bury (7v, London, 1896-98); *Autobiographies,* ed. J. Murray
(London, 1896); *Memoirs,* ed. G. B. Hill (London, 1900); *Journal
to January 28, 1763,* ed. D. M. Low (New York, 1929); *Journal à
Lausanne, 1763-1764,* ed. G. Bonnard (Lausanne, 1945); *Private
Letters,* ed. R. E. Prothero (2v, London, 1896); J. C. Morison, *Gib-
bon* (London, 1878; English Men of Letters); R. B. Mowat, *Gibbon*
(London, 1936); D. M. Low, *Edward Gibbon* (London, 1937);
S. T. McCloy, *Gibbon's Antagonism to Christianity* (Chapel Hill,
1933); G. Keynes, *The Library of Edward Gibbon* (London, 1940);
G. M. Young, *Gibbon* (New York, 1933).

EDMUND BURKE (1729-1797)

Burke was the greatest genius ever produced by the
Anglo-Irish culture which has so largely enriched British
life and letters. His father was a Protestant lawyer, his
mother and many of his kinsfolk Catholics, his favorite
teacher a Quaker. Though he learned important religious

and political lessons in Ireland, his education at Trinity College, Dublin, was in the English Augustan tradition. As an undergraduate he read the classics, enjoyed the theater, and wrote an Addisonian essay-periodical *The Reformer* (1748). He does not seem to have been acquainted at this time with his fellow-student Oliver Goldsmith. In the 1750's Burke studied law as a resident of the Middle Temple, and was drawn at the same time into London literary life and into politics. Early publications showed his originality and speculative power: his *Vindication of Natural Society* (1756) is a *reductio ad absurdum* of Bolingbroke's attack on revealed religion. Just as Bolingbroke had used the corruption of the Church to support his argument for natural religion, so Burke ironically adduces social wrongs and injustices to support an argument for merely "natural" society. Rousseau was soon to use such an argument in good earnest, but Burke here announces his lifelong opposition to fine spun political theorizing. *A Philosophical Enquiry into the Origin of our Ideas of the Sublime and Beautiful* (1757) is a pioneer study in the psychological basis of aesthetic enjoyment; Burke's doctrine that "a mode of terror or pain is always the cause of the sublime" indicates the growing preference for the "Gothic" and the wild. The range of Burke's interests is shown by his numerous contributions of reviews and summaries of current events to Dodsley's *Annual Register* for more than thirty years from 1758. In 1764 Burke, with Johnson and Reynolds, had a main hand in forming the famous Club, and he is thereafter one of the principal figures in Johnson's circle, though Boswell does not record his conversation so fully as we could wish.

Burke began his career in politics as secretary to William Gerard Hamilton, chief secretary for Ireland, but the two parted company when Hamilton wanted to monopolize his services. He then became a lieutenant of Lord Rockingham,

the leader of one of the Whig factions, all in opposition
to George III and all at odds with one another. Thus Burke
could not get on with the elder Pitt, and stayed outside
his last administration (1766-68). A series of unwise measures by George III's ministers was making it certain that
the Empire would lose America. Yet while America was
being lost India was being won. Throughout all these events
Burke remained the commentator and parliamentary critic;
he was never the administrator. His comment was magnifi-
cently eloquent and philosophical, going to the roots of
political theory. Most of his important pieces were in the
form of orations, but called for sustained attention and
close reading. He did not indulge in mere personal abuse,
like Junius, though he used invective more and more as
time went on. His central principle, clearly formulated in
Thoughts on the Cause of the Present Discontents (1770)
and constantly restated and reapplied, was that politics is
an art, not a science, that it deals with men and nations in
actuality, never with bloodless abstractions, pure theories
or principles. This put him in opposition alike to parliamentary legalists and French *philosophes*. Until the end
of the North ministry (1782) it led him to recommend
practical, moderate, and conciliatory policies. He deplored
the long feud between the government and Wilkes; he tried
to relieve Irish Catholics of the oppressive Penal Laws; he
supported the repeal of the Stamp Act, though with the
passage of the Declaratory Act (declaration of the right to
tax). In two of his most famous speeches, *On American
Taxation* (April 19, 1774), and *On Conciliation with
America* (March 22, 1775), he developed his magnificent
view of an America fired with the English love of liberty in
comparison with which the claim of an abstract right to
tax sinks into insignificance. Here Burke is positive, constructive, and profound; his view of an empire based on
Anglo-Saxon traditions of liberty, though it did not alter

and probably could not have altered the course of events in the eighteenth century, still bears on the problems of the twentieth. In the practical politics of the day Burke did not stand supreme; when his party came into office in 1782 he was not taken into the Cabinet; he went along with the unfortunate Fox-North coalition of 1783, and his opposition to the younger Pitt, as to the elder, was partisan. But he always centered on the great issues of the Empire—England's relations with America and Ireland, and in the last twelve years of his life England's relations with India and France. If we substitute Russia for France, one revolution for another, we see how up to date much of this is.

Burke's concern with India came to a climax in the great prosecution of Warren Hastings. As governor general of India, Hastings had built up British power, but he had played a corrupt financial and political game, and his political opponents, especially Sir Philip Francis and Edmund Burke, tried to make him the scapegoat for all the abuses connected with the régime of the East India Company. The impeachment of Hastings, a long drawn out process which ran from 1788 to his acquittal in 1795, was a last great field day for eighteenth-century oratory. From 1785, with the *Speech on the Nabob of Arcot's Debts,* Burke rose to heights of eloquence on the subject, but his zeal and indignation carried him beyond the facts. His fine style was becoming somewhat strained and exaggerated.

Lastly, the French Revolution called forth all his heavy artillery. His *Reflections on the French Revolution* (1790) fuses moral and religious feeling, political philosophy, literary power, and personal feeling in such a way as to form the great classic of British conservatism. Burke was now with his old foes, the Tories, against the "New Whigs," the pro-French wing led by his former friend and ally Charles James Fox. Burke had interpreted the Revolution of 1688 and the American Revolution as just assertions of rights guaranteed by the British constitution; he opposed the French Revolution because, he thought, it broke the framework of tradition altogether. Against the philosophical radicals and the Foxite Whigs Burke "proclaimed the sacred continuity of the social fabric." Externally the established order is protected by all the accumulated sanctions of society, church, and state; internally it should be protected against mere theory or speculation by the instincts, emotions, habits, and prejudices of man. For the divine right of kings is substituted the divine right of established institutions. Burke's final conception of the state leaves scope only for the most gradual change, development, or adjustment to new conditions. As Lord Acton says, "The authority of history devoured all the rest of his principles." Thus Burke was a traditionalist, like his friends Johnson and Reynolds, but he looked toward the past with an imaginative ardor which had the color of Scott's romantic Toryism, the heightened sense of the national past which came in the romantic period. England recoiled against the Revolution, but Burke was not happy. He proudly defended himself against the impudent Duke of Bedford in his finely written *Letter to a Noble Lord* (1796), and continued to the last his campaign against revolutionary France in his *Letters on the Proposals for Peace with the Regicide Directory of France* (I-II, 1796; III, 1797).

Works (8v, London, 1852); (12v, Boston, 1897); *Select Works,* ed. E. J. Payne (3v, Oxford, 1866); *Letters,* ed. H. J. Laski (London, 1922); A. P. I. Samuels, *The Early Life, Correspondence and Writings of Edmund Burke* (Cambridge, 1923); John Morley, *Burke* (London, 1879; English Men of Letters); Robert Murray, *Edmund Burke* (Oxford, 1931); J. MacCunn, *The Political Philosophy of Burke* (New York, 1913); A. Cobban, *Edmund Burke and the Revolt against the Eighteenth Century* (London, 1929); D. C. Bryant, *Edmund Burke and his Literary Friends* (St. Louis, 1939); Philip Magnus, *Edmund Burke* (London, 1939); Annie M. Osborn. *Rousseau and Burke* (New York, 1940).

JUNIUS

>>

The violent political controversies of the first ten years of the reign of George III must be kept in mind as we follow the dashing career of Churchill in satire, the protracted agitation of John Wilkes, Smollett's journalism, Burke's course in politics, and many an argument and remark in the pages of Boswell. Innumerable newspaper writers and pamphleteers had their angry words, but the one master of sheer invective was the unknown writer whose usual signature was "Junius." His letters appeared in Woodfall's *Public Advertiser* beginning in January, 1769, and he vanished in January, 1772. He was evidently an ardent Whig partisan close to the Grenville faction, a bitter opponent of the administration of Grafton and the succeeding administration of North. He had inside information about the politics of the day, and expressed his rancor in a polished, terse, antithetical style which made much use of irony. His daring address to the King brought a libel suit against his printer, but a London jury refused to convict. Though bitterly partisan, Junius served the cause of true patriotism by his attacks, however malevolent, on personal vice and political corruption and jobbery.

Junius, ed. John Wade (2v, London, 1850); *Letters of Junius,* ed. C. W. Everett (London, 1927); Charles Wentworth Dilke, *Papers of a Critic* (2v, London, 1875), II.

CHARLES CHURCHILL (1731-1764)

>>

Churchill, the son of an obscure clergyman, was educated at Westminster School, where Robert Lloyd and William Cowper were his contemporaries. Though he never attended a university he took holy orders and held small curacies. Like other young and ambitious writers, he deliberately sought publicity by launching a satire to startle the town; his *Rosciad* (March, 1761), a pungent review of the actors of the day, created a great sensation. With money in his pocket, a taste for dissipation, a reputation as a literary slasher, and an overweening sense of his own power and importance, Churchill was now embarked on a short and brilliant career. He attacked Smollett and the *Critical Review* in the *Apology,* threatened Garrick but allowed a truce to be patched up, proclaimed his creed as a satirist in *Night,* and entered into a close personal and political alliance with John Wilkes. He collaborated on Wilkes' *North Briton,* which was directed against Smollett's *Briton* and the Bute administration, and paid off various grudges in *The Ghost* (1762-63), which attacks Johnson, *The Prophecy of Famine* (January, 1763) , an anti-Scotch satire, the *Epistle to Hogarth* (July, 1763), *The Duellist* (January, 1764), *Gotham* (1764), and *The Candidate.* On his way to join Wilkes in Paris he died at Boulogne, November, 1764, and was buried at Dover.

In Churchill the professedly lofty principles and indignation of the satirical tradition ring hollow. The satirist claims privileges which he has not earned, and talks grandly about "liberty," meaning vaguely political freedom, freedom or license of speech and action, and liberation from the musty rules that are supposed to cramp original genius. He expresses satirical scorn not only for pride and pretence but

also for bourgeois respectability. He has much in common
with the cheap politician who must always be denouncing
something or somebody. Though he uses the formulas of
reason and good sense, he is actually an irresponsible bohemian and a cynic. It would be unfair to Churchill not
to recognize, however, the impressiveness of his boisterous
and virile personality. The self-portrait of the satirist is
more nearly authentic than Pope's, and points forward to
the tormented self-consciousness of Byron. Much of his work
was written hastily and carelessly, and was of ephemeral
interest. He is saved from oblivion, however, by his fine
command of the heroic couplet. In a notable passage of *The
Apology* he exalts Dryden's vigor above the smoother and
tamer beauties of Pope, and he even looks back to the pre-
Dryden tradition of rough and snarling satire. His use of
the run-on couplet and of variations of pause and accent
within the line is freer than Dryden's. Though there is some
affectation in his quest for "the generous roughness of a
nervous line," he comes off pretty well when compared with
the attenuated and bookish work of contemporary pre-
romantic poets. There is critical value in his contemptuous
survey of his romantic and Scottish contemporaries in the
posthumously published fragment called *The Journey*. He
rises far superior, too, to the mere scurrility of many minor
writers who were trying to attain his vigorous effects.

Poems, ed. J. Laver (2v, London, 1933); *The Rosciad* and *The
Apology,* ed. R. W. Lowe (London, 1891); J. M. Beatty, "An
Essay in Critical Biography—Charles Churchill," *Publications of
the Modern Language Association,* xxxv (1920). 226-46; W. C.
Brown, "Charles Churchill: a Revaluation," *Studies in Philology,*
xl (1943). 405-24.

PHILIP DORMER STANHOPE, FOURTH EARL
OF CHESTERFIELD (1694-1773)

▶▶

Chesterfield was primarily a man of the world, absorbed in the idea of social and public success. Son of the third Earl, and on his mother's side grandson of the great Earl of Halifax, he was educated at Cambridge, made the grand

CHESTERFIELD

tour, and on his return sat in the House of Commons as a Whig, though he was soon in the anti-Walpole wing of the party. He was Ambassador at The Hague 1728-32 and during this time formed a liaison with Elizabeth du Bouchet, who bore him the illegitimate son to whom his most important letters are addressed. During the 1730's he continued to be a principal leader of the opposition to Walpole. After Walpole's fall he went to Dublin for a time as Lord Lieutenant of Ireland, and later held office as secretary of state under Newcastle, but retired from active politics in 1748.

Chesterfield wanted for his son the same high place among wits and men of the world which he himself had attained, and in an attempt to polish this uncouth lad he wrote him the famous letters. The solicitous father begins with elementary education and etiquette and goes on to a subtle and witty exposition of men and manners, the most remarkable formulation in English of the ideal of the *honnête homme*. Chesterfield had formed himself in spite of physical defects and social inadequacies. His program derives from the courtesy literature of the Renaissance, but in some respects fits the Frenchified gentleman of the Restoration rather than the ideal of the Christian gentleman set up for the English ruling class in the eighteenth century. Chesterfield lays great emphasis on externals and endlessly inculcates the graces. He sets a fine example of literary culture by his flawless style, though his formal ideas on literature are conventionally neo-classic. He is untouched by the philanthropy and sentiment which were coming to characterize the good man of the eighteenth century. He recommends genuine urbanity, based on a shrewd estimate of human nature as susceptible to flattery and controlled by ruling passions. His emphasis on elegant manners and his latitude in sexual morality (particularly his advice to the young man to have a liaison in high life) antagonized English puritanism. Chesterfield's reputation has also suffered from the rebuke which Dr. Johnson administered in his famous letter repudiating tardy patronage; but the nobleman hardly deserved this assault, for he had never denied Johnson or turned him away. Yet the contrast between surly English virtue and insincere suavity in the French style was only too easy to play up. Dickens likewise caricatured Chesterfield as Sir John Chester in *Barnaby Rudge*. However, the attitude toward human nature and society which we find in the letters is realistic rather than cynical or insincere. It is certainly equal in morals and far superior in intelligence and style to the modern pseudo-art of salesmanship, and to the shoddy psychology of the "how to win friends and influence people" school. Chesterfield is wise and shrewd, though his is a worldly wisdom. His affection for his son and his uniform good nature and undeniable capacity for true friendship suffice to vindicate his character and integrity.

S. L. Gulick, Jr., *A Chesterfield Bibliography to 1800, Papers of the Bibliographical Society of America*, XXIX (1935); *Letters,* ed. Bonamy Dobrée (6v, London, 1932); *Letters and Other Pieces,* ed. R. P. Bond (Garden City, 1935); *Some Unpublished Letters,* ed. S. L. Gulick, Jr. (Berkeley, 1937); W. H. Craig, *Life of Lord Chesterfield* (London, 1907); P. E. More, "Chesterfield," *Shelburne Essays,* Fifth Series (Boston, 1908); Roger Coxon, *Chesterfield and his Critics* (London, 1925); S. Shellabarger, *Lord Chesterfield* (New York, 1935); W. Connely, *The True Chesterfield* (London, 1939).

HORACE WALPOLE (1717-1797)

>>

Horace Walpole was the fourth son of the great prime minister. Though his fastidious and sensitive temperament contrasts with that of the coarse and robust Sir Robert, he was always devoted to the family interest and the Whig tradition of the Walpoles. At Eton he was bookish though not studious, and here he made important friendships, especially as a member of the "Quadruple Alliance"—Walpole, Richard West, Thomas Ashton, and the future poet Thomas Gray. Eton always meant more to Walpole than his years at King's College, Cambridge. He was promptly given political sinecures which assured him a comfortable income for life. With Gray as a companion he traveled in France and Italy from 1739 to 1741, making long stays at Florence and Rome. Both young men were already incomparable letter writers, and this is the most brilliantly recorded grand tour of the century, though the two companions quarreled and parted at Reggio. They were reconciled a few years later. On returning to England Walpole entered Parliament just as his father's administration was on the point of being overthrown. He was never an active politician, though always interested in political intrigue.

In 1747 he rented the small house at Twickenham which he afterwards bought; enlarged and redesigned, this became the famous Strawberry Hill, the seat of his connoisseurship. With the aid of friends (Richard Bentley, John Chute, George Martyn) whom he called a "committee of taste," he undertook to "build a little Gothic castle at Strawberry Hill," collected various art-objects, relics, books, and manuscripts, and gardened in the English manner on his fourteen

STRAWBERRY HILL
From the *Universal Magazine*, 1793.

acres. He carried on his hobbies with amateur enthusiasm, and with considerable pride in his own fastidiousness. Besides his pursuits in architecture and gardening, his interests as antiquarian and virtuoso were expressed in his *Catalogue of Royal and Noble Authors* (1758), his *Anecdotes of Painting in England* (1762-80), based on Vertue's manuscript collections, and his famous Gothic romance *The Castle of Otranto* (1765) (see p. 282). Walpole's ambitions as an author were on the whole disappointed; though *Otranto* was influential, his tragedy of incest, *The Mysterious Mother*

(1768) , must be considered a misguided effort. But the effect of his taste in furthering the Gothic revival was considerable. Another hobby was the printing press at Strawberry Hill, which began work with the printing of Gray's *Odes*. Eighteenth-century connoisseurship was often trivial and superficial, as Walpole himself recognized when he commented on the weaknesses of his contemporary William Shenstone. But Walpole was very close to the heart of his age. He always kept a town house, first in Arlington Street and then in Berkeley Square, and for many years he observed and recorded the social scene in his inimitable letters. What is missing is the bourgeois and low life of the town, which Walpole despised both in literature and actuality; but the life of the magnate and the man of fashion is recorded by him in his lively and informal style, with its endless variety of people and topics, its wit and light malice. The body of Walpole's letters, now being re-edited by Mr. W. S. Lewis in the great Yale edition, combines literary value and social documentation in a way unique even in an age which is rich in such matter. Walpole's untiring pen wrote whole volumes of letters to such correspondents as Sir Horace Mann, the English resident at Florence—George Montagu, William Cole, and from 1765 Mme du Deffand, the elderly, blind, and witty Frenchwoman who loved him ardently and whose affection he returned in a curious way. Of this important correspondence we have only Mme du Deffand's letters, not Walpole's. He outlived many of his friends, but found new interests and correspondents; his last years were colored by an emotional friendship with the charming sisters, Mary and Agnes Berry. He succeeded to the family title as Earl of Orford in 1791.

Letters, ed. Mrs. P. Toynbee (16v. Oxford, 1903-05); *Supplement* (3v, Oxford, 1918-25); *Correspondence,* ed. W. S. Lewis (New Haven, 1937-   ; Yale edition); *A Selection of the Letters,* ed. W. S. Lewis (New York, 1926); *Fugitive Verses,* ed. W. S.

Lewis (New York, 1931); W. S. Lewis, *The Genesis of Strawberry Hill* (New York, 1934); Austin Dobson, *Horace Walpole* (4th ed., rev. P. Toynbee, London, 1927); P. Yvon, *La vie d'un dilettante, Horace Walpole* (Paris, 1924); Dorothy M. Stuart, *Horace Walpole* (New York, 1927; English Men of Letters); R. W. Ketton-Cremer, *Horace Walpole* (London, 1940); A. B. Mason, *Horace Walpole's England* (London, 1930); *Journal of the Printing-Office at Strawberry Hill,* ed. P. Toynbee (London, 1923); A. T. Hazen, *A Bibliography of the Strawberry Hill Press* (New Haven, 1942); Isabel W. U. Chase, *Horace Walpole, Gardenist* (Princeton, 1943).

CHRISTOPHER SMART (1722-1771)

>>>

Christopher Smart makes his first literary appearance as a scholarly but dissipated fellow of Pembroke College, Cambridge, with a turn for Latin and English verse. By November 1747, probably earlier, he had issued proposals for a collection to include *The Hop-Garden,* various odes, and Latin versions of *L'Allegro* and *Il Penseroso* and Pope's *Essay on Criticism.* These pieces, finally published in 1752, and his Seatonian prize poems on the attributes of the Deity are not remarkable. From 1749 he was a London hack writer, contributing to periodicals (*The Student, The Midwife, The Universal Visitor*), doing other work for the bookseller John Newbery, forming literary friendships and engaging in personal controversies. His quarrel with Dr. John Hill resulted in the *Hilliad* (1753). A religious mania overtook him, perhaps at the beginning of 1756, and he spent five years in a relatively mild confinement (when one considers the treatment of the insane in the eighteenth century), partly under the care of his friends and partly in hospitals. During this period he planned his translation of the Psalms, wrote the incoherent but fascinating *Jubilate Agno,* recently published as *Rejoice in the Lamb,* and may have planned and begun his one great and famous poem, *A Song to David*. The old legend that Smart scratched the lines of the *Song* on the walls of his madhouse is to be rejected, but unquestionably his religious mania was closely connected with the rhapsodic enthusiasm which produced the poem. When it appeared in 1763, soon after Smart's release from an unidentified hospital or asylum, the *Song* was regarded only as an aberration of ruined genius. It was deliberately omitted from the edition of Smart's poems published in 1791, was first reprinted in 1819, and rediscovered and justly praised by discriminating nineteenth-century readers, Rossetti, Palgrave, Tennyson, and above all Browning, whose lines on Smart in *Parleyings with Certain People of Importance* (1887) are a deserved and brilliant tribute. The Victorians, ill informed though they may have been about the eighteenth century, were justified in their surprise at finding *A Song to David* there; recent studies of Smart's life and the new evidence provided by *Rejoice in the Lamb* do not explain the inspiration which produced the simple, intense, beautifully ordered and sustained lyricism of the *Song*. Smart never recovered his sanity completely, lived on in poverty and drunkenness, and died at last in a debtors' prison, yet there are fine touches in some of his later verse, notably in *Hymns for the Festivals of the Church of England* and *Hymns for the Amusement of Children*.

G. J. Gray, "A Bibliography of the Writings of Christopher Smart," *Transactions of the Bibliographical Society,* VI (1903). 269-303; K. A. McKenzie, *Christopher Smart, sa vie et ses oeuvres* (Paris, 1925); *Rejoice in the Lamb,* ed. W. F. Stead (London, 1939); R. B. Botting, "Christopher Smart in London," *Research Studies of the State College of Washington,* VII (1939). 3-54; E. G. Ainsworth and C. E. Noyes, *Christopher Smart: a Biographical and Critical Study* (Columbia, Mo., 1943).

PRIMITIVISM

>>

Primitivism is the exaltation of a state of life in which man depends on his natural powers exerted in a simple society and an uncomplicated environment, rather than on a high degree of training and on an environment greatly modified by civilization. Primitivism thus presupposes some form of the theory of man's natural goodness, whether this be taken to reside in instinct, common sense, spontaneous feeling, or in some or all of these. To be primitivistic, such a view of human nature must be connected with a stage or phase of human life different from that in which the writer or thinker lives, either in the past or in some contemporary society. Lovejoy calls the former "chronological primitivism," the latter "cultural primitivism." The two are often connected; contemporary primitive peoples may be taken to illustrate an early and desirable stage in the life of the race. Classical antiquity handed on such ideas and attitudes —the legend of the Golden Age, the admiration for simple unspoiled peoples such as the Germans of Tacitus. Lovejoy further describes primitivism as "soft" or "hard," according as the primitive life is described in terms of the gentle social virtues or in terms of rigor and severity. Applied to chronological primitivism, this distinction points a contrast between the soft virtues of the Golden Age and the barbaric virtues of a heroic age; applied to cultural primitivism, this distinction depends largely on descriptions of the environment: in general, inhabitants of tropical regions will be soft, while those who live in desolate regions and severe climates will be hard. Any form of primitivism implies that man may or must grow worse: chronologically he degenerates from an earlier happy state; culturally society deteriorates as it grows more complex. But this does not mean that man may not get back to a happier state. The impulse underlying primitivism is the desire to escape from a corrupt and sophisticated civilization, or the desire to reform such a civilization by bringing it into conformity with an ideal of virtuous simplicity. It is thus opposed to the idea of progress in the sense of a further advance along the lines that have produced the complexities of civilization.

While the impulse to primitivism always finds some expression in any age, several causes make it a prominent part of modern literature. The emphasis on classical literature gave prominence to such ideas. Political theory, often based on the supposed social contract made by man in a state of nature, sometimes dwelt on the advantages of an early stage in the process, though not necessarily the *earliest* stage. A growing philosophical emphasis on self-evident common sense or reason, the "light of nature," weakened esteem for traditional authority, established institutions. And the great literature of travel which developed in the age of discovery often described happy peoples in distant climes, so that cultural primitivism was encouraged and richly illustrated.

With higher standards of living and increasing prosperity, the propaganda against luxury often took a primitivistic form. This might be just a heightening of the impulse that leads people to praise the simpler life of their forefathers, or it might be extended into an attack on civilized society. It could compromise with the idea of progress. Progress is desirable up to a point, as Brown's popular *Estimate of the Manners and Principles of the Times* (1757) argues, but beyond that point corruption sets in. Thus Thomson, Goldsmith, and many others could praise simplicity and British prosperity at the same time. Similarly, evidence for and against a "state of nature" could be gathered from the travelers. There was a strong impulse to idealize, but in real life few people were found ready to prefer the savage or the barbarian in all respects. A moderate position was to point out that simple peoples like the Indians or the Lapps enjoyed certain advantages (health, social virtues, freedom from anxiety over money and property) which are denied to civilized man. These advantages could be described as compensating more or less for the obvious disadvantages of such a state. Professor R. H. Pearce points out that this balanced view appears in the Scottish writers on cultural history (Adam Ferguson, John Gregory, William Robertson), and cannot be called fully primitivistic.

AMERICAN INDIANS
As portrayed in Beverley's *History and Present State of Virginia*, 1705.

Neither do Rousseau's doctrines in the *Discours sur l'inegalité* and the *Contrat social*, so often mentioned in this connection, clearly exalt the noble savage; they point out the disadvantages of the earliest stage and most emphatically the evils of an over-developed civilization, placing man's happiness in an intermediate patriarchal stage. The cult of the noble savage which becomes so prominent is not to be attached to Rousseau, but is to be explained as the coloring of the traditional dream of the Golden Age by an actual change in ethical theory. The extreme doctrine of sensibility, that goodness consists in the spontaneous expression of social sympathies, led primitivists to discover such qualities in the savage, whether the stoical Indian, the Negro, the Laplander, or the South Sea Islander so popular in the England of the 1770's.

The application of primitivistic ideas to the history of poetry was important for eighteenth-century criticism. This aspect is well illustrated by one of Gray's notes to *The Progress of Poesy*:

> Extensive influence of poetic genius over the remotest and most uncivilized nations; its connection with liberty, and the virtues that naturally attend on it. (See the Erse, Norwegian, and Welsh fragments, the Lapland and American songs.)

Blackwell's *Enquiry into the Life and Writings of Homer* (1735), though not fully primitivistic, is a brilliant study of the relation of early poetry to its environment; similar theories lie back of Ossian. The general doctrine is thus stated in William Duff's *Essay on Original Genius* (1767): "That original poetic genius will in general be displayed at its utmost vigour in the early or uncultivated periods of society which are peculiarly favorable to it; and that it will seldom appear in a very high degree in cultivated life." But since Homer, Hebrew poetry, Ossian, and Shakespeare were generally treated on the same level as great originals, it is evident that the cult of originality and simplicity was at a great distance from true literary history. Such ideas, under English influence, were enthusiastically cultivated in Germany by Hamann and Herder. The most drastic type of English primitivism appeared at the end of the century, when the cult of the noble savage was connected with educational reform and political radicalism, but was still, even more emphatically than in an earlier generation, blended with the idea of progress, that is, a movement toward perfection which consists in the re-attainment of an ideal of simplicity.

A. O. Lovejoy and George Boas, *Primitivism and Related Ideas in Antiquity* (Baltimore, 1935); G. Chinard, *L'Exotisme américain dans la littérature française au xvie siècle* (Paris, 1911); *L'Amérique et le rêve exotique dans la littérature française au xviie et au xviiie siècle* (Paris, 1934); C. B. Tinker, *Nature's Simple Plan* (Princeton, 1922); H. N. Fairchild, *The Noble Savage* (New York, 1928); R. W. Frantz, *The English Traveller and the Movement of Ideas, University of Nebraska Studies,* XXXII-XXXIII (1932-33); Lois Whitney, *Primitivism and the Idea of Progress in English Popular Literature of the Eighteenth Century* (Baltimore, 1934); "English Primitivistic Theories of Epic Origins," *Modern Philology,* XXI (1924). 337-78; A. O. Lovejoy, "The Supposed Primitivism of Rousseau's *Discourse on Inequality,*" *Modern Philology,* XXI (1923). 165-86; R. H. Pearce, "The Eighteenth-Century Scottish Primitivists," *ELH,* XII (1945). 203-20; D. M. Foerster, *Homer in English Criticism* (New Haven, 1947).

THE MEDIEVAL REVIVAL AND BISHOP HURD
>>>

The medieval revival was not a single concerted movement; the term covers diverse interests and activities. The Scandinavian death-song in Temple's essay *On Heroic Virtue* was connected with "hard primitivism" (see p. 361) and the cult of liberty, and this thread can be traced through the Scandinavian odes of John Campbell's *Polite Correspondence* (1741) and the elder Thomas Warton's *Runic Ode* (1748), taken directly from Temple. At this stage interest was stimulated largely by the fascination that Germanic and Celtic origins had for students of English history. Early Celtic and Scandinavian antiquarianism dwelt on a pre-chivalric heroic age, as in Ossian, but from the 1760's the emphasis came to be more and more on the chivalry of the later Middle Ages. Interest in the Gothic architecture which almost every Englishman had before his eyes, in English history, in balladry, and in earlier stages of English literature naturally led to this development. No line was drawn between the Elizabethan period and the Middle Ages: the study of Shakespeare, Spenser, Milton, and Chaucer alike promoted "Gothic" themes. Much of this appears in the poetry and criticism of the Wartons (see p. 227), and the way was fully prepared for a return to chivalry in the 1760's, with the appearance of Gothic and historical romance (see pp. 282-84), and with Hurd's *Letters on Chivalry and Romance* (1762).

Richard Hurd was a tame and scholarly bishop who rather suddenly proceeded from conventional Augustan criticism to enthusiasm for medieval themes. The third of his *Moral and Political Dialogues* (1759), "On the Age of Queen Elizabeth," represents Addison and Arbuthnot discussing feudalism and chivalry in the ruins of Kenilworth. The *Letters* themselves begin with a plea for an historical approach: we must understand both Greek and medieval romance in terms of the societies that produced them, and certain parallels between the two appear. Here Hurd's doctrine is much like that of Blackwell's *Enquiry into the Life and Writings of Homer* and Warton's *Observations on the Faerie Queene*. But the contrast between classic and Gothic proves to be of more importance than the parallel: each is to be justified by its own rules, but if the highest thing in poetry is an imaginative appeal to the sense of the marvelous, then the Gothic is superior, intrinsically more poetical, even though French taste and modern rationalism condemn it.

What we have gotten by this revolution, you will say, is a great deal of good sense. What we have lost is a world of fine fabling, the illusion of which is so grateful to the charmed spirit that, in spite of philosophy and fashion, *Faery Spenser* still ranks highest among the poets.

Tasso and Ariosto were for Hurd the great masters of the marvelous, along with Spenser and Shakespeare. At this stage literary and antiquarian enthusiasm for the Gothic outran creative power (Hurd disliked Walpole's *Castle of Otranto*). For the next generation the medieval movement was largely occupied with the superficially picturesque. It readily took on a sentimental coloring, though it did not blend easily with democratic and drastically primitivistic strains of thought. Eventually, of course, it was taken up into the larger humanity and more vigorous intelligence and imagination of Walter Scott.

K. Clark, *The Gothic Revival* (London, 1928); F. E. Farley, *Scandinavian Influences in the English Romantic Movement* (Boston, 1903); R. Haferkorn, *Gotik und Ruine in der englischen Dichtung des 18. Jahrhunderts* (Leipzig, 1924); Hurd, *Letters on Chivalry and Romance,* ed. Edith Morley (London, 1911); A. L. Smith, "Richard Hurd's *Letters on Chivalry and Romance,*" *ELH*, VI (1939). 58-81; H. Trowbridge, "Bishop Hurd: A Reinterpretation," *Publications of the Modern Language Association,* LVIII (1943). 450-65; A. D. McKillop, "A Critic of 1741 on Early Poetry," *Studies in Philology,* XXX (1933). 504-21; E. D. Snyder, *The Celtic Revival in English Literature, 1760-1800* (Cambridge, Mass., 1923); E. R. Wasserman, "The Scholarly Origin of the Elizabethan Revival," *ELH*, IV (1937). 213-43; R. Wellek, *The Rise of English Literary History* (Chapel Hill, 1941); P. Yvon, *Le Gothique et la renaissance gothique en Angleterre* (Caen, 1931).

JAMES MACPHERSON (1736-1796)

>>>

Macpherson, the supposed translator of the once famous Ossianic poems, was born in southern Inverness-shire, in a remote region associated with the feuds of Highland clans and the rebellion of 1745. He grew up with a smattering of Gaelic, though without detailed knowledge of that difficult language. He was educated at Aberdeen and Edinburgh, and wrote mediocre verse. In 1759 he met John Home, who was moved to enthusiasm by a supposed translation of a fragment of traditional Highland poetry, "The Death of Oscar." Home and his scholarly friends in Edinburgh then encouraged Macpherson to publish *Fragments of Ancient Poetry Collected in the Highlands of Scotland, and Translated from the Gallic or Erse Language* (1760). There was already a well-defined idea that a great body of traditional verse had been preserved by the bards in Wales and the Scottish Highlands. John Campbell's *Polite Correspondence* (1741) had spoken of the heroic virtue and primitive enthusiasm of Celtic poetry, and suggested that "remains of this poetic spirit" should be sought in Wales, Brittany, and the Highlands. The "runic bards" in Collins's *Ode on the Superstitions of the Highlands of Scotland* (written in 1749 and addressed to John Home) represent the same idea. A young schoolmaster, Jerome Stone, had published a letter on Gaelic poetry with a specimen translation in the *Scots Magazine* (1755-56). Macpherson was now virtually ordered by the Edinburgh literati to travel in the Highlands at their expense and find this primitive poetry. The Reverend Hugh Blair, Professor of Rhetoric and Belles Lettres at Edinburgh, was convinced that the fragments pointed to a Highland epic, and would be satisfied with nothing else. Macpherson was somewhat reluctant, but after two short Highland journeys he duly produced *Fingal* (1761, dated 1762), and *Temora* (1763).

Macpherson's later life is of no importance for literary history except for the long controversy that raged about the authenticity of the Ossianic poems. He cut a poor figure in these quarrels, and was never able to produce his alleged Gaelic originals. The question of the relation of Ossian to Gaelic literature lies outside the English field. The conclusion now is that Macpherson's work has a slender traditional basis but does not rest on traditional texts. What is denied, of course, is not the existence of traditional High-land poetry, but Macpherson's actual connection with that tradition. Quite apart from the question of authenticity, the enthusiasm with which the Ossianic poems were received and the influence they exerted throughout western Europe are historical facts of great importance. Ossian now seems to be merely bombastic and rhetorical prose, yet it could move a fastidious critic like Gray to write, "Imagina-tion dwelt many hundred years ago in all her pomp on the cold and barren mountains of Scotland.... She reigns in all nascent societies of men." [1] Gray and his generation were moved by preconceived ideas of early or primitive poetry. Macpherson succeeded because he gave what was expected, but gave it in a superficially novel way. His poetic prose is obviously influenced by the Bible, and follows the parallel style of Hebrew poetry; his pseudo-simple style, with its stock similes and epithets, was taken to be Homeric. The Ossianic pieces have little concrete detail of character, manners, physical objects, or topography. In these respects they are the very opposite of Homer. Shadowy figures, such as Ossian, the great hero turned blind bard in his old age, and the young and tender Malvina move against a vague background of mountain, seashore, forest, and sky, the austere landscape of the Highlands. Simple feelings of regret, loyalty, tenderness, and heroism are expressed with pseudo-archaic simplicity and monotonous repetition. The generality and vagueness of Ossian gave an elevation which contemporary readers and critics found sublime.

But there is a complex fusion of moods here: the poetry of melancholy was already encouraging the somber-sublime, but also blended with softer emotions so cultivated for their own sake as to be sentimental. The narrative interest of

[1] Gray, *Correspondence*, ed. Toynbee and Whibley (Oxford, 1935), II. 797.

Ossian is slight; the appeal is that made by graveyard poetry, the Gothic, and the sentimental cult of noble feelings. As Blair put it: "The general character of his poetry is the heroic mixed with the elegiac strain, admiration tempered with pity." [1] The supposed historical significance of Ossian was also important; not only did Macpherson set up the Caledonian against the Irish, and thus appeal to Scottish patriotism—he appealed also to a cult of ancient simplicity and heroism. Even the historian Gibbon, though he was no primitivist and did not believe in the authenticity of Ossian, admired the contrast between "the untutored Caledonians, glowing with the warm virtues of nature, and the degenerate Romans, polluted with the mean vices of wealth and slavery." [2] Perhaps it was this aspect of Ossian which later captivated Napoleon. The continental vogue of Ossian, as great as that of Richardson and Young, lies beyond our field. Cesarotti's Italian version and Le Tourneur's French version are only two among innumerable documents which attest the wide diffusion of Ossian. Goethe's references in *Werther,* including a translation of the "Song of Selma," should be remembered. There is some justice in Scott's verdict: [3]

While we are compelled to renounce the pleasing idea that 'Fingal lived and that Ossian sung,' our national vanity may be equally flattered by the fact that a remote and almost a barbarous corner of Scotland produced in the eighteenth century a bard capable not only of making an enthusiastic impression on every mind susceptible of poetical beauty, but of giving a new tone to poetry throughout all Europe.

G. F. Black, "Macpherson's Ossian and the Ossianic Controversy: A Contribution towards a Bibliography," *Bulletin of the*

[1] *A Critical Dissertation on the Poems of Ossian,* in *Poems of Ossian* (London, 1807), I. 213. First published 1763.
[2] *Decline and Fall of the Roman Empire,* ed. J. B. Bury (London, 1912), I. 130. Chap. vi.
[3] *Edinburgh Review,* VI (1805). 462.

New York Public Library, xxx (1926), 424-39, 508-24; *Poems of Ossian*, ed. William Sharp (Edinburgh, 1896); *James Macpherson's Ossian*, ed. O. L. Jiriczek (3v, Heidelberg, 1940); B. Saunders, *Life and Letters of James Macpherson* (London, 1894); J. S. Smart, *James Macpherson* (London, 1905); B. Schnabel, "Ossian in der schönen Litteratur England's bis 1832," *Englische Studien*, xxiii (1897). 31-70, 366-401; R. Tombo, *Ossian in Germany* (New York, 1901); Alexander Gillies, *Herder und Ossian* (Berlin, 1933); P. van Tieghem, *Ossian en France* (2v, Paris, 1917); W. A. Craigie, "The Ossianic Ballads," *Scottish Review*, xxxiv (1899). 260-90; A. Nutt, *Ossian and the Ossianic Literature* (London, 1899).

PERCY AND THE BALLAD REVIVAL

⟫⟫⟫

In our time the popular ballad is considered by many scholars to be definitely separated from the poetry of literary art, and the controversy as to its ultimate origin, whether communal or individual, still goes on. In its present form this debate comes down to us from the romantic movement, particularly from the Brothers Grimm in Germany. The eighteenth-century interest in ballads was connected with other themes, with the doctrine of the universality and uniformity of poetic inspiration, with the cult of simplicity, and with the interest in medieval antiquities. Thus Addison's famous papers on *Chevy Chase* (*Spectator* Nos. 70 and 74) praise the ballad for conforming naturally to the rules of the epic, though the critic also has a genuine and unpedantic liking for these familiar pieces. Addison also fosters the cult of simplicity by his comments on *The Babes in the Wood* (*Spectator* No. 85). A successful *Collection of Old Ballads* (1723-25), doubtfully attributed to Ambrose Philips, contains mostly broadside pieces connected with English history. The special Scottish interest in ballad material appears in Allan Ramsay's *Tea-*

Table Miscellany (1724-27). The favorite ballad of the century, David Mallet's *William and Margaret,* a remaking of a genuine popular ballad, was published in the *Plain Dealer* in 1724. In the next generation a growing interest in the bard or minstrel as composer of authentic primitive poetry was common to the Scandinavian, the Celtic, and the ballad revivals. It was no accident that Thomas Percy's *Reliques of Ancient English Poetry* (1765) was published soon after the appearance of the Ossianic poems.

BISHOP PERCY
With the folio manuscript in his hand.

Percy was an intelligent clergyman of wide though desultory antiquarian and literary interests, a correspondent of Shenstone and Thomas Warton, and an associate of Goldsmith and Johnson in the famous Club. He was later Dean of Carlisle and Bishop of Dromore. In 1761 and 1762 he published specimens of Chinese poetry taken from Du Halde's *History;* his *Five Pieces of Runic Poetry* (1763) and *Northern Antiquities* (1770), a translation of Mallet's influential *Histoire du Dannemarc,* give him a place in the Scandinavian revival. In 1764 he wrote to Evan Evans, who had just published *Some Specimens of the Poetry of the Antient Welsh Bards,* that his original purpose was "to exhibit specimens of the poetry of various nations in a series of literal translations." The Chinese, the Runic, the Song of Solomon, Evans's specimens from the Welsh, are to be continued, Percy says, by specimens from Arabia, Greenland, Lapland, North America, and Peru.

The underlying interest in this plan is primitivistic.

But Percy's greatest contribution dates from the time when he found the famous folio manuscript lying neglected and torn in a Shropshire country house. This was a miscellaneous collection of pieces copied by some unknown person, not highly educated, in the seventeenth century. Only about one quarter of the *Reliques* is taken from the manuscript, and that part is freely refined, rewritten, and mixed at times with lines and stanzas of Percy's own composing. Percy combined the rôles of editor and composer of ballads; thus he rewrote *Sir Cauline* and composed *The Friar of Orders Gray*. Beside the ballads the *Reliques* included many Elizabethan and seventeenth-century pieces. Percy gave his material a form acceptable to the public, and his success and influence were great. His *Essay on the Ancient Minstrels* argued that the medieval minstrels were the successors of the Celtic bards and Scandinavian scalds; erroneous though this theory was, it stimulated the historical imagination of the age. Other important collections followed—David Herd's *Scots Songs* (1769), Thomas Evans's *Old Ballads* (1777-84), John Pinkerton's *Ancient Scotish Poems* (1786), and Joseph Ritson's *Select Collection of English Songs* (1783). Sounder editorial methods and a better taste in ballads were still needed. Meanwhile Herder's philosophy of popular literature, based largely on Percy and Macpherson, marked a new era, and Bürger's *Lenore* was the most successful of all artificial ballads. Percy's conception of the antiquarian miscellany and the rôle of the ballad editor was handed on to Walter Scott, and the *Reliques* pointed the way to the *Minstrelsy of the Scottish Border*.

Alice C. C. Gaussen, *Percy; Prelate and Poet* (London, 1908); *Letters from Thomas Percy*, etc. (Edinburgh, 1830); *The Percy Letters*, ed. D. Nichol Smith and C. Brooks (Baton Rouge, La., 1944-); *Reliques of Ancient English Poetry,* ed. H. B. Wheatley

(3v, London, 1891); ed. M. M. Arnold Schröer (Berlin, 1893); *Bishop Percy's Folio Manuscript,* ed. J. W. Hales and F. J. Furnivall (3v, London, 1867-68); H. Hecht ed., *Thomas Percy und William Shenstone* (Strassburg, 1909); I. L. Churchill, "William Shenstone's Share in the Preparation of Percy's *Reliques," Publications of the Modern Language Association,* LI (1936), 960-74; Leah Dennis, "The Text of the Percy-Warton Letters," *ibid.,* XLVI (1931), 1166-1201; "Thomas Percy: Antiquarian *vs.* Man of Taste," *ibid.,* LVII (1942), 140-54; H. Lohre, *Von Percy zum Wunderhorn* (Berlin, 1902); S. B. Hustvedt, *Ballad Criticism in Scandinavia and Great Britain during the Eighteenth Century* (New York, 1916); L. F. Powell, "Percy's *Reliques," Library,* Fourth series, IX (1928), 113-37.

THOMAS CHATTERTON (1752-1770)
>>>

   The brief career of Chatterton brings together two aspects of romanticism, the return to the Middle Ages and the escape of the individual from an uncongenial bourgeois world. The former makes his work of intense interest for the antiquarian movement of the time; the latter has made him for later times a symbol of martyred genius. Between the two it is hard to approach his work directly and estimate its value.

   Chatterton's life centered in the neighborhood of the noble church of St. Mary Redcliffe in the great port of Bristol. His immediate ancestors had worked in or about the church. Thomas Chatterton, Senior, who kept a small school, died before his son was born, and the boy was educated at Colston's Hospital, a charity school, where he found the practical curriculum of writing and accounts very dull. His apprenticeship to the scrivener John Lambert was also dull, but gave him free time for his own strange studies. His imagination dwelt on local antiquities, the medieval architectural remains of Bristol, and he spent much time over some old parchments which his father had taken from a chest in the muniment room of St Mary's. The documents he handled were legal, not literary, but they stimulated his imagination. By steps unknown to his biographers, he evolved a romance of fifteenth-century Bristol, centering about William Canynges, a merchant who became Lord Mayor and had been a benefactor of City and Church. About him Chatterton conjured up a group of learned priests, particularly Thomas Rowley of St. John's, whom Chatterton made a poet and antiquarian like himself. For the actual poems represented as those of Rowley and his circle he devised a vocabulary drawn largely from the dictionaries of Bailey and Kersey and from Speght's edition of Chaucer, and couched in elaborately archaic spelling. It was thus that he began to fabricate the "originals" of the Rowley poems.

In 1768, when the new bridge was opened in Bristol and there was a flurry of interest in local antiquities, Chatterton published his first spurious documents and was soon giving or selling his manuscripts to two Bristol antiquarians who repaid him with little sympathy or help. We cannot apply modern standards of literary honesty and historical accuracy to Chatterton; literary imposture was frequent in his time, from the fabrications of Macpherson and the later Shakespeare forgeries of Ireland down to the common practice of slipping modern pieces into collections of ancient literature. Scott himself may have planted a ballad or two of his own. Chatterton was indulging his poetic bent and his antiquarian enthusiasm, and resorting to a device to attract attention. In 1769, after an unsuccessful attempt to offer his wares to the bookseller James Dodsley, Chatterton sent Walpole a specimen, "The Ryse of Peyncteynge yn Englande." Walpole wrote a cordial answer, but on getting more Rowley material was warned off by Gray and Mason, and after some delay sent the manuscripts back

with some good advice. He was justified in doing this,
though when he was later blamed for Chatterton's disappointment and death he was goaded into an indiscreet
defense. In 1769 and 1770 Chatterton turned suddenly to
miscellaneous writings on current models, *African Eclogues*
after Collins, imitations of Ossian, satires in Churchill's
style, and political letters on behalf of Wilkes. Many of his
contributions appeared in the *Town and Country Magazine,* and when he left Bristol for London in April 1770
it was with the hope of earning his living as a hack writer.
Despite enthusiasm and hard work he remained miserably
poor, and in August he committed suicide in his London
lodgings.

The controversy about the authenticity of the Rowley
poems was soon settled in Tyrwhitt's edition (1777-78) and
in Thomas Warton's *History of English Poetry* (1778),
though some people continued to argue that Rowley was
too good to be written by Chatterton, just as Ossian had
been considered too good to be written by Macpherson.
The best of the Rowley poems stand on their own merit—
the dramatic interlude of *Aella,* with its remarkable lyrics,
the poem on freedom in *Goddwyn,* the *Bristowe Tragedy
or the Dethe of Syr Charles Bawdin* (a ballad which is
the only conspicuous example of the influence of Percy's
Reliques on Chatterton), and the last of the Rowley poems,
An Excelente Balade of Charitie. Chatterton's skill in free
and irregular meters and his quaintly simple diction, Elizabethan and Spenserian rather than medieval, influenced
later poets, particularly Coleridge. His personal history and
fate counted for much also. Every one knows the references
to Chatterton in Wordsworth's *Resolution and Independence* and Shelley's *Adonais;* Coleridge's *Monody,* an early
sonnet by Keats, the dedication of *Endymion* to the memory of Chatterton, Alfred de Vigny's drama *Chatterton,* and
Rossetti's intense admiration should also be remembered.

Poetical Works, ed. W. W. Skeat (2v, London, 1875; Aldine edition); ed. H. D. Roberts (2v, London, 1906); *Rowley Poems,* ed. M. E. Hare (Oxford, 1911; reprint of Tyrwhitt's edition); J. H. Ingram, *The True Chatterton* (London, 1910); E. H. W. Meyerstein, *Life of Thomas Chatterton* (London, 1930); Esther P. Ellinger, *Thomas Chatterton* (Philadelphia, 1930); A. Watkin-Jones, "Percy, Warton, and Chatterton," *Publications of the Modern Language Association,* L (1935), 769-84; Frances S. Miller, "The Historic Sense of Thomas Chatterton," *ELH,* XI (1944), 117-34.

JAMES BEATTIE (1735-1803)

>>

Beattie was born at Laurencekirk, a small town about thirty miles south of Aberdeen. He won a scholarship at Marischal College, Aberdeen, taught school, and studied for the ministry. From 1760 he held the chair of Moral Philosophy at Marischal College, and came forth as an orthodox opponent of the skeptical Hume, against whom he directed his *Essay on Truth* (1770). This work was much overpraised, and won for Beattie the patronage of Mrs. Montagu and others. Hume was so far superior in philosophic power that the pretensions of his critics now seem ludicrous. At Aberdeen Beattie was in contact with the exponents of the Scottish "common sense" school of philosophy, and with a school of rhetoricians and critics who exalted taste and original genius. Among his teachers was Thomas Blackwell (see p. 364); Alexander Gerard, author of *An Essay on Taste* (1759), was both teacher and colleague, and George Campbell the rhetorician was also a colleague. Beattie, always academic and docile, got from these men what we might call an official doctrine of pre-romanticism. While at work on his *Essay* he diverted himself by writing *The Minstrel,* which he thus described in 1768: "It is a moral and descriptive poem, written in the stanza of

Spenser, but not much in his style. The hint of the subject was taken from Percy's 'Essays [*sic*] on the English Minstrels.' " [1] In the preface to Book I (1771) he says: "The design was to trace the progress of a poetical genius, born in a rude age, from the first dawning of fancy and reason, till that period at which he may be supposed capable of appearing in the world as a *Minstrel,* that is, as an itinerant poet and musician." Beattie does not break fresh ground in this work; he does not, like Wordsworth, give us a study of the growth of a poet's mind, but puts his vaguely conceived young minstrel Edwin in the midst of sublime and picturesque scenery based to some extent on the Scottish landscape though not vividly localized. In Book II (1774) Edwin, under the instruction of a sage hermit, passes from the dreams of youth to a survey of moral duties, and is told at length of man's cultural progress. This didactic survey combines the idea of progress with the idea of the excellence of primitive simplicity. A similar pattern of themes occurs in Thomson, who influenced Beattie directly here. *The Minstrel,* now completely neglected, was once very popular because it set forth currently acceptable ideas and images in a smooth though undistinguished style. Though Beattie has a certain academic good taste, he falls far short of Thomson in imaginative and artistic power, and at the same time he lacks the scholarly enthusiasms of his friend Thomas Gray. Unlike his younger countrymen, Burns and Scott, he makes no significant use of the traditions of his native land.

Poetical Works, ed. A. Dyce (London, 1894; Aldine edition); Sir William Forbes, *An Account of the Life and Writings of James Beattie* (2nd ed., 3v, Edinburgh, 1807); Margaret Forbes, *Beattie and his Friends* (London, 1904); *London Diary, 1773,* ed. R. S. Walker (Aberdeen, 1946).

[1] Margaret Forbes, *Beattie and his Friends,* p. 56.

WILLIAM COWPER (1731-1800)
>>

There is much that is normal and representative in Cowper's poetry and letters; his best work is plain, sensible, and sensitive. He was a conscientious, devout, refined Englishman, and this largely accounts for the popularity of his work down to Victorian times. His *Task,* like Thomson's *Seasons,* was long within reach of almost everyone in school and at home. Yet Cowper was abnormal, a victim of a mania that drove him to despair and more than once to the verge of suicide. In his life, as later in the life of Charles Lamb, playfulness and domestic comfort are subtly connected with an underlying terror and despair.

Cowper was born at Great Berkhamstead, Hertfordshire; left motherless at the age of six, the sensitive boy was unhappy at a school in Hertfordshire, but tolerably happy at Westminster School and then as a solicitor's clerk and resident of the Middle Temple. He enjoyed the friendship of his cousins Harriet and Theodora Cowper, and fell in love with the latter. He did some minor writing in partnership with literary friends—Thornton, Colman, and Lloyd. But a painful break came when, to meet the requirements for a clerkship in the House of Lords, he was called to appear at the Bar of the House for examination. Fear of this ordeal drove him to attempt suicide, and his mania took a religious form. Under the care of Dr. Nathaniel Cotton at St. Albans he made a partial recovery, and in 1765 settled at Huntingdon with the Unwin family. On the death of the Reverend Morley Unwin, Cowper and Mrs. Unwin moved to a commonplace village, Olney, Buckinghamshire, in the valley of the Ouse, to enjoy the religious ministrations of the Reverend John Newton. Newton was a firm but not extreme Calvinist of the Evangelical

COWPER'S HOUSE AT WESTON, BUCKINGHAMSHIRE

group within the Church of England; he was a devout and sincere man, but by forcing Cowper to incessant religious exercises he subjected the poet to a nervous strain which brought on another attack of insanity in 1773. During this period the *Olney Hymns* (1779) were written. With religious despair in the background, he devoted himself to the simple pleasures of the country, the details of the household, the pleasures of gardening and of watching his pet hares. His gradual convalescence at this stage marks the beginning of his most important work as a poet. The *Poems* of 1782, however, still show the conventional censorious attitude of the satirist, and do not fully express the rare quality of his personality. From 1781 the stimulating friendship with Lady Austen helped to bring out this quality; she told him the story of *John Gilpin* (first printed in the *Public Advertiser,* 1782) and also started him on *The Task.* Because Mrs. Unwin did not get on well with Lady Austen, this pleasant relationship was broken off, but his cousin Theodora, now Lady Hesketh, played a like part in 1785-86. At this time Cowper and Mrs. Unwin moved to Weston, Buckinghamshire. He occupied himself with translating Homer and made some new friendships, especially with the poet William Hayley, whom he visited in Sussex. Mrs. Unwin died in 1796, and the poet's last years were darkened by failing health and incurable religious despair, expressed in his tragic poem *The Castaway,* written a year before his death. But his life should not be painted in too somber colors; he found a refuge, though not a permanent one, and at his best he took constant delight in the world around him. It should be added also that despite his secluded life he took a comprehensive view of the late eighteenth-century scene.

THE TASK

The Task (1785) is the most informal and personal of
the eighteenth-century descriptive-didactic poems. Cowper
was right in saying that his blank verse was unlike Milton's
or Thomson's, unmistakable though his debt is to his predecessors. He often uses Miltonic diction for playful and
humorous effects, and he extends the descriptive and genre
work of Thomson by using more minute realistic detail and
much more local color. In his treatment of the tame and
gentle Midland landscape we find an interest in realism for
its own sake, more moderate and delicate than Crabbe's—
in Book I, for example, the view of the valley of the Ouse
(ll. 154-80) , and the descriptions of rural sounds (ll. 181-
209) and of the color of the bark and leaves of trees (ll. 300-
20). Cowper, says Hussey, "had no need of the picturesque";
he does not describe the country in terms of the contemporary romanticized landscape or sympathize with the new
styles of gardening. Some of his most characteristic work
is the description of domestic comfort and retirement (especially in Book IV). Nature itself may be said to be an
important part of the social or the domestic situation in
the English village and countryside.

Cowper expresses at length his opinions on man, society,
nature, and religion, though his ideas are of less importance
than his style, tone, and imagery. He avoids the extreme
-isms of his day: he describes the hardships of the poor
(Book IV), but this does not carry him to the sentimental
excess of saying that the poor are always innocent and virtuous; he loves rural simplicity and retirement—"God made
the country and man made the town"—but he rejects the
primitivistic cult of the South Sea islanders (I, 592 ff.) and
the pastoral poets' Golden Age (IV, 513 ff.). He deplores the
corrupting effects of industry, militarism, imperialism, and
aristocratic fashion, and this leads him to sympathize with

the early stages of the French Revolution. His Christian orthodoxy, his insistence on the fallen state of man and on a God found necessarily in revelation and not merely in nature make him bitterly hostile to deism and limit his sympathy with the physico-theologist's program of using scientific discovery to prove divine design. There is much of interest in Cowper's opinions and doctrines, but more in the subtle personal and artistic qualities which the less doctrinal and satirical parts of *The Task* have in common with the poet's charming letters.

Works, ed. R. Southey (15v, London, 1836-37); *Complete Poetical Works,* ed. H. S. Milford (3rd ed., London, 1926); *Correspondence,* ed. T. Wright (4v, London, 1904); *Unpublished and Uncollected Letters,* ed. T. Wright (London, 1925); *Poetry and Prose,* ed. H. S. Milford (Oxford, 1921); *New Poems* (Oxford, 1931); *Letters: A Selection,* ed. E. V. Lucas (London, 1911); Goldwin Smith, *Cowper* (New York, 1880; English Men of Letters); T. Wright, *Life* (2nd ed., London, 1921); H. I'A. Fausset, *William Cowper* (London, 1928); Lord David Cecil, *The Stricken Deer* (London, 1929); Gilbert Thomas, *William Cowper and the Eighteenth Century* (London, 1935); L. C. Hartley, *William Cowper, Humanitarian* (Chapel Hill, 1938).

GEORGE CRABBE (1754-1832)
>>

Though Crabbe's life and work extend beyond our chronological limits, they are really of the eighteenth century. He has earned a secondary but important place in literary history by his effective use of the plain style of eighteenth-century verse for the purposes of literal and disillusioned realism. Early experiences prepared him for this approach to poetry. He was born at Aldeborough, a little seaport in Suffolk, where he saw and shared the struggles and troubles of the poor. He became a surgeon's apprentice, began prac-

384 ENGLISH LITERATURE—DRYDEN TO BURNS

tice in Aldeborough, and resolutely continued to educate himself by studying the classics, theology, and botany, and by trying to write poetry. A few months after he came to London in 1780 he was reduced to desperate straits, but he found a good patron in Edmund Burke, who helped him to publish a mediocre poem, *The Library* (1781), encouraged him to take orders and look for preferment in the Church, and soon got him a place as chaplain to the Duke of Rutland at Belvoir Castle. *The Village* (1783) justified Burke's faith in Crabbe and showed his full power. Here he makes a direct attack on the pastoral tradition, and sets over against the happy swains of the Golden Age the wretched inhabitants of Aldeborough. The artificialities of the pastoral convention had long been a commonplace of criticism, and in particular a favorite theme with Dr. Johnson, who read and admired the poem in manuscript and contributed a few lines (Book 1, ll. 15-20). Crabbe attacks the whole sentimental concept of "the simple life that Nature yields," and his poem has often been taken as an answer to Goldsmith's *Deserted Village*. His work also connects with a tendency to minute and precise description in late eighteenth-century poetry. He approaches the naturalistic novelists of a later time in his grim transcription of physical detail and his picture of man bogged down in his own nature and his environment. He keeps his pity for the poor clear of sentimental idealization, and directness and surly honesty give him peculiar power.

After the publication of *The Newspaper* (1785) Crabbe printed nothing for twenty-two years, though he continued to write. In *The Parish Register* (1807) and *The Borough* (1810) he elaborates the theme of *The Village,* studying various phases of life and character within the same or a like community. *Peter Grimes,* one of the most powerful tales in *The Borough,* is the subject of a tragic opera by Benjamin Britten, successfully produced at Sadler's Wells in 1945. In *Tales in Verse* (1812) and *Tales of the Hall* (1819) Crabbe studies human character, particularly its limitations and disappointments, in simply plotted narratives with more widely varied settings. He was greatly admired by many readers and critics of the romantic generation, and has been praised by a minority of discriminating readers in later times. Thus the fastidious American poet Edwin Arlington Robinson pays tribute to Crabbe's "hard human pulse," his "plain excellence and stubborn skill."

Poetical Works, with his Letters and Journals and his Life by his Son (8v, London, 1834); *Poems*, ed. A. W. Ward (3v, Cambridge, 1905-07); *Poetical Works*, ed. A. J. and R. M. Carlyle (London, 1914); A. Ainger, *George Crabbe* (London, 1903; English Men of Letters); René Huchon, *Un Poète realiste anglais* (Paris, 1906), trans. by F. Clarke as *George Crabbe and his Times* (London, 1907); J. H. Evans, *The Poems of George Crabbe: A Literary and Historical Study* (London, 1933); Varley Lang, "Crabbe and the Eighteenth Century," *ELH*, v (1938). 305-33.

ALLAN RAMSAY (1685?-1758)

>>

Ramsay was born in a barren mining region in Lanarkshire; he was apprenticed to a wigmaker in Edinburgh, and seems to have begun his literary career as a member of the Easy Club, a group influenced by the social standards of the *Tatler* and the *Spectator,* with an added touch of Scottish conviviality and folkways. From songs and occasional pieces published as broadsides he went on to put together collections largely made up of rewritten versions of earlier Scots pieces—*Scots Songs* (1718), *The Ever Green* (1724), *The Tea-Table Miscellany* (1724-27). The preface to *The Ever Green* shows his nationalistic spirit:

When these good old bards wrote, we had not yet made use of imported trimming upon our clothes, nor of foreign embroidery in our writings. Their poetry is the product of their own country, not pilfered and spoiled in the transportation from abroad; their images are native, and their landskips domestic, copied from those fields and meadows we every day behold.

In his curious series of mock-elegies and epistles, based on models set by Robert Sempill of Beltrees and Hamilton of Gilbertfield, and in his continuation of the old poem *Christis Kirk on the Green* he prolongs the Scots tradition of coarsely humorous verse. The immediate predecessor of his collections was James Watson's *Choice Collection of Comic and Serious Scots Poems both Ancient and Modern* (1706-11). Ramsay's lyrics garble traditional songs, and show something of the method though not the skill of Burns, but he anticipates the greater achievements of Burns and Scott in his patriotic pride and his dependence on national tradition. His humorous pastorals, *Patie and Roger* (1720) and *Jenny and Meggy* (1723) became part of a pastoral drama *The Gentle Shepherd* (1725), made into a ballad-opera in 1728 and in this form long read and acted.

In the 1720's Ramsay became a bookseller and the proprietor of a circulating library, and in the 1730's he even started a dramatic company—all this to the horror of the austere Presbyterians of the town. Until the appearance of Fergusson and Burns, Ramsay was thought of as the leader of Scots poetry. In 1791 R. Cummings could still publish an *Essay on the Question: Whether have the exertions of Allan Ramsay or Robert Fergusson done most honour to Scottish Poetry*.

Works (3v, London, 1852); *Poems*, ed. J. L. Robertson (London, 1887); Andrew Gibson, *New Light on Allan Ramsay* (Edinburgh, 1927); Burns Martin, *Allan Ramsay* (Cambridge, Mass., 1931); *Bibliography of Allan Ramsay* (Glasgow, 1932).

SCOTTISH LITERATURE

>>

Earlier Scottish literature, discouraged and repressed in the seventeenth century, was revived and imitated in the movement already briefly referred to under Allan Ramsay. Vernacular poetry, broadly comic, vividly realistic, or echoing with genuine pathos, brought educated and uneducated closer together in Scotland than in England, particularly in the second half of the century. The best pieces were written by educated Scots who caught the spirit of popular poetry and popular music, the folksong rather than the ballad: here belong Lady Wardlaw's *Hardyknute* (1719), Hamilton of Bangour's *Braes of Yarrow* (1724), Grisell Baillie's "Werena my heart licht I wad dee," versions of *The Flowers of the Forest* by Mrs. Cockburn and Jane Elliot, John Skinner's *Tullochgorum,* and innumerable others, many of doubtful authorship and date and many anonymous. The example of Percy's *Reliques* was of the first importance for collectors of Scottish ballads and songs, from David Herd to Walter Scott himself (see p. 373). The immediate predecessor of Burns in humorous genre poetry was the unfortunate Robert Fergusson (1750-1774), a student at St. Andrews and frequenter of Edinburgh taverns and clubs, who died insane at twenty-four. He is the poet of Edinburgh low life, but the range of his subjects suggests Burns time and again—*Leith Races, The Hallow Fair, The Farmer's Ingle.* Ramsay and Fergusson took from earlier writers and handed on to Burns certain traditional stanza forms: thus the stanza of Burns's *Holy Fair* goes back to *Christis Kirk on the Green,* the opening of *The Jolly Beggars* to Montgomerie's *Cherry and Slae,* the familiar six-line stanza of Burns to a whole school of humorous Scots writing.

But the genteel tradition in Scotland tried to eliminate broad Scots, and to ape English speech and ways. The literati of the universities, especially at Edinburgh and Aberdeen, were for the most part out of sympathy with the speech and literary traditions of their own country. Many great and familiar names belong here, and are for the most part discussed elsewhere in this book—Thomas Reid, the philosophical opponent of Hume; Adam Smith the economist; Adam Ferguson the sociologist; William Robertson the historian; Hugh Blair and George Campbell the rhetoricians. Until well past the middle of the century men like these had bad luck in picking Scottish poets, and professed to admire the Homeric qualities of Wilkie's *Epigoniad* (1757), John Home's plays, and the verses of the blind Thomas Blacklock, who it seemed might qualify as a Scottish Pindar. Intellectual snobbery and a somewhat languid preference for neo-classical formulas cut them off from the native tradition. An interest in literary history makes itself felt as the century advances, and the somewhat confused demands of this group for primitive poetry helped to produce Ossian (see p. 368), and later predisposed men like Henry Mackenzie to welcome Burns. Moreover, some Scotsmen who did not deliberately cultivate their own tradition, and who, while proud of their nationality, tended to become anglicized in style, attained literary success in the standard tongue—notably James Thomson and Tobias Smollett, on a lower level James Beattie and Henry Mackenzie, on a still lower level David Mallet and others of the obscure.

Quite apart at first was the literary tradition of Celtic Scotland, which as we have noted, makes at least superficial contact with English literature in Collins's *Ode on the Superstitions of the Highlands of Scotland* and in Ossian. Even in the great days of Walter Scott Celtic actualities were imperfectly known and understood outside the Highlands. Yet Highlander and Lowlander, Scot and Englishman found more and more common ground. Though national prejudices had in some ways been stimulated by the union of England and Scotland in 1707, and by the Jacobite uprisings of 1715 and 1745, they were colorful but not so deep in the reign of George III, and were overcome in large part by community of interest and by the contagious influence of Scottish song and romance.

Robert Fergusson, *Scots Poems*, ed. B. Dickins (Edinburgh, 1925); H. G. Graham, *Scottish Men of Letters in the Eighteenth Century* (London, 1901); *The Social Life of Scotland in the Eighteenth Century* (London, 1928); T. F. Henderson, *Scottish Vernacular Literature* (3rd ed., Edinburgh, 1910); Agnes M. Mackenzie, *Scotland in Modern Times, 1720-1939* (London, 1941); W. L. Mathieson, *The Awakening of Scotland* (Glasgow, 1910); J. H. Millar, *Literary History of Scotland* (New York, 1903); *Scottish Prose of the Seventeenth and Eighteenth Centuries* (Glasgow, 1912); E. C. Mossner, *The Forgotten Hume, Le Bon David* (New York, 1943); Wallace Notestein, *The Scot in History* (New Haven, 1946); J. W. Oliver, "The Eighteenth Century Revival," in *Edinburgh Essays on Scots Literature* (Edinburgh, 1933); John Ramsay, *Scotland and Scotsmen in the Eighteenth Century* (Edinburgh, 1888); G. G. Smith, *Scottish Literature, Character and Influence* (London, 1919); John Speirs, *The Scots Literary Tradition* (London, 1940); H. W. Thompson, *A Scottish Man of Feeling* (New York, 1931); H. Walker, *Three Centuries of Scottish Literature* (2v, Glasgow, 1893).

ROBERT BURNS (1759-1796)
>>

The late eighteenth century considered Burns first of all as a provincial poet and a humble unlettered farmer. It has been the work of later biography to revise this view, and, without belittling his nationalism or his natural genius, to define his place in British literature. Throughout the century Scottish vernacular verse had been reanimated by Ramsay, Fergusson, and many lesser writers, and Burns inherited his models from these immediate predecessors. The rich treasury of Scottish popular song was open to all, and here at last was one who could take full advantage of it. The profounder side of Burns's racial inheritance cannot be fully described: it appears in the noble and somewhat intractable character of his father, in the poet's own sound sense, rich humor, and strong passions, and in the conflict between this ardent temperament and the rigid rule of the Scottish Kirk. Moreover, Burns had access to standard English writers and was sensitive to ideas and attitudes current in his day; he was a man of the Enlightenment and the Age of Revolution.

BURNS

Our own standards of living must not lead us to exaggerate the tragedy of Burns's poverty. "Ayrshire," writes a recent biographer, President Snyder, "was a good place in which to be born and to live and write poetry." It is only fair to add that another authority, Professor Ferguson, editor of Burns's letters, takes a gloomier view. Externally the history of the Burns family was a continual struggle with barren soil and high rents. From the village of Alloway, near Ayr, where the poet was born, they moved first to one farm and then to another, from Mount Oliphant to Lochlea, and, just after the father's death in 1784, to Mossgiel, near Mauchline. But their minds were not dulled or their spirits broken. Burns's early education was based on the standard works of eighteenth-century literary culture, such as the

Spectator, Pope's Homer, Thomson's *Seasons,* Young's *Night Thoughts,* and some of Shakespeare. He soon came to admire the writers esteemed by the current school of sensibility —Shenstone, Sterne, Mackenzie, and Ossian. His lifelong love of Scottish popular song and music he would, to be sure, hardly think of as literary. He knew too well also the seamy side of Scottish life, the reckless drinking and love-

THE BIRTHPLACE OF ROBERT BURNS, ALLOWAY
From an engraving of 1805.

making that went on under the shadow of the Kirk. In the years 1784 to 1786 his life came to a crisis; his amours, particularly the affair with Jean Armour, brought on him the censure of the church authorities, and in the background is the obscure story of "Highland Mary," about whom we know very little. It seems, however, that this affair, over which earlier biographers grew sentimental, was no more ideal than the others. Yet these troubled years show Burns as a poet at his best; he was now writing freely and easily in forms and styles set by his Scots predecessors. He was filled with a reckless sense of power as he wrote his satires against hypocrites and grim preachers of the old school; he found that he could hold his own with intelligent lairds and professional men like Robert Aikin and Gavin Hamilton; and he made his way to poetry with marvelous directness.

In 1786 a large part of this work of his early prime appeared in the famous little volume published at Kilmarnock. Literary critics hailed the work of the "Ayrshire plowman"; and instead of sailing for Jamaica, as he had planned, Burns visited Edinburgh as a literary lion and traveled through the Borders and the Highlands. To this period belongs his artificial and sentimental love affair with Mrs. McLehose. His career was not deeply or favorably affected by these new experiences; the republication of his poems at Edinburgh did not bring him the money such a success deserved. He now avowed his earlier marriage to Jean Armour and undertook to get a living from the run-down farm of Ellisland, near Dumfries, and from his new appointment as exciseman (collector of internal revenue). Soon he moved to the town of Dumfries, where he continued to live rather recklessly, mingling in the convivial society of the town and indulging his enthusiasm for the French Revolution. He discharged his official duties well. In poetry, the years after 1787 are memorable for the three hundred songs which he contributed freely and enthusiastically to James Johnson's *Scots Musical Museum* and George Thomson's *Select Collection of Original Scotish [sic] Airs.* The one important long poem of this period is the incomparable *Tam o'Shanter* (1790). His untimely death in 1796 was not, as his early biographers thought, the result of sheer dissipation, but of hard work, disappointment, and anxiety.

Burns at first thought of himself as a local bard, "just a rhymer like by chance." Much of his work was occasional, centering about some particular object or person or situation. Thus his early satires were directed against certain clergymen and elders of the conservative "Auld Licht" party with whose theology he disagreed and against whom he had a personal grudge (*The Holy Fair, The Twa Herds, Holy Willie's Prayer, Address to the Unco Guid*). Poor Mailie, for whom he wrote two poems, was a real sheep; no doubt the poet actually saw the louse on the lady's bonnet at church. "That's the field where Burns plowed up the daisy," said a boy to Wordsworth a few years later. His verse epistles on the model of Allan Ramsay are highly informal and personal. His incomparable power of giving definitive literary expression to the feelings and interests which he shared with his own people is shown time and again, as in the *Address to the Deil*, blending popular superstition with the proper theological flavor, in the folkways of *Hallowe'en*, in the humorous bucolic *Auld Farmer's Salutation to his Mare Maggie*. It is in this circumstantial and realistic work that his indebtedness to Robert Fergusson appears. The setting of *The Jolly Beggars*, "Poosie Nansie's" disreputable dive at Mauchline, shows notably how Burns could turn his participation in Scottish low life to the highest account. In the few score lines of *The Twa Dogs* he gives a more graphic comparison of low and high life than can be found in any other of the numerous poems of the time, sentimental or satirical, which dwell on the contrast of poverty and riches.

Burns passed through a very brief prentice stage to direct, natural, and independent expression. Despite his echoes of the cult of sensibility, the painter Ibbotson seriously misrepresented him when he portrayed him as a pensive youth framed in a wide picturesque landscape. His main bent was toward the realistic presentation of social relationships, and

in this he was greatly helped by his use of his native Low-
land Scots speech, which intensifies his humor, realism, and
unaffected human feeling. He had a literary command of
standard English also, but in English he would have been
only a competent secondary poet. The favorite *Cotter's
Saturday Night* is almost entirely on this secondary level,
with conventional sentiment and diction and conventional
use of the Spenserian stanza. Likewise, the familiar lines
To a Mouse and *To a Mountain Daisy* are touched with
the affected language of sensibility. Of course the merit of
a poem does not vary directly with the number of Scots
words; the folk poems are saturated, many of the best lyrics
merely flavored. Burns at his best is never excessively preoccupied with his diction, and does not give the impression
that he is hunting or choosing words. This is remarkable
when we consider how many difficult rimes his stanza forms
call for. If he succeeds better in the vernacular, it is because he is there treating subjects which he commands
more completely. Like Chaucer and Byron, he is a great
master of the difficult technique of using conversational
rhythms in poetry.

Burns always stood for the rights of man, and expressed
what passed for democratic and subversive opinions—"A
Man's a Man for a' That." His enthusiasm for the French
Revolution, which got him into trouble with his superiors,
was real but comparatively superficial. His religion was
the deism which many enlightened men had substituted for
the old orthodoxy. More important than his formal opinions in politics and religion was his spiritual democracy:
he was a friend of humanity not because he held certain
views but because he shared the life of man and expressed
what all men felt. The songs are occasionally autobiographical, but more often they represent general experience, not
merely the sentiments and feelings of the "luckless bard"
or "rantin' dog." His best lyrics are almost too familiar to

the English speaking world, but nothing can stale their simplicity and economy, their remarkable range and variety of mood, their integrity and sincerity. Burns almost always wrote to an old tune for which he sought appropriate words; often he improved traditional texts, pieced out fragments, or supplied new stanzas for an old chorus. He had a rich national heritage of song, but we may say in the words of Goethe that what he inherited he earned anew, in order that he might possess it aright.

The Poetry of Robert Burns, ed. W. E. Henley and T. F. Henderson (4v, Edinburgh, 1896-97; Centenary edition); *Complete Works* (Boston, 1897; Cambridge edition); *Complete Poetical Works*, ed. J. L. Robertson (3v, Oxford, 1916); *Songs*, ed. J. C. Dick (London, 1903); Sir James Wilson, *Scottish Poems of Robert Burns in his Native Dialect* (London, 1925); *The Dialect of Robert Burns as Spoken in Central Ayrshire* (London, 1923); W. A. Craigie, *A Primer of Burns* (London, 1896); A. Angellier, *Étude sur la vie et les oeuvres de Robert Burns* (2v, Paris, 1893); F. B. Snyder, *Life* (New York, 1932); *Robert Burns: His Personality, his Reputation, and his Art* (Toronto, 1936); *Letters*, ed. J. D. Ferguson (2v, Oxford, 1931); J. D. Ferguson, *Pride and Passion* (New York, 1939); Hans Hecht, *Robert Burns, The Man and his Work*, trans. Jane Lymburn (London, 1936); R. T. Fitzhugh, ed., *Robert Burns: His Associates and Contemporaries* (Chapel Hill, 1943).

MINOR AUTHORS

»»

Christopher Anstey (1724-1805). Anstey was a Cambridge wit, educated at Eton and King's College, and long resident at Trumpington, just outside Cambridge. After frequent visits to Bath, he took up his residence there and published *The New Bath Guide* in 1766. This is a series of verse epistles written by Simpkin Blunderhead and other members of his family, humorously describing life at Bath from various points of view. The device was taken over by Smollett in *Humphry Clinker*. The brisk and playful verse of the *Guide* and its light satire were immensely popular, and it ran through more than a score of editions up to 1800. Anstey wrote other light verse, and was one of the coterie that contributed to Lady Miller's famous Batheaston vase, but he is remembered only for the *Guide*.

W. C. Powell, *Christopher Anstey: Bath Laureate* (Philadelphia, 1944).

John Armstrong (1709-1779). Armstrong, a Border Scot, practised medicine in London and gained some reputation by his *Art of Preserving Health* (1744), an example of somewhat pompous Miltonic blank verse applied to a didactic theme in a manner made standard by Philips's *Cyder* and Thomson's *Seasons*. As a boy Armstrong is said to have written independently of Thomson a blank-verse fragment on winter which aroused the admiration of Thomson, Mallet, and their circle. This piece was first published in Armstrong's *Miscellanies* (1770). His friendship with Thomson is also commemorated by a few stanzas contributed to *The Castle of Indolence*. He was a literary and personal friend of Smollett and for a time of Wilkes.

L. M. Knapp, "Dr. John Armstrong," *Publications of the Modern Language Association*, LIX (1944). 1019-58.

William Beckford (1760-1844). Beckford's eccentric literary career is unique, but may be treated under the general heading of prose romance. His immediate forebears were West Indian planters of great wealth, and his father was Lord Mayor of London. His private education and continental travels developed his brilliant vein of dilettantism, at once imaginative, sensuous, and playful. The oriental romance *Vathek* is the best-known expression of his amazing talent. It was composed in French in 1782. Beckford's tutor

Samuel Henley published an unauthorized translation in
1786; variant French texts appeared at Lausanne (1786,
dated 1787) and Paris (1787). The associated *Episodes of
Vathek* remained unpublished until our own time. Beckford's vast fortune and his unrestricted whims led him into
extravagant building projects centering about his modern
Gothic Fonthill Abbey in Wiltshire.

Guy Chapman and John Hodgkin, *Bibliography* (London,
1930); *Vathek, with the Episodes of Vathek*, ed. Guy Chapman
(2v, Cambridge, 1929) [French text]; *Vathek*, in *Three Eighteenth Century Romances*, ed. H. R. Steeves (New York, 1931);
Vathek, trans. H. Grimsditch (London, 1929); *Episodes of Vathek*,
trans. F. T. Marzials, introd. by Lewis Melville (London, 1912);
Travel-Diaries, ed. Guy Chapman (2v, Cambridge, 1928); *The
Vision, Liber Veritatis*, ed. Guy Chapman (Cambridge, 1930); M.
May, *La Jeunesse de William Beckford et le genèse de son Vathek*
(Paris, 1928); J. W. Oliver, *Life of William Beckford* (London,
1932); Guy Chapman, *Beckford* (London, 1937).

Aphra Behn (1640-1689). The first professional woman
writer in English drama and fiction is a rather mysterious
figure. Doubts about the facts of her life are involved with
the question as to the autobiographical basis of her famous
story, *Oroonoko, or the Royal Slave* (1688). Her own account
was that her father had been appointed lieutenant governor
of the South American colony Surinam (British Guiana), and
that she traveled thither and saw the slave rebellion which
she describes. The best opinion now seems to be that she
went to Surinam as an adventuress, and thus got some details which were used in her extravagant romance. Later
she seems to have been a government agent in Holland.
She began to write for the stage in the 1670's, and then
turned to the writing of short pieces of fiction, called
"novels," which tried to blend the loftiness of romance
and the excitement of sensational drama with intense and
facile sentiment and luscious love themes. *Oroonoko* repre-

sents also an attempt to heighten realism by the use of local color and the report of a supposed eye-witness. The story centers about an African prince who after an ardent love affair with Imoinda is sold into slavery and dies a bloody death in a rebellion in Surinam. The theme is not the horror of slavery, but the exaltation of this heroic and ferocious figure. His story is not primitivistic, though there is a primitivistic passage on the innocent natives of South America. *Oroonoko* was given a sentimental turn in Southerne's drama (1696), which remained popular through the eighteenth century.

Works, ed. M. Summers (6v, London, 1915): E. Bernbaum, "Mrs. Behn's Biography a Fiction," *Publications of the Modern Language Association,* xxviii (1913). 432-53; "Mrs. Behn's *Oroonoko,*" *Kittredge Anniversary Papers* (Boston, 1913), 419-33; Victoria Sackville West, *Aphra Behn* (London, 1927); H. G. Platt, Jr., "Astrea and Celadon: An Untouched Portrait of Aphra Behn," *Publications of the Modern Language Association,* xlix (1934). 544-59.

Sir Richard Blackmore (?-1729) . Sir Richard Blackmore, physician and poetaster, incurred the contempt of Dryden and the other wits for his bad epics, *Prince Arthur* (1695) and *King Arthur* (1697) , and for his campaign, somewhat parallel to Collier's, against literary immorality (*Satire against Wit,* 1700). But his *Job* (1700) and *Creation* (1712) earned him a place among serious religious poets in the estimate of Watts, Addison, Johnson, and even his old enemy John Dennis.

Robert Blair (1699-1746). Robert Blair, a Scottish clergyman, is remembered for one poem, *The Grave* (1743), written independently of Young but published shortly after the first book of the *Night Thoughts.* The two poems were often published and read together, but there are considerable differences between them. Both, of course, indulge in religious and moral reflections inspired by the thought of death, and so may be said to belong to a "graveyard school," but Blair is much more interested than Young in painting "the gloomy horrors of the tomb." In a fairly terse and vigorous blank verse derived from Shakespeare and later tragedy he restates the commonplaces about death which come down from the tradition of Puritan sermon and elegy and religious treatise, and raises this popular religious vein to a somewhat higher literary level. *The Grave* was reprinted more than fifty times in England and America before the end of the century.

Poetical Works of Blair, Beattie, and Falconer, ed. G. Gilfillan (London, 1879); Carl Müller, *Robert Blairs Grave und die Grabes- und Nachtdichtung* (Weimar, 1909); J. W. Draper, *The Funeral Elegy and the Rise of English Romanticism* (New York, 1929); P. van Tieghem, "La poésie de la nuit et des tombeaux," in *Le Préromantisme,* II (Paris, 1930).

Henry Brooke (1703-1783). A cultured and benevolent Irish country gentleman who touched the literary life of his time at several important points. His *Universal Beauty* (1735-36), a long and turgid poem in heroic couplets, embodies much scientific detail for physico-theological purposes. The play *Gustavus Vasa* (1739), a manifesto of the opposition to Walpole and forbidden under the Licensing Act, deals with the struggle for liberty in ancient Sweden, and connects with the widespread doctrine that among the northern or "Gothic" peoples is to be found the origin of the free constitutions of Europe. *The Fool of Quality* (1765-70) is a long and confused novel, describing the education of the young hero in the principles of sentimental benevolism and mystical religious enthusiasm. This work was adapted by John Wesley and highly praised in the next century by Charles Kingsley.

The Fool of Quality, ed. E. A. Baker (London, 1906); Helen M. Scurr, *Henry Brooke* (Minneapolis, 1922).

Tom Brown (1663-1704). A clever, harsh, and dissipated Grub Street hack, who did much work in controversial pamphlets, translations, and miscellaneous literary adaptations. His *Amusements Serious and Comical* (1700) is one of the best of the realistic "trips" through London, and invites comparison with Ned Ward's *London Spy* (1698-1700), a similar coarse and graphic piece. Another interesting work to which Brown was a principal contributor is *Letters from the Dead to the Living* (1702-03), in the tradition of the *Dialogues of the Dead* of Lucian and Fontenelle.

Benjamin Boyce, *Tom Brown of Facetious Memory* (Cambridge, Mass., 1939).

Michael Bruce (1746-1767). A Scottish theological student born of humble parents in Kinross-shire, on the shore of Loch Leven. He died young. John Logan edited a posthumous volume of his poems in 1770, and has been accused of claiming some of Bruce's work as his own, notably the fine *Ode to the Cuckoo*.

Works, ed. A. Grosart (Edinburgh, 1865); *Life and Complete Works*, ed. J. Mackenzie (Edinburgh, 1914); *Life and Works*, ed. J. G. Barnet (London, 1927).

Gilbert Burnet (1643-1715). A Whig bishop who was one of William's principal lieutenants. He belongs to political and religious history rather than to literature, but his partisan memoirs which appeared as *History of His Own Time* (1724-34) contain much spirited narrative and characterization.

T. E. S. Clarke and H. C. Foxcroft, *Life of Gilbert Burnet* (Cambridge, 1907); *History*, ed. O. Airy (2v, Oxford, 1898-1900).

Thomas Burnet (1635?-1715). This learned clergyman is remembered for his *Telluris Theoria Sacra* (1681-89), translated as *The Sacred Theory of the Earth* (1684-90), an imaginative piece of cosmology written in elegant prose. Though opposed by many scientists, this work was admired by poets from Thomson to Wordsworth and Coleridge.

Richard Owen Cambridge (1717-1802). A witty and versatile country gentleman who wrote a heavy mock-epic the *Scribleriad* (1751), some excellent essays in the *World*, and some agreeable light verse, but is more noteworthy for his sociability and wide acquaintance, especially in the groups associated with Johnson and Walpole.

R. D. Altick, *Richard Owen Cambridge: Belated Augustan* (Philadelphia, 1941).

Henry Carey (1687?-1743). A struggling song-writer and music-teacher who did a good deal of work for the theaters. His burlesque *Chrononhotonthologos* (1734) has already been mentioned, and he also wrote a burlesque opera, *The Dragon of Wantley*. His poem *Namby Pamby* probably fixed this nickname on Ambrose Philips. Best known of all is his song *Sally in our Alley* (composed before 1719, first known publication in *Poems on Several Occasions*, 3rd ed., 1729). So little is known about Carey that a contemporary satirical description may be quoted:

The next object is a little fat sonnetteer who went mad for the love of *Sally in our Alley*. This poor soul runs up and down wild from one end of the town to the other, singing and smiling to himself, and cannot see a card but he'll make a Song upon it. He is a walking library, carrying always a porter's load of music books *(Law Outlaw'd, 1726)*.

Poems, ed. F. T. Wood (London, 1930); R. G. Noyes, "The Contemporary Reception of 'Sally in our Alley,'" *Harvard Studies and Notes*, xviii (1935). 165-75; "'Sally in our Alley': Plays of Henry Carey," (London) *Times Literary Supplement*, Oct. 9. 1943. p. 490.

Thomas Day (1748-1789). A somewhat eccentric enthusiast for liberal and philanthropic ideas. He wrote against slavery and in favor of the American cause, and took some part in the Whig campaign for electoral reform, but his chief interest was in the application of the educational theories of Rousseau's *Emile*. Taking some hints from Brooke's *Fool of Quality* also, he worked out his educational program in the story of *Sandford and Merton* (I-1783, II-1787, III-1789), which became one of the most popular children's books in the language. Day opposed luxury and fashion and inculcated virtuous benevolism and rigorous simplicity. He was a good friend of the Lichfield group (Erasmus Darwin, Anna Seward), of the Birmingham scientists and inventors (Boulton, Priestley), and of the Irish philanthropist Richard Lovell Edgeworth, whose daughter, the famous novelist Maria Edgeworth, was influenced by Day's educational program.

G. W. Gignilliat, Jr., *The Author of Sandford and Merton* (New York, 1932).

John Dyer (1699-1757). John Dyer was born in Carmarthenshire, in southern Wales; as a young man he studied painting under Jonathan Richardson, traveled in Italy, and about 1725 was a member of Aaron Hill's literary coterie in London, along with James Thomson and Richard Savage. In 1726 appeared three versions, one in Pindarics and two in Miltonic octosyllabic couplets, of his charming prospect poem *Grongar Hill*. Like his younger fellow countryman, the landscape painter Richard Wilson, Dyer no doubt came under the influence of the Italian picturesque tradition in painting, and carried over the results of these studies to poetry. He thus takes a modest but significant place in the history of the poetic treatment of landscape. Later he became a gentleman-farmer and eventually a clergyman. His *Ruins of Rome* (1740) invites comparison with Thomson's *Liberty;* his *Fleece* (1757), an account of sheep-raising and the great British woolen industry, is one of the better descriptive-didactic blank-verse poems of the time, handicapped though it is by its subject.

Poetical Works of Mark Akenside and John Dyer, ed. R. A. Willmott (London, 1855); *Minor Poets of the Eighteenth Century,* ed. H. I'A. Fausset (London, 1930; Everyman's Library); H. S. Hughes, "John Dyer and the Countess of Hertford," *Modern Philology,* XXVII (1930). 311-20; *Grongar Hill,* ed. R. C. Boys (Baltimore, 1941).

Sarah Fielding (1710-1768). A sister of Henry Fielding and a member of Richardson's circle. These personal relationships are more important than her own novels, of which *David Simple* (1744) was the best known.

H. O. Werner, Jr., "The Life and Works of Sarah Fielding," *Harvard University Summaries of Theses, 1939* (Cambridge. Mass., 1942), pp. 250-55.

Sir Samuel Garth (1661-1719). A successful physician, a prominent member of the Kit-Cat Club, and an early friend of Pope's. His mock-heroic *Dispensary* (1699) attacks the apothecaries and their allies who opposed the opening of a free dispensary for the poor. The poem is loaded with allusions to this forgotten controversy, and though once popular is now neglected, yet it is a competent piece of work, one of the more rewarding of the secondary poems of the age. Pope respected and imitated Garth's command of the balanced couplet and the pointed line. *The Dispensary* occupies a significant place in the history of the English mock-epic: it largely imitates Boileau's *Lutrin* and in turn passes on some features of style and method to *The Rape of the Lock;* equally important is its elaboration of the "stupidity" theme of *Mac Flecknoe,* which made it contributory to the *Dunciad.*

The Dispensary, ed. W. J. Leicht (Heidelberg, 1905).

Joseph Glanvill (1636-1680). Joseph Glanvill, educated at Oxford and long rector of the Abbey Church at Bath, was eminent for his keen and fresh philosophical thought and his excellent prose. He was influenced by the Cambridge Platonists, Cartesian rationalism, and above all by the Baconian program of the Royal Society. In his *Vanity of Dogmatizing* (1661), called *Scepsis Scientifica,* or *Confest Ignorance the Way to Science* in the revised edition of 1665, and finally included in his *Essays* (1676), he commended "skepticism," not in the radical form of a denial of the possibility of knowledge, but as a tool to help man to attain well grounded knowledge. Skepticism cuts away mere speculation and "confidence in opinions" and insists on the test of experience. This is the anti-dogmatic and anti-speculative program of the Royal Society. Self-explanatory is the title of another of his works, *Plus Ultra, or the Progress and Advancement of Knowledge since the Days of Aristotle. In an Account of Some of the Most Remarkable Late Improvements of Practical, Useful Learning* (1668). In his religious thought, however, Glanvill kept to the Cambridge Platonists' exaltation of reason, and he argued vehemently, both on religious and scientific grounds, for the traditional beliefs in witches and apparitions (*Sadducismus Triumphatus,* 1681).

The Vanity of Dogmatizing (facsimile repr. New York, 1931); F. Greenslet, *Joseph Glanvill* (New York, 1900); M. E. Prior, "Joseph Glanvill, Witchcraft, and Seventeenth-Century Science," *Modern Philology,* xxx (1932). 167-93.

Richard Graves (1715-1804). For many years rector of Claverton, near Bath, a close friend of Shenstone and Dodsley, and author of *The Spiritual Quixote* (1773), a satire on the Methodist movement which is also one of the most genial comic novels of the period.

C. J. Hill, *The Literary Career of Richard Graves* (Northampton, Mass., 1935).

Matthew Green (1696-1737). A clerk in the London Custom House who diverted himself and his friends by writing verses. His posthumously published *Spleen* (1737) treats the somewhat hackneyed question of how to avoid ill health and boredom and live contentedly, but, as a friend remarks in the preface, it has a "peculiar and unborrowed cast of thought and expression." Green's work in the octosyllabic couplet is as fresh as Prior's, and his wit was deservedly admired by Gray, Walpole, and others.

Minor Poets of the Eighteenth Century, ed. H. I'A. Fausset (London, 1930; Everyman's Library); *The Spleen,* ed. W. H. Williams (London, 1936).

George Savile, Marquis of Halifax (1633-1695). An eminent statesman and one of the wisest Englishmen of his generation. His public career belongs to history: though a Whig, he opposed Shaftesbury in the crisis of 1680; though he held office under James II, he warned the Dissenters against the King's pretended zeal for religious toleration (*A Letter to a Dissenter,* 1687; *The Anatomy of an Equivalent,* 1688). He was a leader in the Revolution, and as has been said above (pp. 7-8), expounded his political doctrine of compromise in his famous *Character of a Trimmer* (written 1685, published 1688). Like his celebrated *Character of Charles II,* this piece shows his mastery of the portrait-character as a literary form. His *Lady's New Year's Gift* (1688), addressed to his daughter, applies the practical ethics of compromise to the problems of married life; it assumes the domination of the husband, but urges the advantages of cleverness and good temper. Halifax was master of an urbane, clear, and witty style, strongly influenced by the French masters (La Bruyère, Montaigne); he avoided the affectations of fashionable Restoration wit, and on the other hand he had much of the good sense of the eighteenth century without its pervasive sentimentality.

Works, ed. W. Raleigh (Oxford, 1912); H. C. Foxcroft, *Life and Letters* (2v, London, 1898).

James Hammond (1710-1742). A protégé of Chesterfield's and a member of the literary group gathered about Frederick, Prince of Wales. His *Elegies,* closely imitative of Tibullus, were published in 1743. They seem to modern readers merely vapid and smooth, but probably had some part in helping to make the iambic pentameter quatrain standard for eighteenth-century elegy.

Eliza Haywood (1693?-1756). Following in the steps of Mrs. Manley, Eliza Haywood wrote short tales of intrigue and passion and "secret histories." Pope attacked her in the *Dunciad.* After the success of Richardson's *Pamela,* she turned from the older forms to the novel of manners, in which she did mediocre work (*Betsy Thoughtless,* 1751; *Jemmy and Jenny Jessamy,* 1753).

G. F. Whicher, *The Life and Romances of Mrs. Eliza Haywood* (New York, 1915).

James Hervey (1714-1758). Though his position was not identical with Wesley's, Hervey was an ardent evangelical. His *Meditations and Contemplations* (1746-47), one of the most popular religious works of the century, is written in an inflated rhetorical prose. It is often put in the graveyard school, but the contents include not only "Meditations among the Tombs" but pieces on a flower garden, night, winter, the heavens, and a "Descant on Creation." Hervey quotes and imitates the poets freely, and follows the physico-theological treatises which use the new findings of science to glorify God.

William Law (1686-1761). Law's best works are unfortunately buried among neglected religious treatises, but he
was eminent for his piety, vigorous intelligence, and fine
command of prose. As a Non-juror—that is, a Jacobite who
refused to take the oath of allegiance to George I—he cut
himself off from a career in university and Church. Yet he
entered largely into the life of his time; he wrote against
Hoadly in the Bangorian controversy (see p. 207), against
Mandeville, against the corruptions of the stage, and against
the deists; but he was not a mere controversialist, and his
Serious Call to a Devout and Holy Life (1728), despite a
title which suggests dreary piety, has the crispness, clarity,
good taste, and wit of eighteenth-century prose at its best.
"When at Oxford," said Johnson to Boswell, speaking of
his early indifference to religion, "I took up Law's 'Serious
Call to a Holy Life,' expecting to find it a dull book (as
such books generally are) and perhaps to laugh at it. But
I found Law quite an overmatch for me." His religious zeal
influenced Wesley and the Methodist movement. In his
later years he became increasingly enthusiastic and mystical,
under the influence of Jakob Böhme. He was long associated with the family of Edward Gibbon, who pays him
high tribute in his *Memoirs*.

Serious Call (London, n. d.; Everyman's Library); J. H. Overton, *William Law, Nonjuror and Mystic* (London, 1881).

Charlotte Lennox (1720-1804). The one book for which
Mrs. Lennox is remembered is *The Female Quixote, or The
Adventures of Arabella* (1752), a satire on a romance-reading heroine which interested and amused a generation
increasingly conscious of the claims of prose fiction. The
works which turn Arabella's head are, however, the French
heroic romances of the seventeenth century, not modern
novels. The story was praised by Richardson and Fielding.
Though comparatively obscure as a writer, Mrs. Lennox

was highly admired by Dr. Johnson. Since she was born in New York, and lived in America until she was fifteen years old, she has some claim to be considered the first American novelist.

Miriam R. Small, *Charlotte Ramsay Lennox* (New Haven, 1935).

George Lyttelton, Baron Lyttelton (1709-1773). Lyttelton was one of the group of young men connected by birth and marriage, including Pitt and the Grenvilles, who were led by Richard Temple, Viscount Cobham, in opposition to Walpole. In the 1730's Lyttelton was the chief political aide of Frederick Prince of Wales (see p. 90). He wrote *Letters from a Persian in England* (1735) in imitation of Montesquieu's *Lettres Persanes,* a fine monody on the death of his wife (1747), *Dialogues of the Dead* (1760), and much else in verse and prose, but his chief claims to distinction were his cordial relationships with Thomson, Fielding, and other writers, including his Warwickshire neighbor Shenstone. Though sometimes derided for his seriousness and self-importance, as by Smollett, Lyttelton seems on the whole to have shown generosity and tact in combining literary patronage and personal friendship. Thus he helped Thomson to revise *The Seasons,* and to him *Tom Jones* is dedicated.

Rose Mary Davis, *The Good Lord Lyttelton* (Bethlehem, 1939).

Henry Mackenzie (1745-1831). Mackenzie was a genial and intelligent Scot who for two generations played a leading part in the literary life of Edinburgh. He showed talent with his excellent ballad imitations *Duncan* and *Kenneth* (1764 and 1765), but turned from the medieval revival to sentimental fiction, earning a reputation as an arch-sentimentalist by his famous *Man of Feeling* (1771). In this work he follows Sterne in writing "episodic adventures" keyed to moods and sentiments, but for Sterne's unpredictable humor and ingenuity he substitutes the somewhat banal delicacy and ethical commonplace of Shenstone. His other two novels, *The Man of the World* (1773) and *Julia de Roubigné* (1777) have recourse to the more violent stimuli of seduction and jealousy. In his essay-periodicals, the *Mirror* (1779-80) and the *Lounger* (1785-87) he does some of the best late eighteenth-century work in this form, writing sentimental tales, sympathetic humorous sketches, and at least one important piece of literary criticism in his essay on Burns (*Lounger* No. 97). His responsiveness to literary currents also appears in the paper on German literature which he submitted to the Royal Society of Edinburgh and which stimulated the young Walter Scott.

Works (8v, Edinburgh, 1808); *The Man of Feeling,* ed. H. Miles (London, 1928); *Anecdotes and Egotisms,* ed. H. W. Thompson (New York, 1928); H. W. Thompson, *A Scottish Man of Feeling* (New York, 1931).

David Mallet, originally **Malloch** (1705?-1765). Mallet and James Thomson were fellow-students at Edinburgh, and belonged to the literary club which produced the *Edinburgh Miscellany,* where some of their earliest verses appear. When he came to London Mallet attracted attention with his ballad *William and Margaret* (written before 1723, published in Aaron Hill's *Plain Dealer,* 1724). For his later collaboration with Thomson in *Alfred,* see p. 197. Of his other miscellaneous labors, the best known was his edition of Bolingbroke's works (1754). He probably deserved the amusingly hostile sketch of his career which Johnson gives in the *Lives of the Poets.*

D. M. Little, "The Letters of David Mallet," *Harvard University Summaries of Theses, 1935* (Cambridge, Mass., 1937), 278-81.

Mary De La Riviere Manley (1672-1724). Mrs. Manley, sensational and somewhat disreputable like Mrs. Behn before her and Mrs. Haywood after her, was notorious for her *New Atalantis* (1709) and its continuation *Memoirs of Europe* (1710), a scandalous chronicle of contemporary politics and society which jumbled fact, fiction, and gossip with intent to help the Tories, and was widely read, mere trash though it is. She was active as a political writer during the Tory régime of 1710-14, and was well known to Swift. References in *The Rape of the Lock* and *Spectator* No. 37 help to perpetuate her memory. Her best work is perhaps a piece of epistolary fiction published as *Letters* in 1696 and reprinted as *A Stage-Coach Journey to Exeter* in 1725. The romanticized autobiography *Rivella* (1714) is of some interest.

P. B. Anderson, "Delariviere Manley's Prose Fiction," *Philological Quarterly,* XIII (1934). 168-88; "Mistress Delariviere Manley's Biography," *Modern Philology,* XXXIII (1936). 261-78.

William Mason (1725-1797). Mason well represents the type of liberal and literary-minded clergyman who plays so prominent a part in eighteenth-century culture. His Miltonic, Spenserian, and Pindaric verses have little value; his dramas on the Greek model, *Elfrida* and *Caractacus,* though Gray took them seriously, are dull and wooden. *The English Garden* (1772-81) is an interesting document on its subject. His long friendship and correspondence with Gray resulted in his *Memoirs of Gray* (1775), a pioneer work in documented biography and thus an important forerunner of Boswell.

J. W. Draper, *William Mason* (New York, 1924).

Thomas Parnell (1679-1718). Parnell was an Irish clergyman, Archdeacon of Clogher, who became a friend of the Tory wits and a member of the Scriblerus Club, and was also on good terms with Steele and Addison. He contributed an *Essay on Homer* to Pope's *Iliad*. After his premature death Pope brought out his collected verse with a fine dedication to the Earl of Oxford (1722). Parnell was evidently fascinated by Pope's poetry, but his own work is of a somewhat different kind, including the once famous moral apologue *The Hermit,* meditative poems in octosyllabic couplet (*A Hymn to Contentment, A Night-Piece on Death*), the playful *Fairy Tale,* and some graceful lyrics.

Poetical Works, ed. G. A. Aitken (New York, 1894; Aldine edition); *Minor Poets of the Eighteenth Century,* ed. H. I'A. Fausset (London, 1930; Everyman's Library).

Ambrose Philips (1674-1749). Ambrose Philips, a very minor poet, is remembered chiefly because of Pope's hostility. The first four of his *Pastorals* were published in Fenton's *Oxford and Cambridge Miscellany Poems* (1708); when all six appeared in the Sixth Part of Tonson's *Miscellanies* (1709) they invited comparison with Pope's *Pastorals* in the same volume. Pope thought they were overpraised in the Whig *Guardian,* edited by Steele, and contributed to that paper ironical praise of the weakest passages in Philips's pieces. This episode helped to bring to a head the feud between Pope and Addison's Whig coterie at Button's, of which Philips was a prominent member. Gay's *Shepherd's Week* may have been intended as a parody of Philips. Pope and Swift pursued Philips with their scorn, and Carey's *Namby Pamby* (1725) satirized his pretty but sometimes mawkish poems to children, and thus fastened a nickname upon him. Philips spent the latter part of his life in Ireland as a Whig office-holder. Other works of his were an adaptation of Racine's *Andromaque* as *The Distrest Mother,* praised by Addison in *Spectator* No. 335, and an essay-periodical called the *Freethinker* (1718-21). His editorship of *A Collection of Old Ballads* (1723-25) is very doubtful.

Poems, ed. Mary G. Segar (Oxford, 1937); R. H. Griffith, "A Variorum Text of Four Pastorals by Ambrose Philips," *University of Texas Studies in English,* XII (1932), 118-57; A. J. Bryan, "The Life and Works of Ambrose Philips," *Harvard University Summaries of Theses, 1936* (Cambridge, Mass., 1938), pp. 313-16.

John Philips (1676-1709). John Philips, educated at Winchester and Christ Church, Oxford, made an important contribution to eighteenth-century verse by showing how the Miltonic manner could be adapted to moderate or playful literary projects. His *Blenheim* (1705), planned as a Tory tribute to Marlborough's victory, unfortunately shows only the bombast of the misapplied Miltonic style. But he had already done better in *The Splendid Shilling,* a humorous and skillful burlesque of Miltonic blank verse which appeared in three collections of 1701, in an unauthorized edition of 1705, and finally in an authentic text in that same year. Addison praised this piece as "the finest burlesque poem in the British language" (*Tatler* No. 249). In *Cyder* (1708) Philips uses the same style to treat the theme of the orchards of Herefordshire. This is an expository poem on the georgic model, but it admits the widest digressions, descriptive, geographical, historical, and personal, and so did much to set a model for the blank-verse descriptive-didactic poem. As exposition, it points forward to Dyer's *Fleece* and many other poems of the kind; in its broad and leisurely style it points forward to Thomson's *Seasons.* Thomson duly pays tribute to Philips when he hails him as

> Pomona's bard! the second thou
> Who nobly durst in rhyme-unfettered verse,
> With British freedom sing the British song.
> (*Autumn,* ll. 645-47)

Poems, ed. M. G. Lloyd Thomas (Oxford, 1927).

John Pomfret (1667-1702). John Pomfret, a young clergy-man with a Cambridge degree, wrote for the most part mediocre religious and philosophical verse (*Poems,* 1699; *Reason,* 1700), but won a place in all the anthologies and miscellanies by his poem *The Choice* (1700). This piece is an undistinguished but representative account of a way of life: the poet would have a small country house with pleas-ant grounds, a modest income, a library stored with classics, a small but well-stocked cellar, a few congenial friends, especially some "obliging modest-fair," "for I'd have no wife." The last stipulation got Pomfret into trouble with his bishop. Johnson, Southey, and Leigh Hunt all bear witness to the continuing popularity of *The Choice.*

Richard Savage (1697-1743). Savage wrote nothing of much importance, but his claim to be the illegitimate son of the Countess of Macclesfield and Richard Savage, fourth Earl Rivers, though stubbornly denied by his supposed mother, was generally accepted by the London public, and helped the ne'er-do-well poet to get a precarious living. He was a sturdy literary beggar, always seeking pensions and patronage and airing his grievances. He had many literary friends, such as Dyer, Hill, Thomson, and above all the young Samuel Johnson, whose *Life of Savage* (1744) is a superb piece of biography and affords a remarkable view of the literary underworld of the time. Savage edited an important miscellany, *Miscellaneous Poems and Trans-lations* (1726); his poem *The Wanderer* (1729) follows the trail of Thomson.

S. V. Makower, *Richard Savage* (London, 1909); "Poet and Interloper: Richard Savage," (London) *Times Literary Supple-ment,* July 31, 1943, p. 368.

Elkanah Settle (1648-1724). Settle began to write heroic plays in the 1660's, and won much patronage with his

Empress of Morocco, which succeeded both on the court
stage at Whitehall and at Dorset Gardens (1671). It was
notable chiefly for its elaborate staging and scenic effects;
the engravings in the 1673 edition give important evidence
about the physical stage of the Restoration. The preface
attacks Dryden; Mulgrave and Rochester were evidently
backing Settle against the greater poet. Shadwell and
Crowne joined Dryden in a reply, *Notes and Observations
on the Empress of Morocco* (1674), quoted at length in
Johnson's *Life of Dryden.* The quarrel was personal, and
had little critical significance. Settle soon lost his patrons, but
reappeared as a Whig partisan in the political crisis of the
Popish Plot. He wrote an anti-Catholic play, *The Female
Prelate* (1680), and a reply to *Absalom and Achitophel*
called *Absalom Senior* (1682). He is the "Doeg" of *Absalom
and Achitophel II.* But soon he was with the Tories again,
finding himself on the losing side at the Revolution. From
about 1691 Settle worked as "city poet," preparing pageants
for the Lord Mayor's shows. He had already been engaged
in the humble task of supplying drolls for Bartholemew Fair.
He lived on to become a by-word in the Augustan period
as a drudging rimester, and has a prominent niche in the
Dunciad.

F. C. Brown, *Elkanah Settle* (Chicago, 1910).

William Somervile (1675-1742). A fox-hunting Warwickshire squire—not a Squire Western, however, but an Oxford
man of considerable literary culture. In his best poem, *The
Chace* (1735), he used the Miltonic blank verse and the
digressive georgic pattern of Philips and Thomson to describe his favorite sport. His accurate knowledge of country
life and his wholesome enthusiasms are set forth with considerable vividness in this artificial form. Another interesting blank-verse poem of his on country life is *Hobbinol,*

or the Rural Games (1740), though here the burlesque epic form is too elaborate for the theme.

"Guide to the Hunt: William Somerville, 1675-1742," (London) *Times Literary Supplement,* July 18, 1942, p. 358.

Thomas Sprat (1635-1713). Sprat, Bishop of Rochester, wrote inferior Pindaric odes in imitation of his literary master Cowley, and the important *History of the Royal Society* (1667), an official defense of the new science. The point of view is completely Baconian and practical: the coöperative gathering of experimental data is to take the place of speculation and hypothesis, and toward this end English diction and style are to become simple, objective, and clear. The whole program, he points out with patriotic pride, is particularly appropriate for an enlightened, practical, commercial people like the English.

Thomas Tickell (1685-1740). The part Tickell's proposed translation of the *Iliad* played in the Pope-Addison quarrel has already been mentioned (pp. 167-68) . Tickell was always prominent among Addison's Whig followers, and to his edition of Addison's works he prefixed the famous lines *To the Earl of Warwick on the Death of Mr. Addison.*

R. E. Tickell, *Thomas Tickell and the Eighteenth Century Poets* (London, 1931).

William Warburton (1698-1779). A self-educated scholar who by sheer weight of learning and arrogant will-power won a prominent place in the Church and the literary world, and became Bishop of Gloucester. His political and religious works are now forgotten (*The Alliance between Church and State, The Divine Legation of Moses*) . He thought of himself as dominating the Christian apologetics and literary scholarship of his own time, and looked down on such contemporaries as Hume, Fielding, Richardson,

Sterne, and even Johnson. But posterity has not taken him at his own valution. He is best remembered as Pope's friend, defender, and literary executor.

A. W. Evans, *Warburton and the Warburtonians* (London, 1932).

Isaac Watts (1674-1748). Isaac Watts was born at Southampton and educated at a dissenting academy at Stoke Newington. The Independent congregations which had played such a prominent part in earlier religious and political struggles had now settled down to a quiet, prosperous, and relatively unenthusiastic existence. Cut off largely from political and professional interests, the middle-class Dissenter was likely to be a zealous man of business. Watts represents the best intellectual and spiritual interests of Dissent in the first half of the eighteenth century, and became the leading dissenting preacher and man of letters of his day. He held a theory of the religious inspiration of poetry illustrated in his *Horae Lyricae* (1706); he revolutionized the Protestant hymn, and some of his hymns are still sung throughout the English-speaking world; his *Divine Songs for Children* (1715) have gone through hundreds of editions. In terms of actual use and familiarity Watts may fairly be called the most popular English author of the century. His textbooks and educational manuals and his expositions of a moderate Calvinistic theology also had wide currency. Though he kept apart from the Methodist revival, much of his influence was concurrent with that movement.

A. P. Davis, *Isaac Watts: his Life and Works* (New York, 1943); T. Wright, *Isaac Watts and Contemporary Hymn Writers* (London, 1914); W. M. Stone, *The Divine and Moral Songs of Isaac Watts* (New York, 1918).

Gilbert White (1720-1793). White was born and died at Selborne, Hampshire, and his whole life centered about that secluded village. His *Natural History and Antiquities of Selborne* (1789), which grew out of informal letters to interested friends, has become a classic for its accurate observation and charm of style. White's work as a field naturalist is of high scientific value, particularly his observations on birds, and his whole career shows us the cultivated English country clergyman of the eighteenth century at his best.

Walter S. Scott, *White of Selborne and his Times* (London, 1946).

Anne Kingsmill Finch, Countess of Winchilsea (1661-1720). Anne Kingsmill was maid of honor to Mary of Modena (James II's Queen) and married Colonel Finch, later Earl of Winchilsea. She and her husband went into retirement after the abdication of James. Her verse, written under the name of "Ardelia" and circulated in manuscript in her own group, expresses at its best a fine observation of natural detail, and delicate, pensive, and devout feeling, though it includes much conventional work. Wordsworth laid the foundation of her modern fame by praising her "Nocturnal Reverie" in his Preface of 1815, and since then all the anthologies have included that piece and also her "Petition for an Absolute Retreat," "The Echo," and "The Nightingale."

Poems, ed. Myra Reynolds (Chicago, 1903); *Poems* [selected], ed. J. Middleton Murry (London, 1928); *Minor Poets of the Eighteenth Century,* ed. H. I'A. Fausset (London, 1930; Everyman's Library).

BIBLIOGRAPHY

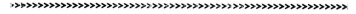

Bibliographical references for special fields, topics, and periods and for individual authors have as far as possible been given at appropriate places in the text. Thus, for political history, see above, pp. 8, 93, 318-19; for the history of thought, pp. 25, 134; for classicism, romanticism, and related topics, pp. 33-34, 217; for drama, pp. 71-72, 84-85, 312-13; for prose fiction, pp. 284-85. The following is a brief selected list of studies considered to be of broad significance and general usefulness.

GENERAL BIBLIOGRAPHICAL AIDS

"American Bibliography—English," annually in *Publications of the Modern Language Association,* xxxviii (1922)—.

Annual Bibliography of English Language and Literature (1920—, Cambridge, 1921—). Modern Humanities Research Association.

Arber, Edward, *The Term Catalogues, 1668-1709* (3v, London, 1903-06).

British Museum, Department of Printed Books, *Catalogue of Printed Books, 1881-1910* (repr. Ann Arbor, 1946).

———, *General Catalogue of Printed Books* (London, 1931—).

Cambridge Bibliography of English Literature, ed. F. W. Bateson (4v, New York, 1941).

Crane, R. S., and Kaye, F. B., *A Census of British Newspapers and Periodicals, 1620-1800* (Chapel Hill, 1927).

Crane, R. S., "Materials for the Study of English Poetry, 1660-1800," in *A Collection of English Poems, 1660-1800* (New York, 1932).

Cross, T. P., *Bibliographical Guide to English Studies* (8th ed., Chicago, 1943).

"English Literature of the Restoration and Eighteenth Century. A Current Bibliography," *Philological Quarterly,* v (1926)—. Compiled successively by R. S. Crane, L. I. Bredvold, R. P. Bond, and L. A. Landa and Arthur Friedman.

Kennedy, A. G., *A Concise Bibliography for Students of English* (2d ed., Stanford University, 1945).

Library of Congress Printed Cards, Catalog of Books Repre-sented by, (167v, Ann Arbor, 1942-46).

Moore, C. A., "Bibliography," in *Restoration Literature* (New York, 1934).

———, "Bibliography," in *English Prose of the Eighteenth Cen-tury* (New York, 1933).

———, "Bibliography," in *English Poetry of the Eighteenth Cen-tury* (New York, 1935).

Northup, C. S., *A Register of Bibliographies of the English Language and Literature* (New Haven, 1925).

Spargo, J. W., *A Bibliographical Manual for Students of the Language and Literature of England and the United States* (2d ed., Chicago, 1941).

Tobin, J. E., *Eighteenth Century English Literature and Its Cultural Background: A Bibliography* (New York, 1939).

Union List of Serials in Libraries of the United States and Canada (2d ed., New York, 1943); *Supplement* (New York, 1945).

Wing, Donald G., *Short-Title Catalogue of Books Printed in England, Scotland, Ireland, Wales, and British America, and of English Books Printed in Other Countries, 1641-1700* (New York, 1945–).

Year's Work in English Studies (1919–, London, 1921–). English Association.

GENERAL LITERARY HISTORY AND CRITICISM

Babbitt, Irving, *Rousseau and Romanticism* (Boston, 1919).

Beers, H. A., *A History of English Romanticism in the Eighteenth Century* (2d ed., New York, 1910).

Beljame, A., *Le public et les hommes de lettres en Angleterre au dix-huitième siècle, 1660-1744* (Paris, 1883).

Bernbaum, Ernest, *Guide through the Romantic Movement* (New York, 1930).

Bosker, A., *Literary Criticism in the Age of Johnson* (Groningen, 1930).

Bredvold, Louis I., "The Tendency toward Platonism in Neo-classical Aesthetics," *ELH*, I (1934). 91-119.

Cazamian, L., *L'Évolution psychologique et la littérature en Angleterre, 1660-1914* (Paris, 1920).

Cruse, Amy, *The Shaping of English Literature and the Readers' Share in the Development of Its Forms* (New York, 1927).

Dennis, John, *The Age of Pope, 1700-1744* (London, 1925).

Dobrée, B., *Variety of Ways* (Oxford, 1932).

Dobson, A., *Eighteenth Century Vignettes* (3 series, London, 1906-07).

———, *At Prior Park and Other Papers* (New York, 1912).

———, *Later Essays 1917-1920* (London, 1921).

Durham, W. H., *Critical Essays of the Eighteenth Century 1700-1725* (New Haven, 1915).

Dyson, H. V. D., and Butt, John, *Augustans and Romantics* (London, 1940).

Elton, Oliver, *The Augustan Ages* (Edinburgh, 1899).

———, *A Survey of English Literature, 1730-1780* (2v, New York, 1928).

———, *A Survey of English Literature, 1780-1830* (2v, London, 1912). I.

Elwin, W., *Some XVIII Century Men of Letters* (2v, London, 1902).

Fairchild, H. N., *The Romantic Quest* (New York, 1931).

Folkierski, W., *Entre le classicisme et le romantisme* (Cracow, 1925).

Gallaway, F., *Reason, Rule, and Revolt in English Classicism* (New York, 1940).

Garnett, R., *The Age of Dryden* (London, 1895).

Gillot, H., *La querelle des anciens et des modernes en France* (Paris, 1914).

Gosse, Edmund, *A History of Eighteenth Century Literature (1660-1780)* (London, 1898).

Green, F. C., *Minuet* (London, 1935).

Hettner, H., *Literaturgeschichte des achtzehnten Jahrhunderts* (3 parts in 6v, Brunswick, 1872).

Legouis, E., and Cazamian, L., *A History of English Literature* (New York, 1929).

Maar, H. G. de, *History of Modern English Romanticism,* Vol. 1 [all published] (London, 1924).

Millar, J. H., *The Mid-Eighteenth Century* (Edinburgh, 1902).

Minto, W., *The Literature of the Georgian Era* (Edinburgh, 1894).

Monk, S. H., *The Sublime* (New York, 1935).

Nichols, John, *Literary Anecdotes of the Eighteenth Century* (9v, London, 1812-16).

———, *Illustrations of the Literary History of the Eighteenth Century* (8v, London, 1817-58).

Phelps, W. L., *The Beginnings of the English Romantic Movement* (Boston, 1893).

Pinto, V. de Sola, *The English Renaissance, 1510-1688* (New York, 1938).

Price, Mary B., and Price, L. M., *The Publication of English Literature in Germany in the Eighteenth Century* (Berkeley, 1934).

Reynolds, Myra, *The Learned Lady in England, 1650-1760* (Boston, 1920).

Saintsbury, George, *The Peace of the Augustans* (London, 1916).

Schöffler, H., *Protestantismus und Literatur* (Leipzig, 1922).

Seccombe, T., *The Age of Johnson 1748-1798* (London, 1900).

Stephen, Leslie, *English Literature and Society in the Eighteenth Century* (London, 1907).

Stern, B. H., *The Rise of Romantic Hellenism in English Literature, 1732-1786* (Menasha, Wis., 1940).

Sypher, Wylie, *Guinea's Captive Kings: British Anti-Slavery Literature of the XVIIIth Century* (Chapel Hill, 1942).

Thüme, Hans, *Beiträge zur Geschichte des Geniebegriffs in England* (Halle a.S., 1927).

Tinker, C. B., *The Salon and English Letters* (New York, 1915).

Van Tieghem, Paul, *Le Préromantisme* (2v, Paris, 1924-30).

Yvon, Paul, *Les crises de la morale et de la moralité dans l'histoire de la civilisation et de la littérature des pays anglo-saxons* (Paris, 1937).

POETRY

Aubin, R. A., *Topographical Poetry in Eighteenth Century England* (New York, 1936).

Bateson, F. W., *English Poetry and the English Language* (Oxford, 1934).

Bond, R. P., *English Burlesque Poetry, 1700-1750* (Cambridge, Mass., 1932).

Boys, R. C., "Some Problems of Dryden's Miscellany, and A Finding-List of English Poetical Miscellanies, 1700-48, in Selected American Libraries," *ELH,* VII (1940). 130-62.

Bradner, L., *Musae Anglicanae* (New York, 1940).

Bragg, M. K., *The Formal Eclogue in Eighteenth-Century England* (Orono, Me., 1926).

Bredvold, L. I., "The Element of Art in Eighteenth Century Poetry," in *Selected Poems of Alexander Pope* (New York, 1926).

Brie, F., *Englische Rokoko-Epik, 1710-1730* (Munich, 1927).

Broadus, E. K., *1 he Laureateship* (Oxford, 1921).

Bush, Douglas, *Mythology and the Romantic Tradition in English Poetry* (Cambridge, Mass., 1937).

Case, A. E., *A Bibliography of English Poetical Miscellanies, 1521-1750* (Oxford, 1935).

Chapman, R. W., "Dodsley's Collection of Poems by Several Hands," *Oxford Bibliographical Society*, III, iii (1933). 269-316.

Courthope, W. J., *History of English Poetry* (6v, London, 1911-13), V-VI.

Deane, C. V., *Aspects of Eighteenth Century Nature Poetry* (Oxford, 1935).

Doughty, Oswald, *English Lyric in the Age of Reason* (London, 1922).

———, *Forgotten Lyrics of the Eighteenth Century* (London, 1924).

Draper, J. W., *The Funeral Elegy and the Rise of English Romanticism* (New York, 1929).

Durling, D. L., *Georgic Tradition in English Poetry* (New York, 1935).

Fairchild, H. N., *Religious Trends in English Poetry*. I: *1700-1740, Protestantism and the Cult of Sentiment* (New York, 1939); II: *1740-1780, Religious Sentimentalism in the Age of Johnson* (New York, 1942).

Goad, C. M., *Horace in the English Literature of the Eighteenth Century* (New Haven, 1918).

Grierson, H. J. C., and Smith, J. C., *A Critical History of English Poetry* (London, 1944).

Griffith, R. H., "The Progress Pieces of the Eighteenth Century," *Texas Review*, V (1920). 218-33.

Haas, C. E. de, *Nature and the Country in English Poetry of the First Half of the Eighteenth Century* (Amsterdam, 1928).

Haferkorn, R., *Gotik und Ruine in der englischen Dichtung des 18. Jahrhunderts* (Leipzig, 1924).

Havens, R. D., "Changing Taste in the Eighteenth Century: a Study of Dryden's and Dodsley's Miscellanies," *Publications of the Modern Language Association*, XLIV (1929). 501-36.

———, *The Influence of Milton on English Poetry* (Cambridge, Mass., 1922).

Howard, W. G., "Ut Pictura Poesis," *Publications of the Modern Language Association*, XXIV (1909), 40-123.

Kitchin, G., *A Survey of Burlesque and Parody in English* (Edinburgh, 1931).

Lange, V., *Die Lyrik und ihr Publikum im England des 18. Jahr-hunderts* (Weimar, 1935).

Larrabee, S., *English Bards and Grecian Marbles* (New York, 1943).

Leavis, F. R., "The Augustan Tradition and the Eighteenth Century," in *Revaluation* (London, 1936).

Lee, Rensselaer W., "Ut Pictura Poesis," *Art Bulletin,* XXII (1940). 197-269.

Moore, C. A., "The Return to Nature in English Poetry of the Eighteenth Century," *Studies in Philology,* XIV (1917). 243-91.

———, "Whig Panegyric Verse, 1700-1760: a Phase of Sentimentalism," *Publications of the Modern Language Association,* XLI (1926). 362-401.

Neff, E., *A Revolution in European Poetry, 1660-1900* (New York, 1940).

Pottle, F. A., *The Idiom of Poetry* (2nd ed., Ithaca, 1946).

Quayle, T., *Poetic Diction* (London, 1924).

Renwick, W. L., "Notes on Some Lesser Poets of the Eighteenth Century," in *Essays on the Eighteenth Century Presented to David Nichol Smith* (Oxford, 1945).

Reynolds, Myra, *The Treatment of Nature in English Poetry between Pope and Wordsworth* (2d ed., Chicago, 1909).

Shuster, G. N., *The English Ode from Milton to Keats* (New York, 1940).

Sickels, E. M., *The Gloomy Egoist: Moods and Themes of Melancholy from Gray to Keats* (New York, 1932).

Smith, D. Nichol, *Some Observations on Eighteenth Century Poetry* (London, 1937).

Swedenberg, H. T., Jr., *The Theory of the Epic in England, 1650-1800* (Berkeley, 1944).

Tillotson, G., "Eighteenth-Century Poetic Diction," in *Essays in Criticism and Research* (Cambridge, 1942).

———, "Matthew Arnold and Eighteenth-Century Poetry," in *Essays on the Eighteenth Century Presented to David Nichol Smith* (Oxford, 1945).

Walker, H., *English Satire and Satirists* (London, 1925).

Williams, G. G., "The Beginnings of Nature Poetry in the Eighteenth Century," *Studies in Philology,* XXVII (1930). 583-608.

Wolfe, H., *Notes on English Verse Satire* (London, 1929).

PROSE

Cole, G. D. H., *Politics and Literature* (London, 1929).

Douglas, D. C., *English Scholars* (London, 1939).

Hazlitt, Wm., *Lectures on the English Comic Writers,* in *Collected Works,* ed. A. R. Waller and A. Glover (12v, London, 1902-04), VIII.

Hearnshaw, F. J. C., ed., *The Social and Political Ideas of Some English Thinkers of the Augustan Age* (London, 1928).

Hornbeak, Katherine G., *The Complete Letter Writer in English, 1568-1800* (Northampton, 1934). Smith College Studies in Modern Languages, XV, 3-4.

Leonard, S. A., *The Doctrine of Correctness in English Usage 1700-1800* (Madison, 1929). University of Wisconsin Studies in Language and Literature, No. 25.

Longaker, J. M., *English Biography in the Eighteenth Century* (Philadelphia, 1931).

Major, J. C., *The Role of Personal Memoirs in English Biography and Novel* (Philadelphia, 1935).

Murphy, G., *Bibliography of English Character-Books, 1608-1700* (Oxford, 1925).

Quennell, Peter, *The Profane Virtues* (New York, 1945). [Boswell, Gibbon, Sterne, Wilkes.]

Read, H., *English Prose Style* (London, 1928).

Saintsbury, George, *A History of English Prose Rhythm* (New York, 1922).

Stauffer, D. A., *The Art of Biography in Eighteenth Century England—Bibliographical Supplement* (2v, Princeton, 1941).

Sutherland, J., "Some Aspects of Eighteenth-Century Prose," in *Essays on the Eighteenth Century Presented to David Nichol Smith* (Oxford, 1945).

Thackeray, W. M., *The English Humourists of the Eighteenth Century,* ed. W. L. Phelps (New York, 1900).

Walker, H., *The English Essay and Essayists* (London, 1928).

Whittuck, C. A., *The "Good Man" of the XVIIIth Century* (London, 1901).

A TABLE OF DATES

▶▶▶

English History		Continental History and Literature	
1660-1685	Charles II	1661-1715	Personal government of Louis XIV
1661-1665	Clarendon Code		
1662	Royal Society's Charter	1636-1674	Dramatic career of Corneille
1665-1667	Naval War with Holland	1653-1673	Dramatic career of Molière
1665	Plague in London		1659 *Les Précieuses Ridicules*
1666	Great Fire of London		1664 *Tartuffe*
			1666 *Le Misanthrope*
		1660-1691	Dramatic Career of Racine
1667	Dutch Fleet in Medway		1667 *Andromaque*
			1677 *Phèdre*
1668	Triple Alliance— England, Holland, and Sweden		1690 *Athalie*
1670	Treaty of Dover	1660-1710	Literary Career of Boileau
			1674 *Art Poétique*
1672-1674	Third War with Holland	1668-1680	La Fontaine, *Fables*
1678	"Popish Plot"		
1681	Arrest of Shaftesbury		

English History		Continental History and Literature	
1683	Execution of Russell and Sidney		
1685-1688	James II	1685	Revocation of Edict of Nantes
1685	Monmouth's Rebellion		
1688	The Revolution		
1689-1702	William III		
1689-1694	Mary	1689-1725	Reign of Peter the Great of Russia
1689	Bill of Rights Toleration Act		
1690	Battle of the Boyne		
1694	Establishment of Bank of England		
1695	Press Licensing Act dropped		
1697	Peace of Ryswick		
1701	Act of Settlement	1700	Foundation of Berlin Academy of Sciences
1702-1714	Anne		
1702-1713	War of the Spanish Succession		
1704	Battle of Blenheim Capture of Gibraltar		
1706	Battle of Ramillies		
1707	Union of England and Scotland		
1708	Battle of Oudenarde		

English History		Continental History and Literature	
1709	Battle of Malplaquet	1709	Defeat of Charles XII of Sweden at Pultowa
1710	Trial of Sacheverell Fall of Whigs, and beginning of Tory government of Harley and Bolingbroke		
1713	Peace of Utrecht		
1714-1727	George I		
1715-1716	Jacobite rebellion	1715-1774	Reign of Louis XV
1720	South Sea Bubble		
1721-1742	Ministry of Walpole	1721	Montesquieu, *Lettres Persanes*
1722	Patent for Wood's halfpence	1714-1778	Literary career of Voltaire
1729	Beginning of Methodist movement (at Oxford)		1734 *Lettres anglaises* 1751 *Siècle de Louis XIV* 1753-1758 *Essai sur les moeurs* 1758 *Candide*
1727-1760	George II		1764 *Dictionnaire philosophique*
1733	Settlement of Georgia Walpole's Excise Scheme		
1737	Licensing Act Prince of Wales in opposition Death of Queen Caroline		
1739	War declared on Spain	1740-1786	Reign of Frederick the Great

English History		*Continental History and Literature*	
1745	Battle of Fontenoy Jacobite Rebellion	1741-1748	War of Austrian Succession
1746	Battle of Culloden		
		1948	Montesquieu, *Esprit des lois*
1752	Change of calendar from old to new style Clive in India	1750-1778	Literary career of Rousseau 1755 *Discours sur l'inégalité* 1761 *Nouvelle Héloïse* 1762 *Emile—Contrat social* 1781-1788 *Confessions*
		1751-1780	*L'Encyclopédie*—important contributors Diderot, Voltaire, d'Alembert
1755	Braddock defeated	1755	Lisbon earthquake
1756-1763	Seven Years War—"French and Indian War" in America		
1757	Beginning of Pitt's ministry Battle of Plassey		
1759	Fall of Quebec British Museum opened		
1760-1820	George III		
1762	Beginning of Bute's ministry	1762-1796	Reign of Catherine the Great of Russia
1763	Peace of Paris	1750-1781	Literary career of Lessing 1766 *Laokoon*

English History		*Continental History and Literature*	
c.1764	Spinning jenny invented		
1765	Stamp Act		
1768-1779	Voyages of Captain Cook		
1769	Arrest of Wilkes Watt's first patent for steam engine		
1771	First cotton mill		
		1773	Bürger, *Lenore;* Goethe, *Götz von Berlichingen*
1775-1783	War of American Independence	1774	Goethe, *Werther*
1777	Battle of Saratoga	1774-1792	Reign of Louis XVI
1778	Franco-American Alliance		
1781	Surrender of Cornwallis	1781	Kant, *Critique of Pure Reason*
1780	Gordon Riots		
		1782	Schiller, *Die Räuber*
1783	Beginning of ministry of the younger Pitt		
1786	Impeachment of Hastings		
1788	Settlement of Australia		
1789	Debates on Regency Bill	1789	Fall of the Bastille Outbreak of French Revolution

INDEX

>>>

This index lists significant references to writers, historical events and figures, topics in literary criticism, and some other recurring topics and terms. Individual books or other literary works are entered only when discussed at some length. The principal notice of a subject is indicated by **bold-face** type.